MAGIC CIRCLES

MAGIC CIRCLES

THE BEATLES

IN DREAM AND HISTORY

DEVIN McKINNEY

HARVARD UNIVERSITY PRESS
Cambridge, Massachusetts
London, England

2003

Publication of this book has been supported by the generous provisions of the Maurice
and Lula Bradley Smith Memorial Fund.

Frontispiece: Skyline, London Airport, 1966. Photo by Rex Features.

Library of Congress Cataloging-in-Publication Data
McKinney, Devin.
Magic circles: the Beatles in dream and history / Devin McKinney.
p. cm.
Includes discography (p. 392) and index.
Contents: Rude noises from the bog: the Beatles in Liverpool and Hamburg—
Ascension/sacrifice: a hard day's night and help!—Meat: the Beatles in 1966—
The unintelligible truth: the Beatles and the counterculture—
O.P.D. / Deus est vivus: the Beatles and the death cults—
Fantasy into flesh: a life and an afterlife.
ISBN 0-674-01202-X
1. Beatles. 2. Rock musicians—England—Biography. 3. Music—Social aspects.
4. Rock music—England—History and criticism. 5. Rock music—United States—
History and criticism. I. Title.

ML421.B4M34 2003
782.42166'092'2—dc21   2003047854

For Kathy

—

and John Barrett

ACKNOWLEDGMENTS

First thanks go to my mother and father, who never told me I couldn't or shouldn't; to my sister Dawn, who gave me the gifts of love and silliness; and to my grandmother, Neva Minehart, the finest teacher who ever lived.

Love to Rhoda, Mark, and Lori; Nietzsche the cat; Will; Robin; and my fellow toilers in the typing pool. For their kind words, I'm grateful to Melanie Jackson and Tracy Flynn. For his generosity, paeans to Fred LaBour. Peace all over Farah Kidwai, the truest musical eclectic I know, for responding vigorously and being an irreplaceable presence in the world. And a Celtic salute to my constant reader, pugnacious critic, and fellow Irishman Tim Joyce: to paraphrase Dylan, you was the brother I never had. Burn on.

Eternal gratitude to Chuck Musse of Rex USA, who allowed this book to come alive visually. For their mighty labors, unfailing patience, and high spirits, I honor Lindsay Waters, Tom Wheatland, and Maria Ascher at Harvard University Press. A special thanks to those at the Press who worked so hard to make the book, and its author, look good: designers Tim Jones and Marianne Perlak, and production coordinator Heather Shaff.

This book wouldn't have been published without the gallant intercession of Luc Sante. Luc responded to an unsolicited manuscript delivered on the tenuous premise that he and I had once belonged to the same Brooklyn food co-op; ever since, he has been unstinting with his time, talent, counsel, and enthusiasm. He is a gentleman, and I owe him a pint.

I dedicate this work to my wife, Kathy Berenson. Kathy has fanned my flame, nourished my heart, kept me working, thinking, laughing, and believing. Her insights into human behavior have pushed this book in directions I couldn't have taken it alone, and shaped it more than any single influence. For the six years she has chosen to live with me, she has had no choice but to live with the Beatles. I only hope that when the long day closes she will allow that we were not, perhaps, the *most* uncongenial of roommates.

CONTENTS

ILLUSTRATIONS

I trust the reader appreciates the strangeness of this, because if he does not, there is no sense in writing poems, or notes to poems, or anything at all.

—Vladimir Nabokov, *Pale Fire* (1962)

So we sailed

On a night in early 1966, Paul McCartney lay in his London bed.

"There's a nice twilight zone," he said years later, "just as you're drifting into sleep and as you wake from it."

Within this twilight zone he conceived a new piece of music: a children's song. "I just made up a little tune in my head, then started making a story, sort of an ancient mariner, telling the young kids where he'd lived and how there'd been a place where he had a yellow submarine."[1]

Soon the Beatles were in the studio, recording the song Paul brought back from the twilight zone. Titled "Yellow Submarine," it became a communal free-for-all. Ringo sang while John blew bubbles; George and others ran about the studio ringing bells, honking horns, shaking chains. There were nautical rattlings, a brass band, rushing waves, shouting voices. The result was clangor, cacophony, fun for the whole family. Few records could have been simpler; few as thick and exuberant with action.

On August 5, the song was released as the B-side of the Beatles' latest single. Before the month was over, 1.2 million people had bought the record.[2] As summer became autumn, millions more heard the song on radios, turntables, and jukeboxes. Children learned to play it on their kazoos. The yellow submarine had sailed out of the twilight zone and into the world.

1

RUDE NOISES FROM THE BOG

The Beatles in Liverpool and Hamburg

I sang in my chains like the sea.
—Dylan Thomas, "Fern Hill,"
Collected Poems, 1934–1952 (1957)

The Beatles began underground, in dirt and darkness. They sprouted in squalor. Their cellar walls ran with postindustrial sweat; their dressing rooms crept with fungus. Dim bulbs, gray sheets, and rats. Dirt and darkness turned them into beetles as well as Beatles, into patient burrowers and cunning foragers—collectors of detritus. It taught them how to subsist on the fringes of a trash-laden pop scene; how to infiltrate another's realm and remake it from the inside; how to thrive on the currents of desire and sensation crackling between themselves and their audiences; and how not to die as a group until history itself became the only thing that could kill them.

They would have to create themselves; their culture would not do it for them. With little native rock and roll to call their own (Cliff Richard? Duffy Power?), the Beatles listened to America and lived on fantasies of everything their culture lacked. They never sought to be bigger than the Shadows: no, their ambitions were fixed on a holy trinity of American pop—the Everly Brothers, then Goffin and King, then Elvis. But in the meantime, as cultural parasites, the Beatles had to piece themselves together from remnants of George Formby music hall and Lonnie Donegan skiffle and Little Richard roadhouse. As they stole equipment from competing Liverpool bands, so they stole rhythms from Tennessee rockabillies and eccentricities of harmony from uptown girl groups. Their peculiar notions of pop melody were validated by the contract songwriters who were shrink-wrapping teen heartbreak in the cubicles of Manhattan's Brill Building. All the time they prowled and huddled in their dungeon discotheques, feelers out for every variance in the air of the underground.

They were, like beetles, prepared to eat shit to stay alive. The metaphor, though coarse, is borne out by the remarkable recurrence in early Beatle days of a bodily-fluids motif: toilet seats around the neck, public urination, venereal disease, the famous flaming condom. These are familiar parts of the legend, and no less meaningful for being partially or wholly apocryphal. It would appear that someone in or around the Beatles was always leaking something; or maybe it only seemed that way at the time. "The four of us sleeping in the same room, practically in the same bed, in the same truck, living together night and day, eating, *shitting* and *pissing* together,"[1] was one Lennon version of the story (emphasis his). And how astonishing, yet obvious, is the excremental reference—how simply it cuts through the myth and even the music to the biological imperative of bodies in close and constant proximity in the toilet of miserable beginnings.

Let us dive into another, even coarser metaphor:

The Beatles' music from this early period is the very sound of the toilet. That is not a put-down but an encomium. The toilet is the essence of rock, and a factor in the genius of anyone who ever remade this music as something it hadn't been before. Rock and roll has passed through many periods of powder and perfume, but the sound of the toilet circles back again and again, a primal memory, stretching from Elvis' Sun singles to John Lennon's first solo album to the ultra-modern machine music of techno and hip-hop. It's a contradictory sound, both resonant and flat, eerily distant and uncomfortably near, electronically distorted and emotionally direct. Mostly, though, this ur-noise of rock is simply dark, dirty and dark.

But once something is discovered in a toilet, nothing but an act of total force will release it into the world. No one wants to reach down, pull it up, fling it about. Especially when, as with early rock and roll, it is rank and lascivious, an agglomeration of fluids; when it is an un-named thing dreamed into being by the disconnected energies of white hillbillies and big-city blacks; when it slithers from juke joints on back roads and drips from illicit sex in back seats; when it is the natural product of tight, dim places. That so many recoiled when the Great American Toilet yielded this funk as its latest obscenity upon the hygiene of a good and faithful populace was its badge of realness: those in the majority gazed piercingly upon rock and roll and saw in it the sacking of every social, sexual, and racial formulation that had determined their lives.

Puritan prophets, they were not wrong. If there were millions of kids thrilled by the new sound, maybe even a few ready to fight in the street for it, there was a much stronger armature in place to squash it. The stereotype of a smug, contented American 1950s, white and calcified as milk, has passed into cliché as a fact; but the decade had its deep pockets of alienation, expressions of unease that could not have taken form at any other time. The '50s began with the Kinsey reports and ended with *Naked Lunch,* had its Kerouac Beat and Mailer's White Negro, its *Feminine Mystique* and Mattachine Society; there was Brando, there was Dean; movements from Civil Rights to Ban the Bomb were born in the crevices between Eisenhower's bland peace and Allen Dulles' secret wars. Not all were happy: some were even willing to *say* that they were not—that their nation's consciousness was corrupt and deranged.

But a fringe is not called a fringe for nothing. The American '50s were shaped by complacency, and even more by fear: of the Russian, certainly, but mostly of the enemy within—the native Communist, the black man and woman, the sexual deviant. The 1950s prepared for the years that followed by being a scientific decade, science culminating in a magical moon landing; but it was also the science of the bomb, shadows of the recent bombs and auguries of the new war, groundwork for napalm and defoliation. Eventually, there was bound to be a great social gagging at the prolonged inhalation of such military-industrial fumes. As the '40s babies grew into '50s teenagers, much plastic was poured, much metal tortured into gargantuan forms; and all in the name of peace of mind. Fear encased in science: what a noxious combination. Bomb shelter was the result—to survive apocalypse in one's own piece of the underground.

Rock and roll was synthesized of this world, by this world. Its sources can now be traced in many directions, its development codified in the straight logic of a syllogism, yet its character was spontaneous, its appearance inexplicable. No one knew where it came from, but it came. *Out of where?* the American wondered, idly at first. He watched white kids shake ass, heard mad black voices shouting from transistor radios, and shifted in his seat with a cool concern which held the promise of hot fear. *Out of here,* was the answer returned by secret knowledge: *Out of us—we—you and me. Them.* That was the first fear it excited. Adults tightened up as a new quiver was added to the bulging middle-aged vein, while kids found that suddenly there was a choice to be made, with some sense of consequence and reward. Commitment was felt necessary to this music, so new, so suggestive of an undecided future. Every atomic adolescent turned on by the sick humor of *Mad* magazine or EC Comics while guarding the tender buds of the utopian dreamer could pin his hopes on this art. This art could validate and inspire those on both sides of the apartheid line who suspected that black people ought not to be mutilated for failing to eat white waste with sufficient gusto. Rock and roll in its first surge might even awaken the nascent politics of those girls who glimpsed a day when intersex communication would be more than a whisper of formalities through the smog of hair treatments, punctuated by the odd date rape.

So rock was great, and yet . . . it was a set of first testaments, not a revolution. The fact is that this music—as both art form and personality vehicle—lacked the materials to change the world. It was a legitimately new language, synthesized from older languages separated by great distances in society and geography. It dealt in lingo, and quickly accrued a store of basic mythic images that to the unimpressed meant nothing but to those eager to be reached by something beyond themselves meant everything. *Blue suede shoes.* The loner claimed his place at the center of the landscape. *Don't step on my.* The loner made his threat against the world. *You can do anything but.* The loner made it clear he would relinquish everything to maintain his identity, his individuality. And all the other loners in radioland, actual or aspiring, heard the word.

That defiant ethos, defiance finding community, was early rock's widest opening for cultural innovation. But in another way it was only another definition of hipness as the right clothing—an old story even then—and so came with its own conformity built in. *Where are your blue suede shoes?*

Pop culture is always style-oriented, but the more rigid its biases the less its power in the world at large. Early rock (as costume, attitude, physical noise) was organically and decidedly a minority culture, self-referring and self-obscuring; excluding more than it included, it denied the Other—that is, the Grownup. This became the first article of rock and roll faith, that the Others *must not like it,* certainly must not like it too easily. If the young are admitted free, the Others must be made to pay some price—in worry, property, propriety. For if everyone is given equal chance to respond, if there is some plurality of the ear, democracy of the spirit, where is our specialness? What do we control? *Who gave you those blue suede shoes?*

In the '50s this was not noble piety but unquestioned conviction. And it is why early rock did not—perhaps did not even desire to—transform the world: it deliberately excluded too much of it. The most it could have done, as a collection of conscious and unconscious aims spreading from Sun Studios to Chess Studios to New Orleans to Los Angeles, was to have brought a new diffraction to that world, set slipstreams moving. Validated longings and triggered ambitions; sprung a new intimation of possibility before the eyes of someone who might straddle that possibility and ride it into the center of the earth.

Then there is the plain fact that early rock was a primitive, repetitive music, not bottomless in its riches. The pioneer squalls of Presley, Berry, Holly, and Little Richard were either love lyrics that threw back to the '40s more than ahead to the '60s, or they were rages in a tin can, referencing issues of sex, race, and identity in code so deep it was all but invisible. Berry's Brown-Eyed Handsome Man and Richard's Long Tall Sally are tantalizing as pop symbols for the black hero and the gay provocateur, but there is only so much a symbol can do without being both seductive and subversive, a purveyor of pleasure and excitement, a good time, which under its mask personifies the feared thing itself—and there were too many who would never be seduced by these sounds. The sounds themselves were strong, sometimes brutal, but the brutality was contained: mad dogs on leashes. In an art of the instant, passion is more important than formal originality, but to have both is the most important of all. Just as Swing music did not survive its time though its forms were brilliant, rock and roll had slim hope of survival (forget metamorphosis) if all it could feed from was its own rebel code, its teenage concerns, throaty discontent, and raw sex.

Early rock was a music made to astonish, to tease, and even to touch the perverse, but it needed someone foolhardy and ignorant of limits to pull it from the toilet of its parochial origins and thrust it into the world, where it would either mark that world forever or run silently down the impervious wall of culture. Rock had to start in the toilet; it then had to emerge. In all its harshness and lack of class, it had to brave something like a full engagement with the greater world that scorned it. It had to beckon all passersby, no matter their clothing. It had to trample lines of color, class, and educational attainment. It had to at least tease the ear of everyone who might conceivably hear it, offer nutrition to a broad range of hungers, add a twinkle to the star of every wish. It had to magnetize an audience of a size no single art had ever commanded, and then provide the field for that audience's lowest and highest desires. Finally it had to concentrate all of this intensity in one place, lay its burden upon a single entity, not two or five or twenty: rock and roll needed a hero with a thousand faces. And it had to run the risk of believing itself important enough to take in the world—not merely take it on.

Of course, things weren't understood this way at the time, and only a fool will dismiss the pioneers for not seeing past what were then the outermost limits of popular intercourse between artist and audience. But my modest suggestion is that this may be where the first wave of rock broke and fell back, why in its first great push it never quite reached the shore to cover the earth: there was no unifying talent complete and obsessive enough to work the transformation it made its fan desire.

Its geniuses could not do all that it took. Elvis was early rock's godhead and figure of broadest appeal; though his audiences remained segregated, he was the first to suggest such a broad comity of taste among people who presumably had nothing to say to one another. But from the start there was lard at the heart of his judgment (the ersatz jazz of "Heartbreak Hotel"), schmaltz in the boil ("Love Me Tender"), and aside from two aberrant skirmishes with need and doubt in later years (his 1968 comeback music, side one of *How Great Thou Art*) he did not extend his pioneer moves into music of psychological complexity.

Buddy Holly: As a writer and producer ambitious beyond his peers, had he lived he might have made the first mark on some of the Beatles' later innovations. (The demos he recorded in January 1959, just weeks before his death—"Crying, Waiting, Hoping," "That's What They Say"—sound like Lennon/McCartney compositions, circa late 1963.) But as a hard rocker he was only inconsistently hard, and his politeness had no edge: he would never say "Boo," let alone "Fuck you."

Chuck Berry *would* say it. This hard man of effortless style had the hubris to notch himself as the usurper of Beethoven and Tchaikovsky. But though he had all the charismatic contradictions of star quality (edge, charm, duck-walk), his songcraft was too genre-bound to truly threaten the heritage of those great corpses. For every prick of a Berry lyric in the skin of teenage experience, every two-edged rendering of America as sinister supermarket and risky highway, there was a tune and arrangement of thudding sameness—airless danceband dynamics, and a lack of melodic invention to numb the brain.

Little Richard and Jerry Lee Lewis were restricted by personal madnesses of race, region, sex, and psyche. In their frenzy there was no room to breathe or think, and they had no hint of romance; they were noise or they were nothing. As for all the minor figures—the Everly Brothers, Carl Perkins, Fats Domino—they were minor for a reason. Without question, they were irreplaceable; for them and their music, any fan feels terrific love. What one doesn't feel is conflict—in them or about them. No audience could poise its myriad fantasies upon Fats's eternal grin or Perkins' square journeyman shoulders, and their records were too perfectly what they were to be mistaken for anything else. In them there is never the distant rumble of the earth shaking—as there is in "Hound Dog," as there is in "She Loves You."

And: it is necessarily redundant and a necessary redundancy to say that for Berry, Richard, and Domino, another barrier to massive popularity and wide social influence, more impassable than any limitation of talent, was the fact of their race.

It may be that the early rockers felt their own limits in some form, or that, in the confusion and hustle of scouting new territory without a compass, they merely lost their way. The result was the same: tacitly acknowledging its inability to change the world as it stood, rock and roll hesitated, then withdrew. Elvis, the only one with power and position sufficient to keep the movement moving on a mass level, did his national service in 1958 and came back two years later with sneer smoothed and pelvis locked. The other stars got killed, or jailed, or pious. Rock and roll shriveled as pop went dry and nearly blew away in the polite caucasian breezes of the New Frontier. Percy Faith and Lawrence Welk had number 1 hits and flushed the toilet. The new pop sound was expansive and airy, but, with only a few exceptions (Sam Cooke, Phil Spector), not in any way that suggested freedom. This was the insulated expansiveness of American consumerism, without any of its color, push, and invigorating near-madness: the precise formula for mainstream middlebrowism.

By 1960, fans were forgetting there had been a rock and roll, and wise heads were already past-tensing it as the fad they'd always desperately hoped it was. *And what rough beast, its hour come round at last, slouches towards Bethlehem to be born?*[2]

□

The city sprouts like a huge organism, diseased in every part, the beautiful thoroughfares only a little less repulsive because they have been drained of their pus. Liverpool.

—Stuart Sutcliffe, quoting Henry Miller; in Robert Cording, Shelli Jankowski-Smith, and E. J. Miller Laino, eds., *In My Life: Encounters with the Beatles* (1998)

The British critic Nik Cohn once put Liverpool this way: "a strange town."

"Outside of Glasgow," he wrote, "it's the rawest, most passionate place in Britain. It has a certain black style of its own, a private strength and humor and awareness, real violence, and it is also grim, very much so. . . . This is America in England: a night out ends almost inevitably with a punch in the nose."[3]

For Americans, it is also the town outside of America with the greatest freight of rock and roll mythology. Relatively few of us on this side of the Atlantic have seen Liverpool up close, yet we all have imagined it as the exotic crucible of something extraordinary. For us it is, like the Beatles, a field for the play of imagination. Through secondary sources, we have absorbed its stories; studied its industry, character, perceived freedoms and constraints. And for all that, we must fill in the rest to make it worthy of what came out of it.

We have seen the pictures of postwar Merseyside, its narrow side streets and tottering sooty buildings; the docks which through pentimento of age and grain look like harbors for ghost ships; the provincial gloom that casts even the Town Hall in shades of slate gray; the spotty, hungry look of the kids, brought up under wartime rationing and looking avid for overstimulation. We've absorbed the stories of gang violence, Lime Street prostitutes, invasions of drunken sailors from invisible distances carrying American R&B and exotic VD; races and nationalities mixing in a community kettle heated by fantasy and frustration. We know it as a place where music was not luxury but identity, voice, weapon against inertia and violence under bomb-rotted towers, with ferocious followings behind jazz, Caribbean, and country-western. We know it as the birthplace of rockers, footballers, and comedians; as a place where, in Lennon's words, "people had a sense of humor because they're in so much pain."[4]

As a depiction of a real place where real people lead real lives, the picture may be distorted and unfair. But as pop mythology a place could situate itself no better, because it contains the elements common to all mythologies, pop or classical: the grip of the familiar, and the lure of the strange. To the extent that we may identify these images of Liverpool with the provincialisms, decay, and petty brutalities of our own American towns, the images are as real as the street outside our window. Yet in their foreignness they exist at a remove, in some parallel universe not really knowable *except* in the imagination. Therein lies all the romance of this "strange town." It is us, we feel, but we've never seen it before—and we're fascinated by it. The grass is always greener, the slate always grayer.

So the Beatles as we imagine them arise from a place of weird properties: multicultural and violent, bomb-riddled and hard-scrabble, land of welfare lines and a thousand beer brawls, a place you might leave but never escape.

In the mathematics of mythic exchange, it makes perfect sense that an American should mythicize Liverpool this way. What were the Beatles' beginnings but an attempt to rewrite in their own tongue the myths of a foreign land? America in England: a mythos of America enlarged and invigorated by foreigners' love and hate and envy of America, their desire to outdo the land of dreams itself, hurled back at its progenitor as a whole new myth—full of the grip of the familiar, and the lure of the strange.

Ask first what the familiar might be. What essential temper did Britain and America share in the 1950s? What was it that connected one to the other to provide a common frame of memory as both entered the 1960s? This could well enable our first creep upon the outer rim of the more essential questions: What did four English teenagers of the '50s do to American kids of the '60s, and how were they able to do it?

Fear was the sputtering engine beneath the gleaming Cadillac hood of the American 1950s, but Britain's feeling of fear spiraled back into dusty and unglimpsed anterooms of colonial history. For America's oil of technology, Britain substituted its sense of natural superiority to all its dark colonies. The country wrote its official history over a long cruel line of oppressions and dominations, hatreds buried under manners, a ruling class freakish with incest and madness. Beneath the white man's burden, there was surely a stomach filled with ulcerous self-loathing at having to administer his empire while feeling small beside the noble and potent savage. Fear drives the deed that feeds the fear: colonization abroad paralleled colonization at home, the whole system of public school and school tie, social class as predestination, children reciting like math tables the names of their country's conquered provinces. Over centuries, the subjects of a dissolving empire were made to absorb the fear of their rulers.

But fear to the Beatles and their generation was more than an abstraction of history. Their era had been on close terms with it since the first thump of a Nazi boot at the far end of the European corridor. Bombed almost ceaselessly between 1940 and 1944, Britain's major cities were brought to the edge of infrastructural collapse; the threat of death hovered in the silence of national blackouts, crept through all the windows shattered by last night's Blitzkrieg. Waves of paranoia followed the invasion of Poland and the fall of France. Allotments of food, clothing, electricity, and heat were stretched; mass starvation was averted by cabbage and pigeon pie. John Winston Lennon was born in the midst of a bombing raid, took first breaths in a world of fearful screaming females, and found the first name of his country's revered prime minister affixed patriotically to his person.

No American can imagine a Briton's relief once the war was won, or how long it took for all those embedded tremors to settle, the dreads to quell. What follows quickest upon relief but complacency? Back on safe ground, Britain settled into a cautious, porridgy contentment that drained the economy of vigor, the clothing of style, the arts of rascality. The old decade of terrors and prides devolved into a new one of uncertain goals, vague promises of national renewal, and very little in the way of thriving indigenous culture. The Beatles came out of fear into something that was perhaps worse: boredom. The Conservative government was inefficient at home and inept abroad, Prime Minister Anthony Eden a magnet for charges of political impotence. Unlike America, which was gearing up for its confrontation over civil rights, Britain had no social issue sufficiently near the rawest anxieties of the populace to seize a major share of its preoccupation. Elsewhere the British film, awaiting its kitchen-sink renaissance, was a lace hanky waved in the direction of Hollywood. Avantgarde art was the province of a few Marxist schemers.[5]

But there was action in the outlands. The kids in Liverpool were doing what kids everywhere do when unexcited by their environment: they were making their own noise. In the process, they made their own culture. True enough it was tattered culture, second-hand, a Frankenstein operation built of parts almost totally American. But if it was not, properly speaking, a movement, it was definitely *movement*, and of a kind not seen in Britain before: a fast-moving dialectic which discovered, rejected, and recombined an array of jarring influences. The kids were making themselves ugly. They became goons, greasers, and punks. Mock-Edwardian Teddy-boy garb (long coats and drainpipe dungarees) overlapped with cowboy fringe, which overlapped with motorcycle leather, all pressing together in an inelegant mash. There was no grand aesthetic to unify the rogue styles, and this left the Liverpool kids looking just plain weird. Weirder by half than their American cousins, for whom the looks and sounds were all homegrown.

In that weirdness—the Liverpool kids' lack of shame or system in their borrowings, their eagerness to move away from torpor and toward a mash of strange and thrilling combinations where they might find a new style—right there lay the beginnings of the Beatles' own weird history. We study the Teds and pseudo-Texans and embryonic Rockers of that time for a glimmer of personal style, some pose not appropriated from across the water. We study even the Beatles' earliest photos for that. We fail to see it. What we do see, and plainly, is youth in the process of finding its own pose; and in its very ugliness it is something to behold: the wet, squealing birth of culture. The clothes are American but the faces are English. The stances are stolen but the eyes tell their own story. *I'm English and my face is pasty and fuck yer arse.*

What was identifiably British in the clatter of these sudden obsessions was skiffle music, which is what John Lennon's Quarry Men were playing on June 6, 1957, the day he met Paul McCartney at St. Peter's Church Garden Fete on Church Road in the Woolton section of Liverpool.[6]

□

I came out of the fucking sticks to take over the fucking world, it seemed to me!

—John; in *Lennon Remembers*, ed. Jann Wenner (2000)

John and Paul stepped into a scene with no center. In fact skiffle itself had no center, drawing from American strains of folk, blues, and country, the sex and rough humor of its sources flattened into a grinning, folksy kitsch. But it had one undeniable thing: its tempo raced. This first intimation of what speed could do, the attack it could make, may be what most attracted Lennon and McCartney to it. The first big skiffle hit, Lonnie Donegan's "Rock Island Line" of January 1956, is not rock and roll, but the song itself as handed down from Leadbelly is an ancestor of Chuck Berry's "Too Much Monkey Business" and Bob Dylan's "Subterranean Homesick Blues"—fast, nervous songs whose lyric lines spin out with incremental rhymes, kick inward in hiccuppy hesitations. It would be months before "Heartbreak Hotel" hit Liverpool and nearly a year after that before Lennon put together his first group in March 1957.[7]

In their first form, Lennon named them the Quarry Men. The title was innocence itself: derived from the name on his grammar school,

1. **Notes from underground: the Beatles at the Cavern Club, August 1962.**

it was a crude image containing many meanings. "Quarry Men" spoke of rock (as in roll), sweat, back-breaking work; the mining of old stone for new objects, objects not found but burrowed out; the push and pull between destruction and creation. Organic process and rapacious commercial enterprise. Men underground, grinding for their pay, waiting to emerge.

Quarry Men, went a line from the school song, *old before our birth.*[8]

After dark at that Woolton garden party of June 1957, Liverpool teenager and Lennon friend Bob Molyneux lifted the microphone of a Grundig recorder to the stage as John sang the new Donegan hit, "Puttin' on the Style."[9] The tape that survives is a mere thirty-second shaving, and more than half its sound is surface noise, ambient racket, the cross-calls of Liverpool kids. You hear a hot, active summer night inside a provincial gymnasium. Pounded out for the dancing teenagers, the Quarry Men's beat is admirably certain, a consistent thud—the beat is really all there is to the music. Except for the ghost of Lennon's vocal: his sixteen-year-old voice, even half-heard, is simply not to be mistaken for any other. It flies like the cockiest, the looniest of birds over that low, dull thud; whines like a freighter steaming out of Liverpool Harbour. Is this genius? What could be seen in Einstein's first equation?

Brief as it is, this sliver of tape may be an accurate capture of how the music sounded that night to anyone standing more than twenty feet from the stage. The music, though it *resembles* rock and roll, sounds as if it owes nothing to any form, because it is so completely itself. It feels like ugly British kids make it, and sounds as if it comes from under the ground.

Somewhere in the time just before or after this noise is recorded, John meets Paul.

They were conscious that making the top meant starting from the bottom; that being born meant first becoming old. The band may have started in the flush of a fad, but soon their tenacity took the shape of an obsessive dues-paying. And there were comical dues to be paid in those first years. Did they know when they began that in order to create themselves they would also have to create the scene in which they could thrive? These Quarry Men were gone on rock and roll, but their town was not. The Liverpool clubs were ruled by Trad (what Cohn called "a definitely sick bowdlerization of New Orleans jazz, all banjoes and fancy waistcoats and boozy vocals"[10]—and you thought *American* pop was in trouble?), folk music, West Indian steel bands, country-western hokum, or at best the blues. Music both blatantly sexual and proudly commercial was derided as unpure.

So it was that they had to make their own scene. They sought out their city's demimonde. In a word, they went underground. They hung out in coffee bars and cellar clubs, absorbed deafening sounds in subterranean squats and silty alcoves, learning chords, deciphering the words of American records, writing their first songs, cutting their fingers and stretching their throats: all the gruntwork of learning the game. This was their down-home version of the toilet—or bog, in English working-class slang. Characteristic was a place called the Morgue, a skiffle cellar which Mark Lewisohn tells us "held 100 people and had no facilities. A single bare blue bulb and one white fluorescent strip light provided the only illumination, and one electric fan supplied the only 'fresh' air." One month after its opening it was raided by the Liverpool police in midshow, and soon after the building was condemned as uninhabitable.[11]

Their haunts were all funk and sweat, but that stink was theirs, they were in it by choice, and they were confident it held prizes for them. Just as Elvis only a few years earlier had transgressed race and religion to walk Beale Street by night because he knew it was where he would locate a vital part of himself, the Quarry Men removed themselves from the environment they had known in order to make themselves what they knew they could become. They eschewed securities of class and college and submitted to the certain degradation of slamming themselves against doors that were solidly shut, playing music it was supposed no one cared to hear. John, Paul, and their rotating bandmates—George soon to appear—consumed experience hungrily, wherever it offered itself. They worked church dances, garden parties, neighborhood fairs, wedding receptions. They performed in shacks and atop coal wagons. They played for ten minutes in a golf course clubhouse and entertained slaughterhouse swells at the Stanley Abbatoir Social Club—all the while thumping on the cardboard-box Spanish guitars and tea-chest bass of skiffle, dressed in bolo ties and aspiring pompadours. Musically they were all effort and adenoids, while visually they were not lovely, caught as they were on a fashion cusp between Teddy boy and Eddie Cochran casual. Paid engagements were few, return appearances fewer.[12]

The Quarry Men made a record. Just to hear themselves, see how good—or bad—they really were. In early 1958 they set up their gear in the Liverpool parlor of one Percy Phillips, who owned a tape recorder and a record-cutting machine and was paid a small fee by locals wishing to commemorate themselves on ten-inch 78-rpm discs.[13] John, Paul, and George, along with a pianist and drummer, recorded two songs. The first was "That'll Be the Day," Buddy Holly's signature hit, the title of which he took from a line John Wayne spoke in *The Searchers;* the other was something called "In Spite of All the Danger," a love song written by Paul and George, with John singing lead.

Were the Quarry Men searching, or had they found? Listen closely—the disc has two sides, and tells two stories. "That'll Be the Day" is to rock and roll what evaporated chocolate is to chocolate. After a quick introduction, the band bears down on the Holly song, but not into it. Their version is competent and dead: they never get their hands near the bratty meat of the song. Very nasal, Paul's harmonic interjections a series of priggish commas marking the group's bland musical syntax, it carries an echo of the honking, thumping sound they must have made at the very first, and suggests a band whose search for a sound had already come to rest on the weary flats of something not terribly interesting.

But perhaps they meant only to get it out of the way fast, because on the flip-side was laid something different: a coherent statement of purpose. *In spite of all the danger,* they sing, voices rising with an odd, gloomy solemnity. This schoolboy ditty is pure pop masquerading as near-blues, slow tempo and serious intentions, a vow of devotion dragging itself toward an affirmation more convincing for the effort behind it. Harrison plays a simple guitar, secure in its fall and rise, its smiling arpeggios. McCartney's voice, holding loosely to one note—

venturing a step up or down, then going home—is like a streak of
cloud through the sky, with Lennon's under-vocal moving in considered steps across a very real earth. Together they put weight and serenity into the song's formulaic promise of eternal bond. It sounds
not quite like anything to be heard in England then; it suggests precious few counterparts in America. Every element speaks of youth
and future, a looking forward; every element speaks equally of decisions formed and made, certainty of motive and meaning, a center
firm and growing harder. It is an old record by young men, boys old
before their birth.

Hearing it at the time, few would have rushed to lade this record's
makers with riches, but today it speaks with a different voice. "In
Spite of All the Danger" is not merely a wistful diversion dreamed up
by three youths of modest ability who, but for many favors of fortune, might well have left the stage of history without a sound. It is
the Beatles, and so it has meaning. The sound is of a group more interested by what it has yet to search out than what it has too easily
found; a group excited by the danger of staking every hope on nothing but their talents, themselves, each other; a group willing to brave
its fear of failure and horror of obscurity on the long, long chance
that their voices will be heard. Listening to it now, we hear John, Paul,
and George forging a vow from the mettle of their ambitions—*I'll do
anything for you*—and addressing it to a single person. *If you'll be true
to me.*

Is it a girl, the traditional object of phallocentric popsong? Is it
Percy Phillips? Is it Liverpool, the rest of England, all the unseen millions in all the mysterious lands across the straits and oceans? Is it
me? Is it you? And what do these singers want from us—do they want
us to love them, follow them, invest our dreams in them, with the
promise that they'll be repaid a hundredfold? Do they wish us to rise
to meet their ambition, become an audience with its own ambition,
to challenge and push them as they push and challenge us? Do they

wish us to lock fates and agree to change one another in ways that will breed magic, hysteria, transformation, occultism, violence, death, resurrection?

These are only questions. Gravity calls.

□

A vow, like an ideal, means nothing if it goes untested. Surely they reminded themselves of this more than once in the year after cutting their vanity disc, as they came closer to failure—the real, final thing—than they ever would again. As if in conspiracy against the edicts of history, Liverpool bookers neglected them. Jobs dried up over the rest of 1958, and 1959 was their lowest point: for the better part of the year they did not formally exist. George drifted, playing sporadically with another local band. John cohabitated with his painter friend Stuart Sutcliffe, an abstract expressionist of febrile gifts; Lennon would eventually con him into buying a bass and joining the band, despite his manifest lack of musical acumen. John and Paul spent this period scheming, commiserating, writing new songs, playing and singing head to head, holding to the vow.

It can't have been easy. Certainly it was harder for British kids than American to preserve any faith that rock and roll would be their means of self-realization. Rock and roll had set off the odd riot in a British moviehouse, but it lacked the numbers and a certain natural resonance with social conditions to become what it was in America. Proximity, obviously, counts for a lot. An American teenager nursing wild desires could go to an Elvis show—or better (in a sense), an Elvis movie, where the object was not distant flesh but immediate phantasm, protected and well-lit, passive and perfect. In Britain the same kid had Cliff Richard and the Shadows. For film, the best domestic product he could count on was the 1959 *Expresso Bongo,* a good sour movie starring Laurence Harvey as a hustling East End talent agent, and Richard as the crooner he hawks. The American had *Jailhouse*

Rock, convicts with five o'clock shadow dancing around the cellblock: the return of the repressed. (Albeit a decorous, choreographed return—the American '50s, in sum.) Hapless British youth had Richard singing bizarre teen-idol material like "The Shrine on the Second Floor," a sad cry of love to dead Mum. Hapless youth who sits through a good sour movie's good sour sarcasm at the expense of teenage gullibility, all for the blessing of a Cliff Richard funeral hymn.

The Quarry Men had models for their hopes, those who had seen the same dream and followed through; but they were, as the song said, somewhere beyond the sea. What they did not have that Elvis to some degree had—what they would ultimately need to create throughout England as they were already creating it in Liverpool— was a milieu in which all possibilities seemed open, where personal pop-related fantasies were validated by a broad marketplace in which they could be sold to and shared in and built upon by others. This simply did not exist in Britain: there was no English Elvis telling the Quarry Men it was all right to do what they were doing. Everything they did they did on faith.

In these dead months between surges of activity, John and Paul— George too, his thoughts elsewhere as he strummed joylessly on another stage, in another group—must have thought fondly of the pathetic joints they had lately played, that no longer existed or were rejecting them for the latest Trad outfit. They must have hungered for just another chance at momentum, another toilet; longed for someone to exploit their music and their youth, favor them with some real rock and roll humiliation. Anything but this, which was nothing.

Then the Casbah Coffee Club opened in the basement of a large Victorian house in the West Derby section of Liverpool. It needed a band; George pulled the others together, and the Quarry Men played opening night. Their first famous toilet. They were a hit, and did a seven-week stand through October 1959.[14] Pictures show John and

Paul performing in the club, wooden planks forming a wall behind them, electrical cord knotted on a hook, scarcely any headroom: it looks like a treehouse, or a chicken shack, primitive enough to impart Palladium splendor to the rankest roadhouse on Route 66. Paul sings out of his wide eyes at two grinning girls, while John pouts pensively and fingers the upper neck of his guitar. But here again, look at the faces: they are already different—still young but a stage less awkward. They wear poses, but the poses do not wear them.

In the spring of 1960 they made another recording, and it shows what they had learned about being a band since the Percy Phillips session. Produced in the living room of Paul's house, these tapes consist largely of interminable instrumentals—Sutcliffe humping his three notes, dreaming of canvas as he stares into a corner; George trying out riffs and running scales; John and Paul working toward a shared rhythm. But there are a number of actual songs, and these come straight from the bog: they are damp and uncouth and have a funny smell. They are hard to listen to and tough to make out. Discernible melody lines and comprehensible sentence formations—*Hallelujah I love her so* and *Have courage and follow me* and *You just don't understand*— emerge intermittently from a congestion of bad acoustics and aged tape, only to retreat again, each song abrasive and ungraspable, a phantom with acne. Voices are high and hollow, lonesome whistles behind three cheap guitars going by as fast and metallic as trains. Much of the Beatles is already here, particularly the Beatles of the very near future: the first recording of "One After 909," one of the earliest John-and-Paul originals; the blues treatment given a pop standard like "The World Is Waiting for the Sunrise"; the howling-dog harmonies that finish off an improvisation usually titled "I Don't Know"; the good time of "You'll Be Mine," with its absurd doo-wop melodrama and spoken interlude pivoting on a girl's glass eyeball.

On the Duane Eddy instrumental "Movin' and Groovin'"—still

only three chords, but a fast three—they hit on precisely the sharp dirty sound that would soon make them the darlings of drunken Nazi sons and daughters up and down Hamburg's Grosse Freiheit. Fed up with a straight fiber diet of leisurely blues-based improvisations, George tears off an ear-piercing intro. He is not casual; you can hear his concentration, feel the good pain in his fingers. Heading into the song, he doesn't lay back and wait for his moment; he attacks. John and Paul, perhaps surprised, realizing the kid means it, speed to catch up on their rhythm guitars. The attack stays high and tight for four action-packed minutes, capped with a classic rockabilly windup.

Bad tape or no, it is thrilling. Maybe it was one moment among all the other moments when they suddenly fell back and realized they weren't posing anymore—that an hour ago they'd been in one place, and now they were somewhere else.

History picks up the pace. They got themselves a drummer (Tommy Moore, older than the rest, with a day job, playing for kicks), a manager (Welsh bantam cock Allan Williams, a small-timer with low Liverpool cunning), and a job backing a second-tier heartthrob named Johnny Gentle. They toured Scotland for five weeks, grinding out the would-be idol's middling pop in decrepit ballrooms and isolated corners of the cold island, Clackmannanshire and Nairnshire and Banffshire, one shire after another.[15] So what if Scotland was even farther from the hot nucleus of the rock and roll sphere than England herself? So what if they were in darkness even here, the darkness of the stage's back reaches? It was action: they were back in the bog, the lower pits of show business, getting dirty. The logic of ambition says they drank in all the second-rateness of their station as proof of everything that was in store for them.

No coincidence that they changed their names just at this point— from unglamorous Quarry Men to mercurial Silver Beetles, with personalized *noms de stage* to match (Paul Ramon, Carl Harrison, Stuart De Staël, Long John Silver).[16] Not only name but identity: they were

starting to see themselves in the mirror of their audiences, their success, their first very small scrap of real success.

Allan Williams, who knew how to operate in toilet environs, made
things happen for them. After the Gentle tour he installed them as
regulars at his own basement club, the Jacaranda; and he booked
them for a solid two-month run at Liverpool's Grosvenor Ballroom,
where they played sets in between titanic rumbles among rival gangs
and unaffiliated stompers. John, Paul, George, Stu, and Tommy often
went in fear of their lives, and without doubt that fear put a new edge
on their music, the music sharpened by the fear even as it drove the
wild energies of the audience. The Silver Beetles' final Grosvenor date
was canceled when the ballroom itself was shut down over the violence attending the Saturday-night rock shows.[17]

The Silver Beetles left Liverpool on August 16.[18]

They returned as the Beatles, and on December 27 killed the crowd
at Liverpool's Litherland Town Hall—the Beatle date generally held
as witnessing the first flash of real riot: Beatlemania, ground zero.
"Their music was raw," Allan Williams writes, "almost savage, compulsive, and it knocked the Merseyside kids sideways. . . . The bounc-
ers on duty on the door thought a riot had broken out and went
rushing in to stop the trouble."[19]

Obviously it must be wondered what had happened to them between August 16 and December 27. Some hypothesis must be ventured regarding the place where it happened. And if the hypothesiz-
ing seems imaginative, remember what the Beatles became and ask if
any hypothesis too sensible can explain them.

□

The Beatles climbed down out of the van to stretch their cramped
legs. They breathed the air of sleazy Hamburg, looked around,
their eyes popping. They took to it immediately. It was their kind
of town, all right, all right.

—Allan Williams; in Allan Williams and William Marshall, *The Man
Who Gave the Beatles Away* (1975)

The year 1962 saw the release of *Mondo Cane* ("It's a Dog's World"), a Technicolor travelogue exhibiting the varieties of human and animal savagery around the globe. Though insistent on extreme depictions of death and dismemberment—and despite much of it being clearly staged—the film was a huge hit; its theme song, "More," even became a standard on the order of "Moon River." Among all the passages obviously faked, we find one that just as obviously was not: a glimpse of low-life along the Reeperbahn, Hamburg's roughest thoroughfare, and the spine of its red-light district. Over shots of boisterous beer-swilling in a Reeperbahn bar, the suave Italian-accented narrator lightheartedly interprets the revels: "And now let us do as these wild Germans of Hamburg do, and drown the memory of so many cemeteries in beer. In this gay German beerhouse of the Reeperbahnstrasse, our attention is attracted not by the cult of death but of life. Life is joy, is gaiety, is mental deftness; is physical fitness, social grace, serenity, and the power to forget. But most of all the absence of any memory, or sense of death."[20]

Initially the views are innocuous. The bright lights of the street, looking like any raunchy strip in any U.S. town. In the bar, patrons flash ugly faces, men sleep off their drinks at the bar, two women—one black, one white—lock tongues in a soul kiss. Then the bartender pushes a senseless man into the street, and the mood grows unstable, nightmarish. To the strains of stormtrooper music—"More" re-orchestrated as an ironic victory march—people stumble out of doors and wander into the dark. We are thrown into the middle of one hellacious fight, a blank-faced woman pulling a man's hair, the man's eyes bulging and wild, his face half-covered in blood.

Suddenly it's the morning after: gray light over the Reeperbahn. A small crowd watches as a man calmly and viciously beats a cowering victim. Three youths stand at a corner, one of them urinating into the gutter. A man vomits in an alleyway as his woman mouths curses at the camera. An old crone makes ballerina moves and smiles like a Teutonic Blanche DuBois. A wasted rocker tries to sleep standing up.

Men hide behind walls and posts, peeking out, mumbling paranoid mumbles.

It seems a land of the crazed. The Hamburg we see is a pit of undirected tension, tension a step away from nihilism; a culture—or anyway a subculture—that is drunken and stumbling in the dark, trembling with a hostile energy forced backward. With these images in play, we can daydream of the world the Beatles stepped into just as the Reeperbahn's red lights were flaring up in the dusk of August 1960.[21]

Those words of the Italian narrator are supercilious in their irony, but they point to something that feels true. What did every battered nation want in the years following the war but to "drown the memory of so many cemeteries"—to neutralize fear by whatever means were at hand? America used technology, chemical disinfectants, kitchen appliances. Britain retreated into the security of boredom. Perhaps these Germans used beer.

Perhaps these Germans would have used beer even if there'd been nothing to run from; and perhaps they used beer more obsessively and ritualistically because they knew running would not help. It's unthinkable that any other country bore a greater weight of irresolvable emotion, impacted angers, guilts, and frustrations, in the years after World War II. Germany had never gotten over its defeat in the First War; Hitler's stated objective at the dawn of the Third Reich, after all, had been a recapture of national pride, anti-Semitism merely one instrument among many. Only in time did his personal pathology surface as explicit program, whereupon extermination came to be the very diseased soul of national pride, its pivot and purpose. Once it did, Germany gave in to itself and tried to topple human life from the pedestal it had always occupied in the refined halls of Western civilization—to effect a radical reformation not merely in the ethnic makeup of Europe but in the mentality of the world at large. Who can say that it failed? In redefining the known bounds of human atrocity, Hitler's Germany left a curse on the consciousness of history.

In its mass madness the nation had sworn itself to a totality of victory, and so when defeat came instead it was not mere defeat but abject defeat—more humiliation. Having gone farther, they were obliged to fall harder. Germany was left in rubble, and the world spat on the rubble. Walled in on the east by the Soviets, controlled on the west by the victor nations, it was doled an allowance by American beneficence, blanketed in benign occupation by foreign military bases, and made to know that it would never again be allowed to choose its destiny, good or evil. It crept toward a factional democracy that was never convincing to the rightists, monarchists, and neo-Nazis left in the wake of the war.

When Allan Williams brokered with Hamburg club owner Bruno Koschmider to import the Beatles in 1960, Germany was closer to the Holocaust than America is now to Vietnam. "Some of them," Williams wrote of the Germans, "were still very sensitive about the war years and wore their national pride where their Iron Crosses had been."[22] Fear may have been the unidentified scent in the American air of the '50s, but surely it was everyday miasma to the German. (Some have said it took years for the crematorium stench to leave the valleys.) How do the citizens of a nation breathe this air, conduct a collective life under the weight of such a recent past? The forward-looking mass will put distance between itself and the past, work on the economy, modernize and beautify the cities, design, construct, create. But what of that minority which sees no place for itself in this project, those who fly as if instinctively from the comforts of their culture but still must deal with its poisoned common memory, and these German memories more poisoned than any? Well, they will choose their own poison, *danke schön,* and drink beer.

The Germans in *Mondo Cane* are playing roles—the rocker, the ballerina, the muscle man, the life of the party—which are implied by their clothes, their acts, their stances. And yet there is an emptiness to the faces, a flatness of affect that belies all that, that makes it seem as if their only true roles are as walking corpses in a living graveyard. So one plays the role all the harder—invests it with a conviction close to mania. One drinks longer, fights dirtier, fucks kinkier; buys a gun, a knife, brass knuckles. In the absence of some sense of self-determination, one will gravitate to an underground where the roles are fiercest and freest and the lower creatures of a desexed and disempowered society can run and shoot and screw in a shadow society of their own making.

This was the Reeperbahn at just the time the Beatles were playing it. This was their audience—first at Koschmider's small Indra Club, and then at his big room, the Kaiserkeller, with a few unauthorized drop-ins at the rival Top Ten Club.

And this is where we hear the first real crunching noise in the Beatles' story: the crunch of new history being made as existing histories collide. This is different from any noise we've heard before in this tale, and the first sign of what the tale will become a few years into the future. We've seen the birth of culture, the sprouting of new limbs from the body of old culture, the drift of alien culture to leave its specter upon another across the water. But this new phenomenon, unique in rock and roll to this point, lies in the collision between one irresistible force (the Beatles) and one immovable object (Germany), each with its own freight of history, memory, psychology, passion, prejudice. New culture is not the result in this brute collision, as it is when two forces meld together gradually, each yielding something to the other. The result is more sudden, more violent than that, the transformation of what already lives into a form it could never have anticipated, that is not "natural": a mutant, a monster. Not an osmosis but a grafting, under heat, with a rusty blade. A German eye grafted to the Beatles' British foreheads.

Their Hamburg stints are legendary for their chaotic character:

love and hate passing between performer and audience in barely controlled currents. This hot and scratchy relationship was inevitable, given the whole setup. It must have been what Koschmider sought, because he knew his patrons sought it, and the Beatles for all their hicky innocence were clearly hungry for corruption. So they would not quail at playing four and a half hours a night Monday through Friday, six hours Saturday and Sunday. Beer would be gratis, and amphetamines would help them hold the pace. Physical fires at a constant chemical stoke, no money, scant food, noise and shoving everywhere, whorehouse the readiest recreation, fear on top of excitement on top of drugs on top of sex, John on top of Paul on top of George on top of Stu on top of Pete in a moldering two-room cupboard behind the screen of a fifth-rate moviehouse. The Beatles grew skinny and manic. Suddenly their tempos were very fast indeed: they were not after speed—speed was after them. The stage act became a marathon stomp as they competed with Rory Storme and the Hurricanes to burst a hole in the Kaiserkeller's rotten stage. They traded curses and outrages with their crowds. Lurched about like cartoon cripples, hollering holy hell into the sunrise. Lennon in particular must have found it a kind of heaven: demented mind theater, Goon Show without censor or good taste, as he goose-stepped and played Der Führer to the crowds.

It was a bigger, hotter, riskier toilet than they'd found back home, and they had their dirty fun in it. The Hamburg days are rich in scatological apocrypha, a twisted lore of excrement and ejaculate that is probably half-fact, half-embroidery, and like all mythologies impossible to resist at either end: five Scouse rockabillies find they have wandered into *Tropic of Cancer*.[23] The boys urinate upon a flock of nuns passing beneath their balcony. They sculpt a Jesus, hang a beer-swollen condom between its legs, and erect the icon for the awe of Sunday churchgoers. About to be deported for lack of work papers, pissed-off Paul and Pete set a condom on fire and—whoops—nearly burn down the hovel they have called home. Williams even claims that "heaps of excrata" are to be found on the floor of said hovel, hidden under newspapers and spiked decoratively with cigarette ends.[24]

In Liverpool it had been up to them to shove destiny along. In Hamburg they and their audience, joint experimenters in the laboratory of bog aesthetics, shared the shoving. This was their first great audience, and no wonder: they and Hamburg were made for each other. A port town like their own, proud and provincial, rough and alcoholic, an open city: Liverpool on the Elbe. Could it be that the krauts looked at the limeys and saw themselves in a warped mirror—and vice versa—and there was recognition? Recognition of war, hunger, deep hostility, and fellow feeling between the undergrounders of two nations so lately striving to ruin each other? Could this be why band and audience got so ferociously intimate—why each side was jostling closer to its freakish foreign reflection for a harder look at something too hard to look at straight?

Germany gave the Beatles their first audience with ambitions of its own, one that rose to meet them in *their* ambition. The first audience to challenge the group, force them past their limits; to urge and adore them in their wildness, their profanity and ecstasy. Angry drunks, American sailors, student existentialists, ladies and gentlemen slumming; whores, pimps, junkies, gangsters, perverts, thrill-starved punks, dazed spooks out of *Mondo Cane:* these patrons were out for a bruising good time, a flash of knife, the night's fix of danger. They were not about to ease back and take in a show—it was a given that they would in part *make* the show. They would dance as other audiences danced, but they would also holler abuse at the band, tell it what to play, buy it beer when it did well, threaten it when it flagged. They would get drunker and drunker and the music would have to drive them all to the end of the night. No invisible wall separated the Beatles from those who had paid to be stimulated by them.

So these long nights changed them. Apparently they hadn't moved much onstage, pre-Hamburg; the Germans got them to move. Apparently the Beatles had been a skilled but not outstanding live group, pre-Hamburg; by the time they left, they were a buzz saw—no group on the scene could match them. Set eyeball to eyeball against a volatile crowd with a talent for confrontation and a hunger for raw meat, the Beatles could have quivered and retreated; their tonsilly yells might have turned to squawks. Fear might have eaten them. Instead it obsessed and propelled them—as it may have in some of the lower Liverpool joints, but never like this. In that fear, the midst of this noisy toilet, they found the growl at the bottom of their voice and the violence their music was capable of. And on returning home, they were able to force that same violence upon a crowd that, up to then, had *not* been pushing them.

There, I am guessing, is the seed of all that came later: the mania. The Beatles pushing; their audience pushing back.

What remains is to hear the music, the little there is of it: an hour or so out of the eight hundred the Beatles played in Hamburg,[25] an hour of tape that is as much a fundamental rock and roll document as Jackie Brenston's "Rocket 88," the Sun singles of Elvis and Howlin' Wolf, or Johnny Ace's "Pledging My Love." Like them, this music is both an obvious product of everything that fed into it and indefinable as anything other than itself: a hot piece of chaos we can hold in our hands, still bristling from a past we might otherwise doubt ever existed.

We leap from 1960 to two years later, to a moment that now predicts much of the future beyond it, and contains everything essential about the past that created it.

The last of the Beatles' five Hamburg trips was in December 1962. By then a lot had happened, and fast. Unquestioned dominance of the Liverpool beat; Sutcliffe dead; first studio sessions, under Bert

2. John at the stage door, early 1963.

Kaempfert in Hamburg, backing Tony Sheridan; dozens of hard sweaty sets back at Liverpool's Cavern Club; Brian Epstein at the cellar door with love and dollar signs in his eyes; out of leather, into suits; a failed audition for Decca Records, a successful one for EMI; Pete Best out, Ringo in; record contract; first single. Chartwise and otherwise, middling success. Measured from their toilet beginnings, terrific success. Everything that awaited them was just over the rise of the next hill: if they'd been able to see their own greatness far back in Liverpool and steel themselves with its certainty over the long Hamburg weeks, surely by December 1962 they were tumescent with expectation.

Then why, when playing their last show on the Reeperbahn—at the precipice of the year that would turn them into other people, "Beatles," strange faces in their own mirrors—why were they *still* playing as though everything hung on this one show? Why did they attack their music with the density and drive of a band with nothing to lose, hell-bent, willing to play as if for the last time?

The Star-Club recording was made on New Year's Eve, 1962, during the Beatles' evening show—taped reel-to-reel by Ted "King Size" Taylor, lead singer in a Liverpool combo that sometimes shared the stage with the Beatles. The tape was lost and forgotten, then in 1972 found beneath a pile of clutter in an abandoned Liverpool office; it was released five years later, just as punk was kicking at the bloated body of post-Beatles rock and roll.[26] The Star-Club tape had never been bootlegged, or even rumored: this piercing noise from a past that to many seemed prehistoric—that is, pre-Beatles—arrived with the suddenness of suppressed memory. Had there truly been a time when rock was that wire-drawn and fat-free, that *immediate?*

The immediacy, the drama, lies in the Beatles' attack—on the audience and on the music. Strangely for a New Year's Eve, the crowd sounds glum: there is a brazen catcall here and there, a woman who laughs a bit louder than society prefers, but mostly the roomful of voices combines and melts down to a motley hum. To the German MC's hurried introduction of the band, the ringsiders respond with applause too scrawny to qualify as a smattering.

If it is indifference they feel, or exhaustion, or if they are only pacing themselves against the drinking to come after midnight, it doesn't matter: the Beatles will throw indifference back in their faces and force a response. It will be an honest response—not merely grateful or surprised, but exhilarated. Along the way, Paul will play the toastmaster, the unflappable compere, the Latin lover, ready to parody his own love of kitschy masks as he suaves it up for song introductions, dedicates a tune to barmaid Bettina ("Your Feet's Too Big" his ungallant selection), and favors the lazy hand-clappers with endearments rendered in German. John, of course, will crouch behind him and soil the display, acting the spastic, the id, the evil echo. Irked at an early point by who knows what, he will declare in a tone of utter gravity to some unrecorded interloper, or perhaps the whole bloody audience:

"I don't know whether you can understand me or not, but piss off. You got that? Christmas or no Christmas."[27]

The show takes off from there. Listen to how the Beatles brutalize everything they touch. It's indicative of both the band's limits and its powers that although the songs range fairly widely in terms of sources, from Chuck Berry to Fats Waller to Marlene Dietrich, everything is turned into rockabilly. Usually on the staider material it doesn't work. If Paul's mush-mouth mewling on the *Hit Parade* perennial "I Remember You" gives a ridiculous pleasure—as does Lennon's harmonica, which wheezes drunkenly, wobbles happily—the Beatles are wrong in thinking something like "Red Sails in the Sunset" is served best or even decently by a rock treatment. Their desire to encompass all of popular music within the short reach of their rockabilly sound shows that their capabilities are not unlimited. They stumble here and there, their judgment is not quite as exquisite as it will one day be. On a version of Dietrich's "Falling in Love Again"—shades of *The Blue Angel* to appease whatever Weimar nostalgia resides in this shifty crowd—they waltz clumsily to a futile end, integrity of the song split between a McCartney vocal that wants to care and a group performance that is dissonant without being exciting or absurd.

But the Beatles' take on rockabilly was singular and, applied to songs that were made for it, irrefutable. Even at its most pounding, the rockabilly that came out of the Sun Studios had plenty of air and light in it, hollows for those Southern ghosts of country and blues to whistle in and out. The beauty of that music is not in its force but in the space it allows for the creep of ordinary mystery. The Beatles were not interested in making mystery—not yet. They were interested in stripping a song to its parts, exposing its frame, then retooling it with what was theirs: a group dynamic, a oneness of instruments and voices that made four discrete noises into one great noise, a syncopation of chaos; and a driving quality of hysteria, derived from the closeness of their crowds, the potency of their pills, the quickness of their ambitions, their desire to holler the world into submission.

Among other things, this means that many of the Star-Club songs, though eccentrically American in verbal content—especially Berry's, full of indigenous references—become new, odd things, songs without a country, or even a provenance: innocent objects with no sociology behind them, no shared cultural landmarks. Sung by a British band to a crowd of Germans, the Americanisms of "Sweet Little Sixteen" cannot mean much, even as symbols, even if they could be heard. But goddamn, how they swing this song! How they put across every excitement Chuck Berry dreamed it to express, and more. Hear how John flies into the heart of the chorus—*Ahhhllll over St. Louie*—and how Ringo's thunderous fills push him to go higher and harder, finally exploding the tension with an honest exhausted crash of the brass. The Beatles have beat the song to within an inch of its life, and the Germans know it is good. Not because it has told them something of what they are about—which it can do for Americans—but because it has rocked.

What's happened isn't the same as an American artist performing for Americans in America, where rock and roll is taken for granted because this is where it comes from, and therefore it is already mine—I don't have to *make* it mine. A vital clue to the Beatles' essentially indefinable specialness is that they simply had to work harder. Foreigners playing a foreign music, they couldn't assume it as a national birthright, or absorb it in all its Americentric detail; and so, driven to somehow own it, they were forced to absorb it as pure feeling, then to relay it to their audience in the same form. For the Beatles a song had to be reduced to a vehicle for expression with all emotional meaning—the song's power to connect in some deep way with whoever heard it—implied by the performance. Either it would rock, or it would do *nothing at all.*

But "implied" is such a weak, weak word. Nothing is implied in "Twist and Shout," which, unlike the vaunted version the Beatles would record in a few weeks for their first LP, does not take time building to its highest point but attains it immediately and stays there. Nor in Ringo's drumming on "Lend Me Your Comb" and "Matchbox" and all the way through: there are times when the drums alone whiten King Size Taylor's tape, distort and reconfigure the whole band's thrust. George's guitar produces the snide, cutting sound which is at the core of rockabilly—the sound of metal tearing, but tearing with style, marvelous elan, even wit. So many moments of breathtaking intensity on this tape. The coda to "Long Tall Sally," drums doubling, Paul wailing, the band lunging and devouring. "I Saw Her Standing There," a Lennon-McCartney original, and so pure a piece of rock it could pass for its own archetype. Even "Besame Mucho," that piss-elegant mock-Latin bit of macho. It may be kitsch, Paul may love it *because* it is kitsch, but they don't perform it as kitsch: unlike Elvis, they don't condescend to songs they know are beneath them. Instead they drive this lemon at top speed until it crashes into a real wall, into genuine things like power and release, and bellow joyfully as it explodes.

In this way, the show builds. The night deepens. The crowd is louder now, no longer indifferent, though they are yet to be won. The Beatles finish a number, pause to tighten strings, drink beer, throw back Preludin, do whatever needs doing between songs. The pause continues, Beatle mumbles passing under the microphones.

Finally a voice shouts, *Come on!*

For answer, George drills a familiar run on his guitar. He makes two or three passes at a tough opening solo, and then: "Roll Over Beethoven," faster, harsher, intenser than anyone has ever heard it. More rampaging in its sound, more of a weapon. George's ludicrously youthful voice, full of yelps and gulps and glottal curls, tosses off the lyric with a callow confidence that says: *Roll over, Beethoven. I needn't argue about this; I'm right and will be proved right.* Terrific suspense as the heart races with the beat—Can they hold this maniac rhythm, not fall back dumb and watch as it flies apart, its works fluttering with a tinkle of anticlimax over the crowd?

The rhythm holds to the very finish. You are twisted and breathless. These boys have something.

I'm a road runner, honey! Paul cries, at full throat.

Star-Club schnitzel-slinger Horst Fascher, big-bodied and tin-eared, steps up to front the band on a couple of tunes. His English is imperfect, his timing less than that. Crowd loves happy Horst anyway. "Be Bop a Lula" really gets 'em going, but—What was that he sang? *She's the king of all the queens?* Nah.

Lennon introduces what may be the most powerful single performance by saying, "We'd like to do one for the Negro sailor . . ."[28]

"Where Have You Been All My Life," a song from the Brill Building hutch of Barry Mann and Cynthia Weil, found its way to the Beatles in Arthur Alexander's 1962 version. Alexander was a deep well of painful talent who never found the mass audience he deserved, who sang with a choke in his voice that made you wonder if he saw failure and obscurity bearing down on him every instant. A soul man with a country singer's hurt heart, Alexander drained the song's organizing inquiry of all rhetoric and remade it as a real emotion. His rendition was at once a beautiful, expressive act and a commercial pop record. There was no way John Lennon could fail to love it, want to own it.

But mere replication is not enough; it could never be enough. Lennon must do his own number on it. Again he returns to that base level of pure feeling where words don't signify and action does—in fact so close to the base that the question, genuine in Alexander's mouth, is no longer a question but an outcry. Lyrically the song is made incoherent, since it no longer speaks of romance, but emotionally it is made to live in a way it never has before. Alexander was still wounded by his years of loneliness, stunned and grateful at finding love; Lennon is enraged, frightened, confused, as if in finding one thing he feels all the keener how much he still lacks. But anyway the band moves too fast for the words to matter. George and Paul, singing backup, do not encourage, they taunt—they are Lennon's furies given voice. The recriminations lie in the growing hostility and desperation of John's singing more than in the stock phrases, and by the final chorus which is pure white noise, a dense block of frustrated wanting, he is screaming. Hearing it, I wonder one thing: Is it possible to care this much? About a song?

There is one other Star-Club performance that to me says the most—that says everything. Lennon is again at its obsessive center, though the obsession he voices belongs to all of them. The song is "To Know Him Is to Love Him," the Teddy Bears hit of 1958, written and produced by Phil Spector. In its original version there was no song worthier of being sung by people calling themselves Teddy Bears, but in the Beatles' treatment it is barely credible as a high schooler's fulsome daydream of wedded bliss. Their whispered verses are low, controlled, sinister: the sound of a secret wanting to reveal itself. It's not a high school kind of love they're singing of—in fact this love isn't quite placeable on any map previous pop has provided. It simply is what it is; and whatever it is, it binds you to it. The audience in the Star-Club, by now perhaps halfway through the Beatles' set, listening harder with every song, holds its breath to see what will happen.

For this is the Beatles' promise: that something will happen. That there will be that point of breakout, when the noise coming from under the ground thunders through the crust to shake everything free of itself. The Beatles were suckers for the breakout. "To Know Him Is to Love Him" has a dramatic bridge that in the original, holding to Top 40 pop-song form, occurs once; the Beatles use it twice. They can't resist: they are in love with what they've done to it. Ringo pounds his sticks, lifts the band on his shoulders to the breakout: *Why . . . can't she see—How blind . . . can she be?* Paul and George support John with a rhythmic vocal figure that rises on the heartbeat of the audience and the new hard march of the instruments; we imagine them both transfixed with the audience as Lennon sings from a deeper place than he has reached tonight. John is the one who must sing the words of the breakout because he is the Beatles' breakout factor, forever the voice of their communal will, of their arrogance and ambition:

Some—day—she will see (as the chord sequence reaches its plateau and the singer squares off with his image of the absent lover, with the audience, most of all with the self to whom he is making these oaths) *that she—was meant—just for me.*

Of course. Some day they will *all* see. There is such a note and twist of triumph in John's voice as he reaffirms this to himself. *In spite of all the danger . . . if you'll be true to me . . . some day she will see.* It all adds up.

With a circular *da-da-da-da-da-da* and shattering cymbal, the Beatles spiral back down into the calm and sinister. But only until the next breakout: if one climax is good, two will be killer. So they try it again, the impossible—lifting song and audience again to that same height, pushing the song and their performance and their luck to their limits. Do they bring it off? Do they—the second breakout is everything the first was, only more so. And when the song is finally done, the Germans applaud. They whistle, they howl, they cheer. They are moved. They are won.

What have the Beatles just done? Well, they have performed a brutality on something they love. They've taken a song that on its face means little, is a sweet sentiment, sweet tune, they've ripped that bland face off to show the skull underneath, and—holy shit!—there *is* a skull. There is an inside to the song, and it is able to hold the very personal meaning with which the Beatles are compelled to invest it. The Beatles make the words of the song mean everything they conceivably can—so that now the words not only avow an eternal union but damn its absence, dare its defiance, take the last stand against any possibility of its failure—and suddenly there is more behind the words than anyone knew. Simple words of love have been wrung for their every emotional meaning; their power has been pushed to the surface and let loose.

There is one thing clear and evident about this Star-Club music when taken as a block: it is not just music, but the sound of deep emotional experience pressed into the tightest, most intense space imaginable. In other words, it is something like life. Not a scrap of life or a stolen glance at life as in most pop music—a moment's epiphany of connection to a cosmic oneness. Heard as a whole, the Beatles' last Hamburg performance is a large, weighty chunk of real existence. Existence in a toilet, the toilet rendered in full dimensions, with focus and specificity; a liberated mix of bodily fluids, an exchange of rough pleasure. In this music we hear a start and a finish; fight and victory, struggle and reward, everything given and taken along the way.

In its primitive forms, this early performance contains so much of what the Beatles would become, so much of what they would give. Certainly it tells us what millions would find so transfixing in their music: the sound of deep emotional experience pressed into the tightest, most intense space imaginable.

□

Collarless jacket as castration symbol?
—A note I once scribbled

It's always interesting to see what a minority passion does once it enters the world. Will it grow or wither, change form or stagnate, absorb its neighbors or die in the act of eating itself? Will it stand monolithic and self-important, touching nothing, or will it show a talent for subtlety and subversion, its fingers spidering out in a hundred directions to touch a mind here, a heart there, put bodies in synchronized motion across great distances?

It is too easy to say, as John Lennon did, that the Beatles left the best of themselves behind in the cellars of Liverpool, the dance halls of Hamburg. The experience they gained in those places was deep and irreplaceable, but it was only one kind of experience; it was their bedrock, but nothing grows in bedrock. Whatever their ambitions for it, the music they had learned to make was nothing if not a minority passion: it was produced by a few to be received by a few others. Knowing that, yet knowing that a minority success could never begin to satisfy their wants, they had to choose that full engagement with the world that the first wave of American rockers had probably not even envisioned. Engagement, not capitulation; not castration but intercourse. Intercourse meant pushing, resisting: to become bigger than Elvis they would have to resist what he did not resist, which amounted to being rewarded too highly for doing too little. But it meant, as well, allowing themselves to be pushed. If the Beatles were to change the world, they would have to agree to let the world change the Beatles.

It is important to remember how much of this happened not by chance but because of the choices they made at each stage. In Liverpool, John, Paul, and George had made their first choice: they chose to be big. They then made all the less spectacular choices entailed by the first. If they lost weight it was because they chose not to eat; if they squatted in hovels it was because they chose to squat. If they became the greatest thing in rock and roll it was because they chose to live in filth and perform in fear, and then make music that was undeniable because it had been put daily to that test. They were, after all, scions of the middle classes, with homes to return to and honorable trades to enter. But as a function of their desire and the work ethic it demanded, the Beatles elected to switch strata and become working-class; while in their drive forward they took nothing for granted, except that forward was the only place to go.

For them it was likely no choice at all, whether to enter the world or remain cloistered in their regional dominion. What would have happened to them had they not gone for engagement? Probably much the same as what happened to many of the early rock fathers: obscurity and slow decline in the fabled backwater of fame. Conceivably they could have gone on for a few years, shouting the same songs in the rear recesses of dives smelling more and more like tombs, the sound bleeding up the stairs to the street where those walking the cobbles above would scarcely register it. They would have split apart, drifted back to their neighborhoods, never been known. The world would have gone untouched by their boggy hands.

The years since 1957 had been a wholesale investment in the belief that such an abysmal end was not an option. The time came for them to leave their toilet workroom and blink their eyes against the light, and see if the noise they had worked up could survive in the world.

We know that it did. Look at their record jackets from 1963 to see one version of how. The cover of the first album, *Please Please Me,* is a colorful commercial confection of its time: a splash of cereal-box graphics, the LP title given not once but an overemphatic twice, at the center four small faces beaming. Far from being underground, or under-anything, they look down from a great height. But this is the moment just before they've made it, and it represents the push of the world upon them. Soon enough they are doing the pushing. They first fully announce themselves to the world on the cover of their second album, having reached that apogee they have always *known* is theirs to assume—you, the world, are now *With the Beatles*—and it's no mere pass at faddish style but a statement of reality that the faces have the rocky grain of stone busts; or that they are half-hidden, even yet, in dirt and darkness.[29]

Now go back to the records to hear how closely the Beatles' 1963 sound, still so near its toilet antecedents, held to the principles of bog rock while integrating them with fresh inspirations. The music is bright, inventive—yes, and sometimes it is that dreaded thing, cute. But what is remarkable is that its *madness* is just barely contained. Listening into these records is like nothing so much as that last shot of Polanski's *Repulsion*—a long meandering track, ending on a photograph which at any ordinary distance is a happy family portrait, but in burgeoning close-up reveals a child who radiates the livid glare of a psychopath.

The madness whirls at the center of a sound that encompasses the Beatles' entire toilet-dwelling past and foretells their future. Against the American pop of its year, it comes on like a seizure. There are raging adenoids, hot shrieks, near-to-grating slivers of harmony, and other irritants in the sound; more than a suggestion of the ugly, skinny, spotty English war-baby teenager, a *hysterium nasalis* that had no place in the sweet hums of Sam Cooke or Dion, the thunders of Spector, or the bitter tea of Roy Orbison. The singles, especially "She Loves You" and "I Want to Hold Your Hand," are monumentally crazed: clearly made to singe the frayed cloth on a million walnut-box English radios.

But delve past the hits into the B-sides and LP tracks, the less glamorous bones and organs supporting their cheeky hits. Love songs go at a gallop ("Ask Me Why"), introspection is a hurried moment between Star-Club sets ("There's a Place"). "Hold Me Tight." "Devil in Her Heart." The desperate peaks of the "Anna" refrain. In "This Boy," John's near-loss of emotional control on the word *cry*. Even a song called "Misery" is fanatical in its heartiness. Two Motown covers, "Please Mr. Postman" and "Money," are perhaps the maddest of all. Lennon and the band go so far past the songs' textual preoccupations with romantic and pecuniary fulfillment that they cease to be *about* anything other than the unprecedented lunacy of the people performing them.

Save for a pair of aberrant and deeply refreshing McCartney forays into Pop Standardland ("A Taste of Honey," "Till There Was You"), there is no Beatle song in 1963 that does not partake of audial insanity in some form or guise—that is pure cool, indifferent to its own breakout potential. This is the sound that soon would be dumped on America all at once, as a whole, not an evolving but a formed phenomenon: several years' worth of accumulated shrills, amphetamine highs, first excitements. Why did this music have as its destiny the inspiration of a mass madness? Because, formed in an ecstasy of aggression and energy, driven higher by wild popularity, it was itself madness, physical madness. I sing the body hysterical.

Thus, ambitions of Melvillean size came in sight of their realization; the undergrounds of Liverpool and Hamburg sang to seventy-three million on "The Ed Sullivan Show"; fantasies unimagined were set in motion; and a sound born of the toilet emerged to take over the world.

□

In this orgiastic technological fantasy in which our lives are led for us, it is all too easy to assume that basic human needs are altered or radically modified. Basic needs merely go underground.

—Ihab Hassan, *Radical Innocence: Studies in the Contemporary American Novel* (1961)

3. Calm before the storm: outside EMI Studios, July 1, 1963—the day they recorded "She Loves You."

It will have been guessed well in advance that this vaunted toilet is not meant to signify merely the objective flush contraption, or even the symbolic toilet where rock and roll started. We've been talking about the national toilets of the postwar years—toilet being a place everyone goes at least once a day, a place necessary for the disposal of the wastes of surface life. That is, the underground, which is where waste goes, and where it sometimes turns into something else.

Most of us privileged types in the West, if we touch an underside at all, touch one; and then we run. Consider all the undersides the Beatles not only touched but lived in, embraced. They came out of American rock and roll: product of the hot, fluid underside of American society in the '50s as it grew from the '40s, all the rage and discontent beneath the congealed pudding-skin of God's country. They came out of Britain: the nonoccupied nation that came closest to internal collapse in world war, memories of terror and dirty human wants driven under cover of ritual and the pull away from public excitation. They came out of Liverpool: scarred, provincial, polyracial, hidden in an inconspicuous corner of an increasingly marginal nation. They came out of Germany: the country that in this century grew most hellish with the fascist underworkings of the collective mind. They came out of the Reeperbahn: a danger zone where guilts and lusts rose from beneath social surfaces to emerge as beer culture, fringe culture, freak culture, something violent and begging for a smash-up.

The Beatles absorbed each of them thoroughly, and left having taken what they needed. They were amalgamated of secret madnesses, hidden torments, the bogs of the Western world in the years of war and after-war; they became dwellers in toilets, hinterlands, undergrounds. They then had the monumental audacity to attempt to bring that buried force to the surface. Why? Because such a thing was there to be done, and they could do it. And if their action wasn't total, if they were not committed to realizing the absolute, there would be no point in acting at all.

"We could handle anything," John said years later, remembering his thoughts as the Beatles, primed with fame and acclaim, cast eyes on their land of dreams. "We were new. When we got here you were all walking around in fucking Bermuda shorts with Boston crewcuts and stuff on your teeth."[30]

No way for America, or the world, to resist the changes they would bring with them. Like a flower or an orgasm or a mushroom cloud—anything whose birth, growth, and machinery are underground but whose nature compels it upward—how could the Beatles have failed to burst and spread, blanket and engulf the surface upon reaching the light and air of the greater world?

In December 1966, a group of students in Berkeley, California, met to discuss antiwar strategies. Someone started singing "Solidarity Forever," a perennial of the unionist movement. It was quickly supplanted by a newer song, one equally though more obliquely expressive of unity in tight conditions: "Yellow Submarine." On October 21, 1967, war protesters at the Pentagon in Washington D.C. would also sound this song, with its foursquare beat (perfect for marching) and inspirational verses (heavy on "we," "us," and "our"), in the moments before rioting broke out.

"With a bit of effort," a writer deeply involved in such events said years later, "the Beatles' song could be taken as the communion of hippies and activists, students and nonstudents, all who at long last felt they could express their beloved single-hearted community." Although there was, he acknowledged, an exact obverse to that interpretation: "It did not cross the collective mind that 'Yellow Submarine' might also be taken as a smug anthem of the happy few snug in their little utopia."

Michael Rossman, a Berkeley activist, had been at the sing-along that night in 1966. Heartened by the unison of like voices, he found himself filled with renewed drive and optimism. The flier he produced and distributed the next day depicted a yellow submarine floating over a small sea of hopeful words:

"The Yellow Submarine was first proposed by the Beatles, who taught us a new style of song. It was launched by hip pacifists in a New York harbor, and then led a peace parade of 10,000 down a New York street. Last night we celebrated the

growing fusion of head, heart, and hands; of hippies and activists; and our joy and confidence in our ability to care for and
take care of ourselves and what is ours. And so we made a resolution which broke into song; and we adopt for today this unex-
pected symbol of our trust in our future, and of our longing for a
place fit for us all to live in. Please post, especially where pro-
hibited. We love you."[1]

2

ASCENSION/SACRIFICE

A Hard Day's Night and Help!

Dear Paul,
   I think you are very sexy and I don't even know what it means.
Your little fan,
Shirley D.
Louisville, Kentucky
   —*Love Letters to the Beatles,* ed. Bill Adler (1964)

The words used to describe this country's first response to the Beatles have always implied violence. *Conquer. Invade. Rule. Dominate.* These took root in the early days of American Beatlemania, when they were employed by veteran newspaper reporters—men conditioned to translate any big story, from missile crisis to heavyweight title fight, into metaphorical war. But as ideas meant to encompass the meaning and convey the impact of the event, these words are all wrong: they reduce and simplify the identity of the event as it led out of and into other events. The language of warfare does not describe what occurred when the Beatles landed at JFK Airport in New York on February 7, 1964.

Had those reporters been women, the defining words of Beatlemania would have been different. (The British Seduction?) The lan-

guage on the distaff side—heartthrob rags, gossip columns, fan letters—may have been just as clichéd as the war talk of the men, but
today it does speak honestly, because it speaks emotionally; and emotion, the Beatles' and the crowd's, was what it came down to. *Giggle.*
Swoon. Love. Obsess. America's response to the Beatles is found in the
wet eyes of a fifteen-year-old schoolgirl straining to touch Beatle baggage outside the Plaza Hotel. The skeptical eye examines every extant
artifact of the first American trip—studies film, absorbs analysis, examines testimony, factors in every expression of something less than
enchantment—and nothing seriously qualifies the impression of romance and fascination on a gigantic scale.

Many who would have assumed no commonality with a British
pop group, from a fight promoter to a cop, found there were things
they could take from the Beatles, things they could give. The promoter was Harold Conrad, who was publicizing, in Miami Beach, the
first match between heavyweight champion Sonny Liston and chal-
lenger Cassius Clay. When the Beatles came to town, a week after
landing in America, he inveigled them into a photo session with Clay
and wound up engineering one of the key iconic encounters of the
decade. The cop was Buddy Dresner: charged with Beatle security in
Miami Beach, he found himself watching TV with Paul McCartney.

> We were watching a show called "The Outer Limits,"
> and I said, "If I had one of those guns, I could zap all the
> criminals."
> Paul said, "What did you say?"
> "Zap," I said. They never heard that word before. I heard
> they put that word in one of their songs.[1]

Less than two months later, improvising a scene in the Beatles' first
film, Paul extemporized Shakespeare by way of Buddy Dresner:
"O, that this too, too solid flesh would melt. *Zap!*"

It may have been with that *Zap!* that the Beatles first fully engaged their world, their audience, and their history. How strange that people like these—so removed from them in age, culture, concern—should find themselves stepping into, and changing, the Beatles' story.

But that fifteen-year-old girl—she *was* the story. And such was the depth of her feeling that it could absorb all negative opinions, parental sneers, and critical dismissals: for love, as every girl knows, is not love without the challenge of those who would dismiss it as infatuation. The Beatles' musical spectacle, said a New York *World Telegram* editorial, "seems to be a haunting combination of rock 'n' roll, the shimmy, a hungry cat riot, and Fidel Castro on a harangue." *Newsweek,* less allusive, went straight to words like "nightmare," "disaster," "catastrophe," and "preposterous."[2] But these were reasonable adult squeaks in a squall of unmediated adolescent emotion, pieces of newsprint at the bottom of an inner page of an afternoon paper that stopped existing years ago.

Not that skeptical and even contemptuous voices weren't heard. In fact they were the ones most often heard: their owners were the ones sitting before the cameras on news shows and talk shows and even game shows, joking about long hair and predicting, as all sensible people did—as the Beatles themselves did, lying through their teeth—that this Beatle thing wouldn't last. That the Beatles, heh-heh, well, they're a symptom, you see, of our nation's post-assassination anxiety/depression/confusion/frivolity. These voices—Chet Huntley's, Dr. Billy Graham's, your father's—were heard loud and clear. They simply failed to shape the event in any way. The fifteen-year-old girl, along with the Beatles, did the shaping.

Because it was her event as much as it was theirs. She makes up the bulk of the audience at the Sullivan shows, poised eagerly on her seat to see everything and more, clapping hands not upon the beat but with the spontaneous surge of her feelings as the middle-aged men around her squirm and grin. She is a brunette, a redhead, curly, straight-haired, plump, skinny, she wears glasses or doesn't. Beautiful or plain, cheerleader or bookworm, she is equal to every girl around her. She is consumed with a fantasy that has dropped itself in her lap, and it makes her jump from her center. The girl's is the one image that is effectively synonymous with the Beatles': often TV and newspapers, pressed for the one picture that would say a thousand words about something for which there really were no words, would show a picture of one sobbing girl, or a hundred.

There's nothing dark or negative in her energy. She seeks to be part of the event, release herself in it, and wants nothing from the Beatles, really, but the pleasure they offer. Tom Wolfe, in 1964 a reporter for the New York *Herald Tribune,* wrote of watching as a group of girls set upon a policeman who, exiting the Plaza, was claimed to have touched the Beatles. "The girls jumped on the cop's arms and back, but," Wolfe is quick to point out, "it wasn't a mob assault. There were goony smiles all over their faces."[3]

The Beatles, co-conspirators, wore the same goony smiles. If they gave their audience joy, it is equally apparent that, at this stage, they were getting it back. Watch them in the Maysles brothers' fly-on-the-wall documentary of the American debut: whether suffering the disc-jockey jiveries of devout Beatle-booster Murray the K, flinging their arms wide for "spontaneous" photos in Central Park, or mocking American cigarette ads on the train to Washington, they are serene in their fame. They do not strike antisocial poses or play at being resentful in the teeth of the attention they have sought; they seem even to love the reporters and photographers who are their constant companions and querulous chroniclers. It seems inconceivable that the Beatles could appear so innocent—could *be* so innocent—after the mean, scraping days and nights that have brought them to this place. But their delight is clearly the real, youthful thing.

Perhaps the Beatles, who had eagerly surrendered so much of their innocence to the toilets of Liverpool and Hamburg, again look so innocent in February 1964 because they are absorbing the innocence of

4. Wired up for *Another Beatles Christmas Show,* Hammersmith Odeon, London, December 1964.

those around them, reveling in the last time that they will ever be so new to an audience, that any audience will be so new to them. Watch them perform on "Ed Sullivan" and see a kind of interaction with the audience that simply does not exist anymore. Note the way Ringo drums without a hint of self-sacrifice on his face because he sees the *rightness* of the whole event: this thing he is doing, this place he is doing it in—everything about it is right. Follow the chain of interlinking pleasures forged as Paul's grin incites a communal scream—which causes him to grin a little wider—which brings on a bigger scream. See the assurance with which Lennon, from the floor of a Miami Beach hotel ballroom, can bark at the Paul-squealing cuties, *Shut up when he's talkin'!*, in full knowledge that the squeals will only rise higher, the ecstasy peak on his harshness. The Beatles have been in America a few days, and already they have achieved an intimacy and ease with their audience unlike anything that existed before them, unlike anything that exists today.

That's the way it happened; that's how fast it happened. In a swim of goony smiles given and gotten, they played "Sullivan," the Washington Coliseum, Carnegie Hall, "Sullivan" again in Miami Beach. Posed for photos with the likes of Don Rickles. They made themselves rich and famous. Then after two weeks they left, as mysteriously as they had come, but with a promise to return in the summer for a full-scale tour of the States. America was left exhilarated and confused, millions of its children huddling in classroom congeries, dreaming open-eyed into their pillows, and walking their schoolyards in excited circles, not knowing what to do with their excitement.

This was the Beatles' honeymoon with their audience, and it lasted, all told, a few months. Then things began to get strange.

But this is Memory Lane, the stuff of someone else's nostalgia—just what we seek to avoid in thinking clearly about the Beatles at the turn of the twenty-first century. So why the rehash of old hash? Just to pause and appreciate the verity of what could be too easily cast off as another precious, self-massaging boomer cliché: that in its first flush Beatlemania really was a very innocent thing, something naive and without guile. It was what it appeared to be to anyone looking on—erotic and emotional fantasy of a fine grade; intense, yet uncorrupted by any suspicion of what maturer forms the fantasy might take. Its implications (sexual, social, mass-psychological) were sufficiently well hidden so as not to trouble anyone's thrill. For the Beatles, it was the opening-night performance after a long and arduous period of dress rehearsals. For the fifteen-year-old girl, it was the best first date imaginable with the boy she would never get over. For everyone, it was action without immediate consequence, the party without a morning after.

The Beatles made and released their first movie immediately after their initial trip to America, when they and the world were still on such uncomplicated terms, each in the glow of its first discovery of the other. So their film debut would reflect that. The reckonings could wait for later, and later was thought to be a long time off, if it was thought of at all.

□

Q: Got any analogies to elucidate this whole tongue thing? I still think you chew the root.
A: Okay, take the scenes in *Hard Day's Night* where the boys escape all the time by running away from the pack pursuing them and then, upon realizing there's no way out, they do it by going right back in the same direction they came from. Or you could take a photo of the earth and the moon and fold it in half and punch a hole in it and unfold it and stand in wonder. Good enough?

—"R. Meltzer Interviewed by A. Warhol," in Richard Meltzer, *A Whore Just Like the Rest: The Music Writings of Richard Meltzer* (2000)

A beginning—

Simultaneous with the chain-banging sound of a twelve-string electric guitar, and a flicker of white over the screen just as the image appears, three Beatles are shown running from their fans. Where they are running *from* is not indicated, nor why they are on foot at all; but no questions occur in the madness of the dash and dart of the camera eye, the hysterical laughter of John, George, and Ringo, the silent screams of the pursuers. The boys run and hide, leap and evade, and as they make their circuitous way to the train that will carry them to London they are driven through a succession of ever smaller, tighter enclosures. From street to alley to instant-photo booth to telephone box to train station to train corridor to train compartment, we watch as their world narrows before our eyes.

—and an ending:

Sunny Bahamas, and the Beatles are safe, for the instant, from all the mysterious characters who have been after them lately with guns, bombs, and artillery. Close by, all hell breaks loose. The scene blurry and imploding with the helter-skelter of cultural and ideological collisions (white-black, scientific-religious, Christian-Hindu, East-West), its action by now so free of finely directed passions that it represents not just chaos but Chaos, the Beatles stand apart from the fray that has spun itself up around them. In the water, washing red paint off their drummer, they frolic in the overcast of eight enormous arms rising from the body of a female deity appeased only in the ritual of human sacrifice.[4]

A beginning and an ending: two depictions of a mass hysteria. But the change in character from one to the other could not be more striking.

Some of this change can be explained logically. It was to be expected that *A Hard Day's Night* and *Help!* should represent some of the more obvious changes in Beatle lives between early 1964 and the year following—new standards in clothing and hair-length, increases in adulation and money and exhaustion. The films were manufactured as Beatle products in a Beatle world and were bound to reflect, within the limits of good mass-market taste, the reality of those for whom they were tailored as vehicles. What was not to be expected was that they should be such uncanny *symbolic* enactments of those changes, bracketed by echoes from the past and portents of things to come— the heightening into occultism and madness of Beatlemania as it mutated from its beginnings in youthful fascination into something larger and scarier, a familiar beast with new heads.

The progression goes something like this: lingerings of the old toilet amid the first bright burst of Beatlemania; evolution of the Beatles from dirt-stained humanness to something godlike; beginnings of retreat as they become objects of morbid obsession; and development of a volatile bond with their audience that, beyond the films' bounds but predicted by their subtexts, will result in a year-long tug of war between the Beatles and the world.

In one way, it is absurd to claim that movies like *A Hard Day's Night* and *Help!* have their dark sides. As texts, these films are anything but incoherent: they are conceived as commercial vehicles for the worldwide transmission of pure personality, made by and for people who sought no contact with demons. And yet they reveal themselves to the skeptical eye, the fairy-tale eye which knows that nothing is quite so benign as it seems, and that charm always has a reason. Both films are what they are, but they are also what they are not: each is a positive underprinted with its own negative. *A Hard Day's Night* is as open-hearted and cheering as any movie musical that exists; it is also damp and dismal, preoccupied with bare white bulbs and imprisonment. *Help!* is pure splash, deep color, and King's Road corduroy; at the same time it's cynical about itself, weary and mean, its bent to the morbid at odds with the shopwindow pop milieu which gives it its look and sensibility. These movies are natural twins not merely because one was sequel to the other but because they are united by the through-line of a common dream life: that of the Beatles' evolving relationship with their audience.

Logic won't take us closer to this. The real nature of the change in

Beatle hysteria requires a search for symbol, the traces of unconscious apprehensions left upon the image.

Plotwise, *A Hard Day's Night* is straightforward enough. The Beatles are to perform their spot on a television show; their own natural rambunctions coupled with Ringo's brief defection at the prodding of a mischievous senior citizen conspire to . . . It's as silly, on paper, as any sockhop tedium ever produced by a Skid Row studio—but innovation was never the point. For United Artists, the point was to finance ninety minutes of United Artists–owned film showing the Beatles doing whatever it was kids wanted to see the Beatles do, in the process of which United Artists would sell a few million soundtrack albums. For the director, Richard Lester, the point was to show the Beatles moving and speaking and singing, running, jumping, and standing still: to make an artful pop movie. As for the Beatles, they were determined to be the stars of a "real" movie—as real as might be achieved within the borders of the jukebox musical, a form limited on one side by romantic convention, and on the other by standards of filmmaking so malnourished as to lie starving in the B-movie's lowest depth.

For the group, "real" meant, if not truth-telling per se, then not lying to their audience egregiously: portraying their own essence in a way that was rough and immediate, and light on the pop-idol sugar. Their ethic results in a picture that is proudly ordinary, with a visual style that not only avoids gloss but is drawn in the other direction, toward something approximating squalor. Its project is to place the Beatles both physically and psychologically in situations that will emphasize their commonness, their Liverpudlian toilet whiff, their life size. They are limned in a precise but unromantic, un-*noir*ish black and white; they are shown not luxuriating in their rewards but earning them; and most of their time is spent in either the literal underground of tunnels or the figurative one of tight rooms and jostling compositions.

Until its very last shot, the film takes a resolutely antimythic stance with regard to its subjects, and pursues qualities of clutter and cruddiness. From the baggage cage in which the Beatles share space with a dog to the catacombs beneath the TV studio to the wet mud and hidden pits of a construction site, the film is styled in North Country Drab. Even in cheerier environs—nightclub, hotel room— the picture's psychic gravity pulls toward the banal, the stale air of overpopulated spaces. As a piece of filmmaking, it leaves exposed the unpolished edges of staged fiction (John's swimming trunks in the bathtub), as well as the process of visual reproduction itself (the klieg lights, video monitors, and technicians mediating between the Beatles and their concert audience). The cinematography, despite its focal clarity—we can read the made-in-Madrid imprimatur inside George's Spanish guitar—leans toward plain-faced realism and unheroic arrangements in which the stars' bodies tend not to dominate any others.

Narratively the film is a series of encounters between Beatles and non-Beatles, the point of any given exchange being how unimpressed each party is with the other. In this blasé democracy, the Beatles are shorn of "specialness" even as their charisma is magnified. Just as the credit sequence drives the group from open space into airless confines, the ensuing train-compartment encounters dress them down from sleek, self-possessed idols to defensive teenagers with their tongues stuck out. They are made to seem like lads in the cadaverous presence of Paul's grandfather, and assume a schoolboy irreverence when lectured by the road manager. Further regression comes with the arrival of a dyspeptic, derby-wearing fussbudget whose Edwardian hauteur dwarfs them as in a Freud scenario of the castrating father. After Lennon makes a spontaneous pass ("Give us a kiss," a familiar British endearment not endearing in this context), they are forced from the sanctuary of their compartment, the scene ending with boy-Beatles on the other side of the glass and crying, *Hey mister, can we have our ball*[s] *back?*

More in this vein is to follow. The Beatles are objectified, reduced, and ridiculed, the result being that they are kept clear of any pedestal while respect for their self-assurance grows. George's session with a pop promoter—whose attitude goes beyond cynicism to an absurdist misanthropy worthy of a Dickens character—plays like an update of *Expresso Bongo,* both the exploiter and the exploited fully clued in to the scam, with Harrison as a Cliff Richard who won't play ball. Though the group score points off their neurotic TV director, what comes through equally is his perception of them as purely visual objects ("Try not to jiggle out of position"). The press reception opens on a montage of reporters devouring food as they would devour the Beatles; each vignette that follows shows a reporter gagging on a Beatle who will not be eaten. (Subliminal comedy throughout the movie is provided by the scrape of the Beatles' glottal Scouse against the assonances of educated Londonese.) The group's only natural allies are those as comfortably déclassé as themselves: the grandfather, the road managers, the elderly hotel waiter who sits reading an Elvis movie mag in his underwear. Ringo commiserates with a truant schoolboy, the two familiarly trading working-class gibes and slang— a scene in which Lester is as faithful to the real sneer and smudge of an English boy-face as Fellini was to the sweat of an Italian circus performer.

The point is made: the Beatles are not gods but men; and not long ago they were boys, boys who came from a dirty place. Dirt lingers in their voices and in their manner. The world makes of them what it will. In *A Hard Day's Night* the Beatles are despised as well as loved; but this is the Beatle dream in action. They are caught in the process of engaging with the world, and objectification, reduction, and ridicule are part of the bargain. Again, Elvis is the only precursor. Certainly he braved stronger ridicule and harsher dismissals as the first rock and roll freak to push something genuinely new and outlandish upon America's gray, Depression- and war-conditioned taste. But when it came time for him to make his devil's pact with the movies,

5. "Try not to jiggle out of position": George and Paul with director Richard Lester, March 1964.

he buffered ridicule by retreating behind fictional personae and plots in which he was no freak but a race-car driver, a circus roustabout, a hip ghetto doctor, the natural embodiment of cool surrounded and supported by characters who were a Hollywood version of the Memphis Mafia.

For years, Elvis was off the concert stage and the movie Elvis was the only one people saw; in the public mind, the two became one. In that sense he substituted a fiction for himself, and the fiction was not real or even "real" but pure ectoplasm: his films may have been garbage, but they were plainly designed to extend, or at least maintain, the Elvis myth of social and sexual mastery. The Beatles play themselves in *A Hard Day's Night,* just as they played themselves in public life and on the stage; and so, aside from their wits and their unity, they have far less buffer against the various ways the world chooses to engage with *them.* This is not to diminish Elvis by claiming the Beatles were more courageous than he; they were not. But it is to suggest one reason the Beatles went farther with a mass audience: they obliterated the boundaries of a performer's ability to change people's lives by consistently placing themselves, not a mythos of themselves, on the chopping block of world response. The singular wonder in their journey derived from this eschewal of self-protection—as did the danger.

The point is made again: *A Hard Day's Night* seeks to place the Beatles, pretty much as they are, at the center of a portrait approximating their real lives and true selves. The film will soften a harsh truth but not polish an ideal: it seeks, essentially, to quash Beatle myth before any can be born. But amid all this conscious and unconscious demythifying there are subtle signs of harsher things brewing, of a time when myth will become too powerful to deny.

This is where the humanism of the first film shades into the secular deism of the follow-up. The signs are so subtle because they have to do with the Beatles' fans—and in *A Hard Day's Night* the Beatles, among their myriad encounters with the unimpressed, are shown in head-to-head relation to their fans scarcely at all. Fans are a rolling wave or flying wedge forever haunting the streets outside, their common shriek an audial constant stitching itself through the soundtrack. Nothing is explicitly made of the audience as a malign factor; if the Beatles have fear of the fifteen-year-old girl, at this early point it is tucked safely away in their dreams. Yet there is an odd moment when Ringo, drumming inside the baggage cage with the schoolgirls outside, jerks his head away from two creeping schoolgirl fingers. It is a reflex move of terror and self-protection, like the sudden pivot of a hunted animal at the snapping twig, and it just barely corrupts the surface of an otherwise enchanted interlude.

More red flags in a scene which has John mistaken by a wardrobe lady for someone never named—her ambiguous love object, his features said to be hauntingly similar to Lennon's, but perhaps imaginary given the games-playing nature of the dialogue. Wardrobe Lady's immediate and passionate insistence that "Oh, you are, yes, you are" is met with Lennon's feeble "No, I'm not," and ends with her realization upon closer examination that "You don't look like him at all." This Pinteresque compression of the stages of love affairs both private and public—fixation on "recognized" object; refusal of object to conform; rejection of object—is achieved in perhaps a minute and a half of screen time.

Interesting for its further implications along these lines is the scene of Ringo alone, snapping photographs of milk bottles along a deserted street. He is spotted by two girls; he runs. Slips into a second-hand clothing store. Emerging dressed in docker's cloth cap and soiled overcoat, he tests the disguise by placing his famous schnoz in the face of a passing beatnik girl, who cuts him dead in a voice dripping of East End: "Get out of it, shorty." In context it is clearly the soil, not the schnoz, that turns her off. The moral: as far as the audience is concerned, divest a Beatle of his Beatle trappings and he is one more common geek. Let the object refuse his role and affirm his ugly uniqueness by sticking his very specific snout in your face, and the result might be not unconditional love but something altogether more ambivalent, from confusion to hostility to something as yet unglimpsed. "You don't look like him at all."

The film perceives the sexual component in Beatlemania; but as with its other ambivalences, sex is hardly something to be faced directly. The Beatles are held clear of overt sexual associations, yet the associations are there. In fact they are displaced onto the film's own Fifth Beatle and comic prophylactic, the grandfather. "Sex-obsessed," as he is pegged, he functions as the Beatle id, embodying all that they wish at this point in their public lives, and everything they fear privately: old and crusty ineffectual rebel, representing the specter of age and withering of beauty, but also anarchic and confrontational, acting out the Beatles' own fantasy of an open defiance they don't quite dare. An id is by definition contained only half-successfully, an irritant always at the edge of consciousness. Like the Beatles, the grandfather looks "clean" but his thoughts are lewd; his actions, like theirs, are calculated in the direction of disruption and breakout; and the longer one knows him, the less his surface hygiene obscures his baser knowledge.

More than anything, Grandfather carries the deeper psychic currents of the Beatles' sexual presence: their erotic play with the audience, and their maintenance of an image that by unspoken agreement is *not* explicitly sexual, but "clean." His double-entendres are at least as direct as Lennon's; and at the concert's climax the old Irishman, old spirit of rowdy Liverpool, pops through the stage, quite erect and penis-like, only to be shunted offstage by an embarrassed Harrison. Just before the concert John lectures Grandfather, and behind the old man sits an enormous tilted blow-up of John's face. Taken from Dezo Hoffman's 1963 collarless series, the face is a smirking reminder of gamier times. "But I'm clean," Grandfather protests in his role as Beatle proxy. "Are you?" John asks, interrogating himself. And through it all the magnified Lennon mouth grins, a vertical gash on the scene, drawing attention to the humor inherent in the moptop persona, the id behind the id, the dirty smirk in the Liverpool toilet that lies at the bottom of the Beatles.

6. Clean Englishman and sex-obsessed id—but who is who? Paul with Grandfather (Wilfred Brambell).

But these are only ambivalences; they remain vague no matter how long we try to bring them into focus. They are suspicions of complexity, and slivers against the grain of the whole film. Certainly they stand in opposition to the concert that both ends and defines the picture, in which the picture resolves or at least defers these fan-based doubts and secures itself in an affirmation: an innocent exchange of love. Love of the Beatles for their audience, as much as the reverse; and innocent because this love knows only what it is at the moment it is felt, with no regard for what it may become. These are screams of joy, not violence; these mouths are open in wonder, not hunger. This is all honeymoon, no marriage, pure communion between the Beatles and the fifteen-year-old girl, and a great climactic moment in movies.

It starts with a flourish: a hail of female arms flying, and Ringo's drums rolling out the opening bars of "Tell Me Why." Then a series of shots, each of which shows a girl mouthing the name of her favorite Beatle. The band, viewed from every angle, sing abbreviated versions of songs already heard. The camera prowls the stage like a journalist taking notes; not quite involved, it regards the audience from behind the drum riser and casts the show as impersonal spectacle. It does not venture too closely to any band member's face, and the shots of girls weeping and shrieking are static, though beatific. The neurotic director bounces happily in his box.

But as the performance continues the cutting quickens, more intent upon capturing every point of view—the Beatles', the fans', from overhead, low, sideways, straight on. The camera comes in close: Lennon's salaciously grinning, singing lips fill the screen. And though the concert is an epiphany of innocence, this does not mean it isn't sexual. It is: there is crescendo and climax and a pervading wetness to it. We are treated to close-ups of authentic Beatle sweat. Girls' faces turn to spongy masses of tears and mucus. Features are blurred with accelerated movement. The camera's lens zooms in and out.

Booming sounds from Ringo's kit herald the final number. "She Loves You," maybe the greatest performance of the Beatles' early years, is the climax of the climax. Grandfather appears, is suppressed: the priapic suggestion is enough. Now the camera loses all objectivity. It spins and darts in sudden upheaval, trying to capture an instant of sense in those faces, failing to center itself upon each open mouth. It sweeps and swoons, cuts from Beatle to fan and back with each thump of a Ringo floor-tom, coming to detumescent rest on a full-stage shot of four Beatles sighing as one upon the eternal *Yeah*, and behind them there is a burst of incandescence:

BEATLES

They are off running again.

You may not articulate it but you sense it, you know it: a transformation has occurred. The Beatles are not what they were when we first saw them, just ninety minutes ago. They have reached an apotheosis, and a point of no return. With every day that passes, they will be less what they are and more what they are seen to be by those whose lives are bound up in theirs. They will lose identity as they gain ubiquity; in place of their reality will appear any number of autonomous fantasies. In place of a band there is now a word, a presence, an idea: BEATLES. They are gods now—*How did that happen?* they are asking each other. And so a sense of just completion attends as the Beatles take off for their next show in a helicopter, and we witness, from mere ground level, their ascension into a new realm.

It's true that, as one watches, this does not quite register as a move into the mythic. It comes with no visual signifier (celestial cloudburst, say, or *Oz*-like shift into Technicolor) that it should be taken more seriously than what has preceded it, and it flows naturally out of the rhythm the film has built. Besides, the Beatles have another show to do, and air is the speediest travel. But hindsight robs everything of its simplicity. Out in the real world, the Beatles were already in the process of becoming something other than they had been; and the people who made the film had to feel this, even if their brief was to maintain the group's human dimensions. This antimythic film ends with a mythic dénouement because it knows what is happening, but doesn't know it knows.

□

Dear Beatles—
   I saw you when you landed at Kennedy Airport in New York. I was almost killed and I was just six feet away from you. Everbody went crazzzy. I had an ankle sprained, my dress torn, a slightly scratched face, and a black eye.
   Isn't it WONDERFUL?
   I adore you all,
   Cookie E.
   Queens, N.Y.

   —*Love Letters to the Beatles,* ed. Bill Adler (1964)

Meanwhile, back in Paradise:

Between June 4 and September 20, 1964, as they ran, laughed, sang, and ascended on the world's movie screens, the Beatles mounted its concert stages and sang the same twelve-song set-list to audience after audience on their first international tour. They performed in Denmark, the Netherlands, Hong Kong, Australia, New Zealand, England, Sweden, and England again. On August 19 they went to America and played thirty-two concerts in twenty-five cities in a little less than a month.[5] Most concerts were sold out. The flick was boffo. Lennon had a best-selling book. The Beatles were cleaning up on all fronts; by any measure they were the most popular thing in the world. Naught but love rained on their shoulders.

But other, not just loving things were beginning to occur; bizarre and, in what should have been the afterglow of global coitus, unaccountable things. In Sydney, Australia, fans dramatized their love by pounding the Beatles with a hailstorm of jelly babies. Now this was nothing new. The story had gone round back in England that the Beatles, to a man, loved the candy; for at least a year they had felt the sting of the little missiles. But now, it would seem, there was a shift in intensity, for the band elected to speak out. "I keep asking them not to chuck those damned things," Paul told a Sydney daily in an uncharacteristic snit, "but they don't seem to have the sense to realize we hate being the target for sweets coming like bullets from all directions." No use, said the reporter, for Paul to stop the show and beg a reprieve: "Each time his request has been greeted by screams and another shower of sweets."[6]

The day after their September 18 performance at Dallas' Memorial Auditorium, an article by staffer Larry Grove appeared in the *Morning News*.[7] The article is both a conventional wrap-up on the concert and an inscrutable text. At the preshow press conference Paul is asked if he is an anarchist, and a reporter wonders what Ringo will do with his recently removed tonsils. Yawns all around. Then someone asks, "Are you scared when crowds scream at you, John?"

"More so here [in Dallas] than other places, perhaps."

There is a sidebar photo of Lennon, and its caption says: *"Beatle John . . . Will he regret the remark?"*

What can this mean? That Lennon will, or ought to be made to, regret admitting that he is more paranoid in Assassination City than anywhere else? (George had already refused to inaugurate the U.S. tour by riding through San Francisco in an open motorcade.) Who might make him regret it, and by what means? Is it a warning to Lennon and whoever else might speak plainly to watch what you say, because someone else might be listening? Search the article again and it answers no question; it only blandly predicts the future.

There were weird scenes on this tour, harbingers of weirder to come. Upon landing at the Sydney airport, they were driven to their car atop a truck in a violent rainstorm. Film exists of this. The truck is open and the Beatles are on display. We stare in pity and complicit misery as they manfully brace their umbrellas against the torrent, offering a wave, a grin, making like Beatles as George's umbrella is ripped away by the wind and they stumble and huddle in a pathetic real-life parody of *Hard Day's Night* slapstick.

Bomb threats were lodged as the Beatles flew across New Zealand, and again before a show in Las Vegas. At least twice they rode into town in the wake of disaster: in Philadelphia they played Convention Hall just days after a race riot, while a Jacksonville concert followed the destruction wrought by Hurricane Dora. Shows were halted midway through in Cleveland and Kansas City as fans breached crowd-control barriers and police cordons. Psychic forecaster Jeanne Dixon, who a year earlier had won the ghouls' lottery by hinting at JFK's demise, added to the gaiety by announcing that the Beatles' chartered plane would crash and burn somewhere between Indiana and Pennsylvania.[8]

So the honeymoon was over. The marriage had begun.

On top, with its surface hijinks and air of frivolity, *Help!* scarcely seems to know any of this has happened. If anything it has less gravity than the first film, which seemed lighthearted enough. But underneath, it is defined—far more than *A Hard Day's Night*—by a compulsive apprehension of what it cannot consciously realize. It scores real life as farce, disguises concrete and well-grounded fears in a series of tossed-off jokes springing from a premise that places the Beatles as moving bull's-eye for a band of religious zealots.

Whatever its cartoon quality, the violence this movie visits upon the Beatles is remarkable in its variety and volume. Castration fear, which reared its head in the earlier film's encounter with the stuffy Londoner, is a powerful theme in the preliminary stages of *Help!* Ringo, because he wears the sacrificial ring, faces first the loss of his hand—a drummer's emasculation. But past a certain point, only the *death* of "he who wears the ring" will satisfy Kali; at which time castration anxiety is replaced by a more generalized fear of violence emanating from who knows where. For plot purposes the Beatles are shrunk, drenched in paint, thrown through glass and into water; encaged and electrocuted; strapped to mad-science machines and operating tables; pierced, poked, and prodded; chased, fired upon, blowtorched, and blown up. They become the target of everyone's animus, and spend the movie trying to survive. With a wink and a song, but trying to survive.

Help! is therefore a comic strip of what the Beatles' real lives were becoming; and not surprisingly it shows them recoiling from the world's burgeoning demands, receding from the audience even though in their madcappery they appear to be in constant forward motion. The film is even an instrument in their retreat: it defines itself in every way as *unlike* the real world—anyone's real world—by inhabiting a self-referential sphere of mod satire, hip clothes and hip spoof and everything hip. Likewise the Beatles are spherically encased, and unmoored from any but a symbolic sense of their relationship to the real world. Much of the lingering emotional taste of *A Hard Day's Night* comes from its insistence on the unglamorous,

7. Stranded in a limousine: the Beatles take refuge in *Help!*

which enables it to ground an inexplicable present in the stone and mortar of a very real, very dirty past. Whereas *Help!* is insistent upon knowing only its own evanescent moment: it bears no weight of Beatle history, no sense of their having come from anywhere or up through anything, and is anxious in its slapstick to evade the implications it raises for the future.

Richard Lester and his gifted movie artisans spackle this absence with shining surfaces and primary colors. *Help!* is tacky and noisy, from the Beatles' domestic décor to the outsize toilet brush crowning the ceremonial headgear of Clang, high priest of the Kali cult. The group alight from their limousine to unlock four doors along a quiet street of row houses, each door its own bold color; the doors are shown to lead to the same apartment, and we want to believe they represent unique passages to a common heart. But the interior is spiritually impoverished—like summer-camp accommodations for the children of the super-rich, or the museum installation of a fatuous sculptor who believes he is decrying the kitsch that in fact dully entrances him.

The movie persists in displaying the Beatles', and its own, commercial affluence. The having of money is scarcely inimical to good rock and roll or good rock and roll stars, but in *Help!* money buys them the style they once created out of themselves. *A Hard Day's Night* showed the Beatles in implicit opposition to the cult of mindless consumerism, not because they were Marxist but because in their new fame they realized they had become its latest tool. *Help!* shows them to have become the most conspicuous hoarders of useless gadgetry outside of James Bond's MI-5. For Paul, a multicolored pump organ laden with comic books; windup false teeth to clip George's carpet of grass; for Ringo, an armada of airport-lounge food-vending machines. Soon enough, the Beatles' regressive preoccupation with costly diversions will become that of the film itself, scene after scene pushing machines and expensively designed antics to the fore in a gross display of clanking tin and dull fun-making.

This is a function not just of scripted narrative or a bloated budget but of Lester's camera strategy. In the sequence accompanying "Another Girl," the editing moves the Beatles around at will, picking them up, putting them down, with cutting providing the only physicality as movie magic makes chess pieces of four inert bodies. The Beatles miming "You're Gonna Lose That Girl" is a lovely passage for its visuals, a soft-edged montage of faces shot through colored gels and cigarette smoke. But it communicates neither passion in perfor-

8. Their magnificence as objects: in *Help!* the Beatles are sleek and
   beautiful, but also indivisible, inbred, and inaccessible.

mance nor the furtive interrelations of a tight unit—as did the musical sequences in the first film, without apparently trying. Throughout, the Beatles are employed as simply four more colors, objects to
be shadowed and filtered and poised merely for their magnificence as
objects.

Visually, a queer thing happens as the film cranks along on its rusty cogs: the Beatles themselves turn mechanical—become toys. "My gosh," says Clang of the four, "they all look the same, in their similitude and language." And it is hard to gainsay the tubby Indian, because in *Help!* they are more alike physically than they have ever been, or will ever be again. The first film gave each Beatle room to move; each was allowed his differences, however glib or stereotyped. In *Help!* they are hastened as a bloc from one crisis to another, indivisible, inbred, and inaccessible. Black-and-white photography seemed to sculpt their unique faces out of light and dark; in color, the same faces become fat blurs. The fringes over their pot-dimmed eyes lack the character of Beatle hair in the first film, where each head had such identity that in the film's advertising it was visually acceptable to crop each face from bridge of nose down, identifying its owner by nothing but staring eyes and silhouetted crown. And though their *Hard Day's Night* costumery was more identical, here the clothing on one Beatle body is interchangeable with that on another, for they even *wear* their Carnaby Street fashions identically.

What we see in *Help!* is the "real" Beatles at a double remove—once by the falsification of fiction, again by the vicissitudes of the fractured Lester style—and so twice as alienated from any vital, breathing portrayal of a true Beatle essence. The film, though it never comes close to owning this, is onto something dreary and self-indicting: the extent to which the Beatles have already become mechanical puppets in their own processional. The most obvious difference between the two films is that whereas in *A Hard Day's Night* the Beatles determine the plot, in *Help!* the plot determines them. Persona in the first is subsumed under "personality" in the second, and Beatles are found to be less important than "Beatles."

Sacrifice, remember, is the theme. In the course of the movie, the Beatles are driven to relinquish ever more of themselves in order to remain insulated from the madness they've inspired—which is now

9. On the run from Clang's artillery—and the gathering forces of hatred and obsession.

other people's madness more than their own. They sacrifice essential parts of themselves even as they gain materially and are allowed to roughhouse at some of the world's more extravagant tourist sites. Part of this has to do with the Beatles' vulnerability, as exposed public figures, to a certain humiliation. "One has to completely humiliate oneself to be what the Beatles were," John once justifiably bitched,[9] and in *Help!* the humiliations they have undergone in life are replayed in comic costume. One scene situates the boys in a toilet (remember it?) and has them buffeted about rag-doll style by a supercharged hand-dryer, and soaked by a water-spout. If the Sydney airport humiliation had an echo of *Hard Day's Night* knockabout to it, jarring because it was not being acted for laughs, this wet episode in a very different kind of bog is an instance of art imitating life imitating art.

Then there is the specter of sacrifice as something literal: physical violence, the explicit wish to destroy. This is where *Help!* begins to intimate, like the Dallas *Morning News* article, that weird and dangerous desires are abroad in the land, and that they are focused hard upon the Beatles. Kali is the correct choice of savage deity. She is Female—standing in for all of the female horde whose love, hunger, hysteria, and jelly babies assail the Beatles. Her arms wave like those of the girls who kicked off the *Hard Day's Night* climax. In effigy she is enormous, her size representing the shadow of the Female over the Beatles. Kali represents the audience, and its threat: like Kali, the threat is without personality, faceless and many-faced, but manifest in the outbreak of sudden, specific hatreds. (Thus, Clang throwing colored darts at the Beatles' black-and-white images harks back to the innocent jelly babies of 1963, prefigures the physical and verbal attacks to fall upon the Beatles in 1966, and connects one to the other.) Like Kali-worshipers who kill to renew their vows, the Beatles' audience is beginning to respond to them in ways that suggest violence as a natural result of adoration. Toward the end of the decade, this Thanatotic impulse will make its return in far grislier forms; yet here it is, as early as 1965, nestled at the very core of this comic-strip enterprise, this commercial machine.

The sacrifice at stake has to do with objectification. At the same time that they construct an elevation of Beatle status from human to god, *A Hard Day's Night* and *Help!* on another level chart the course of a dissolution: the dissolution of the Beatles as a public phenomenon with self-defined features into one that is increasingly defined by the feelings the audience projects upon it. The audience discovers hostility and hunger mingling with love in its well of feelings, and the Beatles withdraw into the guarded bubble of their private entertainments. In the cause of self-protection—from physical harm as well as "mere" humiliation—they are close to canceling themselves as individuals.

Danger. It may be that gods-in-waiting assume their Valhalla at precisely that point when they are perceived to have no personality, no stubborn eccentricities left, and no shield against the hunger of the mass for an uncomplaining repository of its own desires. If in *Help!* the Beatles have ascended to new heights of wealth and fame, they are also powerless to control the movements they have set in motion. As worship blurs their individualities, melds four persons into a single nonperson, the audience will increasingly be left to write that part of the story which the retreating Beatles have abrogated—to scheme and dream in a roomful of Beatle posters, Beatle 45's on the spindle, Beatle dolls as bed partners. Ultimately the audience will go beyond dreaming into active mythmaking, begin to scrawl its own narratives, carve its initials, upon the passive bodies of its idols. "Try not to jiggle out of position."

These are the dynamics of the Beatle drama as it builds to its peak. As celebrities, individuals who must live the better portion of their lives in public, the Beatles feel themselves evaporating. The audience is making demands upon them that go well beyond the bounds of mere entertainment. The audience is making symbols of them. The Beatles in the next year will exist beneath the crushing excesses of love, hate, fear, and pathology that symbols from Jesus to John F. Kennedy have been invented to absorb. The audience will demand that they lie still as they are strapped to the slab and this surgery of symbology is performed under the white light of an international arena. But the Beatles—and one of them in particular—whether out of contrarian reflexes or conscious strategy, will find no choice but to resist, to jiggle out of position in an attempt at sabotaging the entire lunatic process.

□

Recall: the Beatles had made a vow all those years before. The vow had been returned when they engaged with the world and were in turn engaged by it. *I'll do anything for you . . .* Singing those words in Percy Phillips' parlor, they were addressing their ideal respondent. That, it turned out, was the fifteen-year-old girl, and the Beatles' vow was a prophesied proposal: an investment of their dreams in the depth of her feelings, her receptivity, her capacities for excitement and passion, her willingness to go all the way. The first joyful American encounter was their courtship. When the girl sang her own song back to them—title it anything, title it "We Love You Beatles," "Little Beatle Boy," or "I Want a Beatle for Christmas"—it was her way of saying Yes.

A Hard Day's Night ended with the honeymoon. Hence, Ringo turns up in the Beatles' next movie wearing a ring. It has been sent him by a Hindu Beatlemaniac, the fifteen-year-old girl in her Indian guise; it is a wedding ring, symbol of their vow. Red and oversized, it's also the girl's heart and soul, blood of her youth, color of her passion. *Help!* goes on to depict the turbulent early stages of the marriage. Everything in it that is dangerous, from religious mania to Professor Foot firing his handgun at John's chest, grows from the red heart of that red ring—from the unfathomable complexity of the Beatles' intercourse with their audience.

Even in its happier forms, marriage can enforce unwholesome dynamics: domination and submission; sacrifice of self; balance of power; a certain assumption of ownership on both parts. In marriage each partner gives up something, takes something; each learns when to lead, when to follow. Each attempts to mark the other as a kind of property. Contented marriage defines itself on a happy resolution of these interrelationships, or at least enough of them. Contentious, vital, evolving marriage—of the kind shared by the Beatles and their audience—depends on an ongoing examination of how to live richly and justifiably within these extremes of give and take, the human process of needing to recast, in accord with one's own private needs, the persona of the loved one.

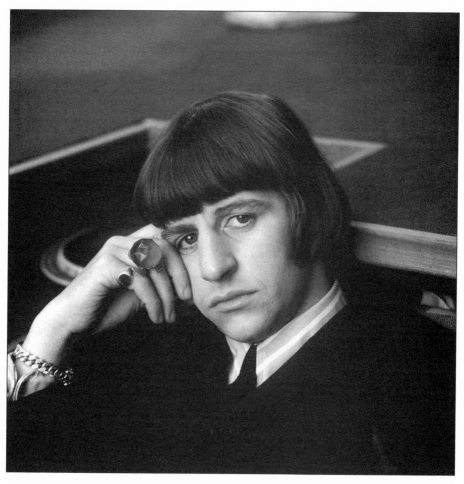

10. Sacrificial lamb, sacramental blood: Ringo and the glowing talisman at the center of *Help!*

Another thing about marriage: there are always in-laws. The fifteen-year-old girl had them in abundance: a Bible-thumping, record-burning uncle down South; zealously nationalistic brothers in the Far East; and more shrieking sisters than could finally be counted.

11. Ascension: Hammersmith Odeon, December 1964.

This dialectic became operative in the Beatles' story almost imme-diately—starting in Hamburg, where they found their first great audi-ence, were pushed by it, and learned fast how to push back. *A Hard Day's Night* links the process, now in further evolution, with those toilet-bound pre-phenomenon days when the ambitions were grand but the stage infinitely smaller. *Help!* shows the process in full blaring action. Both express tensions of the sort that always grind in those hidden connections between a beautiful fantasy and its grimmer reality. Therefore they capture, albeit by accident and against their will, something more essential about the Beatles than can be contained in the standard judgment that *A Hard Day's Night* is moptop joy and *Help!* a depressed and sluggish failure. Driven by the fantasy-reality frictions that haunt the Beatles' story—which, in the terms of this telling, *are* their story—*A Hard Day's Night* is not pure joy any more than *Help!* is mere exhaustion. Put quite simply, they are, to paraphrase a line from the latter, not what they seem.

This is the region from which *Help!* in particular derives a surprisingly disturbing undercurrent. Strange that a pop vehicle explicitly designed and manufactured for the purpose of propagating love— that is, the audience's love for the Beatles—should all throughout its length acknowledge and anticipate, even if only in comic form, the imminence of real hate. Strange that it would recognize in the deeper part of its frivolous candy-colored self that the same psychological mechanisms that produce deep love also produce fear, resentment, and the will to destroy the object of that love. That the Beatles, by accident of history, force of personality, or an inexplicable hybrid of both, are a constant and irritating provocation to the precarious sense of cosmic right residing in millions of dogmatic hearts and minds. That in addition to being an organic magnet for love, they are inevitably to become a natural locus of hatred.

In mid-1968, Jean-Luc Godard was in London making a movie.[1] *One Plus One* aspired to be an impressionistic collage anticipating the pop-political revolution that was sure to be coming soon—to your theaters and your streets. But ultimately it looked more like a revolution sitting around waiting to happen.

Everyone is up to something and not accomplishing anything. Black radicals stockpile arms and read aloud from Eldridge Cleaver, in between raping and murdering white virgins. An offscreen narrator reads passages from an imaginary porno-political novel written in hardboiled prose—de Sade by way of E. Howard Hunt. A mystery woman spray-paints word-mutations on sidewalks, shopfronts, billboards, cars: CINEMARXISM; FREUDEMOCRACY; SOVIETCONG. The Rolling Stones, communing in their studio, manage to work up a new song ("Sympathy for the Devil") and emerge as the only ones in town with any follow-through.

Guevara, Castro, Ho Chi Minh, Malcolm X, Kennedy, Cassius Clay: each totemic male rebel-god of the time makes his guest appearance in the violent porn fantasy that coats the stream of images like a poison frosting. Godard's revolution is promiscuous and star-obsessed: a radical-chic fantasy of murder, deface-ment, and name-dropping.

At the end, a title card alludes to the radical catchphrase of Paris' May '68 uprisings: "Beneath the pavement, a beach." But on the beach Godard shows us, a war is playing itself out. Activity is split into discrete pockets; impossible to tell what is going on or why. People run—a woman falls, aping agonized death—a camera crew strains to catch every twitch.

You cannot tell what is happening here, but you do get the idea that the revolution has failed. Soon it will be escape time for the survivors—for every failed revolution has its survivors. But where will they go? What magical ark will spirit the radical remnants to their new Heaven on Earth?

"Now I was standing on the beach," the narrator says, "waiting for Uncle Mao's Yellow Submarine to come and get me."

You figure it out.

3

MEAT

The Beatles in 1966

Summer 1966. A female fan—fifteen, maybe, going on sixteen—is being interviewed by a television reporter. She holds a painting she has done. It shows Paul McCartney, with large head and elfin body, amid greenery and hills; oversized and sponge-like, he seems to be rising from the earth. The girl describes the painting and explains its meaning.

"And the name of it is 'A Sprout of a New Generation.' It shows Paul McCartney comin' up from the earth, like sproutin'— a sprout. A start, a new dawn. You see, the Beatles are the original. They started the look, everything. And they are the greatest group ever. And here is the thing—if you notice, he's like growin'."[1]

Dream is the only form of experience that allows consciousness to wrap itself around the impossible. So we're magnetized, when thinking about the Beatles, by the dream analogy. The story itself is so fantastic as to compel us away from the banality, the single dimension of fact, and toward the dream—its logic, its symbols, its states—as the only source of sense.

What the Beatles touched off was dreamlike in particularly deep and intricate ways. Their mania became a huge, open arena for the unregulated discharge of submerged energies—their own, and the audience's. Within it the symbolisms of desire, fear, and foreboding ran wild. Under its proscenia, acts were committed which could not be consciously acknowledged for what they were. And under its sway, the dreamer had no power over its components, its direction, or its outcome.

The year 1964, at least in its first months, had been a time for sweet dreams, mass dreams unprecedented in size and spontaneity but still obvious, perhaps, in meaning. In 1966, the obvious meanings of the Beatle dream were eradicated by others which, up to the instant they were made—if even then—were anything but obvious. This was their year of living dangerously, the harrowing passage leading them into the meaty, complicated center of everything: the year they located, lived out, consumed, and regurgitated the nightmare that lay coiled inside the Beatle dream. These months were a succession of crunching noises, amplified by universal attention and the instant meaning that was now attached to Beatle movements, Beatle opinions.

As a result, the rules of pop engagement were forever changed. Again and again in 1966, specific segments of the observing world used this mere pop group as an outlet for enormous social anxieties; in the process, the Beatles were laden with a range of symbolic roles the variety and weight of which no performer had ever been made to carry. Symbolic, but the dangers were real enough. The mania had never been higher—but now it found its readiest expression in action that was violent, destructive, negative, rather than romantic, transcendent, positive. Which merely means that the Beatles and their audience spent the year inhabiting a very different kind of dream state from the one that had enraptured them two years before. In this year symbolism, as in a dream, ran wild; acts were committed which could not be consciously acknowledged for what they were; and the dreamer had no power over the dream's components, its direction, or its outcome.

For the Beatles, it was a defining impasse: a hero's impasse. Were they fully the pop heroes they had imagined themselves to be? Were they strong enough to carry their ambition as far as it might go, into the unlit outer reaches of the vow? This was the test—and no one yet knew the questions, let alone their answers. At one far-off time the Beatles had had exemplars of success, but past a certain point no precedent existed to offer them a model of sanity and self-determination amid a surge of public feeling both pro and con. Past that point, they were in a zone no entertainer had entered. Forced back on each other and into themselves, they had to recreate the Beatles as they once had created them, though now for different reasons. In 1966, the Beatles found that evolution meant competing with the images and interpretations of others; and that they would need to do their evolving not in the sheltering dark of a Liverpool cellar but under the teeth of a devouring world.

Either docilely serve the audience, or draw it into a deeper engagement—these were their choices. They had chosen engagement in the beginning; and in 1966, at a turning point in the world's history and theirs, they chose it again. Despite feeling paralyzed at the center of the mania, the Beatles would draw their audience in by pushing it to new places. They would speak contentious, unprecedented words; offer upsetting, incomprehensible images of themselves; make disorienting musical noises. Just as their music would be the best and most challenging they had yet made, their collective persona would be more provocative, richer in dimensions than ambition or circumstance had previously allowed—or required. They would answer and interpret their suddenly hostile world in the language of symbol, the logic of dreaming; and they would, by accident and intent, seduction and aggression, tumult and meditation, sound early shots in the ferocious battle over consciousness which consumed the latter half of their decade.

12. Wild eyes in Boston, August 18, 1966: a dark year of meat and dreams.

It was certain that in this process, as one version of the Beatle dream crossed another, the dream in its first form would die. What was *not* certain—what the Beatles and their audience would have to determine together in this dark year of meat and dreams—was if something new might be born of that death.

□

The noise zeros in fast: blurs sideways and expands as disconnected sounds synthesize themselves within a stereophonic vacuum. First a metronomic drum throb consisting of one solid thump and its stuttering echo; then electronicized whimpers evoking the cry of hungry gulls reeling over a barren shore. Somewhere between the crash and flutter of these elements the song takes its swirling shape. The Lennon voice enters, layered, its affect more schizoid than godly.

Solid bars of backward-running noise flare up and die out in the spaces between lyric lines; reversed guitar phrases form and vanish like smoky invocations in the song's constantly shifting air. The voice now crackles, a ghost in the machine. The sound-collage achieves summation, lingers briefly, and then simply expires, echoing with vaudeville piano and the mad cawing of those starving sea-birds.

Extraordinary, contradictory, this piece of music: evolving and constant, claustrophobic and expansive. Although the product of a placeable historical moment and style of mind, in its randomness it floats free. While it is all trickery, a cacophony of contrived randomness, it is also genuine, a piece of reality in the form of stylish artifice: the Beatles gaze through the lysergic window to view their world, and ours, in all its tempest and monotony, its richness and starvation.

With some few exceptions the shelf life of artistic experiments is fleeting, and nothing dates faster, and worse, than a self-conscious innovation. To the extent that "Tomorrow Never Knows" retains fascination, it is because its somersaulting tape loops and revolving Leslie speaker touch reality—and take it over. The song ends, and the reality one returns to is changed. It matters less that a Beatle fan could hear his or her direct experience of reality evoked in "Tomorrow Never Knows" than that the fan knew there was now a whole new version of reality on sale, and that their $3.98 could buy it. The new version came with new mysteries; but the clues were there. They might yield a solution or they might not, but the crucial thing was that, here and now, *the game was on.*

In its initial version, "Tomorrow Never Knows" was a mesmerizing monotony of hard-packed electronic sound: far denser than its successor, it was also less open to the encroachment of any listener's unique imaginings. That the Beatles opted for the remake, with its broadening of the stereo picture, more specific colors, gaping canyons of sound, suggests that they were explicitly inviting the making of personal meaning. It says that they were clearing a new territory in which any fan's self-made sense could breathe and live. The Beatles were provoking their audience to engage with them on a deeper level than before: to enter the play and shape it not just as fans but as collaborators. "Tomorrow Never Knows," as radical, as exotic as it sounded in 1966—sounds *now*—has nothing to do with drugs or half-digested mysticisms and everything to do with where the listener fits in the Beatle scheme: what that listener might contribute to the journey the Beatles are on, the social drama they are inventing and carrying out, day by day. It demands participation. The song is not dead artifice but living experience, experimental surgery performed on a conscious patient.

"Tomorrow Never Knows" was the first new music the Beatles recorded in 1966. The album it eventually consummated was nothing if not a fabric of contradictions which—because it was stitched so furiously tight by musicianship and commonality of theme—gave the appearance of a unified whole. *Revolver* was multicolored music in a black-and-white wrapper, terse pop songs of dream, escape, cynicism, forebodings. It was bright, brilliant, experimental, lively, mold-shattering: full of wit and the marvels of modern chemistry. It was also distinctly morbid and death-obsessed. By its exploratory nature an affirmation of life and possibility, a bold and radical advance upon the new horizon, the album was at the same time fourteen kinds of oblivion served on a Top 40 platter: nostalgic about what had been, and paranoid about what it saw coming.

□

"It's not Madness, ma'am," replied Mr. Bumble, after a few moments of deep meditation. "It's Meat."

—Charles Dickens, *Oliver Twist* (1838)

On March 25 the Beatles convened at the London studio of their photographer, Bob Whitaker. The afternoon had been set aside for the taping of publicity interviews and a photo session. As Whitaker and his assistants huddled in a corner of the studio, engaged in secretive business with a boxful of dolls, the group recorded a number of interviews—including a long, free-form ramble in which John spoke of discovering his penis ("They called it *diddy-winky*"), and Paul of his first sexual experience. George spoke to an Indian journalist about the sitar, while reporters noticed that Lennon kept breaking away to confer with Whitaker on matters of meat.[2]

Finally the journalists were cleared out, and the studio lights turned on. The shoot began formally, with the Beatles against a bare white backdrop. Whitaker covered them from the usual angles, commemorated the one-year-older version of their familiar faces. This battery of shots was to be distributed as official publicity material for the new year, informing the world what the Fab Four looked like in 1966.

At that point, professional obligations disposed of, Whitaker and the Beatles started to play. Props were brought out, and a set of spotless white knee-length coats. It was a bizarre, self-indulgent form of play, and in terms of usable images an almost total write-off. It isn't certain the photographer or his subjects knew what they were after, or if they were after anything other than something unusual. In the event, they spent the afternoon creating a series of photographs most of which went, for many years, unseen—save one, which has been seen in some form by many millions.

You know the one: the Beatles, grinning, covered with hunks of meat and parts of baby dolls—the "butcher" photo. The meat has been described as *red, raw, bloody*. It comes in *slabs, joints, loins, haunches*. The dolls are *naked, broken, dismembered, decapitated, mutilated*. The Beatles are grinning—no, *leering—sadistically, maniacally*. In some descriptions, we find the writers' memories embroidering gore upon gore. One claimed that the Beatles were shown against a "sickly scarlet backdrop," rather than the plain dirty white of reality; another that the hunks of meat had "spiky bones sticking through the flesh"; still another that the babies were covered with cigarette burns.[3] Compared to the routine pop jacket, the butcher cover was imbued with differentness: its finish not glossy but dull, its texture not smooth but coarse. The photograph was overprinted with stitches, like a canvas. Overall it had a smudged, filthy look, with gray its dominant hue, and even the streaks of red were dull and neutral in impact.

Fans can recite its history like a catechism. Three months after the Whitaker session, Capitol Records released a hodgepodge album, *Yesterday and Today,* with the butcher shot on its cover. The album was issued to radio stations; and immediately, gagging noises were heard, along with cries of "Poor taste" from the famously taste-conscious ranks of Top 40 disc jockeys. Capitol withdrew the record instantly and put its assembly lines to work over a marathon weekend, destroying the butcher cover and slipping the old records into a new jacket—this one showing the leaden-eyed Beatles loitering around a trunk. But a handful of employees at the regional Capitol factories in Scranton and Los Angeles saved themselves trouble, and the company expense, by pasting the new cover slick over the old, thus recycling the jacket. And so a small army of butcher sleeves escaped the incinerator of history and were sent, Trojan horse–style, back into the stores—there to be purchased by fans who found they could use steam, gum erasers, and 100-proof Scotch to remove the new cover.[4] Thus, one of the most familiar and least understood works of Surrealist art survived then as it survives today: as a still-circulating object in the real world—not as an untouchable museum piece or glossy art-text reproduction.

What a swirl of feelings must have come to a 1966 teenager upon peeling away the last of the smooth, glazed, condom-like trunk photo to reveal the raw, scarred sausage beneath: the Beatles sadistically leering from within a bloody-jointed, baby-mutilated, cigarette-burned, spiky-boned horror.

What, precisely, was the big idea? The defacing of all previous Beatle imagery, or the creation of an art statement? Subversion or elaboration? John Lennon's motives were certainly outer-directed, as they usually were: some part of him wished these photos to be seen by the world, hoped to hear all the teenyboppers retching as one. Whitaker's goal, apparently, was more theoretical, but itself naturally subversive. In splaying a host of Surrealist connotations and influences over the figures of the world's biggest stars, he would slip into mass consciousness the sensibility of a despised artistic and intellectual fringe. Lennon's drive was personal, Whitaker's academic, but both shared an impulse: to make the hidden visible, and not to a mere few but to millions. A very different kind of underground would here take its form in and upon the bodies of the Beatles.

A contemporary and countryman of theirs, Whitaker had emigrated in the early 1960s to Australia, where he fell in with a circle of avant-garde artists in Melbourne. His work in this period had been a tentative delve into Surrealism, situating the grotesque in settings that were grimly ordinary. He photographed two of his friends, the Australian painters George and Mirka Mora, upon a plain bed, in plain clothes, amid plain surroundings—only, her face was painted with an aboriginal skeleton mask, and he was bowing before her. Death and worship. Elsewhere, Whitaker posed a fourteen-year-old girl with a box of soap powder and unfathomably despairing expression, and pinned her hair to a clothesline to achieve an image of drab terror: living death within an implacable social role.[5]

All these elements return in the photos of March 25. Whitaker's ambitions were grand: certain of the pictures were to form a sequence, which would bear the suitably Surrealist title "A Somnambulant Adventure." He described the butcher photo itself as part of "an unfinished concept. It was just one of a series of photographs that would have made up a gate-fold cover. Behind the head of each Beatle would have been a golden halo, and in the halo would have been placed a semi-precious stone. Then the background would have contained more gold, so it was rather like a Russian icon."[6] One photo showed George hammering nails into John's head, John holding a spread of nails like a Giacometti bouquet; others situated Paul's and George's heads in birdcages; another had John holding a cardboard box with Ringo's head inside, the box inscribed with the unexplained number *2,000,000*. All, Whitaker said, were meant in some way to show that the Beatles were just like anyone else.

His articulated interpretations of the photos are somewhat corny and reductive, and often fail to acknowledge obvious influences.[7] But his perceptual instincts are extraordinary. Confronted with a phenomenon as complex as the Beatles, he goes for the gut—literally—and finds atavistic truths. In one picture the Beatles face a girl who sits with arms raised, her back to the camera: hair long, features unseen, she is Everygirl, the template Beatlemaniac. The Beatles hold a string of sausages which seems to connect her with each band member.[8] Whitaker saw this as the umbilical cord connecting the group to the fan, "the woman giving birth to the concept of Beatles."[9] It is an interesting perception—particularly for 1966, when such postmodern notions of constructed personae were somewhat off the norm: the Beatles were, to a significant extent, fan-created. But an umbilical cord implies nourishment running just one way, whereas to an equal degree the Beatles created their fans: call the sausage a common airway, then, a lifeline, symbol of push and pull, of the vow. The other side of this affirmation, though, is that the girl's facelessness and raised arms, while semiotically identifying her as "the fan," also conflate her with the goddess Kali of a certain recent Beatle fiction. Kali demanded blood sacrifice; and in this photograph the Beatles, standing in supplication at her altar, surrender it from within themselves. They are holding not a string of sausages, but their own innards.

The most famous of the images is also the richest, because in it the metaphor of meat travels as far in any direction as one cares to take it. Like "Tomorrow Never Knows," and like the signature works of Surrealism, the butcher cover is both provocation for its own sake and a true piece of undigested, unanalyzed dream imagery. All mystery, full of clues and free of solution, its only logic is dream logic.

The picture triangulates three symbols. One is the meat. The meat is sex, obviously, organs and intercourse; but more so, it is the flesh, the hard physical matter of the Beatles themselves. The meat looks like it is protruding *from* them. Paul and Ringo have phallic limbs rising from their groins. A shard of meat creeps from Ringo's breast pocket, while John wears a half-circle of guts and ribs as naturally as a vest. An upper bridge of false teeth bites into Paul's forearm as an ambiguous purple sinew descends from his hand. That the picture is artificially dirtied and drained of highlights means there will be no contrast between the dull meat and the subjects' own slick surfaces. What we have is an X-ray inversion of the typical Beatles publicity shot: the grins are there—though unsettlingly deranged, toothy, hyperreal—but the meat takes us through accrued layers of fab gear, teen dreams, and superstar gauze to the entrails within. As a message to the fans, the meat is both offering and rebuke. The Beatles are saying, *We promised you everything—here are our guts.* At the same time they are saying, very bluntly, *Eat me.*

Just as symbolic are the Beatles themselves. If Surrealism had to do with the radical displacement of familiar objects, the Beatles were ripe for it because they were among the most familiar objects in the world. They were, prior to 1966, felt by most to have a precise and immutable "use"—that is, identity: they were good, safe boys. They were lovable and charming, clever and clean. And with the butcher cover, they and Whitaker mutilated that identity in a way that made no sense. What was the conventional fan to do with the image of George Harrison wearing a broken-jawed grin and raising his hand in an obscene gesture, doll's head in place of the offending finger? To place the Beatles in the context of such an image, on the cover of a record that was predestined for the top spot on every album chart in the world, was to insist on such a confusion, upon all the questions that might lead from it. Such as: What do they think they're doing? Or: Is this deep or is it just sick? Or even: How can I use the Beatles now, given what they've shown me?

The dolls. Whitaker references the German Surrealist Hans Bellmer, creator in the 1930s of a photo book called *Die Puppe* (The Doll). Combining life-sized doll parts in freakish permutations (multiple legs, bulbous stomachs, lolling heads) and situating them in poses that suggested the aftermath of rape and murder, Bellmer began with male fantasies of female perfection, then lay bare the sadism behind them. Fetishes of innocence—hair ribbons, white ankle socks, Mary Janes—were attached to dead eyes, deformed torsos, and absent limbs. The mutation took place in some dim, dismal bedroom of the mind, where an idealized image met its psychological root and reality and fantasy were snapped at their instant of embrace.[10]

The Beatles, as we've seen, were about mutation. British into American; Liverpool into Hamburg; Buddy Holly into Motown; Beatles into audience. The mania and everything that followed from it were the unprecedented results of combinations that had never happened before. What kept the Beatles at the epicenter of rock and roll was that, throughout their existence, such mutations *simply kept happening.* By 1966 the mutation at hand was the one Bellmer had dramatized and Whitaker was now reenacting: reality into fantasy, the twisting of old fetishes and simplicities into shapes that were novel and challenging and sometimes scary—like the songs on *Revolver,* like the butcher cover. The Beatles' broken dolls *are* fantasy and reality; they hold hungers and horrors; they dream dreams of devouring and being devoured. Heads without bodies, bodies without blood, eyes without sight. Mutants. Emblems of innocence now defaced and violated; objects of fantasy placed squarely in the context of their unmediated subconscious origins. In the butcher photo, as in Bellmer, a fantasy is made to stare into the darker part of itself, and the finished ideal of desire is made to countenance its own raw material.

The mutant babies are part of a progression. They speak directly to and of the fifteen-year-old girl—who is now well into the onset of her mature sexuality. Developing in ways she is only half aware of, she perhaps paints a picture of Paul McCartney with baby eyes, baby head, and baby body, and calls it "A Sprout of a New Generation"—displacing the anxiety of inner change onto her most intense and all-accepting love object. Babies enter her thoughts and dreams: after all, she has been told all her life that in having children she will find her fulfillment. She has returned the Beatles' vow, taken them as boy-friend, lover, and finally husband. First comes love, the children chant, then comes marriage—then comes *Yesterday and Today,* covered with raw flesh and babies. This, the Beatles are saying to the girl, is the culmination of our marriage: these are our children. With their smiles of psychotic glee the Beatles are the proud fathers. But in their white coats they are also the obstetrician-gynecologists who have de-livered this mutation into the world.

Here was the push and pull behind the butcher cover—behind the Beatles' entire journey through 1966. They were anticipating a new rule of engagement: that, finally, no one had control. The danger of a mutation left unchecked was that it would eventually begin to mu-tate itself. If it could produce in its participants a sharpened percep-tion and more intense responses to ordinary life, it could also self-multiply, break into parts which would break into other parts; and with each new break, everything would flow farther away from the source. Here was the other side of "Tomorrow Never Knows," which advertised the chances for involvement and adventure that would open to those willing to take the next leap. The butcher cover sent the opposite and concomitant message about the nature of mutations, and that message was: *Watch out.*

The old rules were failing, and the audience had been sending the Beatles warnings of its own: bombs threatened, crowds swelling, police lines breaking, the world shrinking. *Help!* had both obsessed over and denied such warnings; but equivocation wouldn't do in 1966. If the Beatles were to remain imaginatively engaged with the world, they would have to make music and speak words that absorbed rather than deflected the warnings they were hearing, and went them all one better.

□

These thoughts, whether they come from me or spring from things, soon, at all events, grow too intense. Energy in voluptuousness creates uneasiness and actual pain. My nerves are strung to such a pitch that they can no longer give out anything but shrill and painful vibrations.

—Charles Baudelaire, "Artist's Confiteor," in *Paris Spleen* (*Petits poèmes en prose*), trans. Louise Varèse

There is a very nice contradiction at the heart of mid-period Beatle music. Even though in 1965 and 1966 the world was to every appearance theirs for the picking, novelty without end, horizons unlimited, during this period they produced music that was becoming less expansive. Most obviously in the lyrics, more interestingly in the textures. In the days before Beatlemania threw its darkening shadow on the ground, the aesthetic of Beatlepop was about expanding, airing out, opening up. From the tight aggressions of the first two albums through the acoustic highlights of *A Hard Day's Night,* from the generous country and sloppy rockabilly of *Beatles for Sale* to the low-key settings of *Help!,* the music had an increasing quality of air and space. It might take its form in brutality or embrace, a fast dance or a chaste kiss; but virtually always it was free and loose, the production seldom large but usually roomy. Assonance reigned, harmony of all parts. Irritation, when it showed, was merely another angle from which to write a love song ("Don't Bother Me," "You Can't Do That"), while the dissonances were usually the result of evident exhaustion ("Dizzy Miss Lizzie") or old-fashioned blue notes flung cheerfully against the momentum of an otherwise buoyant performance ("Baby's in Black").

With *Rubber Soul*, the dissonances became more purposeful; its notes were not just blue but bruised. The sound began to gnarl in on itself. Though its maturity of feeling was striking, and its moments of simple affection between grown-ups all but inconceivable in the teen-driven heat of 1965 pop, *Rubber Soul* was also a rather ugly-sounding album. The sound at its harshest, in fact, was pure acid—snotty beats, guitars thwacking and stinging, bass bristling with fuzz. "Think for Yourself" and "I'm Looking Through You" and "Drive My Car" and "What Goes On" and others—all had something piercingly, gratingly *wrong* with them, some prickly edge to aggravate the ear. Even "The Word," with its universal love call, was couched in a texture that worked against anyone's notion of what "love" implied, its whining organ held on a single note, guitar stumbling up and down a sardonic scale.

There was nothing here with the physical force of "She Loves You" or "Please Mr. Postman," let alone their pop-perfect single-mindedness. Yet *Rubber Soul* was just as undeniable. It shouldn't have worked; without effort, it worked. And in every way—as pop for the moment, meat for the mind, floss for the teenybopper, and soundgarden for the proto-hippie. Dissonant though it was, as a totality of feeling and spectrum of expression the album was broad and impressively self-illuminant, a collection of refracting shades within which the intricate funky ugliness of "Drive My Car" could lead naturally into the controlled enigma of "Norwegian Wood," or the cool chauvinistic distance of "If I Needed Someone" be shadowed by the threat of "Run for Your Life."[11] The Beatles had produced their first contradictory album, and the contradictions enriched everything: sharpened the record's doubts, elevated its affirmations. The record was pure avant-garde art because in seeking to characterize the complexity of real experience it fashioned its own ideal forms. In it the Beatles took all the ambivalence of their position in the world and, better than commenting on it, expressed it, in every curl and cranny of a rich, minimal sound.

The forms would have been empty without the experience to fill them, and in Beatle music experience translated directly, if not always cleanly, into emotion. The music was coiled with contradictions because this was the nature of the emotion behind it. The Beatles were wealthy, world-renowned, adored, catered to; less obvious to those on the other side of the glass was that they were also miserable, encaged, and endangered. The Beatles' lives were regimented by an overriding fact: no way out. Thus, thorny patches sprout and thrive in the previously weed-free gardens of Beatle music; thus *Rubber Soul*—the crabbing inward creep of their sound even as that sound takes itself in unimagined directions, as if resisting its own constriction.

This culminates in the songs of 1966. Virtually every piece of music they put their hands to this year comes out in some way twisted, acerbic, jagged. Their obsessive use of distorted, thickened guitars is part of this. Another is the sudden flooding into their music of Indian dissonance and diaphonies. Perhaps the Beatles responded to Indian music not merely because it was in pop terms exotic and novel but because its intensities were meaningful to them at this precise point. With its speed and twang of the surreal, its classical form barely containing a chaos of improvisation and clash of energies, it must have chimed upon Beatle ears as something unknown yet immediately recognized—and utterly relevant. If they had not discovered Indian music it's possible they would have made something like it, simply because in their 1966 music it integrates so familiarly with everything around it—pop, hard rock, psychedelics.

Going Indian was another mutation: the grafting of disparate influences which had in common elements that were basic but elusive, something obvious that other people weren't hearing. And as with their past musical mutations, the noise the Beatles drew from Indian music was harsh at first, uneasy with itself, even unpleasant. In 1966 it's a furious component, unstable, always churning in an upward line, introducing not higher calm but an irresolvable tension. "Taxman," the Harrison song that opens *Revolver,* has a livid Indian-styled McCartney guitar solo that tears a hot gash in the heart of the performance. The song is already a vertical construction, centered by a crisp riff moving up and down, and the solo, reprised at the song's fade, heightens the feel of wicked intensity in compressed space: the effect of the Indian element is to further enrage the music by immobilizing it.

That same upward twist is heard in other songs where it emerges just as organically, in every component of the production: in "Rain," a bass part that runs the fingerboard in imitation of an agile snake coiling up a pole; in "Paperback Writer," a melody line that is all vertical raga, set against sheets of harmony that mock the sweetness of earlier Beatle voices. "And Your Bird Can Sing," locked in the same limbo, attempts escape and succeeds only halfway. It is organized around a fast, tight guitar phrase that gnaws a descending line before flinging itself up in a last assertion of triumph over whatever is dragging it down. But the phrase's last repetition ends, with the song, neither high nor low but on an ambiguous middle.

This is astonishing music: nearly forty years on, the edges still cut. Musical experiment serves psychic expression, and each electrifies the other. The verticality, representing stasis, set against the intensity of action within that limit, characterizes the Beatles' notion of themselves as harried public figures attempting to create art in an artless genre, hemmed in on one side by fans, on another by commerce, on others by pressures only they may define. They can move, but only up or down; and then only in the studio, where they at least control the sounds they make. In public, though, they are beholden to the idol's role and are largely powerless to move sideways in and out of it. It is only half an identity, reality split into parts. It is a compromise.

Of course they had compromised before: mastering nonrock genres to broaden their nightclub appeal; changing styles from Gene Vincent to Pierre Cardin. But such early compromises were fully self-defined, ones they imposed upon and resolved between themselves, and the world at large could not have been more indifferent to the outcome. Now, the world cared about Beatle choices. Now it cared to the point that any compromise of the truth on the Beatles' part would occur not out of ambition or the drive to self-actualization—their own choice—but because the world had deigned that it should be so. Nothing new under the sun: such had always been the rule in the realm of pop idolatry, and for the idols themselves it had always seemed a tolerable arrangement.

But the Beatles were not Bobby Rydell. They would be pushed only so far. So we must truly wonder if, at some point in early 1966, John Lennon stared into space—perhaps as a hit of LSD spread its fingers over his cerebellum—and asked Prufrock's question: *Do I dare disturb the universe?*

□

But if I see or meet a great artist, I love 'em. I go fanatical about them for a short period, and then I get over it. If they wear green socks, I'm liable to wear green socks for a period too.

—John; in *Lennon Remembers,* ed. Jann Wenner (2000)

We must also wonder exactly what the Beatles and Bob Dylan took from each other at the peak of the 1960s, as all of them hit the full reach of their genius. If Dylan's influence on their music was deep, it was also mostly implicit: the songs routinely labeled Dylanesque ("I'm a Loser," "You've Got to Hide Your Love Away") are also nothing if not pure Beatles. Lyrically, Dylan and Lennon have virtually no commonality. Early instances of Lennon subjectivity ("Norwegian

Wood," "Strawberry Fields") exemplify a cool, hard minimalism a pole away from Dylan's image catalogs of the same period; while later songs of wordplay and lingual excess ("Mr. Kite," "I Am the Walrus") owe far more to the British tradition of literary nonsense than to Dylan's store of Beat-influenced archetypes. Likewise, though the Beatles may have reawakened his nascent pop instinct, no one but Dylan could have created "Like a Rolling Stone."

Musically and otherwise, he and the Beatles did not mutate—they passed in the night. They were fast friends and wary competitors, and each had something the other wanted: Dylan wanted their power, and the Beatles wanted his feel for the symbolic life beneath the world's surfaces. Finally, each did no more—or less—than to delve briefly into the dream life of the other.

1966 was a great rock and roll year—a year which in our current world of strict demographic segmentation sounds mythical: every brand of pop and rock pushed shoulders with every other. Top 40 radio was everything—various, integrated, contentious, sublime, ridiculous—that middlebrow art pretended to be; that high art didn't want to be; that avant-garde art by definition couldn't be; and that America would never fully and consciously allow itself to be. There were many others besides Dylan and the Beatles who made the radio that way, who collaborated in the fantastic commercial artwork that was 1966 pop, but the Beatles and Dylan that year came closer to the flames than any of their rivals. Seemed most cognizant of what was sinister in the psychology of the mass; felt deepest what was unstable in their own fame and fashionableness; and sensed most subtly what lay just beyond the next rise for the West as its history rushed to be telescoped through the movements of its youth. They weren't simply responding to the times, or even making them: they were reading signs that had not yet appeared.

Motown and Stax were producing good-time music, radio music; pure pop art, but the strangulated drama of Levi Stubbs and Otis

Redding were as close as the soul factories were coming to the deeper regions of Dylan and the Beatles. The Beach Boys with *Pet Sounds* and the Rolling Stones with "Have You Seen Your Mother, Baby, Standing in the Shadow" were exploring themes of solipsistic despair and musical ugliness; but despite its brilliance, their new music strained and strove for its uniqueness in ways the Beatles' and Dylan's did not.

Then there was James Brown, who like Dylan and the Beatles was making music that contradicted itself even while observing a semblance of integrated form. His "Brand New Bag" and "I Got You" grooves were groovy the way *Highway 61 Revisited* was comic or *Rubber Soul* affirmative: on the surface. They got over on their good riffs and sweaty vitality, but they were packed with tension, their syncopations as fidgety as they were masterful, their funk spare and spasmodic. As rhythm, they were inexhaustible. But Brown's music lacked the Beatles' variety of tonal expression and Dylan's fecundity of image; and, more than that, the conscious countenance of nightmare to be heard in both.

What their competitors had in pieces, a song at a time, the Beatles and Dylan had whole and sustained. What the others were straining to touch, they were already shaping. They alone were making a music that was contracting even as their world seemed to expand with possibilities, music that was growing more strident and involuted, less a soundtrack for communal delight and more an interiorized vision of a dangerous world.

In this respect theirs was an equal footing, but as idols Dylan and the Beatles were not equals and never could be. The Beatles' momentum had been building for years. By 1965, when Dylan decided to become a pop star, they were already locked in embrace with their audience, their rock and roll bona fides more than established. Dylan, defecting from folk and starting late, had to run fast to catch up. Even if he privately scorned the Beatles' variety of teenybopper success, he clearly coveted their centrality. Intensely competitive, he hustled to get to the center of the game before the game was played out, and so his life and career in 1965 and 1966 were obsessed with speed and the pursuit of speed in every sense—physical, artistic, pharmacological; consuming and regurgitating as much sensation in as short a time as possible.

This rush to catch up came out firstly in his music. If the Beatles' music was contracting, his was imploding. Without three co-creators and the Beatles' audience to inflect his peculiarities, Dylan was freer to construct an entirely self-bound world of image and ambiance, a quicksilver sound and post-Ginsberg wordplay that, before it exhausted itself in the moribund epics of *Blonde on Blonde,* was as dense an expression of frustration and foreboding as theirs.

It came out secondly in his relationship with his audience. Dylan knew something about pushing and being pushed, and they came directly out of his pursuit of the Beatles' cultural influence, their reach across the pop spectrum, their power. In May 1965 he had emerged from the rock and roll closet at the Newport Folk Festival, sporting English leather and playing fast, sloppy rock in front of the Paul Butterfield Blues Band. Depending on which account you believe, he was either booed off the stage or defeated by a bad sound system, his eventual return to sing an acoustic set either a capitulation to the folkie mass or a grumbling farewell. Either way the performance was a mess, the reaction negative, the line between loyalties drawn. Later that year Dylan came up with *Highway 61,* his best album then as now, and all rock—pure, if not simple. Throughout the summer and fall his half-acoustic, half-electric concerts were edgy cacophonies of discord and discovery, as half the audience cheered Dylan's rock and roll reinvention and the other half cursed his betrayal of their folk-music ideals. By May 1966, when he came to London for the shows that rounded off his U.K. tour, Dylan had spent a year under the weight of this rock and roll martyrdom.

In terms that the Beatles were bound to respect, Dylan had suffered for his art. He had taken a chance—the kind of chance they really hadn't. They had jarred an older generation's sense of what was true and false, but they hadn't risked their supremacy among pop fans by daring real controversy, a radical move, a non sequitur. The Beatles' greatest and most natural energy in their first years was for throwing light, not casting dark; despite having catalyzed the biggest emotional upchuck from the rock and roll audience since Elvis, they could not look back and claim they had disturbed anyone's universe. This must have offered as large a challenge to their sense of themselves as their own popularity did to Dylan. So, for a brief instant, each feeling the heat of the other's pressure, the two main forces in rock and roll engaged in a private push and pull, carried out covertly—in the grooves of their records, the vaults of their egos, the rooms of their dream lives.

Ellen Willis wrote in 1967, "Many people hate Bob Dylan because they hate being fooled."[12] This was because Dylan, as precursor to all the self-conscious self-reinventors of pop, employed his identity masks willfully: shockingly but not exactly spontaneously. It hardly detracts from Dylan's greatness to suggest that each new shift was the result of calculation as much as any "natural" artistic progression. From Guthrie-descended troubadour to shock-haired pop star, frontier aphorist to country crooner, outlaw *manqué* to weather-beaten divorcé and born-again doomsayer, he played roles; and usually the new role seemed designed to cancel out the last. It was a perverse and innovative strategy for pop, dependent on shared memory between artist and audience of the past roles, and eager to deny that they had had much value beyond paving the way for the latest.

The Beatles and Dylan split fan response into imaginative halves, dividing between them the conscious (Dylan) and unconscious (Beatles) of the pop audience. It makes sense that Dylan should do more to create a self-conscious audience than anyone in rock and roll, simply because he was so conscious of himself. His shifts of artistic persona were radical breaks with the past and were meant to affect the audience as such; they were art statements. And Dylan was a characteristic sort of '60s artist in that he insisted on making visible his own capacity for deceit—along with the novelists (Vonnegut, Barth) and filmmakers (Godard, Lester) who spent the decade compulsively exposing the tools and tricks of their own creativity. Conscious of the artist in a new way, the fan was likewise made conscious of himself as a receptor of the artist's assumed role, the artist's interpreter and critic.

Dylan's role playing, because it was so polarizing, kept alive, for a time, the irritant factor any popular medium needs to thrive and to replenish itself. But because his acting was self-conscious, he could not slip beneath the skin of a fan's dreams in quite the same way that the Beatles did by their own mode of performance, which was that of nonacting. Too much analysis is inimical to fantasy in its purest form; and the Beatles were ideal fantasy fodder partly because one didn't have to analyze their music to enter it. Fans were intrigued by Dylan's riddles, but they were inspired by the Beatles' plain talk: while people were trying to figure out what Dylan meant, they were trying to figure out what the Beatles meant *to them.*

Which is the difference between borrowing something and owning it. The audience responded more spontaneously—more inexplicably, in a way more naturally—to them than to Dylan because the Beatles, before and after 1966, however much they changed in outward guise or musical sound, seldom gave the appearance of acting; they simply were what they were, and that seemed to be damn near everything. Even in their obliquest songs of this period the Beatles voiced their enigmas plainly, in terse images and short lines; the riddles they offered sank in, took root, in part because they were so self-effacing. Unlike Dylan's epic constructions of joke, biblical allusion, and poetic reference, the Beatles' songs invited participation without demanding exegesis; whatever meanings they bore arose subtly, organi-

13. Paul and John singing "Baby's in Black" at the Circus-Krone-Bau, Munich, June 24, 1966.

cally, and were at least as much the fans' as they were the Beatles'. Fans were able to draw new formulations out of an all-inclusive well of fantasy without, perhaps, ever being fully conscious of what they were doing.

The difference may be that Dylan's persona was fundamentally closed to the audience, almost antagonistic, whereas the Beatles' was open and collaborative. If fans felt they had to figure out Dylan, it was partly because they felt he wasn't talking straight. This was implicit not only in his changes but in the style of his changes, which made it clear Dylan didn't owe anything to anyone but himself. Perhaps wisely, given the price, he had never sought full engagement with the world: he hadn't promised himself to any audience, let alone *the* audience; hadn't staked himself on a single musical identity, or offered himself through a perpetual diversity of persona as the blank screen for anyone's self-projection. *He travels fastest who travels alone* was Dylan's credo: it ain't him you're lookin' for.

The Beatles had always said the opposite: they've got everything that you want. It was a sexual brag, but they backed it up with emotional devotion: they'll give you all they've got to give—just say you love them too. As with Dylan, their stance was not stated but implied in every aspect of how they held themselves before the world. But their one role was that of the Beatles; and because they had defined themselves such that they could not exist without an audience to feed and be fed by them, "the Beatles" meant not just themselves but everyone else. That's why they penetrated the deeper fantasies of the audience at the same time Dylan was occupying its higher mentations. If anyone hated the Beatles, it was not because they felt fooled by them: they hated them for what they were, not for what they had once claimed to be, because they had never claimed to be anything but what they were.

Dylan and the Beatles made a fine dichotomy. Half the story of any art is written by those figures whose impulses lead them to "betray" the audience in favor of their own passing fancies and lasting obsessions. The other half belongs to those who are largely defined by their attempt at fidelity to an audience—the sculpting of an ongoing relationship in which pacts are entered into, inspiration exchanged, sensations traded.

But there are limits. Some sense of separateness must be maintained, or oneness becomes nothingness. Which means that sometimes in a relationship—between artists and audiences as much as between individuals—only painful confrontation spurs the next growth. In uglifying so much of their sound, from *Rubber Soul* to the new *Revolver* songs, the Beatles had already begun to confront their audience musically; with the butcher cover they were confronting it iconically. Could their resentments now be acted out in the other half of their lives, the public half, where they appeared not as voices or images but as vulnerable physical beings who would be made to account for themselves? Could they take Dylan's cue and become actors in a public confrontation, risking danger in the hope that they and their audience would know each other better on the other side?

□

The people gave their money and they gave their screams, but the Beatles gave their nervous systems, which is a much more difficult thing to give.

—George; in *The Beatles Anthology* (2000)

"Love You To" opens liquescently, the prelude to a dream: the dreamer floating in an eerie corridor of distorted mirrors and dim lights; sitar noises grincing and groaning, snide sounds from a nowhere that is alive with secrets. Fast, twisting flourish on a single string—the dreamer reaches his threshold—and suddenly a rapid pounding tempo catches and throbs: the dreamer steps over. The dreamer steps over into the light, the heat and noise, all the din and danger at the center of his dream. Drumskins sound low and deep; the Hindustani strings drone and dance in the air above. The sound is that of the world funneling itself around the inert form of the dreamer as he snaps into the moment, suddenly aware of himself and where he is.

The dreamer's voice appears, a shaft of cold at the center of the hot swirl. At first it seems calm enough, almost peaceful. But no—the true personality of the voice forms. Without nuance or emotion, reaching for no note beyond what the melody demands, the voice is drugged, dull: what sounded like peace is revealed as paralysis. In its numbness the voice is not quite human.

The voice is George Harrison's, and it had always threatened this numbness, this paralysis—though there is no reason to think that at the start he loved being a Beatle any less than the others. In fact in the old footage his pleasure always appears the *least* complicated, the

14. George performing "If I Needed Someone" at the Circus-Krone-Bau.

most unmediated of any Beatle's, for he is the youngest of them and visibly lacks both Lennon and McCartney's confidence and Ringo's innate composure. His smile is unguarded, and the jaunty roll of his head as he plays for the Sullivan audience utterly spontaneous. His early guitar sound remains one of the most identifiable and inspiriting of rock and roll signatures—and that was where all his happiness seemed to be lodged: in the simple swing and bright sparks of a fantastically catchy guitar break.

But as a singer and songwriter he was, by hardest, most immutable nature, dour and starved of charm. His songs stirred gall into the Beatles' brew: the persona he insisted upon in his words and embodied in his singing was one of arrogance and distance, arrogance in a way even more daunting than Lennon's because it was without humor or heat, Lennon's sense of unquestionable wanting. Probably because he was less complex than Lennon to begin with, the frustrations they both felt could be expressed more directly by Harrison because they were not required to emerge through a genius' shifting layers of double vision and surreal vision and innervision. They could hit the record with a dull plop and be heard—or at least *sensed*—for what they were.

But Harrison's songs, while simple, described their own struggle. Intent upon a façade of emotional inviolability, he could then not help undermining his own pose: the cool of his persona was sometimes hedged by an uncertainty that could not fully acknowledge itself as human weakness. An emotional Machiavellian, Harrison sang about power in relationships and how to hold onto it; yet he was hesitant of embracing the distance he claimed to desire. His first Beatle composition declares distance as his one immediate need: "Don't Bother Me" is the singer's warning to all who might attempt to succor his aching heart. Two albums later, though, he is back among the swingers, and everybody is trying to be his baby. He details in swaggering style the absurd lengths to which people will go to *not* leave him alone: like a closeted homosexual on a banging binge, he over-compensates. When he lowers the iron mask to admit that "I Need You," it sounds more like a depressive's self-pity than an open confession of frailty. The next record finds him saying, "Think for Yourself": an unceremonious directive thrown at the lover herself. But Harrison could not relinquish the security that power gave him, and he often kept his girl on a string: You'll never leave me—why, because "You Like Me Too Much." He might give you a call, "If I Needed Someone." He needs, he can do without; he wants, he couldn't care less; he loves you, leave him alone.

With this as his pedigree, it may be that Harrison was the one best situated by artistic limitation and psychological bent to express in flat musical terms the Beatles' own death-in-life as they moved into the latter, rougher half of 1966: their immobility as prematurely aging mopheads and superannuated heartthrobs, their paralysis at the narrow center of a noisily evolving dream. For the Beatle drama was shaping itself into a power struggle between the Beatles and the world. Lennon could write a song like "I'm Only Sleeping," which dealt with that struggle by displacing Beatle anxiety about ceaseless, senseless motion onto other people, which symbolized (and rationalized) death-in-life as a philosophical choice of somnambulism over action. But Harrison could express, with the dead surface of his unvarying voice, the already deadened chambers of the Beatles' collective heart. As a singer and songwriter he lacked the subtlety, the cleverness, the deceit to disguise his doubts in the form of intricate, masterful pop art; what all the Beatles felt took most direct expression in his unsubtle, unclever, undeceitful songs, was most naturally freighted upon his stoic shoulders.

George's contributions to *Revolver* offer different aspects of Beatle ambivalence toward the world, whether disdain of its administrators ("Taxman"), confusion about how to speak directly in the face of emotional and imaginative flux ("I Want to Tell You"), or paralysis before the clashing facts of Beatle life ("Love You To"). The last is the most unsettling of these three very unmelodious Harrison songs, because though it is direct in its parts, as a whole it is too conflicted to be focused. It is warning, capitulation, condemnation, surrender, expressing the love of death and the death of love: a piece of paranoid mysticism, it goes right to the point, but from a half-dozen different directions. Read the lyrics: aside from a lack of guile and poetry, one line has very little to do with another—except an ongoing desire for the impossible, and an apprehension of death amid the making of love.

"It's as though we were force-grown, like rhubarb," Harrison said of the Beatles' accelerated maturation in the incubator of mass mania. "The truth of it is that we were snatched out of our youth, or we snatched ourselves out of it."[13] If they grew up faster than others twice their age, they would necessarily have come that much sooner to thoughts of death—a finer fear of it, a more intense consideration of how far or near it might be. They expressed this in their acknowledgment of certain practical facts: as noted elsewhere, Harrison was the one who had refused to sit for a ticker-tape procession in 1964, assassination fear behind his refusal. But their music tells us that they felt death as not just physically but existentially near, the way an ordinary person may feel the premonition of death in a particularly brilliant and bloody sunset. They expressed it verbally in a song like "In My Life," which encompassed an explicit foretaste of death within its loving remembrance of things past; and tonally in the transcendent melancholy of "Yes It Is," which employed images of color and sorrowful, hymnal harmony to conjure a dead lover's ghost.

Here is the wonderful, the damnable contradiction. Like sun gods the Beatles were brilliant, but like the sun itself they were destined to set. The anxiety of a mind bearing these facts in mind simultaneously is what quickens "Love You To" from its dreaming prologue to its unrelenting speed and kinetic harshness. Meanwhile the exhaustion that follows from anxiety is what makes it, for all its fury, such a downer: for a song that invokes love, that openly speaks to a lover, it is the sourest of valentines. Harrison sounds irretrievably tired, infinitely drained as he gives in to the lover, the fan, the fifteen-year-old girl one more time—and so the Beatle dream is inverted. Once love was all, was not willed but natural, not extorted but given; and death, when it was felt at all, as it was felt in "Yes It Is," was a weight pulling at the edges of love. Now, in "Love You To," it is the reverse: now it is the apprehension of death that drives the music, while love—its memory as against its present reality—is what drags it down.

Give George his due. Of the Beatle songwriters, only he could have come up with expression as blunt and artless as this, even though both Lennon and McCartney, at different times and for their own reasons, tried. In this case only his bluntness and artlessness, his lack of their capacity for symbolizing the components of the feverish Beatle dream, could have caught so plainly the paranoia they lived with, the love they felt slipping away, the death they sensed approaching.

□

There was no more Star-Club.

—Philip Norman, *Shout!* (1981)

The 1966 world tour commenced in Germany: over four days, they played six shows in three cities. One small spot of ugliness—a minor riot outside Hamburg's Ernst Mercke Halle, Beatlemaniacs in a face-off with anti-Beatlemaniacs—but no one took it as an omen of the scenes to come.[14] The German sojourn isn't remarked much in Beatle history; one only imagines what, if anything, the Beatles themselves thought and felt at revisiting their primal scene.

"It was their kind of town," as Allan Williams put it. They recognized it instantly, and saw that it had something precious to give them: worldly experience, and a sense of danger; the heat against which they could test their music and their unity, and plenty of space for both to become whatever they would. They had had their most complete freedom in those days—the freedom to starve, to work recklessly hard, to create themselves daily. And if they were free to fail, they were free to succeed, to surpass even Elvis on their way to celebrity's outer reach. But how distant were those days, how unimaginable now was the freedom. How could the Beatles have failed to measure their lack of space in 1966 against the limitless range they had reveled in once upon a time? As they vegetated in luxury suites, dressed in their velvets and stripes, how could they not have longed for some decent dirt to stain their brilliant lapels, a bit of honest starvation to pierce their stomachs?

They had last played the Star-Club on December 31, 1962. In the three and half years since, they had not returned to Germany. Perhaps the Beatles feared their memories would be deranged, their sense of their own history upended, when they saw what changes this scene of wonders and beginnings had undergone. If this was indeed a fear, it seems to have been realized. "Like much of the rest of the world," Peter Brown wrote, "Hamburg had lost its charm for them. They could no longer walk the streets unrecognized, gaping at the sex shops and the window-ledge hookers. There were no night-long bacchanals, watching the dawn come up over the Herberstrasse rooftops. The bars and clubs where they once played . . . were closed; the Star-Club was shuttered up with boards. What had once been tempting and exotic in the night was tawdry and tired in the light."[15]

Perhaps here, at the climax of their public lives, they are seeking some reconnection with their squalid beginnings, some reminder of the lean little unit they once were. They may balm this itch by calling it something else: according to Brown, the Hamburg stop is slated "purely for the sake of nostalgia."[16] But they must know that any nostalgic wish is as absurd as any hope that that old Hamburg dirt, even if they can get near it, will still stain rather than run right off their anointed skins. As for their live presentation, its juice has been draining steadily over the past two years, as they cross the continents and cross them again, playing to bigger crowds in bigger venues; and by the time they revisit Germany the spritz of madness that has run through the best Beatle performances, from Star-Club to Stockholm to Hollywood Bowl, is almost entirely gone.

As caught on film by West German TV, the June 24 show at Munich's Circus-Krone-Bau is a dry hump. The Beatles wear black velvet suits, cream-colored silk shirts, and no neckties: they look handsomer, more sophisticated than when last seen, but also older and tireder. They don't give a bad show, not really bad—the fans are getting off, and the Beatles coast affably enough on some residual energy, grinning every time one of them botches a lyric. But the illusion of ease and fellowship does not survive the gloom that deadens this ritual, nor does the copious screaming disguise the ritual's true sound, which is not that old German crunch but a long, grinding groan. Lennon's guitar strikes the tiniest of chords, while Harrison's riffs imitate the perambulations of a robot with badly greased joints. Ringo, though he appears to be working hard, cannot be heard. Paul's show of collegial enthusiasm is so void of spontaneity it borders on the infuriating.

Beatle shows as they came to be in 1964 and 1965 were not settings for the honing of musical craft; but on the right night, given the right distance, the right mood, and perhaps some arbitrary shift of the wind, the Beatles played live music for tens of thousands that was a ratcheted-up version of what, as a bar band, they had turned out for a hundred, or a few dozen. Live music that was steady and solid underneath, flexile and feather-light on top. There were more of these moments than there should have been in the high mania years, given how quickly performance became event, romance ritual, and how little incentive there was for them to press any muscle against the

15. "I Wanna Be Your Man": Ringo at the Circus-Krone-Bau.

screams that would greet their merest whimper. Take the two Holly-wood Bowl shows: their first concert there, on August 23, 1964, culminated with a "Long Tall Sally" that had more than a decent measure of Star-Club swing and roll, and when they returned a year later they were able to produce a "Dizzy Miss Lizzie" which, riding a hot chassis of bass and drums, Lennon's howl shifting the gears, had an excitement, a momentum it had never come near in its studio version.

The Munich fans are not destined to experience a single moment so committed. The performance will be defined, as will most on this tour, by a familiarity of intonation and utter lack of surprise—contempt muffled by boredom and the dulled nerve endings of overworked bodies. The band's sound is raw in the wrong way: so raw there is no meat left, only gristle. Somewhere between the Hollywood Bowl and the Circus-Krone-Bau—perhaps it was the very moment of their appearance this evening, as they mounted the stage to see not the old audience of *Mondo Cane* punks and pervs but only another world-mob of generic teenies—the Beatles have determined, or accepted, that if intercourse is to continue with the audience, it can no longer take the form of public performance. Once upon a time they had to fight for their audience, to win the excitement and secure the surrender they now elicit simply by being. What was once a push and pull between a band and its fans, a communing of energies and intimacies that stretched from *I'm a road runner, honey!* to *Shut up when he's talkin'!,* has become something less complex and quite pointless: a push in one direction. And the Beatles have decided—probably for the first time in their careers—that here, in this place, at this time, it isn't worth pushing back.

But another shift now edges into view. Remember, the rules of engagement are evolving in 1966; and though the Beatles are losing their will to fight the battle on the old stage, there are new fronts to be surveyed. Let the audience push the Beatles off the stage; the Beatles will push back in other realms, those realms that are left to them. Music, mainly—the world waits for *Revolver*—but also talk. The weight of statements, the precise meanings of words, talk as act and symbol: these will, in 1966, take on new importance in the Beatle drama.

□

> *Reporter:* When are you gonna retire, fellas?
> *Ringo:* About ten minutes. [*laughter*]
> —Press conference, Vancouver, August 22, 1964

Talk had always been central to their mystique. The Beatles' gift for talk may have been modest next to that of a gab artist like Lenny Bruce, but it fairly towered in the fertilizer-infested fields of pop chat, where the closest thing to honesty was Elvis' dignified silence. Between him and the Beatles lies a barren stretch of oral history never uttered: rockers post-Elvis and pre-Beatles, it would seem, were not asked for their thoughts—or if they were, failed to produce anything memorable. Among the Beatles' British contemporaries, evidence shows even the leering Stones to have been, in chat situations, possessors of mild voices: Mick Jagger, asked in 1964 who was better, Stones or Beatles, was so much the diplomat that he made Paul McCartney seem a bomb-thrower. Dylan, with his absurdist one-liners and freak images tossed like wafers at a coterie of the hip, used talk as a pop factor, but hewed a different line from that of the Beatles—a narrower line, more private joke than public reconfiguration.

The Beatles, just as they injected the plainest, mundanest of enigmas into their lyrics and so made enigma as humanly accessible as a piece of de Sica neo-realism, reconfigured pop talk in a manner and forum so public, so much the opposite of insular, that no one caring to listen could be excluded. Starting at JFK Airport on February 7, 1964, the Beatles' press conferences had been known as good rowdy affairs: dense with reporters eager to laugh in spite of themselves, they were noisy, rife with excitement, full of jostle and cross-talk, the promise of the golden quip. The Beatles themselves, composed and inviolate behind their microphone battlements, eyed the din like benevolent princes at a court orgy, responding bluntly, and usually truthfully, to every banal question designed to elicit a printable platitude.

Nik Cohn describes Murray the K, caffeinated American DJ par excellence, burrowing his way past the staider press at JFK for his first grab at a tag-end of the Beatles' glory, his play for pop life everlasting through their fab and glamorous agency:

> The journalists huddled together and fired questions. But Murray the K somehow wriggled through their legs and got right to the Beatles' feet, crouched there and just about crawled up them. Stingy Brim hat, maniac leer, and his

16. Amid Christly controversy, reporters pursue the next scoop of the century.

stick mike pushing upward, ever upward. His mouth
shooting questions all the time. And he stole it, he broke it
up. He turned a formal occasion into farce. So Paul
McCartney looked down at him. "Murray the K," said
Paul, "cut out the crap."

Immortality: the nation's pressmen got routine, Murray
the K got exclusives. "Cut out the crap." That's all. Nirvana. Quite possibly, it was the scoop of the century.[17]

What made the Beatles' press conferences dynamic was the flickering
hope in every squint-eyed, chain-smoking reporter's breast for that
scoop of the century, and the promise that the Beatles were capable,
on an instant, of delivering it. It was a kind of talk, both edgy and
straight, by turns sincere and ironic, that had never been known in
pop before; and certainly talk had never factored into how anyone

perceived the matter of music as an influence on life, culture, politics, society. Never before had rock and roll been a realm in which anyone might legitimately speak—even in Cohn's teasingly hyperbolic terms—of there *being* a scoop of the century.

Yet there it was. If "Cut out the crap" was a scoop at all, it was because it somehow *mattered* that a Beatle had uttered those precise words. This was one way in which pop had now been made, by the Beatles, to matter; one significant screw-turn in the dismantling of an old mass consciousness, an expedition toward the discovery of the new.

It's 1966, and the press conferences, like everything else (music, hair, hysteria), have changed. Two days after that glum Munich set, the Beatles return to Hamburg—the gloried, storied town itself, where they are welcomed as honorary Deutschlanders. But it will not be an event marked by any particular warmth. The Beatles will, in private, revisit some of their old haunts and old friends, but in public they will distribute curious—not to say bad—vibes. For West Germany's TV networks and print media, they will hold a large-scale press conference which is the prickliest they have yet given. Not that they have ever been docile in the craggy face of the fourth estate, but there is a new sinister quality to their distance, a readiness to pounce on triviality and scorn incompetence that makes the Hamburg homecoming a notably stormy and negative piece of business.

The welter of questions grows increasingly incomprehensible—not because of language barriers but because the queries themselves are irrelevant. What answers suffice when the questions are absurd? *Where are you going to dance tonight? What about parties? Ringo, will Zak be following you to Tokyo? Does George wear long underwear in the winter?* There is no snap to the exchanges—none of the mutuality, the co-exploitation that carried the better press events of earlier days: no engagement in the old, crass, exciting sense.

A German voice calls to Ringo. "What do you think about your coming back to Hamburg?"

"It's okay."

"That's all?"

"What else do you want?"[18]

No one laughs. That sums up the feeling: the Beatles as a unit seem bent on being unamusing. Their humor is parched and combative, a series of taunts; there's none of the fast-moving, quote-grabbing, excitement-inducing banality of 1964. But then, why should there be? Things have changed in two years. Outside, the world is coming to crisis somewhere between cold war and hot war, white noise and black riot, and no one is shimmying in the Beatle wig anymore.

We should always listen, in the Beatles' talk as much as their music, for the passing detail that becomes a signpost. They sense—have been sensing, surely, for some time—that their dream has gotten away from them, that they are now, at best, its co-owners. That control is falling away, and consciousness is split; that they are like the head of a monster whose tail thrashes free, this way and that, alive with its own set of hyperactive nerves. The Beatles sense it all, and in their idiomatic way they express it. As in their songs, Beatle perceptions are realized in fine lines, phrases unadorned in wording yet subtle in meaning.

> *Reporter:* John, when you arrived in Munich, Paul I think was black-dressed, and you I think wore a white dress, and—
> *John:* Yeah. A shorty mini-skirt.
> *Reporter:* —the other one wore a red dress, and Ringo wore a brown dress.
> *Paul:* Yes.
> *Reporter:* Black, white, red, and brown—did you mean anything [by that]?

John: We never noticed.
Paul: Yeah.
John: It was *you* that was looking at *us.*[19]

Is the reporter implying some ethnic symbolism in the Beatles' choice of colors? That in their sartorial array are represented the races of the world—the African, the Caucasian, the Indian, the Latin? (What else *could* he mean?) The idea is patently ridiculous, yet Lennon doesn't bother to deny it. This can only mean that he, like his silent bandmates, recognizes the *objective* validity of even so far-fetched a notion. Not that the reporter is correct; but that it is inevitable and, in a way, justified that such interpretations be placed upon the Beatles.

"It was *you,*" he says, "looking at *us*"—and *we,* after all, are whatever you want us to be. As Beatles, we have become not what we used to be, nor even what we are, but what you interpret us into. This was in our original bargain, an assumption we schemed by: that we would be the ones to feed your fantasies, no matter how separate from our intentions they might be, and that because of this the rewards we would exchange would be of the intensest, the rarest kind. That *we* would be the ones to give all in the cause of—of what? Changing the world? Fine: call it that. We're the Beatles and we don't analyze ourselves much. That would be your job, Mr. Reporter, Miss Teenage Fanclub, Sir Critic, Reverend Preacher, Dr. Social Psychologist. It's *you* looking at *us.*

Hamburg is no sentimental journey. It is something better: a stumbling step into the future, a new kind of public engagement. With their words, the Beatles have released a toxin of conflict into the simplistic public discourse that has always defined them. They realize they are in part there to *be* defined, symbolized, by others; at the same time they are as real, as unsymbolic, as any four people in the world. In acknowledging the fantasy yet insisting on their reality, they are forcing a contradiction into play—as they are doing visually with the butcher cover, and musically with the imminent *Revolver.*

Another crevice opens.

□

They flew to Tokyo on June 29. In this fervid period, there was something like a dialectic in the constancy of controversy: the group threw out a few offhand provocations in a press conference, and soon they were under threat of death. The relationship between the two, of course, was not causal but atmospheric. The atmosphere of the mania and of the many symbolisms hung upon the Beatles created a miasma in which every good or bad influence mixed with every other—as they learned when they ventured into the political rat's nest of the Far East.

On arrival in Tokyo, the Beatles' camp were informed that an extreme faction of Japan's nationalist wing had promised murder should the band carry out their local engagements.[20] Death threats were not new to them; but this seems to have been the first to arrive attached to a concrete complaint—specifically, that the Beatles would outrage tradition by performing vulgar pop music in a sports arena, the Nippon Budokan Hall, commonly employed for sumo wrestling exhibitions but also consecrated as a shrine to dead war heroes; and more generally, that they represented all that was baleful and insidious in the collision of Western commercialism with Japanese tradition.

Whatever the Beatles' feelings on being so marked, the Tokyo officials took their city's political fringes in deadly earnest: the security measures they imposed on the band were Draconian. Peter Brown: "The entire top floor of the hotel had been cordoned off with army troops, and the elevators were fixed to stop only on the floor below, where a round-the-clock gun-toting platoon screened admission to the penthouse via a single staircase. . . . The Beatles were never to

leave their hotel suite, except to go to the Budokan for performances."[21] At the concerts themselves, the fans were overseen by a
force of armed military, including a Roman guard standing at attention around the base of the stage. Thus was it assured that no gross
audience displays of lust or desperation would disturb the ghosts of
the Budokan.

And anyway the real melee was outside the hall, where zealous fists
were being raised, and banners, and bullhorns: *Beatles go home!*

The Beatles gave the far right a chance to flex its muscle on an international stage. Like their counterparts in Germany, Japanese nationalists seemed to draw a particularly bitter resolve from the memory of defeat and the heritage of postwar occupation. Among their
favored targets was the continuing encroachment of the victorious
West; and "Western" was now taken to be synonymous with "American." As the first Western rock and roll stars to play large-scale concerts in Japan, the Beatles were in the interesting position of representing not themselves or even their own nation of origin but the
United States, whose rock and roll had spawned them and of whom
they were an imaginative product. *Yankee go home!* was the familiar
chant of anti-American protesters in Tokyo, as it had been in Caracas
and Havana and elsewhere; outside the Budokan and the Tokyo
Hilton, *Yankee* was merely replaced with *Beatles*. For all the ideological
difference it made to the nationalists, the Beatles might as well have
been on a goodwill tour for Uncle Sam.

The Beatles discovered Japan at the apex of a decade bracketed by
violent murders committed, in Tokyo itself, in the name of radical
nationalism. In 1960 the Socialist Party leader had been knifed to
death, mid-speech, by a teenage nationalist; and in 1970 the country's
most prominent writer and artist-fascist, Yukio Mishima, after failing in his call for a militarist coup, would commit ritual hara-kiri. In
between was a decade which Edward Seidensticker describes as "in
some respects incoherent": concurrent with an unprecedented hun-

ger for all things Western, there was "a great xenophobic rising," manifested in armed demonstrations, sieges of university buildings, and internecine bloodshed between radical splinter groups.[22] In post-war Japan the extremist elements had multiplied and entrenched themselves; even today "they seem," Seidensticker says, "to be among the institutions . . . which the police are unwilling or unable to contain."[23]

Just as the Beatles were adored by those Far Easterners who looked to the West to define their future, they were the perfect hate object for those who saw Westernization as a perpetuation of defeat. Either way, they were translated, naturally and unconsciously, from pop group to political signifier, from the corporeal to the symbolic: Beatles as symbol of sexual license and loose morals, unbounded commerce and gaudy accessories, Coca-Cola and Cornflakes. These haters were not wrong; partly by inclination and partly just because they played rock and roll, the Beatles did in fact represent all of these. What is important is that the Tokyo militants, like others who saw their worlds changing in 1966, perceived that much of that change was embodied in the Beatles, and so used the group as the ready-made focus for their social anxieties. They realized that to stop change they must stop its most visible agents.

In Manila, where the Beatles flew on July 3, the dynamics of this anti-Western sentiment shifted. The Philippines had the same love-hate relationship with the Western nations, in particular America, that for a time caused such rifts in Japan; but there anti-Westernism proved, for the Beatles at least, a far uglier variable. Its potential was more dangerous because the social abrasions and cultural tensions that in Japan could be vented in often extreme protest were in the Philippines allowed no outlet at all—in fact were subsumed and suppressed by the machinations of a dictatorship calling itself a democracy.

Philip Norman lays the scene: "They were charmed, as are all new-

comers to Manila, by a miniature Texas set down among tropical is-
lands; by the skyscrapers, specially earthquake-proofed, the shanties
and juke boxes and brilliant jeep taxis, the jungle foliage reflected in a
speed cop's Harley Davidson. After dark, as the bats bounced like
shuttlecocks against the rim of Manila Bay, shotgun blasts at random bespoke Southeast Asia's most uninhibited autocracy."[24]

In 1965, the CIA reported on the political situation in the Philippines. With the country's presidential election only weeks away, the
forecast was hard to read. There was "a generalized condition of discontent and lawlessness," "widespread rural poverty," "deep social
and economic cleavage between upper and lower classes," and "widespread graft, corruption, and favoritism in government and business." As for the impoverished masses themselves, the CIA feared that
their miseries, if not properly pacified, were "likely to lend themselves
to leftist exploitation. This would present increasing problems to the
Philippine government in domestic administration and in the maintenance of a strong pro-U.S. and pro-West position."[25]

Ferdinand E. Marcos assumed the presidency of the Philippines on
December 30, 1965. Though he'd served in the senate as a Liberal, he
was elected on the Nationalist ticket. Despite this, he and his wife,
Imelda—the "Steel Butterfly of the Philippines," she of the bullet-
proof brassiere—evinced a delight in Western consumer culture, from
music to Hollywood to clothing and other material commodities,
and did nothing to discourage starry intimations of an Asian Came-
lot. As a political operator, Marcos courted Washington's favor and
promised that, if elected, he would continue mutually beneficial relations with the West; while as a candidate, he inveighed against government corruption and commercial exploitation of the poor, promising infinite varieties of deliverance from social and economic
inequity. He took the election with a broad plurality.[26]

But it soon became clear, to both the CIA and the Philippine poor,
that Marcos was committed to nothing so much as the consolidation

of his own political power and material wealth. He was pro-West because he loved American money, movies, status objects; but that didn't mean he would send troops to support the U.S. effort in Vietnam.[27] Everyone from Lyndon Johnson to the Manila factory worker had thought he had an ally in Marcos, when all he really had was a political mercenary whose hands were suddenly on some very important levers. And now many of those who had chosen to believe in him, whether for purposes of Communist containment or basic human need, were growing disappointed, nervous, resentful—the factory worker at least as much as the American president. Both were powerless; the worker much more so, as the threat of official violence, institutionalized in Marcos' use of torture and execution as secret political tools, intensified and became an instrument of routine repression.

Enter, once again, our small and unassuming band of Beatles. We suspect that they are, like torture and execution, meant to serve their own unique function in the propagation of Marcosism. Given a few facts, they might have guessed that their very presence in Manila would be laden with political significance for the Filipinos. Two shows have been scheduled by the local promoter for July 4, a date honoring both Philippine independence day and (a Marcos directive) Philippine-American Friendship Day. The Beatles will give their preshow press conference in the War Room of the Philippine Navy. And the shows are to be held in the José Rizal Memorial Football Stadium, a 35,000-seat arena named for the revered rebel chief who led a successful revolt against Spanish colonizers in 1898.[28] Obviously the Beatles have not been invited to Manila merely to play their music. At the very least, they are here as an opiate for the masses; at most, they are here to implicitly endorse Marcos' self-described "democratic revolution" by honoring the nation's most vaunted revolutionist on a day commemorating, in a perverse juxtaposition, both its independence and its grim pacts with the West.

On this day they will also attend a reception organized by Mrs. Marcos at the presidential palace at Malacañang, sharing tea and chat with ambassadors, senators, and government ministers, entertaining three hundred specially invited children, posing for photographs with the First Lady—images which, once flashed to the four corners of the globe, will confer that irresistible Beatle bloom upon the social miracle unfolding in Manila, and all manner of cachet upon its architects, the Marcoses.

But of course it doesn't happen that way. The whole PR stunt turns into a huge bollix and no one escapes unbruised. It is an international incident, a significant convulsion in the realm where politics and entertainment sometimes cross. And appropriately for a Beatles story, it is all traceable to a few strands of hair.

Back in 1964, on the Washington, D.C., stop of their first American visit, the Beatles had been compelled to attend an official function in their honor at the British Embassy. In their view, they were welcomed as freaks. The upper crust of two continents was represented by a swarm of drunken aristocrats and condescending diplomats. Autographs were demanded by people expressing amazement that a Beatle could write his own name. Horrified, the band were assailed by groping velvet-gloved hands and heavily liquored breaths, as classist jibes filled the air like cigar smoke. Lennon departed the embassy in a blizzard of curses, but not before one uninhibited matron descended on Ringo with a pair of scissors and stole a lock of his hair. New Beatle policy was made: no official functions, ever.[29]

Dissolve to Tokyo two and a half years later. The Marcos invitation is tendered; and an Epstein aide, per policy, sets it aside.

The sequel will unfold like this:

On July 4, the Beatles will sleep the hours away in preparation for their two performances, unaware of the reception. As time passes and no Beatles appear, Mrs. Marcos will forlornly stroll the halls of her palace, her anguish and that of the invited children faithfully recorded by a crew of photographers and TV cameramen. The Beatles will play their concerts at four and eight to a combined total of 80,000 people, the largest one-day audience they will ever see, and then return to the Manila Hotel for a night of rest. Meanwhile the newspapers will scream with headlines like *IMELDA STOOD UP* and *BEATLES SNUB FIRST LADY,* as the national television station airs heartrending footage of lonely Mrs. Marcos and the many wailing children.

The Beatles will be rousted from sleep the next morning by government emissaries demanding to know why they failed to appear at the reception. No answer will be found suitable. Brian Epstein will rush to the television station to offer an on-air apology and the broadcast will be prevented, by a suspiciously timely attack of static, from entering a single Filipino home. Back at the hotel, Beatle room service will be suspended and Beatle security withdrawn, and the hotel will seem as eerily desolate as a "Twilight Zone" set.

Breaths quickening, the Beatle troupe will make its way gingerly to the airport to find armed soldiers standing sentry before hundreds of angry citizens who line the platforms and scream abuse. Epstein functionaries will dash about in search of flight information and the Beatles will be detained for lengthy passport checks, and when the gate is located they will be manhandled by armed guards and outraged citizenry alike and made to run in terror as obscenities and fists instead of love rain upon their shoulders. Finally the plane will be located and boarded, but it will be detained so that a tax official may extort from Epstein a piece of the concert proceeds which have not been paid them anyway, and detained again for another passport check and detained yet further so that the furious crowd can regroup on the tarmac outside in its force of physical hate and raw curses, and so that the Beatles may watch the whole scene and tremble in their seats and pray for safety well after they are on the wing to New Delhi.[30]

His point made, Marcos issued a formal apology stating that the actions of his military and citizenry had been in no way influenced by him. But the Beatles were not having it. Once at a safe distance from Manila, they informed the world of what had happened there, and for a moment the world was afforded a glimpse it would not otherwise have had of the country Marcos was building. In this way, the Beatles' defiance of Marcos was some sort of heroic act. True it was inadvertent, even picayune relative to the heroisms of those who have survived the torture chambers and institutional nightmares of terrorist governments. But it also exposed, for a moment, the vengeful mentality of a political murderer. If the Beatles are to be admired for nothing else, they are to be admired for this.

All traceable to a few strands of hair. For the Beatles, hair was not fashion or freakishness; it was their refusal of the world's symbolism—because it was a symbol they had chosen for themselves. Ringo surely felt as though he had left a piece of his identity behind at the British Embassy; perhaps that is why, when *A Hard Day's Night* was filmed a few weeks later, he withdrew his head with such apparent fear from the hand of a schoolgirl. With each loss of identity would come loss of power, increased susceptibility to cooptation as someone else's symbol. So the refusal of official functions which engendered the Manila debacle was the Beatles' attempt, on a superficial level, to keep their hair, and, on a deeper level, to maintain a sense of their own realness in unreal circumstances. Manila was important because, brought in as a public-relations coup for a venal politician and his corrupt wife, the Beatles were made to pay a visceral price, a price no pop star had ever been made to pay, for refusing that symbolic role—for maintaining their identity and protecting their hair. The Marcoses had been bested by four Samsons who refused to be shorn.

□

When they played the Far East, the Beatles—as they had in the Hamburg of long ago—stepped unwittingly into social processes that were already in evolution. Japan and the Philippines were attempting to move forward from the war, to urbanize, modernize, capitalize, Westernize; and the Beatles were seen as representing modernity in all its forms—artistic, social, cultural. Because they could be cast as leaders by those seeking change, they could also be exploited as targets by those desperate for stability—whether the stability of Japan's emperor worship or of Marcos' political terror. That the Beatles were so readily and naturally symbolized, so eccentrically *used*, not only by the fifteen-year-old girl or Bob Dylan but by someone like Marcos, speaks of their singular power to stir imaginations, to invade minds.

But what was stirred in the Beatles' collective imagination, not in the cool of later reflection but in the heat of these events as they were happening? Is it outrageous to think that, deep in the unvarying clatter of their onstage cacophony, a clue might lie as to what was going on outside, in the heat and physicality of Manila? Some intimation of what the Beatles saw when they looked upon the adoration of a crowd that, one day later, would be howling for its chance to dismember them? They were artists, after all, and their concerts even at their most perfunctory were expressive vehicles. If their post-1964 live music usually expressed nothing but a desire to be finished, we must listen all the harder for something beyond that, something deeper and more resonant beneath the flat, machine-stamped surface.

There is something of this nuance to be heard in the Budokan shows, two of which—the first, on June 30, and another the following night—were filmed by Japanese national television. The first night's footage shows an uncertain band singing politely to an excited but restrained audience, which goes largely unseen by the cameras. The gestalt is alienation—alienation of performers from audience and vice versa, as if neither has quite met the other. What we are seeing is a formal enactment, under state supervision, of the "typical" Western pop concert, in which any Tokyo teenager's thought of breaking for the stage does not survive the cold air around the Roman guard.

And the music, anyone who hears it will agree, is awful. Especially so because here the Beatles are given a real chance at connection—and blow it. Faced with a challenge this first night in Tokyo, they are caught off-guard and sound paltry, inept, amateurish. The polished hysteria, the detailed aggression that propelled them as the best bar band in England are many eons behind them, replaced with dumb obligatory professionalisms and haplessly mutilated technique. The Beatles' live sound is exposed as a corpse on the slab, its bruises and batterings laid bare. It doesn't matter that the adoring audience gobbles each musical scab like the bread of life. Since when was mere adoration enough? The Beatles have, in every place but the concert arena, been pushing adoration to places where it becomes something else: hence the love, hence the hate. But here, in this place with its small crowd, its comparative calm, its potential for near-intimacy, the Beatles are unable to reach for their audience, let alone push it.

Returning the next night, though, they are not the same band. The music achieves a size and excitement it didn't approach the night before: it is both enormous and nimble, like rolling thunder rolling fast. "Rock and Roll Music" and "She's a Woman," big-bottomed and very, very loud, go by in a white blur: immediately the band is pushing. The performance, each song building on the last, crunches. Gone is the tin riffing of Munich. "Day Tripper" and "Paperback Writer" are anchored by thick, devouring guitar figures, each note its own power chord. "I Wanna Be Your Man" whirls like a three hundred-pound dervish, Ringo even throwing out an *All right, George!* that sounds inspired. With just two guitars, bass, and drums, the Beatles whip up one hurricane after another, and half the time the vocals are lost in the din, as they were back in Hamburg—or even before that, on the Liverpool rehearsal tape, where the voices did not matter as much as the unity and drive the band were finding, creating, on the spot. Here, on a stage a universe removed from those beginnings, they find that to make it they must burrow their way back to the center of that unity, and again find, create, its sound.

There are lulls in this intensity, softer songs that do not generate the same energy; but they don't matter. The Beatles have located the center of the sound they know they *should* be making. The sound is enormous, self-propelling, as deliberate and determined as it is abandoned and brazen.

We respond with shock to the force of this performance, coming upon the progressive slackening of the Beatles' live muscle over the previous two years. The show has force because it has obvious caring. Maybe the Beatles care about the free cameras they were given the night before by Tokyo entrepreneurs; and maybe they care about not disgracing themselves again in the open air of the Budokan. Maybe they care because they are feeling the push of those who would screw them in the ground (as "Love You To" had warned), and cannot deal with their own failure to push back. Maybe their performance is driven by their instinctive need to assert themselves against those who would employ them as mere political symbol and protest fodder, to shout rock and roll at the death that has been promised them. Maybe, like the butcher cover, the fierce performance is the Beatles' middle finger in the air.

Whatever it is that inspires their caring, they push it into the music. Feeling the pressure of change as it is happening, they are, even on the exhausted concert stage, able to summon thunder out of their own problematic proximity to the world. Outside the Budokan, amplified shouts incite the furies of those who hate the Beatles and what they are thought to represent. While inside, isolated screams pierce the music with an ecstatic spontaneity, sharp knives jabbing and prodding the renewal of a flabby stage act, arching to the peak of the judo hall to disturb those sacred ghosts. The Budokan is filled this night with an eerie rock and roll noise: the classic sound of a great live combo filtered through all the mania sounds of shouts and screams, guns and knives.

□

Knives are hidden in the cemetery mist of "Eleanor Rigby." This song is at once an impeccably wrought chamber piece and a twisted, miserable thing. It is as safe as prosodic analysis can make it and as creepy as Marley's ghost, and its tension is between the passivity of the lyrics—stiff as a tableau, even when describing action—and the violence compressed in the music.

"Taxman," in its casual reference to the listener's future corpse, had heralded the banality of death as a *Revolver* theme. "Eleanor Rigby" looks death in its gray face and sees only more banality. In outward appearance the song is not mainly concerned with universalizing the experience it shows: there is scarcely a line which cares about anything more than its own grubby details. Details of two people, spinster and priest, collector and mender, custodians of other lives. Socks, rice, jars, windows: the dumbest familiarities are spied as harbingers of waste and demise, and in the end the spinster is wiped from the Earth as easily as earth is wiped from the hands of the priest. But musically, the opposite is occurring: the string setting shows us the fear in that final handful of dust. As the words describe stasis, the music is all movement, the strings churning in a caduceus of activity. It is the same contradiction that drives other *Revolver* songs—a still, passive center surrounded by chaos. As in "Love You To," the chaos is a concentrated, focused presence, a precise threat: the knives of the world stabbing inward at that center, so hopefully and tenuously founded on façades of inviolability.

Who are the lonely people? At one time much academic ink was spilled over the question, though the answer could not be more obvious, more banal, or more moving. The lonely people are *them,* Eleanor Rigby and Father McKenzie, who we observe in their loneliness; *us,* we as observers and auditors, for *No one was saved* refers not to the Devil but to Death, and "no one" refers to everyone; and the Beatles, who feel knives striking and respond by transforming the rawness of experience into a fineness of sound. They are the Beatles and we are they and the Beatles are we. This song of isolation is finally an attempt at realizing unity.

So it is a love song, but also a dangerous song: its violence will not defer to its melancholy, or to its wisdom. The image of knives persists. George Martin once said his string arrangement was inspired by Bernard Herrmann's soundtrack for the Truffaut adaptation of *Fahrenheit 451,* but his memory is faulty—the film hadn't been released yet.[31] The more striking and likely echo issues from Herrmann's earlier score for *Psycho,* a composition written entirely for strings, strings that shriek and stab at the ear as Hitchcock's knife stabbed at the exposed flesh of anyone who had ever occupied a shower stall. That connection is subliminal but it is there, a sharp edge scraping at the planed surface of the song's poetry, real experience abrading its polished representation. "Rigby" has the fine imagery, the minimalist exactness of polite literature, but it barely conceals itself as a psychotic piece of music.

This contrasts with the straight pop styles, the more conventional glisten of McCartney's other *Revolver* songs; but even in these, the surfaces give away the game, or at least confuse its rules. The music questions what the lyrics say, and no affirmation is above suspicion. As the band's most natural romantic, Paul is also its most instinctive denier of chaos and complication; and so if we do not expect the confrontations with doubt that drive many Lennon songs, we do expect to see the mechanics of denial in action. His love songs at their most complex, then, are hopeful glimpses of bliss compromised by the fleeting perception of doubt.

"Here, There and Everywhere" is a love note plush with harmony, warm and lulling in every detail save one: an electric guitar interjecting sharply, the persistent prick of reality at the soft skin of a dream. Even "Good Day Sunshine," a Lovin' Spoonful–inspired "romp" unweighted by any psychic agony, is made metallic and agitated, somehow *untrustworthy,* by its muffled barroom piano, refrain heavy on

cymbal-crash, and coda of dissonant harmonies probably representing the sun's bursting rays but equally evoking the splintering of
fragile fantasy. "Got to Get You into My Life" fades out on an identical blaring note of shattered focus, and is notable for being as expressive of a simple livid frustration as any McCartney music to date: its
two minutes are a tight mass of constipated fury, an existential an-
noyance expressing itself as romantic confusion.[32]

It would be disingenuous not to concede that each of these
McCartney songs can be heard and enjoyed for what it self-appar-
ently is. But one reason the Beatles' music seems inexhaustible in its
variety is that each song gains when taken as a reflection of what surrounds it; and in the context of their Lennon and Harrison neighbors, Paul's *Revolver* songs cannot register as simple affirmations any
more than the car dredged from the swamp at the close of *Psycho* represents a restoration of moral order. In 1966, Lennon, McCartney,
and Harrison are each coming closer to revelations and personal es-
sences, to contradiction; to the meat of himself as a Beatle. Paul's personal revelation is that, romantic and denier though he is, not even
he can craft a fantasy that believes in itself fully, or construct a resolved center safe from the knives of the world.

What proves this is the sober, rigorous despair of "For No One."
Paul has written sad songs of abandoned love before, but in them disillusion and loss were mitigated by optimism ("I'll Follow the Sun")
or at least a certain cocky energy ("I'm Looking Through You"). Pain
was felt vaguely, defenses against it tightly in place. Now the abrasion
between pain and protection, like every other conflict previously latent in the Beatle world, is nearer the surface than ever before; so this
kind of pain feels different. The pain comes from seeing love reduced
from something fulfilling and limitless to a hard set of gestures
which signify life but do not fulfill it: day breaking / mind aching;
waking up / making up; staying home / going out. "For No One" witnesses the decay of love into symbol, the withering of fantasy into

something less than ordinary life—a life more sorrowful for having known fantasy, for the death of fantasy is equated with eternal imprisonment: *You won't forget her.* It is the most chilling symbol of all, four words expressing death in life. The song's original title was "Why Did It Die."[33]

If George's songs get closest to the weariness and loathing implicit in the Beatles' relationship to the world, Paul's filter the simplicity of first-phase Beatlemania through the complicated, even monstrous thing it has mutated into. His *Revolver* songs have the less-than-real sound of a dream not quite lived but nonetheless remembered. It is a true sound—because what dream, no matter how lovely or promising at first encounter, can survive whole when forced through the sieve of real life, real events? In 1966 the Beatles and the audience, still living the old dream, are half in and half out of the sieve. It's a tortured passage. Love is threatened; past fantasies will not serve; the old promises and excitements linger as headaches. Meanwhile knives approach, and everything that used to be true and certain and safe is, or is about to be, in pieces.

□

In his own person he dramatized their dreams and saw himself acting out the prophecies.

—Dr. Hugh J. Schonfield, *The Passover Plot* (1965)

We're more popular than Jesus now.

—John, London *Evening Standard* (March 4, 1966)

On July 29, the inaugural issue of *Datebook* took its place on U.S. newsstands. It was a standard teenybop rag in tone and design, in its fast grab for the adolescent eye, but it promised something different—an angle toward controversy. The cover of this "Shout-Out Issue" showed Paul McCartney in concert, regarding skeptically the column of pop pronunciamentos printed alongside him. These came from the likes of "1-2-3" finger-snapper Len Barry ("English groups won't last. There is no longevity in dirt!"), Bob Dylan ("Message songs are a drag!"), and McCartney himself ("It's a funny country where anyone black is a dirty nigger!"). Apart from the jarring proximity of a racial slur to the candy colors of a slick teen magazine, the cover's most direct provocation was this: "I don't know which will go first—rocknroll or Christianity!" Signed, John Lennon.[34]

There it was: "Rock and roll or Christianity!" Any history of America's public discourse in the twentieth century must treat that exclamation point as one of the most influential marks of punctuation ever fixed in print. It gave an apparently neutral comment the appearance of righteous glee, turned a seeming rhetorical absurdity into a rabid conviction. It inflamed hatred and ensured that the words which preceded it would survive as long as any popular commentary of the past hundred years.

The Maureen Cleave article containing those words, minus the knife-like emphasis, was part of a series for a London paper in which each Beatle was observed at home in the early weeks of 1966, enjoying his longest continuous vacation in more than three years. Lennon's portrait was scary. It told of Beatle John at home in a bizarre nursery habitat of objects and outlandish artifacts that put one in mind of the gaudy and frivolous *Help!* commune. He had insulated himself well from the outside: his mansion was "heavily panelled" and "heavily carpeted."[35] He was an eager reader, but his literature of freaks and ancient wars and children's stories seemed to have failed to bring him into closer contact with any but imaginary worlds. Ignorant of the day of the week or how to use a telephone, when not functioning as a Beatle the twenty-five-year-old millionaire and beacon of youth moved about as a ghost, haunting his own days and nights.

Though hope, or at least a mild discontent, was spotted near the end. "There's something else I'm going to do," Lennon said, "something I must do—only I don't know what it is."[36]

Perhaps this impulse toward *something else* was what led him to say what he did. He could have asked that his comments on Christianity be kept off the record, but he didn't; could have inserted a preemptive apology or qualification, but didn't. Cleave noted that "he has been reading extensively about religion," and among the artifacts she spotted on display at Weybridge was "an enormous Bible he bought in Chester."[37] Lennon knew the intensity of feeling Christians bore for their Lord. Could he have imagined that his equation of the Beatles—of himself—with the messiah of millions would not alter his world forever? Can we imagine, given the trajectory of his subsequent life, the constancy of his impulse toward *something else,* that this was not his most urgent desire as he sat among his useless Beatle toys?

Most witnesses for the defense have been eager to dismiss the controversy which ensued from the Christ statement as another instance of American insanity in general and Bible Belt fanaticism in particular. Which it was, but it was not only that. To dismiss the controversy means to dismiss the remark, and to ignore the larger implications of each. Mark Lewisohn: "The entire episode seemed ridiculous then, [and] now it's almost impossible to comprehend how so many people could have become so agitated over the purely personal opinion of a pop star." Still, spotting the truth, Lewisohn catches himself, almost takes back his own dismissal: "But then, the Beatles always were considered by others to be more than mere musicians."[38]

Obviously. But the question around the Beatles has always been just what that "more" amounted to. What else were they, if they were not merely musicians?

From "The *Playboy* Advisor":

> It may seem sort of silly, but things have reached the stage where I'm really getting a little worried. My daughter and a number of the other kids in the neighborhood have formed a real cult over the Beatles. They have built an altar in one girl's bedroom and they burn candles and recite

Beatle prayers they have written. Now their project is writing a Beatle Bible which starts out, "In the beginning the Beatles created the rock and the roll." If they weren't so darned serious about this, it would be pretty funny. But when Susan doesn't go to church with us because they are having their own service in their Beatle church, I start to worry a little. Worst of all, we have to listen to that awful music over and over and over. What should we do?

  —M.D., San Francisco, California[39]

From "Hilda M." of Detroit: "Dear George—Have you ever thought of becoming a minister? If you were a minister, everybody would go to church all the time. Love, . . ."[40]

More than anything that has reached us through the medium of popular art—more, perhaps, than even Elvis (and certainly faster)—the Beatles became a religion. Kids, American kids especially, laded the Beatles with the aspirations, the psychic fears and physical intensities which religion had traditionally sought to absorb. Kids knelt in prayer to the Beatles, erected shrines to them. At Beatle concerts these kids found a community of worship, in which many white teenagers experienced the nearest thing they would ever know to the mass ecstasy of a revival meeting. It became common later in the '60s for fans—by this time better described as followers—to play their Beatle records in a churchly environment assisted by candles, incense, mystical chants, even sacramental wafers of LSD; to study Beatle lyrics and Beatle iconography like biblical scholars. And finally to erect around the Beatles myths of creation, miracles, and death, in the dual effort to get closer to their objects of worship and to leave their own stamp upon how others after them would understand the Beatles—as every generation since Saint Peter's has attempted to do with Christ.

The religious aspect of the Beatles' appeal was far from broadly ac-

knowledged in 1966, but Jesus was a metaphor—more like a persona—
that had been forced on them long before Lennon made his modest
comparison. But as with most of the metaphors the Beatles were
made to carry throughout their career, it went unstated *as* a metaphor, as anything but total reality—the plain *truth*. For instance: "the
cripples." Most fans got their first glimpse of a grisly backstage scene
in John's 1970 *Rolling Stone* interview: "When we were running
through, it seemed like [we were] just surrounded by cripples and
blind people all the time. And when we'd go through corridors, everybody would be—they'd be all touching us."[41]

The image—four healthy Beatles running a gauntlet of out-
stretched supplicating hands, Gethsemane wails among the screams
—is legitimately creepy. Press agent Derek Taylor had witnessed the
spectacle in Australia in 1964, and suggested its correlative in a *Saturday Evening Post* interview. "The routes were lined solid, cripples threw
away their sticks, sick people rushed up to the car as if a touch from
one of the boys would make them well again. . . . The only thing left
for the Beatles is to go on a healing tour."[42] The disabled and their
handlers may have been no more than star-seekers who used the
wheelchair as their wedge into the stage door. But they were also employing the Beatles as Christ's surrogates on earth; and this was only
the most extreme version, the obvious physical embodiment, of the
use so many fans made of them.

It will be apparent enough to anyone with a little Beatle history
that Lennon saw himself in Christ, Christ in himself—and not in any
conventional spiritual sense. He identified with Christ as one identifies with another person, as one sees one's prosaic struggles reflected
in another's. To Lennon, Christ was not an icon but an imaginative
presence, role model, and creative competitor, and as useful a metaphor as Lennon himself was to others: in 1969, John announced his
own imminent crucifixion in "The Ballad of John and Yoko," and a
year later claimed to believe in nothing but himself, in a song slyly ti-

tled "God." But until 1966, these were only implied potentials—implied by the cripples, by the secular worship of concert scenes, by all the reaching hands and pathetic pleas for benediction and deliverance. Show business and religion had long had a less than holy alliance, but no one had ever seriously suggested that one could fulfill the function of the other. The messianic aspect of the Beatles was treated as another manifestation of the mass hysteria surrounding them, not as a spontaneous and utterly earnest surge of youth toward an idol which could fill a Christlike role in a day when even the cover of *Time* magazine was asking if God was dead. That the Beatles were, to many, the Christs of their time remained an open secret waiting to be announced.

At some point in early 1966, Lennon figured it out. Figured out where the Beatles were standing in the world, what people were getting from them, and just how far the whole caravan had traveled. It's likely he drew clues to this, subliminally at first, then more consciously, from the grist of his daily experiences as a Beatle, but he found the formulation in an unlikely source. "I was just saying," he told an interviewer soon after the furor, "in my illiterate way of speaking, what I gleaned from Hugh J. Schonfield's book *The Passover Plot*."[43]

Certainly there were any number of parallels for him to find in this boldly heretical reconstruction of Jesus' life and afterlife, a British best-seller in 1965 (as it would be in the United States the next year). As Schonfield tells it, a young man of "dynamic purposefulness . . . proceeds methodically to carry out certain actions calculated to have particular effects and leading up to a predetermined conclusion." Self-taught in the spiritual doctrines of his elders, he is "away from home for protracted periods in an endeavor to learn what 'the Saints' could teach him." He is marked in his formative years by the loss of his father; "today it would probably be said that he had a father fixation." His charisma and vision gain him disciples who elevate him

17. Rocking and rolling: fans gather before the Beatles' concert in Boston, August 1966.

as their natural leader. He is seen to perform miracles. Crowds gather around him, "not primarily to listen to his teaching, but to be cured of their complaints or bring their relations for healing"; indeed, at times, he has "the utmost difficulty in getting about because of the press of people."[44]

Maybe Lennon, drawing the connections page by page, began to perceive the prophet in himself. He'd come out of the fucking sticks to take over the world! As Jesus was confirmed in his mission by John the Baptist, Lennon found Elvis, another long-haired wild man shouting in the wilderness—whereupon he had his vision of rock and roll glory, with everything that that might bring, and gathered around him a band of disciples to give the vision life. It had taken form with a vow which was messianic in its implications, and which continued to build through the Liverpool days and Hamburg nights, always returning in the language of ultimate realization, final conversion: *Some day she will see*—"she" standing in for "they," for the world. And the impulse was still there in 1966. "There's something else I'm going to do . . . something I must do—only I don't know what it is."

Jesus Christ, *c'est moi*. But the parallels continued from there, for Schonfield's book was split into two parts. The first was about the realization of a vision; the second detailed how Jesus' vision escaped from him. How the thing he started was taken over and reinterpreted from the Crucifixion on—reinscribed with the personal emphases of others, from the Nazarenes to the Essenes to the authors of the first Gospels, the journey to Calvary goosed for drama, streamlined for narrative punch, recalibrated for its ethnic implications. Schonfield wrote of "Jesus being magnified and becoming more symbolic" by the "misrepresentation[s] of his followers"; and he showed how Christianity "became transformed by the assimilation of alien ideas and modes of thought. In the process it ceased to be a reliable guide to its own beginnings."[45]

But despite his interest in subsequent modifications of the original, presumably unblemished Jesus story, Schonfield's project was objective and historical. He sought to reconstruct from various ancient sources the processes by which messianic Christianity was disseminated and, occasionally, perverted. He was by no means deploring "misrepresentation" as by definition invidious; the disciples, in his characterization, were not fools so much as half-aware pawns receptive to Jesus' calculations; and in no way did Schonfield speculate that Jesus was less powerful a presence in the world consciousness of the 1960s than he'd ever been. So it intrigues that these are precisely the arguments which John Lennon, in his mania-distorted reading, took from it. He described *The Passover Plot* as being "about how Christ's message had been garbled by disciples and twisted for various selfish reasons by those who followed."[46] But in fact Schonfield gave only the seed of this critique. It was Lennon who grew the seed into a plot of weeds, an all-inclusive condemnation of message garbling—a condemnation that surely would have resonated with him in the limbo between *Help!* and the 1966 tours.

That the Beatles' "message"—their vision of worldwide inclusion— was undergoing all manner of symbolic slice-and-dice was natural, but it could not have been fun. Of all the Beatles, Lennon may have been least amenable to the process, simply because his ego was both the most voracious and the least secure. But 1966 taught him that the process was inevitable, battling it futile. Recall how, in Hamburg a few months after the Cleave interview, when presented with a reporter's symbolic interpretation of Beatle clothing, Lennon sounded almost philosophical. What was expressed as irritation in February 1966 had by May turned into wisdom, a kind of acceptance: "It was *you* that was looking at *us.*"

But whatever the Christ comment meant to John personally, it meant something quite different to those Christians who encountered his words in innocence, blinked their eyes hard, and read them again. What infuriated many was not the rightness or wrongness of the remarks, but the unparalleled chutzpah that lay behind the comparison. Lennon's dazed and anxious retraction was that he "wasn't comparing us with Jesus Christ as a person, or God as a thing, or whatever it is."[47] Well, actually he was. Now, for a fundamentalist Christian who cannot see past the immediate provocation, this is horrifying. For a contemplative Christian who can see religion as both personal creed and only one creed among many, it is at the very least something to consider. But, speaking as no kind of Christian at all, I can say that John's blasphemy was a rather wonderful thing.

Because it was all about belief—Lennon's belief in himself and in the power of what the Beatles were doing to change lives. The real arrogance, the real challenge in the statement is not in the most quoted line but in this one: "I needn't argue about that; I'm right and will be proved right."[48] Lennon had always driven his band on the principle that it—he—was right and would be proved right. He often spoke, and acted, as if belief were all anyone needed to achieve the impossible. In the early days, he believed the Beatles were the best band in the world—"and believing that is what made us what we were."[49] Years later he said, "I really thought that—that love would save us all."[50]

For "love," insert "rock and roll"—because rock and roll was the thing against which he measured everything. It was his hate as well as his love, his toilet and his church, the thing that had saved *his* life; and finally his mission was to make rock and roll matter to the world as much as it mattered to him. How he would bring that about, and in what ways it would end up mattering, were questions unanswerable in the here and now of 1966—because, despite having originated the vision, he was as powerless as Jesus to control it once it was freed into, or loosed upon, the world.

The Christ comment was the *summa* of the Beatles', and particularly John's, use of talk as a means of defining not only themselves as individuals on a world stage, but the stamp rock and roll would leave on the popular thought and hidden fantasies of the time. Maureen Cleave got her scoop of the century. When some form of the Christ quote appears now it appears satirically, as a joke (on Jesus, interestingly, as often as on the Beatles), but Lennon's words have survived because in 1966 they were taken *not* satirically but very earnestly indeed. People were right to take them that way. Lennon's offense against complacency was a truly bold move, a wild association which released unacknowledged potentials of thought and action, brought something hidden straight to the surface of world awareness—and every part of that world, from Cleveland to Vatican City, Moscow to Johannesburg, was forced to in some way respond.

It also forced the craziest, the unlikeliest mutation yet. That the psycho-historical theories of an obscure Jesus scholar found their way into the pages of a glossy American teen magazine is only one of the connections that were made by and through the agency of the Beatles—the gaps that in their passing were not just bridged but made to vanish. Pop crashed into religion, not sideways but head-on, and people were driven to take positions. Ministers and theologians and papal councils now had to deal with pop, even if only to dispose of it; more than that, they had to *feel* some way about it, because it was now firmly on their turf—and to date, it hasn't left.

Christianity had always welcomed the burden of its young adherents, absorbed their adolescent anxieties and desires. So did the Beatles. But Christianity welcomed those inchoate energies so as to quell them, the better to redirect them on a particular path, whereas the Beatles never sought to quell. What made them different from any religion before or since was that, rather than redirecting those energies in the service of doctrine, they gave the fan free reign to explore them, intensify them, take them anywhere. Speaking in the cliché of the '60s, the Beatles were from the Church of Do Your Own Thing; granting their accomplishment the respect it deserves, we recognize that they preached a faith of complete and open possibility that was by its very innocent nature a transcendent vision. That their faith spoke more urgently to the times than did Christ's—garbled as it was in the mouths of his officiators—was another reason the Beatles were so loved, and why they were so hated.

Lennon's words did not immediately inspire anyone to articulate that pop was the new church, that kids had chosen it as such, or that, because they were responding to their times and to the history that was theirs alone to determine, they were making the right choice. But people knew—and many were scared of the changes they saw coming. John Lennon saw the new order coming sooner than most, and by opening his big mouth he forced a lot of people, the Beatles themselves not least of all, to deal with it—years, perhaps, before they were ready to.

□

For the band, dealing with it first meant going to America—pitching *whoooo* one more time as they weathered the righteous fury of those whom Lennon's words had hit hardest. Once again Beatle timing was perverse in its perfection. The Christ quote with its demonic exclamation point hit American radar a scant two weeks before the tour began August 12 in Chicago, when the butcher cover, too, was still a fresh outrage. From the start, this tour was grim business—a dark-spirited late-summer pageant of heat and thunderstorms, burning crosses and bad feelings. If the first U.S. visit had been a quintessential, and touching, display of American insanity—our dizzy infatuation with the new—this last tour was all-American in its ugliness, the raw quality of the hysteria it threw up as Beatlemania plowed across the continent, helpless to avoid leaving scars wherever it passed.

The tour occupied the better part of August 1966. It was the high hot season apotheosized by the Lovin' Spoonful's "Summer in the City" and Billy Stewart's "Summertime," the interregnum commemorated in Simon and Garfunkel's "7 O'Clock News / Silent Night"; the time of Charles Whitman's rifle, Lenny Bruce's needle, and Richard Speck's knife; the summer Rosemary's baby was born. All year, the country rehearsed for greater violences to come. Vietnam protests multiplied in force as atrocities took over the cover of *Life* magazine and the first draft-card burners were convicted. The number of U.S. dead in Vietnam would rise nearly 100 percent before the year was out. In 1966 Bobby Seale and Huey Newton founded the Black Panthers, SNCC chairman Stokely Carmichael first shouted "Black Power!" and James Meredith was shot down on a march across Mississippi. In the month of July alone there were black riots in Chicago, Brooklyn, Cleveland, and Baltimore.[51]

Not a sanguine moment in our history: every boil on America's dogged, hemorrhoidal ass seemed to be bursting at once. Unlike the '50s, with their scheming fringes and hidden minorities: what had gone underground then was now becoming the meat of everyday worry. And it was not only the protesters and troublemakers, the white peaceniks and black marchers, who were itchy in these hot moments before the storm. That indefinite American mass—Richard Nixon would soon label it the Silent Majority—which, faced with the new imperatives of change, seemed to have chosen inaction over action, was getting fed up with the loosening of morals, the relaxing of limits, the sudden intrusiveness of the rest of the world.

So if America seemed to have its knives out for the Beatles, it was partly because those knives were out already. As they had in Tokyo and Manila, the Beatles placed themselves in close range of hostilities and fears that were either already in movement or aching to break out. But they were not coincidental, the protests and attacks that followed them across the country: much of the reaction could be traced back to the spoor the Beatles had deposited on their first American binge—long hair, loud music, musical miscegenation, the icky threat of anything foreign—which was in tune with the other elements (civil rights, antiwar protest) troubling the status quo of the early '60s. The Beatles were returning to reap the bad harvest of everything they had sown in the American mind two years before, at the very moment the nation was making its last tortured break from the flimsy social constructs of the '50s to the chaos that would soon define its daily life.

Lousy luck and stormy weather followed the Beatles from city to city. Urban heat and the stench of the stockyards—carnivorous America in its meaty essence—hung over the inaugural concert at Chicago's International Amphitheater. In Cleveland, thousands of fans broke police control in the worst of all American Beatle riots. In muggy Philadelphia, the open-air performance was accompanied by the rumble of thunder and the flashing of an electrical storm. The Cincinnati date was rained out, and the cancellation, with 35,000 fans already in their seats, nearly set off another riot; backstage, an overtaxed Paul hung himself and his sickened nerves over a toilet and puked. In St. Louis the Beatles played through a rainstorm under a thin canopy, risking death by electrocution.[52] Witnesses in the larger stadiums reported instances of fans reaching the stage, not to embrace their idols but to attack them; while in the tighter venues the Beatles spent their time onstage under a constant barrage of fan-tossed objects—no longer just candies or teddy bears but shoes, scissors, bottles, garbage.[53]

They were shadowed across America by a dull sense of backlash. Hunting for Beatle-hate even where none existed, the press delighted in noting declining ticket sales, counting empty seats. Hot for fresh gaffes, reporters poked at the open sore of the Christ business, asking John to both restate his apology and expand upon the original statement. A New York TV reporter, grilling teenagers before the August 23 return to Shea Stadium, pushes hard to extract a single admission that the Beatles are washed up, uncool, last year's clothes. After several failures, a success: one little girl says she now digs Herman's Hermits.[54]

Bad dream time—but it was also as real as real got. The brutal tour acted out on a very real stage the dream life of the *Revolver* music that came echoing through loudspeakers before every show: a barely organized madness with four glazed dreamers standing passive and powerless at its center. Like that music, the tour was morbid and metal-edged; the fantasies that fed into it were distorted and mad. And like *Revolver,* the final tour was suffused with paranoia—that of the Beatles, and that of the audience.

□

There was an article on the group in a German magazine. I didn't understand the article, but there was a large photograph of us in the middle page. In the same article, there was a photograph of a

South African negro pushing the jungle down. I still don't quite
know what he has to do with us, but I suppose it has some
significance.

—Paul, 1962; in *Mersey Beat: The Beginnings of the Beatles* (1977)

No one will say that, for the group, paranoia was unjustified. The
Christ controversy inspired the tour's ugliest scenes, and grimmest
threats. Anti-Beatle, pro-Jesus demonstrations made front-page news
of images seldom seen since Nazi Germany: bonfires consuming
Beatle pictures, towheaded children beaming goblin smiles over the
flames. There were death threats both implied and direct. The Ku
Klux Klan, its power slipping badly under the advance of civil rights,
was not slow to snatch its portion of the general outrage. A cross
hung with Beatle albums was burned in South Carolina, while the
Memphis chapter and its local affiliates turned out in an almost un-
believable force of 8,000 to picket the August 19 show at the Mid-
South Coliseum. None of the threats leveled in Elvis' adopted hometown materialized, but three songs into the Beatles' performance, a
cherry bomb exploded on the mezzanine over their heads—loudly
enough to drill through the screams and feedback, sharply enough
for each member to dart looks at the others to see who had been
cut down. Three teenagers and a bagful of fireworks were taken into
custody.[55]

The Beatles' is an American story as much as any other kind, and
the anti-Beatle reaction was as apple-pie American as that prank
firecracker. Those towheads were our towheads; those men in pointy
hats represented our very own Ku Klux Klan. If in 1964 the Beatles
had triggered the country's exhilarating and sometimes stupefying
willingness to respond with wonder and delight to something genuinely new, in 1966 they catalyzed a very different form of American
madness. In the anti-Beatle protests, Americans were afforded a
unique view of the fascist potential that has always thrived in the
conflict between the society and the individual—the outward push of

the pioneer versus the inward pull of the community. In the 1960s the Southern racist was forced by the civil rights movement to act out this all-American tension, to acknowledge by his actions the impossible contradiction of a population largely predicated on an ethic of rugged individualism which nevertheless, when the crunch came, reacted violently against the defiance of the community.

It may be that this conflict was at or near the core of each of the larger social collisions of the '60s. Civil rights, antiwar fervor, women's liberation, freedom of experimentation and lifestyle were in one sense all about the hearty band of pioneers breaking from an established community; while those who fought back in the name of the status quo, from the White Citizens Council of Birmingham to the pro-Nixon hardhats of New York City, asserted their love of country by attacking whoever sought to practice America's oldest and best ideals of itself. It was possibly the widest community-individual breach anyone then alive in America had seen, and the Beatles, along with millions of others, fell right into it.

Maybe it was inevitable that, as iconoclasts whose dream was a dream of community, they would intersect with America's identical contradiction as it began to crack apart. The 1950s vision of the American community was a false one, as it usually is at any given time, because it claimed to embrace everyone while excluding or suppressing millions. But it was pervasive enough to be taken as truth: it had good PR, and fit the mood of the majority. Despite brave sorties here and there—from sources as disparate as Allen Ginsberg and Martin Luther King Jr.—the time was defined by its fear of confrontation and of realization, with most pioneers of the coming revolt in hiding, waiting for their moment. Along with the blacks of the South and the students on the campuses, the Beatles reintroduced at full synchronized blast the pioneer's ideal of new community, a spirit America had been missing at least since the 1930s.

If the Beatles had ever embodied any principle beyond the trans-

formative power of rock and roll, it was that every step in their progress would entail the inclusion, through engagement, of yet another
community. First they would form a community among themselves;
this would grow into a community that encompassed an imagined
mass, an ideal audience; and after all the dues were paid and the
foundations laid, the community would include, or at least invite, everyone who wished to play a part. And then—their cultural genius,
their social greatness—they took community a step further. They
trumped all the idealists who had ever sought only to break away,
never to return. Once having tested and sealed their communal ideal
among themselves—in isolation, in the underground—they consciously and ambitiously set themselves to the infiltration, the im-
pregnation, finally the capitulation of the larger community: the
world community, with all its splinters and divisions.

Truly, what precedent was there in twentieth-century popular art—
let alone high, rarefied art—for such an outrageous ambition? Some
have defined the Beatles' communal instinct more narrowly, as a
movement toward mere mass bohemianism—but that dissatisfies because it is only half the story: it accounts for the teenyboppers and
hippies who adored them, but ignores the extremists who detested
and feared them yet were sucked into their vortex anyway. And their
ongoing engagement of new and alien communities was not the
same as hegemony, for hegemony desires and requires a monolithic
response: abject surrender. Their natural goal was, very simply,
wholesale mass *involvement*—in whatever form that might take,
within whatever population. In this way, the Beatles would take the
idea of a mass community to its limit of possibility.

A measure of their success in this is that even those who wished
them destroyed found a place in their continuing story. This, in 1966,
was that limit of possibility—another instance of how the Beatles
opened the field for anyone's participation. And the pro-Christ zealots were obviously overjoyed to cast themselves as actors in the Beatle

drama: look at the news footage and you find that the smiles are simply too broad, the stomping and burning too festive in spirit. Of course they were happy—civil rights had made the lynching party unseemly, and many probably despaired of such open displays of racial hatred ever occurring again. These zealots, like the Tokyo extremists and the Manila mob, had found what they needed to focus and release the tension they felt as the social ground trembled beneath them. Again a very particular group of people found in the Beatles just the symbol they needed, and the placard of one Christian protester made that symbol clear: it showed John Lennon with devil's beard and horns drawn in.

It made such sense. The Beatles in their plenitude had offered themselves as the fulfillment of many wishes, many images. For millions they had served as Christ's surrogate, and now they were Satan's substitute—the Antichrist to whom these Americans could ascribe, in symbolic terms, all that they feared about their own loss of social control in an America gone secular.

Although on another level the burnings had very little to do with religion, and everything to do with how the Beatles fit into what the country was going through at that moment. It meant something that the protests were limited almost exclusively to the Southern states, where the resistance to black equality was fiercest. To white Southerners seeing their racist prerogatives challenged, the Beatles and blackness were part and parcel of the same threat. Never mind that, aside from McCartney's "dirty nigger" jibe, the Beatles had done little to publicly associate themselves with black struggle.[56] In dress and manner they appropriated no part of black style, nor had they ever explicitly impersonated a black sound, as had the Animals and the Rolling Stones and Them. But in the symbolic realm they now inhabited, all that mattered was what they were seen by others to represent. If to the extremist elements of the Far East they had stood for all the ills of Western commercial culture, to the God-fearing racists of the

South they portended the mixing of nations and races—i.e., blacks and whites fucking.

This was, of course, the first social threat ever lodged by rock and roll, which white racists of the 1950s had excoriated in thinly encoded language as "jungle music," "race music." But as the movement for black *political* freedom drew strength around the turn of the decade, the fear of *music* as an interracial channel receded; and such fear was largely obviated by the drift of post-toilet rock into a safe and watery dilution of Elvis' stiff racial cocktail. In that sense the Beatles only renewed a dormant potential, a deferred paranoia. But the differences between then and now were signal. The '50s had never seen antirock demonstrations of this fixed intensity. Never had the violence of a specific population focused so fiercely on a single rock and roll target: these protesters may have been trying to burn integration, but they were using Beatle imagery as the fuel. Anti-Americanism too was a new element: as literal foreign bodies, the Beatles were even more representative of the Other than Southern American rockers of the '50s, even less acceptable as carriers of the interracialist virus. And, perhaps most significantly, it was the first time an antirock attack had been triggered not by what a singer sang, but by what he said.

KKK Grand Dragon Robert Shelton made clear, so to speak, his confusion with regard to the overlap of Beatles and blackness: "From their appearances and from the calomeration [*sic*] of colors that they're involved, I couldn't identify them as whether they're actually white or black. I don't have that knowledge."[57] Obviously, to Shelton, the fact that he couldn't securely identify the Beatles as white meant they were no better than black. The Dragon's South Carolina brethren likewise equated "Beatle" with "black" when they burned their cross, as did those citizens of Memphis and Birmingham and Longview, Texas, who lit fires of their own, well aware of the symbolic power fire held in that time of bombed-out churches and flaming Freedom buses.

The demonstrations were, by one set of symbols, an assertion of white Christian supremacy. By another, they were the most extreme Beatle fantasy yet devised. They showed how far the Beatles had gone in engaging with the world, how deeply they had penetrated even its sickest and most ancient passions, and how complex were the burdens their ambitions had forced them to assume. The burnings were deplorable and stupid, but as a social and mass-psychological reaction to a certain provocation they were not without their logic. Fear of the Beatles and fear of social tolerance were not only compatible; each was implied by the other. At certain points in the '60s, the feelings people had for the Beatles and for the world around them came together and formed a circle—a magic circle, a sphere of fantasy within which mutations of thought were formed, the unimaginable was imagined, and action was taken.

□

Why the Beatles were loved seems obvious; why they were hated is trickier. But boiled down, it needn't be very complicated: the haters were jealous—jealous because they so coveted the fifteen-year-old girl. Her fanatic willingness, initially, to follow, to be led and influenced; and ultimately her eagerness to act upon the feelings that had been stirred inside her. They desired her spirit, and wished it for themselves. She was impassioned by the Beatles where she wasn't by the church, or, increasingly, by the securities of bourgeois life. And it was becoming clear that her love of the Beatles was inextricable from, symbolic of, the passions which youth movements were drawing on to change the world.

There had been teen idols before; there had never been Beatles. Frank Sinatra, in his youth, had crooned postwar romance, and the girl had swooned. Ten years later, she had cried out for Elvis—and then pulled back, shocked and ashamed, holding to her chasteness, covering her orgasm with giggles. Confronted with the Beatles, she

18. Stiff arm and flying leg, male constraint and female resistance:
the birth of second-wave feminism? Boston, August 1966.

did all of these things except hold back. The haters perceived the depth of her response, and throughout 1966 felt its gravity widening, from Tokyo to Memphis. Who knew what might result from such action as these girls, in their legions, were incited to? What war might break out, what peace? "Was my friend so wrong," Ralph J. Gleason asked, "who said that if Hitler were alive today, the German girls wouldn't allow him to bomb London if the Beatles were there?"[58]

Writer Elizabeth Hess once proposed a rough starting point for "the second wave of the women's liberation movement":

> My own consciousness snapped into shape in 1964 at a Beatles concert. I still remember melting into a massive crowd of jumping, screaming girls, all thinking and feeling the same lascivious thoughts. It was my generation's turn to let our libidos go public. I was twelve, just beginning to understand that sex was power: my first feminist epiphany. As the '60s tore on, the crowd of girls, now women, was still moving together, marching against the war in Vietnam.[59]

Hess touched upon the hater's basic fear: deep emotional involvement in the sound and being of a pop group translating itself, by process of emotional and psychical mutation, into other kinds of involvement. By virtue of the group's ambitions, which meant demanding everything of themselves, it was only fair to the vow that they demand more of the teenybopper than anyone else, Sinatra or Elvis, had required her to give—and this entailed absolute involvement as both price and reward of her central role. She had rehearsed her screams on other idols; by the time the Beatles arrived, she was ready to translate her scream into social action.

In *Help!* the ring had been coveted as the symbol of this pact. Professor Foot, the mad scientist in that Beatlephobe's wet dream, spoke the haters' secret desire when he said: "With a ring like that, I could—dare I say it?—rule the world. I must have that ring!" The haters, spurned lovers all, hated the Beatles for challenging their natural right to rule the world.

So if the circles drawn in 1966 were magic, sometimes the magic was very bad indeed. Those who lit bonfires for Christ were occupying their own circle, as were the Japanese extremists, Marcos, the fifteen-year-old girl, Bob Dylan, or for that matter the butcher Beatles themselves. Just as much as they, the Jesusites were writing themselves into the story, imposing their meanings upon it. Because it wasn't just a Beatles record these white Christian teenagers were stomping as their parents stood by, stoking the flames; it was black revolt. It was the rush of change, the pain of integration, and the threat of one world. But it was also just a Beatles record.

□

A face to lose youth for, to occupy age
With the dream of, meet death with.

—Robert Browning, "A Likeness"

The relief the Beatles feel upon reaching the tour's end must be comparable to that of a man whose shoulders sag as a cocked gun is removed from his temple. By the evening of August 29, when they enact their final concert—at San Francisco's Candlestick Park, to a less than sold-out house—they have been working at being the Beatles for nearly a decade, effectively without cease. And now a good part of it is over: no more will they appear as exposed objects on the stage of public display, or serve as fleshly targets for either adoration or hostility. Finally all the symbols will be laid to rest. The dream is over.

They know this is the last time they will commune with their audience in this way. That's why John and Paul take their Tokyo cameras to the stage and snap pictures throughout the show; that's why they have asked press agent Tony Barrow to produce a Beatle-sanctioned bootleg of the event. By documenting the moment, they will define it—as an ending.

It might be the primitive nature of Barrow's recording that imparts an almost ambrosiac quality to the music and strips it of the shrillness, the harsh highs, of the typical Beatle concert. It might be the moist Bay air scooping into Candlestick Park that gives the performance its free and open sound. Because it isn't that the performance is particularly good. Most who were there have described it as listless and unremarkable, just another show, the Beatles appearing as black atoms behind wire-mesh fencing, 200 feet away from the nearest fan.[60] Yet it doesn't sound like any other Beatle show one can hear: the sound isn't ear-splitting and unpleasant; it's airy and elusive. The screams provide a vast cushion upon which the music—free of bass and drums, almost all voice and guitar—hovers in space. The Beatles' voices float wraith-like above the music, seeming not to emerge from physical bodies so much as electronic specters.

But in this show they are halfway between specter and flesh, because there's an intimacy here which hasn't existed since their first American appearances. When the Beatles talk between numbers, their words don't sound canned. They are unscripted and of the moment, and imbued with a sense of how much the Beatles and their fans have been through together. George introduces the two-year-old "I Feel Fine" as hailing from 1959. "Day Tripper," John says, was released as "a single record . . . a long time ago."[61] Nine months, to be exact. Secreted in the brief pause and weary voicing of *a long time ago* is Lennon's sudden realization of how old he is at the age of twenty-five.

There are other surprises, small aberrations. McCartney spikes "Baby's in Black" with a series of unrehearsed whoops and shouts; and for a moment all the impacted tension, boredom, and exhaustion that have made constipated hulks of the Beatles' concert songs are dispelled by a lazy rhythmic lope. Introducing another song, Paul sets aside his tired bonhomie as a cluster of boys shakes free of restraints and breaks for the stage, only to be snatched on the infield by security. "Should we just watch this for a minute?" Paul asks, stopping the show dead for a second or five, inviting the audience to join the Beatles in a common gaze upon the spectacle they have created together.[62] These are the rarest of rare moments in mid- to late-period Beatle concerts, where acceptance and love were *faits accomplis* and the group held fast to rigid routine as if the live fantasy were such a fragile thing that any slant into spontaneity might shatter it and send its shards spinning toward the stage.

As a rock show, Candlestick Park doesn't have the hot moment-to-momentness of Star-Club or the pressured intensity of Budokan. Muffled and cloudy and sad, not a beginning but an ending, it is a rapprochement between performers and audience at the far end of this grating, upsetting tour, Beatles singing past all the bad scenes. The depleted thrust of a final fling, the elation and tired smile: finally, there's something like tragedy to be heard in this ending.

Yes: tragedy. Brian Epstein—that tragic figure—saw it happening. Midway through the Shea Stadium documentary, he is heard to say, "To me, in terms of popular music, the Beatles express a cross-quality of happiness and tragedy; and this is basically what the greatest form of entertainment is made up of."[63] That observation sticks—first because it seems so incongruent with the image it accompanies. What is tragic about this youthful convulsion on the green of a baseball diamond? Tragedy implies the death of something, a person or an ideal, and death is the opposite of what we see. But suddenly we realize how many of these faces are twisted, awed, savage with emotion, their images stolen in that moment of release that so resembles agony and death. This must be what Brian Epstein saw from behind all those stages: the mask of tragedy. The private mask beneath the public one, worn so naturally for so long; the shadow of death and loss behind the cult of youth that was the mania.

But you have to go past that pretty image to get at the tragic meat of the Beatles' concert spectacle as it climaxed in 1966. You have to consider that by this time the fans, just as well as the Beatles, knew that what they had shared was dying—and that much of what they had formed their young lives around was going to die with it. In late 1965, Kansas fan Ron Schaumberg looked at the cover of *Rubber Soul* and was "repelled." Only much later did he perceive "what it was that so turned me off. It wasn't the scruffy jackets or the outrageous hair. . . . It wasn't the cold attitude captured by the camera. It was their faces. The Beatles looked old." Schaumberg saw weight and experience sagging the supple skin, the witty features which for him and others had been the first site of so many possibilities. "And I wanted nothing more to do with them."[64]

Even if the teenager could not know what so disturbed him, the Beatles were hip to the inevitable death of mass romance. The Beatles were already saying that it was necessary, even good that it should die: only then could *something else* take its place. In some sense, Ron Schaumberg had to see death in the cover of *Rubber Soul* before Elizabeth Hess could march against the war in Vietnam.

Just before the Beatles left the Candlestick Park stage, John Lennon struck the opening chords of "In My Life," a song he and Paul had written, which they had never performed live. Just a few notes, no explanation, no follow-up, and the stage was empty. It was among the smallest and most ambiguous of Beatle gestures, never to be noted by most in the thronging crowd. But in this atmosphere of endings, it was a dramatic flourish tossed out for whoever might catch it.[65] "In My Life" was not a song about growing older; it was about the sudden realization that you *are* older. If there's tragedy inherent in youth—as poets from Shakespeare on down have insisted there is—it's the realization that nothing beautiful stays as it is. But the song was also about moving on from that realization, because having a history also meant that a life could be sized up, friendships and loves weighed for their value. Far stronger than any tragedy of youth, the song implied, was the richness of maturity, the immeasurable depth of ongoing life.

As they always have, the Beatles invite everyone to take the trip with them. John offers a standard introduction to the Candlestick Park faithful: "We'd like to carry on now . . ." But immediately he

19. Another fainting fan, and the inevitable death of mass romance. Boston, August 1966.

amends the stock phrase, dropping to a baritone of pseudo-sincerity which is nonetheless sincere. ". . . Carry on *together,* and will . . . all together and all for one."[66]

He feels the ending, but knows it is part of a continuity. And if we attend to one small incidental detail, we can hear that continuity already extending itself past the temporal limits of this one night, this one stage. Tony Barrow's recording runs out soon into the final song, "Long Tall Sally"—a song which reaches back to the Beatles' very earliest toilets. The last thing we hear from Candlestick Park is Paul shouting *Baby, some fun tonight,* and screaming—and the scream breaks into silence. An opening exists in this magic circle: an opening for *something else* to slip through. But what? John was stuck for an answer: "There's something else I'm going to do . . . something I must do—only I don't know what it is." It was the unanswered question backgrounding the events of 1966; motivating and irritating the harshness of *Revolver;* ringing through all the year's chaotic, unresolved endings.

To the extent that the Beatles exist in sound and fantasy and symbol, in dream and history, Candlestick Park isn't an ending at all. The Beatles and their audience will remain suspended on the precipice of that final scream: once begun, a scream must be completed. If the Beatles won't do it, the audience will—and the Beatles, at this moment, are encouraging it to take that imaginative leap, to press on into the *something* that is *new.* This is the importance—the singularity—of their demand for involvement, for feeling. That onward press, they imply, is the only way to defeat the tragedy they have experienced together, the irreplaceable bliss of first encounter, the convulsive death of childhood. Into their music they have distilled a poetics of possibility, imagination, action; and in departing the stage, they have left the circle open so that the audience may close it as it chooses. The audience will now need to recreate the Beatles, make coherent myths out of fantasies that from this night on will be inspired only by sound and image, never by live, present flesh. In this way, the evolving drama of Beatles and audience will be kept alive in the separation of the two, the absence of the idols themselves; in this way, the scream will be completed, the circle closed.

And if the new myths born of audience fantasy are to revolve increasingly around death, if the circle is to be completed not just by creative acts of the imagination but by destructive acts of violence both real and symbolic, well—a certain unpredictability of response has always been part of the bargain. More so now that the Beatles have themselves injected a strong dose of death into their mythic mix.

So only one version, one stage of the dream is over; others are just waiting to become.

□

Innocence had gained experience—but the experience did not explain itself. It was a blur of jolts and warnings contained in the events of 1966.

"She Said She Said" was the last song recorded for *Revolver*. In its obscurantism, the song indicates John Lennon wasn't certain that he *cared* to relinquish innocence for experience. "Tomorrow Never Knows" embraces the indiscriminate intake of experience, while "I'm Only Sleeping," uncharacteristic among the great Lennon songs, ignores the choice altogether. Situated between them, "She Said" issues from the teeth of the dilemma. In it, experience is offered as a dark, enticing thing that holds out the possibility of cleansing and rebirth: death itself is a secret the singer has to learn. But in the same instant, he must stop himself from fleeing. Trapped, he stops to weigh the present against what are recalled as the certainties of youth: everything was right, he swears—once upon a time. As it travels its gnarled circuits, the song wonders, at the moment of decision, how easy it can be to let go of the past. How easy can it be to relinquish forever one's younger and less knowing self, to leave behind the time when dreams were born and carried out—especially when the experience one is faced with offers no securities, and even when that uncomplicated past is a lie of the mind? The song asks: What can a dreamer do, now that he is awake?

Circling in upon itself, the song takes shape as a frustrated dialogue with the fifteen-year-old girl.[67] The singer wants to know where
she got her mad ideas, the madness that both feeds and feeds upon
his own. Well, it was the Beatles, of course, who put "those things" in
her head, the fantasies and the fevers; the Beatles who sought to elicit
the very screams that now drive them mad. But the girl is not talking
straight: her gnomic reply—that she knows death, she knows sadness—expresses the dream life behind those screams. Stunned into
life by the Beatles, she gave them her screams for two years—never
realizing that within that well of life was the promise of death. Now
it's easier to see, because there has been death around the Beatles all
summer long: threats of death, songs of death, shades of death in
their exhausted beauty, the sweet voices gone raw. She has tasted the
tragedy in the Beatles' happiness: that even such beauty as theirs de-
cays; that idols soften into flesh, and childhood ends.

The subjects tragedy does not leave dead it leaves stranded—no
moorings, no home. The Beatles and their young fans might have
asked, at this point in time, what would become a great rock and roll
question: *Where do we go from here?* The question echoes against itself
as "She Said She Said" fades on a paralysis of death and sadness,
John's voice split in two to meld the fact of one with the emotion of
the other. Yet again, all is left in suspension.

The strength of *Revolver*—as music, as Beatle-psychological and
pop-historical benchmark—is that it acknowledges this suspension
as a condition; expresses it in music which nonetheless moves, is vital
and committed and engaged, not least with its own morbidity; is willing to waver between hope for the future and immobility before its
unknowns; and lingers on the matter of death, aware that advancing
upon the future means questioning the past. *Revolver* is the first
Beatle album whose capability, in the Keatsian sense, is negative: it
insists upon, lives in, uncertainty.

Hovering over that psychic terrain is an emotional chill. Despite its

20. *Where do we go from here?* The Beatles at London Airport after escaping Manila, July 8, 1966.

furies and frustrations, no one could ignore the record's essential coldness. *Rubber Soul* had been harsh to hear but reassuring to feel; *Revolver* had both a caustic skin and an icy heart. From its opening count-in to its final track of mad animal noise and monotonous drum, the album was not designed to sound lovely, promote simplicities, or stroke the romantic solipsism of the fifteen-year-old girl. It was the first Beatle album to find itself in the dark, not the light.

It's hard not to hear it as prophecy. Formed by all the Beatle experience that preceded it, *Revolver* goes on to foretell the darker, more threatening shapes that experience would take in this most scarifying of Beatle years. In 1966 the Beatles' varied audiences drew circles around themselves and their objects of obsession, spaces of extreme action for carrying out highly personalized fantasies. With *Revolver*, the group drew their own circles; and within each, they themselves were both authors and enactors of a Beatle-centered dream. The dream might be one of surreal invocation ("Tomorrow Never Knows"), macabre portents ("Love You To"), banal tragedy ("Eleanor Rigby"), imagined peace ("Good Day Sunshine"), or existential limbo ("She Said She Said"). But each was its own kind of Beatle fantasy, formed from its author's sense of what the Beatles were, how tall they stood in the world, and how their statements and acts might make that world turn differently in its next revolution.

Revolver was named after the Beatles' own deadpanism for the long-playing record: good title for a record of involutions and turnings—though to American eyes, the word said "gun" and nothing else. Among the alternatives under review was *Bubble and Squeak,* derived from an English vegetable concoction served with meat. Another was *Pendulums.*

They also considered calling it *Magic Circles.* It's anyone's guess where they got that one from, or what they intended it to mean.[68]

□

Like Roy Lichtenstein's comic-strip panels or Godard's agit-prop, the Beatles' music depended on compression. To make it as pop, a Beatle song had to grab the moment and hold it; while to last as art, it had to suggest that there were emotions and implications at work that no moment was sufficient to illuminate. The moment would have to be lived again and again.

This reached back to the first fundament of Beatle music: that it must contain the sound of deep emotional experience pressed into the tightest, most intense space imaginable. In the years between then and now, they'd never ventured far from this holy principle. But as their experiences grew more complex, troubling, inexplicable, and magical, the spaces that contained them would, to be true, have to be tighter and more intense. Everything that happened to them and around them in this year had its precursor in earlier days, but art—

like dreaming—is allowed to shock where real life, in its drawn-out processes, tends to bore; allowed to appease and fulfill the senses by distilling mounting cataclysm into a sudden rupture which leaves everything familiar suddenly strange. A rupture very like the crack that opened in the song that carried the Beatles out of 1966 and into whatever future lay before them.

"Strawberry Fields" originated as a vague, gentle Lennon reverie for acoustic guitar and solo voice, his attempt to speak in the instinctively Surrealist voice of a gifted child. When the Beatles took it over at the end of November, they retained and elaborated upon the song's sense of dazed meditation in a barren setting: their first completed version was spare and metallic in the *Revolver* style, with sighing background vocals and a mercurial interjection of slide guitar. But Lennon realized the song had more to give than they were asking of it. Another rendition was crafted, utterly different—this one gentler, more mellifluous, the guitar sound a golden shower, the chordal abrasions smoothed; in place of barrenness was the sound of a lush acid-fed garden. It was beautiful, but again Lennon nixed it. So further remakes and overdubs and polishings followed, added instruments and effects crowding the song's suddenly active landscape, until the Beatles and George Martin achieved a third realization which was pure bughouse. Thick with lurching strings and harsh horns, bottom-heavy with drums and menace, the sound had the pulse and the sensual fatness of a high-grade fever.

Finally the first half of the second version was joined to the second half of the third. Why had John decided that the child's reverie should be surgically joined to the lysergic freakshow? Because he liked both. The graft was performed by Martin just days before the end of the year.[69]

Heralded by a fluty overture, "Strawberry Fields" comes to limpid focus in some meadow of the mind, its protagonist a somnambular adolescent, a boy Narcissus gazing at himself in the pool. The words he sings are obscure though basic, the sensibility haunted though childlike; a drugged, mumbling guitar follows the voice like a faithful dog. The overall effect is of innocence, a naive fascination. But it isn't to be trusted. The truth is in the rupture: Lennon asks, *Let me take you down,* and as the music descends with him the chords have that dissonant *Revolver* edge, that same sense of being sideways to normality.

Heard at different times, the split that occurs a minute into "Strawberry Fields" can evoke a drop down an elevator shaft, or the low groan of a beast, or that moment in a dream when the earth opens and the dreamer hangs on for life. The sound of cellos on a steep and instantaneous descent into the caverns of the song's violent latter half communicate dislocation, a fall from light into the teeming underground of surface life. *Let me take you down,* Lennon says again, this time in a tape-manipulated voice suddenly vomitous and throaty, and "down" turns out to be a place where bad dreams feed. It's the bottom of Alice's rabbit hole, the final room in the *Psycho* cellar, the place in the Beatle dream where the meat is stored, a kind of Hell.

Every potential suggested in the child's mind-meadow is realized here in its darker form. In this underworld the sensations are pure and unfiltered: noises come flying, the very air weighs a ton, there is too much happening at once. The Lennon voice, so deep it might be channeling Mephistopheles, speaks the words that sounded gentle in the meadow above but which are now frantic and sweaty. Drums pound as horns sound a hysterical, almost human cry. Reversed noises chew rat-like at the background, and the strings are dense enough to choke out the light.

In the suddenness of its chaos, the song continues what was begun on *Revolver.* But there the dreamer was passive at the center of chaos, as much object as subject of the sensations swooping around and through him. Here in this mad dungeon, he feels chaos crawling up his arms: he becomes one with it. Neither fighting nor relenting to it, he is speaking in its voice. *Strawberry fields forever* are the only words as the chaos dims into silence, to come rearing back more chaotic than before, no vestige of melody now, only noise, only rhythm, forever and ever and ever.

Like virtually all Beatle music, "Strawberry Fields" doesn't explain, it expresses. The song is about the nightmare within the dream, and what happens when the two are made to acknowledge each other. It's the collision that pervades the music they will make for the remainder of the decade: the clash between an ineffable dream and its countervailing nightmare—life as it is in a dream, versus life as it is. This is the unanalyzed, undigested meat of Beatlemania, right here in the bowels beneath Strawberry Fields. It contains the underground from which they sprouted, and the dark underneath to all the fantasies they've inspired. It's taken the whole of this bad, magical year for the Beatles to reach this place, to realize it in full. For the rest of their career together, they won't leave it. *Strawberry fields forever.*

But they have ensured that they won't be there alone. Threading, as ever, through the light and the dark of all that they do, is the invitation, the renewal of the vow:

Let me take you down.

□

The splice which breaks the song in two is a melding as well as a divide, and the dream and the nightmare are distorted reflections of each other. Both, after all, speak the same words, sing the same melody, extend the same invitation. It's the quality of the feeling that is different, the intensity and nearness of the experience. The song begins as dream and ends as nightmare; starts in purity and loses itself in perversion. But the material of each is contained in the other.

Just as the nightmare of 1966 was implicit in the dream of 1964.

The violence that greeted the Beatles in Tokyo, Manila, and America may have been a shock, but it shouldn't have been a surprise. Every shift in the strength of anti-Beatle feeling was latent in the mania as it existed in its first triumph: the Jesus connection, the strands of hair foretelling the Manila crisis, the scorched-earth campaign of the American tour. No one would have hated the Beatles in '66 if they hadn't been so loved in '64.

Their mania had always held the potential for a different, darker brand of madness. The jelly babies were a shower of love, but they were also the only form of attack an adolescent, politely British, largely female audience could make upon its love objects. They were not least an assertion of that audience's identity, of its own reality in the midst of a community fantasy. The audience needed to play its part; passive witness was no option, and screams could not touch the idols with proof of the audience's being. So audiences threw things— hard, physical things. The jelly babies turned into garbage; into Clang's darts; into shoes and bottles and light bulbs. In Memphis in 1966 they turned into firecrackers, even as other, more fatal projectiles were being promised outside the stadium. In 1964, an agitated Paul had equated the harmless candy beans with bullets; had he twigged to the correlative of his own metaphor—that each audience member was a symbolic assassin—he might not have complained so loudly.

The vow of limitless love and unending novelty that the Beatles willed into existence had no choice but to reshape itself into grotesque forms once it began to feel the weight of deaths and endings. Of all the Beatles' varied mutations, dream-into-nightmare involved the most people, the most divergent groups; throughout 1966, mutation was incurred upon the audience by the Beatles, by the audience upon the Beatles. *Revolver* and "Strawberry Fields Forever" were its sound, and the remainder of the '60s was its legacy.

□

Wearing the uniform of a British soldier of the Second World War, John sits alone in a vast peaceful meadow, looking pale and tired. A second ago he was running—crouched low, desperately evading the hail of shells. Then he was caught in the gut by a Nazi mortar. He fell to the ground, looked down at his wound, looked up—and looked down again, for a last confirmation. Now, in the silence, he grips his stomach and feels the blood leaving the wound.

But John doesn't seem surprised that he has been shot, or that he is dying. His voice is steady and his face calm as he holds his bleeding stomach, feels the meat of himself, and stares back at the world which stares back at him.

"I knew this'd happen," he says. "You knew it'd happen, didn't you?"[70]

In January 1969, a group of hippies moved into a two-story house in the Los Angeles suburb of Canoga Park. The neighborhood was middle-class and the hippies felt out of place, but they used isolation to their advantage by taking it as a creed. The house was painted a bright yellow, and the group's leader named it the Yellow Submarine. It would allow them, he said, to remain "submerged beneath the awareness of the outside world."

Within its sheltering walls, the group listened to the ravings of its leader. Recently he had become obsessed with race-war and apocalypse. "You know what's gonna happen one of these nights. . . . The blacks from Watts are gonna break into the houses of some rich white piggies in Beverly Hills and start wasting them . . . you know. . . . And it ain't gonna be very pretty. . . . Like they'll be vicious. . . . They'll chop them up and mutilate them and fling blood around; then whitey is gonna retaliate. . . . He'll go into the ghetto and start shooting blacks."[1]

"Life in the Yellow Submarine was intense," one of the followers said years later. "We had to be ready when the shit came down."[2]

4

THE UNINTELLIGIBLE TRUTH

The Beatles and the Counterculture

A weekly news magazine once ran a picture of a row of uniformed men shouldering guns and sporting helmets with Plexiglas visors. They are looking in the direction of a group of young men wearing T-shirts and jeans and holding hands and dancing in a circle before their eyes.

It is obviously the period immediately preceding a clash with the police, who are guarding a nuclear power plant, a military training camp, the headquarters of a political party, or the windows of an embassy. The young people have taken advantage of this dead time to make a circle and take two steps in place, one step forward, lift first one leg and then the other—all to a simple folk melody.

I think I understand them. They feel that the circle they describe on the ground is a magic circle bonding them into a ring. Their hearts are overflowing with an intense feeling of innocence: they are not united by a march, like soldiers or fascist commandos; they are united by a dance, like children . . .

Circle dancing is magic. It speaks to us through the millennia from the depths of human memory.

—Milan Kundera, *The Book of Laughter and Forgetting* (1981)

Once the ooze is out, it's almost impossible to push it back in. But the natural reflex is always to try—and the reflex may be just as characteristic of groups, small and large, as it is of individuals. It's been said that men in combat, grievously wounded, will methodically attempt to reinsert escaping organs, reattach blasted limbs; by the same instinct, a political campaign will create spin to minimize damage, and a government agency falsify the truth to cover its sleazier schemes. There is nothing quite like the power of a community—even a loosely banded one—to construct, elaborate, and promulgate a favorable myth of itself.

We're speaking in each case of something very basic to the human organism, in groups and alone: the reflex to cover up what refuses to square with the ideal.

Cover-ups have always existed—read *The Passover Plot*. But when we refer to the cover-up today, it's usually the 1960s that form our conception. From the U2 misadventure to the Warren Report; from routine fact-fudging in Vietnam to the revelations of the Pentagon papers; from the assassination plots of CIA gremlins to a third-rate burglary at Watergate—all showed groups acting to conceal or obscure truths that had slipped through the mesh of an official story. All sprang from or reached consummation in '60s anxieties—war, assassination, fear of radicalism. All were wounds which, badly bandaged, bled through to the surface of public knowledge—a staining of squalid truth upon oblivious reality. More than television, more than postmodernism, the '60s cover-up robbed the American mind of its ability to view anything without irony.

The time we are entering, the late '60s, lay dead center in this golden age of the cover-up, and showed that the concealing reflex was just as sharp in the youth of America as in their despised elders. The hippie movement was its own kind of cover-up: an escape, an evasion, at best a bargaining with reality. As reality threatened daily to break into chaos, the community became ever more anxious to master events by constructing, elaborating, and promulgating favorable myths of itself—and, by natural extension, of reality.

The Beatles were quickest of all the major musical movers to craft their own false lead. But then they had pushed things farthest, had revealed the most. Their global presence had resulted in more than one community being forced to regard its own true face; and they themselves had come, in 1966, closer to reality's razor edge than Litherland Town Hall could ever have prepared them to be. When the year was over, they descended from the edge and made their retreat into private homes, personal pursuits. What sense did they make of what they had been through, all that had been set free in the realm of the possible? Consciously, probably none: the four minds might have reeled slowly in the process of decompression; each might have wondered how things had gotten so out of hand. But it's certain none of them wasted time theorizing on the implications of Manila or Memphis as they breathed long breaths and reclined on oriental cushions.

Even less likely that the audience worried over such issues. The haters would look to other targets now that the Beatles were in retreat, promising never to occupy the local coliseum again; while the fans, being fans, would busy themselves with minor diversions and temporary obsessions until the Beatles reappeared to state their latest case and centralize the pop discourse.

Fans, in other words, while not obsessing over the socio-pop history recently made, were nonetheless waiting for the Beatles' version of that history. *Revolver* was prediction, not articulation: the audience waited for whatever visions the Beatles would synthesize of those prophesied nightmares now that they had come to pass, what new and flashing forms would be wrought from the violence and the subtle sense of tragedy. Fans wanted a gauge of the creative possibilities now available, of the imaginative dimensions of what they and the Beatles were effecting. Again they had, in their unmapped travel, arrived at a place where their next move would be weighted with meaning: whatever choice the Beatles made would be no ordinary choice but a fresh definition of social and aesthetic terms for millions.

In one way, it seems natural that they should make music that tried to contain the ooze. Such quantities of it had been spilled in 1966: it leaked from *Revolver*—so strong, so insidiously revealing, its revelations hidden in plain sight—and from the ways in which the audience responded to the Beatles in their physical midst. Intensity had risen behind them: with Dylan, James Brown, the Stones, the Beach Boys, Smokey Robinson, the Byrds, the Mothers of Invention, the Supremes, and so many others digging the dirt, pop effloresced in strange and vivid colors. Something called a hippie was mounting a freaks' revolution in Bay Area ghettos; Frank Zappa and Jimi Hendrix were cultivating the scariest hair in show business; Lou Reed was serenading the Warhol clique with an endless song about the unholy rapture of smack; and John Lennon was no longer grinning but bleeding on the world's movie screens. None of these phenomena would enter mass consciousness until well into the next year, but they were all happening *now*. Eighteen months before, the pop paradigm had been Peter Noone, head Hermit, sticking a finger in his mouth.

Like everyone in the mid-'60s with any consciousness, the Beatles felt the ooze. Dylan and the Rolling Stones did too. Only, none of them was certain what to do about it. There were only old questions newly urgent: How to dramatize, crystallize, subjectify this world as we find it? How to go on mattering? How to hide the truth, how to reveal it? First and last: How to make great pop music within this twisted process?

It was impossible for any rock titan—a Lennon or a Dylan or a Jagger—to pretend he was only another worried citizen of the globe. Each had played his part in opening the gap that now yawned so wide; in this opening, new facts had been exposed, issues opened, audiences split. The Stones' sexuality, Dylan's hypertrophic lyricism, the unprecedented multiplicity of popular response to just about everything the Beatles did—all were broad fields of possibility that annexed the equally broad possibilities of social and political life in this time. These artists had a certain responsibility to deal with—or at least exploit, push further—what they had helped to set off.

Part of the nature of art is that, in revealing, it obscures; no art is a newsreel or police file. But questions still abound, such as *how* a given work obscures, and to what degree; or when it does *not* obscure, and why. Whatever the Beatles, the Stones, or Dylan contributed in 1968 would be a brand of cover-up: no music they would make could outstrip reality. It could only enact art's meager process—take in reality, metastasize it, and transform it. The variable in 1968 was how reality would survive that transformation. The titans would be judged on how each spoke of and to their time, past the artist's obscuring impulse and the necessities of the cover-up. Decades later, though, the variable is to what degree a listener is made to feel those 1968 realities despite knowing them only through art, or newsreel, or police file. If at the time it was asked how truthfully they communicated the moment when it was fresh, today we ask how resonantly the rock titans evoke the moment now that it is long past. How do these three speak *to* history when they are heard *as* history, and *through* history?

One has ideas and opinions on these matters; but other matters come first.

The success of any cover-up depends on the faith of those who dream it up and carry it out. That word *dream* creeps in again. In 1967, reality claws closer to the protected center of a Western world which feels but doesn't know what is waiting for it; in 1967, the Beatles and the audience, in common faith, take a last sojourn in the place where dreams can still be harmless, powerful and harmless.

□

Mysteries surround *Sgt. Pepper*. Such as why it was so loved, and why some who had once loved it reappraised it in later years, with evident bitterness, as a failure. Largely unimportant artistically, *Sgt. Pepper's Lonely Hearts Club Band* created a substantial phenomenon around itself; and still today, it reigns among the most recognizable of rock and roll totems. This despite its being quite possibly the most brilliant fake in rock and roll history—Beatles behind the curtain, pulling the Wizard's levers in a din of smoke and echo.

But a fake of its time, and for its time. *Sgt. Pepper* was the Beatles' instinctive cover-up of all that ooze, the bright shining lie they offered to the world—and themselves!—that such a utopia of mind, body, and spirit as the album represented was the natural and only possible culmination of all that had preceded it. But the record's falseness was not solely their doing—not by any means. The hippies, already mounting their own cover-up, inspired and ratified the Beatles': in their collective hands, 1967 emerged as a paradisal fantasy of unity. As far as they were concerned, the year had common shape, was whole and blessed; and the blessing came, as blessings often do, from an ectoplasm—the Beatles, off the stage and into the skies, their new music of the spheres wafting over the planetary transformation that was the Age of Aquarius.

It's taken for granted that necessary to any cover-up is conspiracy. *Sgt. Pepper*—both the music and its cultural triumph—shapes up as a conspiracy among a large, loose band of dreamers, conjured at a state when their common dream was already near its death, worn down by pressures from within and without. The *Pepper* high was the co-creation of the Beatles and their fans, and it drew in many who lay outside both groups. As a cultural centrifuge spinning over the length of a narcotized summer, it drew as respondents and commentators not only accepting hippies but skeptical establishment tastemakers; not only acid-eaters but natural heads; not only Timothy Leary but Spiro Agnew. Once again, people were compelled to take positions, work out personal responses through public exposition, level their excitement by sharing it with others. But the power of this conspiratorial creation lay not in its imaginative truth but in its falseness.

Like a lot of conspiracies, this one formed itself from vague needs and wants that were in the atmosphere, and was the ultimate product of smaller choices that could have gone another way. The Beatles issued a single in late February, one offering a clear choice between equal but opposed creations: "Strawberry Fields Forever" and "Penny Lane." Because both had "Beatles" on the label, both were admitted unquestioned into millions of cars and homes, offices and schools, police departments and prisons, crash pads and high-rises. Everyone heard "Strawberry Fields"; many were intrigued by it. Many others found it vaguely unpleasant, not conducive to daily routine, certainly hard to swallow on heavy AM rotation. Its opposite number—a flavorful wedge of Paul's cheesecake Surrealism and, incidentally, a natural-born hit—soon emerged as the decided favorite of disc jockeys and listeners. "Penny Lane" topped the charts in America, while "Strawberry Fields" barely reached the Top 10 before receding into the radio like the bad dream it was. The conspiracy was on, set to converge from both sides.

The Beatles, in studio sequestration, already weeks into the new album, were—without any conscious complicity—going the same route as those listeners who were forming their commercial consensus between competing Beatle visions. The songs they produced in the months running up to the Summer of Love were of a piece, but not strictly homogeneous: though all were psychedelic in genre, not all positioned themselves on the sunny side of the psyche. There were songs whose capability was positive, others whose tone was comparatively negative. Songs of the former class were jovial, nostalgic, heel-kicking songs, ripe with confidence. The latter were darker-toned, less focused, and sometimes actively bitter.

Like the audience which opted for the sweet candy of "Penny Lane" over the vomit flavor of "Strawberry Fields," the Beatles had a choice. They made it. In line with the forming conspiracy, the music they chose to release under Sgt. Pepper's auspices was almost entirely of that first, positive shade. This meant that it was not directed at pushing the *Revolver* synthesis of cold and hot, suspicion and melancholy, to a new place. Its mix yielded none of those extremes; it was free of disillusion and doubt, with nothing in its glittering pieces to disturb the mythos of the moment.

The new album would be no lurch through the stormier countrysides of the brain, but a gambol down the side streets off Penny Lane. And hearing it, the audience would convince itself of revelations glimpsed along the sidewalk, despite the record's being almost completely unburdened by the true revelations of performer-audience intercourse that should have fed and formed it, twisted it into a trip too scary for the jubilation it made so easy. But this was any conspiracy's prize and payoff—that it faked reality so convincingly well.

The conspiracy theorist recalls that this record had some part of its genesis in the very fan base to which it would one day return to be covered in glory. Its title and vague initial concept, Paul McCartney admitted, were inspired not by some stray breeze of Beatle genius but by the outlandish monikers being adopted by the largely San Francisco–based groups that had begun to emerge in 1966: Country Joe and the Fish, Quicksilver Messenger Service, Big Brother and the Holding Company. The title reified the imaginary persona and fictive charade which were the nominal conceit behind the record: the Beatles would escape themselves by assuming the guise and gauze of a separate entity, Sgt. Pepper's band. "I thought, Let's not be ourselves," Paul has said. "Let's develop alter egos. . . . It would be much more free . . . to actually take on the personas of this different band." Therefore the *Pepper* inspiration presented itself not merely as image play but as psychological wish fulfillment: "We'll be able to lose our identities in this."[1]

But: the "concept" broke down as soon as the introductions were over. After that, you had Beatles singing Beatle songs, the only masks on show identifiably Beatle masks. What we know now is that the

Beatles would never succeed at playing any role other than some very close version of themselves. Which was high among their strengths from the start—that though they were crafters of art, they were not artificers of myth. (The audience took up that slack.) Even when spinning their naivest romantic fantasies, they carried the credibility of realism: each note was an assertion of identity, of singular temperament, and the tensest, truest moments of 1966 had been those in which the Beatles fought to preserve or assert or reshape their identity—but to do it always in the acknowledgment that "the Beatles" *was* their identity, their rightful and only persona. "Much more free" was Paul's hope for the *Pepper* pageant—but what *is* freedom but a sense of danger, of all components in a jarring and volatile interaction? The dangers the Beatles underwent, the uncertainties they admitted in 1966, bent them into new shapes. *Sgt. Pepper* was the sound of the Beatles in hiding, avoiding danger—avoiding freedom.

Yes, and so what. Did that make it a bad record? Of course not—no record so rich and yet so lean could be called bad. Who but the closed-minded misanthrope cannot enjoy its precise and inventive detail, its glaze of confidence and correctness? It had a song sung by Ringo—"With a Little Help from My Friends"—that was blessed with perfect melody, perfect marriage of voice and gentle affect. It had a somersaulting guitar line on "Fixing a Hole," and back of "She's Leaving Home" were cellos capable of both wit and groaning middle-aged woe in support of two abandoned parents' dumb shock. "Lovely Rita" could vie for the funniest thing McCartney would write in his life: full of a sly erectile energy, it bounded out of itself with a grown-up sense of absurd and playful sex. And there was throughout the album an astonishing consistency of tone, of sonic density and aural atmosphere. If this meant little variation in pure impact between lesser songs and better songs, it also meant that even the lesser songs were irreplaceable to a satisfying quality of wholeness.

The album's every angle had texture—there were sparkles within sparkles. Was it a bad record? No, in fact it was good enough, sharp and funny and marvelous enough, to give off the gleam of greatness.

But: *Sgt. Pepper* was the Beatles' concerted if not quite conscious effort to draw a closed circle—around themselves and that portion of the audience which shared its fantasy of the moment. It was not in the great Beatle spirit of wholesale engagement, which had always presupposed an opening in the circle for both the good magic of romantic fancy and the bad magic of chaos. The *Pepper* circle had magic all right, but it was synthetic where others before and after were natural. The true magic, transcendent or terrible, always came through that open end—the hole through which the Beatles reached out to engage that part of the world previously either unconcerned with rock and roll, or concerned far less intensely. It was the hole through which friends' and enemies' fingers of imagination were allowed to reach the Beatles in ways never before achieved, or even conceived.

Pepper had no open end. Not only was it unlikely to cause real offense to its enemies, but it was too fixed and perfect a fantasy to interact richly and inexplicably with its allies. "Fixing a Hole," that marvelous tune, is its signature track. The lyrics, coyly oblique at first, become coherent when read as a description of the creative process within the Beatle-audience interrelation. Each fantasy imagined in that hazy region of imaginative overlap is both beyond conscious direction (the mind wanders where it *will* go, not where it is *told* to go) and so subjective as to be indefensible to anyone other than its owner (so what if he's wrong—he's right anyway). But the music, as elsewhere on *Pepper*, defeats what the lyrics seem to maybe / almost / sort of realize. Instruments click together like tooled parts, while McCartney's voice—which we tend to forget has been capable of conveying nuances of pain, frustration, and anger along with boundless good fortune—fails to suggest that anything might obstruct his

21. Studio One, June 24, 1967: promoting the live international telecast of their Flower Power anthem. "All you need is love," John sang. "Try eatin' off it," Keith Richards was heard to advise.

mind-wanderer's path to absolute imaginative freedom. The words suggest troubles on either side, troubles in the shadows; the music, triumphant, dispels worry with its psychedelic light.

But what of those shadows—what might have crawled through that hole in the head? A very dark song hides inside this glimmering artifact: taken another way, it might have yielded this capacity as thrillingly, as scarily as did "Strawberry Fields." But here the Beatles fix the hole instead of looking inside.

Other songs too go unfulfilled, or are just misbegotten. Two Lennon songs—"Lucy in the Sky with Diamonds" and "Good Morning, Good Morning"—play with hallucination and alienation as nightmare shades, but one is too pretty with psychedelic spangles, while the other loses itself amid quacking horns and animal noises, ending as harmless boogie. "When I'm Sixty-Four" is completely realized, impeccably crafted, and charming enough to rot teeth. "Within You Without You," George's temporal accusation–cum–Vishnu devotion, is cool and mean; but, characteristically for him, only a blunter version of the prevailing Beatle feeling. In posing one of *Pepper*'s too-few questions (you're not one of *them*, are you?), it fixes another hole by drawing the circle tighter around those who would ask the question, and closing out every answer but one.

The album is an optimistic vision, but the optimism lacks weight because it has no negative factor to overcome. The album is about fixing a hole, getting better, getting by, and there is an inescapable thinness of feeling to all of its success. Its creativity is free of, or resistant to, that chaotic underneath roiling below any great and substantial art. One must speak of all that *Pepper* does not do: it does not touch anything violent, incomprehensible, dreadful, or mad; its absurdities are precise, its howls modulated, even its accidents immaculate. It draws virtually none of its breath from the hidden parts of real Beatle life, real audience life, and it returned no poisons but only perfume to the hippie air which had once inspired and now welcomed it.

To this degree, the album's success was a triumph of the Beatles' inherent escapist factor. The audience, leaping to its cue, took it from there. It reveled in the escape that *Pepper* represented because it gelled so perfectly with the escape they were reaching for. The record's natural audience was the hippies: potheads, acidheads, dropouts, collegians, kids who became hippies because they were young and dug rock and roll and the ideas of peace and love; who sensed the possibility of freedom in the air and wanted their share; who were mostly white and middle-class and at a loss to figure out what they could do with and to this world of 1967.

Hippies for the most part were not activists but passivists; usually they were not political except by default, and if they agitated it was through evangelism rather than aggression. They sat in for love, not against Vietnam; held up flowers, not fists. They were characterized not by the Diggers, hippie pragmatists who concerned themselves with mundanities like food and medicine and looked for new ways of meeting basic human needs in a communal setting; nor even by the Merry Pranksters, whose LSD escapades at least constituted a form of engagement, however deranged, with the world outside the hippie ghetto. Insofar as the hippies had a program, it lay in changing the world by changing the individual consciousness—revolution from within. Todd Gitlin defines the sensibility that in 1967 set off the disengagement of the hippie from the confrontation of the activist:

> There were tensions galore between the radical idea of political strategy—with discipline, organization, commitment to results *out there* at a distance—and the countercultural idea of living life to the fullest, *right here,* for oneself, or for the part of the universe embodied in oneself, or for the community of the enlightened who were capable of loving one another—and the rest of the world be damned (which it was already). Radicalism's tradition had one of its greatest voices in Marx, whose oeuvre is a series of glosses on the theme: change the world! The main battalions of the counterculture . . . were descended from Emerson, Thoreau, Rimbaud: change consciousness, change life![2]

It was a hopeful venture, and, who knows, the Emersonian hippie may yet return to redeem whatever is left of the world. *Change consciousness, change life!* Who wouldn't give everything to make social revolution just that simple? But particularly in such a fraught time as the '60s, when a young American dropout's personal choice had inevitably to double as a social position, the venture couldn't have lasted. The hippies were making a choice which their time would not allow as anything more than a digression. Events were hurtling on their course even as the freaks of San Francisco staged their Be-Ins and danced in bucolic raptures, hoping to swerve the massed weight of their country's iron corruption with the stem of a daisy.

This sounds like ridicule. It isn't. The hippies invite parody, but then what doesn't in our day, except maybe the magnificent emotions of Tom Cruise? The hippies were a noble tribe. Theirs was an open and affirmative impulse set solidly in the American grain, a mass defection from straight culture in favor of uncontrived self-discovery in a wilderness of one's own. There was beauty in their wish to float so free. Only later did beauty dissolve in a caustic of hard drugs and sanctimony and mush-brained mysticism. But if the hippie exodus to Haight-Ashbury and its local branches throughout the country was more than an impulse, it was certainly less than a social philosophy, because (like the earliest rock and roll outcast culture) it made the mistake of thinking it could be self-sufficient in an America where no subculture remains inviolate for long, where everything must feed on everything else to live. America ate its hippies fast, and it would not be long before they were just another stomach acid.

The whole adventure came to the end shared by most utopian enterprises. Some of its basic principles went unexamined: the sacrament of drugs, the evil of the city, the benignity of nature. But perhaps failure was built into any ethos based on escape without complication, transcendence without struggle, a fantasy without a reality—free love and free drugs and all things free. Setting themselves apart from the America of rotten politics and a venal war, hippies chose withdrawal over engagement, and paid a price: hard drugs, sanctimony, and mush-brained mysticism came from within hippie culture, not without. The hippies were lovely in their wish, and wrong in thinking they could remain so separate from the society that had created them.

The other fact, more obvious, is that hippiedom was not only defeated by its own insulation, but overwhelmed by the drive of events

which were in natural opposition to it. Its communing doves were de-
fenseless against the circling hawks, its counterculture kitsch a fairy
tale in the engulfing reality of America in 1967—not to mention the
year that followed.

Pepper kitsch, inspired by hippie kitsch, emerged at the height of
the summer to rejoin its inspiration, bless it, confirm it to itself as a
reflection, at once magnified and condensed, of itself. The Beatles
had always served this function for people, but they'd always let *something else* loose in the exchange—some doubt in the affirmation, kinks
jutting from the surface of what seemed organic and effortless. After
all, had their offer of escape always been just what it seemed, they
wouldn't have stayed interesting for long. *Pepper* was a failure of
Beatle vision for the same reason it became a hippie talisman: it offered not the depths its time demanded, but only the escape its moment desired. Though most people didn't feel this way at the time.
Most felt that *Pepper* not only told the truth but was in fact the truth
revealed. The Beatles held their mirror at just the right distance: the
image it returned was too attractive, too ornately framed for any but
the grayest Pentagon head to reject it.

All that being said, this is only one way to view the reaction the
Beatles got with *Pepper*. Another—not necessarily a contradiction of
the first—is to realize that ideas were formed by even such a lesser
Beatle product as this. All over, forms of audience engagement were
derived from the Beatles' brilliant act of disengagement, intellectual
activity from a certain kind of creative absence. We read the contemporary reports of the earliest rock critics to find that they were perfectly aware of our present theme: that the Beatles, in addition to being autonomous creators with a personal agenda, were blank screens
for self-projection. Most commentators realized that to enjoy *Pepper*
meant to partake in meaning-making. Robert Christgau loved the record partly because of what its fans had to say about it, including a
fifteen-year-old girl (seriously) who heard in "Being for the Benefit of

Mr. Kite!" the sound of "life as an eerie perverted circus."[3] Christgau had to wonder: "Is this sad? silly? horrifying? contemptible? From an adult it might be all four, but from a fifteen-year-old it is simply moving. A good Lennon-McCartney song is sufficiently cryptic to speak to the needs of whoever listens. If a fifteen-year-old finds life 'an eerie perverted circus'—and for a fifteen-year-old that is an important perception—then that's what 'Being for the Benefit of Mr. Kite' can just as well be about."[4] On the other side of the country, Greil Marcus spent a night communing with friends and listening to an illicit pre-release tape of *Pepper.* "As the music played we shared rumors, little facts about the Beatles, impressions, interpretations, each adding publicly and taking privately into the myth of the Beatles." Song after song unreeled as a ribbon of wonders; and when it was over, "we all shook hands, and we went to bed thinking about the Beatles."[5]

There was one writer among the longhairs who, largely bypassing the record's pleasures, fastened on its lacks. Richard Goldstein, reviewing for the *New York Times,* made a small phenomenon of his own by judging *Pepper* a failure—and inspiring an epistolary wrath of unprecedented strength from Beatle backers like the fifteen-year-old quoted above. His assessment was blunt, but finally sad.

> In substituting the studio conservatory for an audience, the Beatles have lost crucial rapport, and that emptiness at the roots is what makes their new album a monologue. Nothing is real therein, and nothing to get hung about. Too bad; I have a sweet tooth for reality. I like my art drenched in it, and even from fantasy I expect authenticity. What I worship about the Beatles is their forging of rock into what is real. It made them artists; it made us fans; and it made me think like a critic when I turned on my radio.[6]

Goldstein wrote as one who saw himself in the Beatles' mirror, and only this time felt alienated by what was missing. He sounded lost.

"We still need the Beatles," he ended—like all critics employing the communal pronoun to voice wholly private feelings—"not as cloistered composers, but as companions. And they still need us, to teach them how to be real again."[7]

But though Goldstein spoke one truth, it scarcely canceled out another: that he, Christgau, Marcus, and those they wrote for and to had quick and intense responses to *Pepper*. Real responses portending real complications, spurred by music that in itself really didn't admit of complication; responses of a kind and intensity they did not have to any other music heard in 1967. As a result, new dreams shaped themselves, new oppositions were put in place, and the fifteen-year-old girl suddenly realized that, hey, you know what, life is an eerie perverted circus.

That's what happened in the *Pepper* realm of not-quite-sleeping, not-quite-waking, where all perceptions were brilliant, all pictures clear, and everything the Beatles did meant something because there was no way for it to mean nothing. And that, more than the music, is the import of *Pepper* as historical object and '60s fact. That although as music it was not made of the deepest substance, it was so thoroughly by and of the Beatles and their symbiosis with their audience that it could not help bounding walls of thought and passing into history as another magnificent Beatle dream machine.

This was the short-term success of the *Pepper* conspiracy. That the rock culture and its mainstream offshoots received the record as they did, that like the Summer of Love it was as much media bonanza as spontaneous break of creative force upon gray official culture, shows how eager that audience was to drug its sense of reality with this most wondrous of vinyl chemicals. It also shows that the generation of tuned-in rock fans was in unvoiced conspiracy with the Beatles to spin one last dream of gold before waking, to spin it—unlike earlier dreams—out of cotton clouds and benedictions, not hard candy and screams. If the Beatles were to pose as a band of Edwardian brass-blowers, then, implicitly and equally, their real audience would serve as imaginary auditors to the charade: each actor to his or her part. A conspiracy to favor evasion over reckoning, crystal memory of Penny Lane over deranged present of Strawberry Fields; a memory enhancement in which every bad acid trip was frosted with sugar and there were no slavering reptiles behind the houseplants.

But: the success *was* temporary. In 1967, Marcus found *Pepper*'s musical intricacies "so dramatic that without the genius of the Beatles they'd seem artificial";[8] ten years later he wrote that they *were* artificial—the album had become "a day-glo tombstone for its time."[9] But whose name was chiseled in that stone? Whose hand had helped spread those colors? Marcus was obviously right when he said, after a decade's reflection, that the record was "less a summing up of its era than a concession to it";[10] but it was equally true that the era had conceded to the Beatles. Marcus had conceded, as had Christgau, as had the vast majority of those they felt they were speaking for. It was a concession each side made willingly, each individual to the common dream of the summer.

For the Beatles, the most salient question coming into the next phase had been this: What would grow from the events of '66, the music of *Revolver,* all the violence compressed in that short time? *Pepper* deferred that question along with other, larger ones. The Beatles had undergone wardrobe changes, stylistic shifts, had even taken stage pseudonyms for a short time; but *Pepper,* while not quite *something else* in the terms defined earlier, was decidedly something new. With it, the Beatles, for the first and last time in their lives together, consciously played a fictional role, however half-baked and lacking in "conceptual" fullness—while the audience, in *Pepper* badges and epaulets, allowed itself to be entranced and amazed by music that was brilliant artifice and beautiful calculation, no push or pull on either side.

Pepper posed no confrontation, and demanded none in return: all things free. The hippie ideal, for its instant, held benevolent sway.

□

But what fascinates about the musical cover-ups attempted by the Beatles in their later years is that each was a failure. Each came with disclaimers: not self-protecting ironies, but unconscious equivocations in the face of all absolutes. When the Beatles sang happy in those waning days, they were well aware of the distance between old affirmations and new—even when their audience, it could be argued, was not. They knew the difference between *all I've got to give* and *all you need is*—between what "love," not to mention "all," had been and what it was now. One had felt itself eternal and certain of triumph; the other was embattled and doomed. That was a measure of the distance traveled; and the Beatles, mortal embodiments of that distance as well as its chief navigators, could not but ring the bell, tell the news.

Thus, *Sgt. Pepper* had one passage which put the lie to the conspiracy—stripped, froze, and shattered it. Preceded by a round of applause that constructs a frame around the body of *Pepper,* "A Day in the Life" is not really part of that body at all, but its sorrowful apparition. Like most of the album, it had a nothing where its heart should have been; but its nothingness was majestic and terrifying. It was not a concession to nothingness but a penetration of it.

How often Ringo's drums seem to stir the secret essence of the Beatles, to drive their elusive heart. Here his hollow beats are the steps of the Reaper tailing our dazed dreamer in his reverie, the tunnel-wanderer of "Strawberry Fields" come to ground in a city where the end has been foretold by oblique tabloid headlines and movie screens flickering in empty theaters. The landscape is again that of the dream, but dream as colorless and underpopulated as recent Beatle fantasias both vinyl and physical have been manic, feverish. The crowd is a crowd of hippies, beautiful people, oblivious to the onrush of doom—its attention is not held by the war movie or the celebrity suicide—and as intent as any crowd upon its own selective perceptions, its choice of evasions. The dreamer, for his part, is not anything other than they; he is among them.

Until he makes a choice: as the crowd moves one way, he moves the other—toward, not away from. Silently he breaks apart, held by something barely glimpsed, choosing confrontation with the unspeakable. Reversing the withdrawal of Melville's Bartleby—"I would prefer not to"—he refuses to be fully alienated from that which alienates him: *I just had to look.* Perhaps he looks at the movie, at the image of himself bloodied and dying in green fields; perhaps he is really looking over his shoulder at the footsteps that have been following him, growing heavier, more urgent. Whatever he sees, his act of seeing it compels the quickening of the end.

An ending which swells with disease, swallowing the world as a tumor swallows the host cell—only to transform at its instant of apocalyptic victory into a domestic playlet: *Woke up got out of bed.* (What a displacing turnabout—Now what is being swallowed, and by what? Final judgment by mundane monologue, the Bible by Beckett?) The dreamer awakens as the commuter. He races on panic and eases himself with the belief that his world is real: work waits, the bus is full, lives continue. But it doesn't last: these solid signifiers of real life are only *entr'acte.* The commuter goes back into a dream, and it proves to be the dream from which he believed he had awakened.

Then descent, again descent—all goes underground to reemerge amid the holes of Lancashire County. The enfolding nightmare has been the truth all along, the commuter's fantasy of the normal a memory pebble shaken loose within a brittle consciousness. The nightmare has accelerated. The Reaper footfalls now chase the dreamer as he runs: his reward for having had to look. The crowd of people has been replaced by thousands of holes: *Now they know how many.* Does it matter that *they* now have an accurate Albert Hall–filling count of said holes? Does it matter that the dreamer cannot observe anything more meaningful than that, and does it even matter that he is trying, since he speaks only to an audience of four thousand echo chambers?

I'd love to turn you on. He says it twice, first to the crowd, now to the holes; and again disaster swirls on the dreamer's mere utterance of his hopeless wish, this time to wipe clean the landscape. Death is not the most original thing to hear in this ending; only the most inescapable. Really, it would be sophistry to pretend there is anything else to it. And so even as they sauntered on their stage and accomplished this grandest of illusions, the Beatles in some part of themselves knew that their *Pepper* vision implied decay as much as it celebrated growth, that death awaited it at the end of side two. *Sgt. Pepper* was the prized final product of the Beatle-hippie conspiracy, and in its one passage of real vision it saw its own dissolution.

But though the conspiracy did not last, as a historical fact it remains, because it *happened:* for its moment, it was real. The conspiracy was another circle, and in a nice symmetry the same community that had helped open the circle now gave it, at least for one band member, a symbolic closure. George Harrison visited Haight-Ashbury in August 1967. A year earlier, San Francisco had been the site of another, very different Beatle ending—soon after which, its groups gave Paul McCartney the spark for *Pepper.* In the space between one summer and the next, the Haight became world-famous as the locus of hippie unity, a secular congregation of drug-taking, rock-dancing spiritualists that would welcome every freak into its fold.

Then, as Nik Cohn wrote, "Journalists moved in and started to publicize it."

> And tourists came with cameras to watch the weirdies, and the admen and the record companies moved in for the kill. Within a few months, the whole thing had become a circus. The original hippies had all escaped, and what re-

mained was an acid-burger nightmare. The streets were
filled with beggars and pushers and pubertal panhandlers.
Everything was filthy, decaying, rat-infested. Instant freaks
sat on the sidewalks, munching hash sandwich, and the
tourists took happysnaps.[11]

Writing its history in smoke, the imperfect, escapist hippie ethic used
itself up just that fast. The decline was advanced and inexorable by
the time innocent George went to experience the beatitudes of the
Haight and walk among his subjects as a king. Innocent as all that,
what could he have expected but absolute affirmation of the new
communal ideal in the county seat of the Love Generation—just as
that generation had found its affirmation in the Beatles' offering?

What he found instead, he said a long time later, was "horrible
spotty dropout kids on drugs."[12]

In fact, those kids were Sgt. Pepper's other band: the tragedy faces,
that thing under the mask. The less attractive obverse to everything
Pepper rendered benign—escape, disengagement, the avoidance of a
committed and aggressive relationship with the world. Together with
the Beatles, these kids had produced the fantasy, then bought it back
from themselves. Many went into debt on the transaction, because
they'd bought too much on credit, and what they'd paid for now lay
rotting in a garbage can in the alley behind a head shop. Soon it
would be *heard* rotting in the grooves of the Beatles' latest vinyl:
Haight-Ashbury and *Magical Mystery Tour* would share the same funk
of stale incense and long-gone visions of fly-away bliss.

Acid-burger nightmare, and four thousand holes in San Francisco,
California. George went home. After that, who could believe?

□

The anticlimax that followed, darkening the latter half of 1967 in
shades of failure and dissolution, disguised this decay—decay of ev-

22. Studio One, Abbey Road, June 1967: a final blast of *Sgt. Pepper* brass, with summer's end already in sight. Brian Epstein, center, has two months to live.

erything *Pepper* had represented. The sharp of drugs bled into the dull of the hangover; *Pepper*'s admirable precision of sound became an indefinite morass of post-psychedelicisms. Even the anthem written as benedictory to the Beatle-hippie triumph, "All You Need Is Love," was conflicted: buoyed by an aura of revelry, it was at its core as bone-tired and fuzzy-tongued as the ragged end of a long party. John sang the words of the title with an unmistakable flatness of vocal aspect, laying sarcasm and the smack of chewing gum between the lines.

From summer on down, Beatles '67 was dark and woozy, a gaiety forced into being if it existed at all, the tired drips and dregs of that magic nectar. We're surprised, then, to be reminded that several of the songs characterizing this hangover period were recorded concurrent with or just after *Pepper*. "Only a Northern Song" is a thick, brewing stormcloud on George's psychedelic horizon, its sound-effected sky full of *Revolver*-type predator gulls and other cackling animals of the imagination. The delirious "You Know My Name (Look Up the Number)" sounds less like rich hippies flouncing about than Spike Milligan interpreting King Lear in the last stage of breakdown—its disintegrative effect only enhanced by the unbilled cameo of drug casualty Brian Jones (almost a year dead by the time the song was released). These songs sound like *Pepper*'s distant echo when in fact they are the mutterings barely heard beneath its more confident delivery. Again the cover-up is qualified. Shadows shadow the official story.

Into this set of songs went the sound of creative and spiritual indigestion, desperation unsuccessfully concealed under loads of noise and activity. There was one great song ("I Am the Walrus," vicious, excremental, and running over with grue: this *is* the lizard behind the houseplant), and a Harrison opus that at its full eight-plus minutes was a lyrically prescient, musically excessive, and finally glorious ode to the already domesticated essence of a hippie *Zeitgeist* yet to pass ("It's All Too Much"). Beyond that lay scattered half a dozen ill-considered experiments in washed-out acid imagery and sluggish tape manipulation. A TV theme song like "Magical Mystery Tour" is easily punctured as meaningless, just as disengaged as *Pepper* and twice as false—because while just as evasive of reality, it is not even clever about it. Yet unlike *Pepper*, these songs have their soul. Because if they are evasive of reality, they are equally alienated from their own fantasy; and in their lack of cleverness there is some heavy component, burden of loss and disappointment, ill feeling toward the end of a dream run aground. *Magical Mystery Tour* is in its way stronger than *Pepper*, if only because it is this uncertain of its mission, this cynical about its own presumed meaning.

Loss can often bring to the fore something realer than possession, just as the pleasure of consuming food may be less profoundly felt than the queasiness that follows. The Beatles consumed *Pepper* in addition to creating it, fed on the denial it served, and a song like "Baby You're a Rich Man"—insignificant, tossed off, and still more compelling than most of *Pepper*—was the acidulous grumble that followed in the night. *Pepper* was a self-generating myth which others bought into because it assumed true for itself what they wished true for them—while performances like "Your Mother Should Know" and "Blue Jay Way" have a lack of mastery that is itself purposive and not without substance, a certain sickness of soul despite the songs themselves being trite, precious, or objectively pointless. They stalk the elusive *Pepper* vibe but can't come close to bagging it; they're compelled to undermine the very myth to which they are addenda.

It's the sound of fantasy in decay, decomposing as it reacts to the air of the real world. *Magical Mystery Tour* music, dull and marginal as it is, is psychedelia for that real world, fantasy for the morning after. Dead-flower music.

□

The stakes are higher now—in 1967 I could imagine deadness of a culture, but in 1968 I can imagine only death.

—William Cadbury, "Sgt. Pepper for This Year's Head," *Northwest Review*, 10 (Summer 1968)

Death: that was the face beneath the mask, the stuff of Beatle prophecy, Beatle nightmare. The flowers in all those hippie hands would be dead soon enough.

Many believe that the truest harbinger of what lay ahead was the Pentagon march of October 21, 1967.[13] Conceived as a coalition of Old and New Lefts, middle-aged pacifists and face-painted guerillas, it started as a peace march and ended as a riot. From Virginia across the Potomac to the steps of the war factory itself, a phalanx of young militants served as advance force to an august backfield sporting prestigious names like Spock, Lowell, Chomsky, and Mailer. The more militant of the marchers rained spittle and verbal abuse upon the armed contingents positioned to bar them from entering the Pentagon. As for the hippies, they came armed with flowers, and Norman Mailer spied Sgt. Pepper's colors among their uniforms.[14] But that costume was just as good as any other hippie regalia to the enforcers of law and order, or just as bad—which meant that, no, Pepper haberdashery would not avert a blow to the skull or cushion the floor of a cell. Sticks were swung, teargas lobbed, and many of those who had attempted to live out some version of the *Pepper* principle—who had, with the Beatles, helped dream its birth, fashion its parts, sanctify its significance—were shown how wrong they'd been to believe in anything but the immovable butt of the American institution.

But the Pentagon march, for all its trauma, was only a breeze of that reality, a taste of the cop's baton. As 1968 bore down, all factors were in concert to produce an apocalypse. "For the New Left," Todd Gitlin writes, "the summer of love was the summer of desperation."[15] There'd been race riots that summer in Detroit and Newark, leaving nearly a hundred dead bodies, mostly black. Lyndon Johnson's hawkish liberalism had split his own party down the middle, pushing the radical agenda even farther to the fringes. Meanwhile the war—out of anyone's real control, investments of weaponry and human force increasing monthly—had reached the cancerous point where it was feeding on, escalating, itself. Along with race, Vietnam was the prevailing, unconquerable fact of every American life, even the most insulated. How many comfortable white Americans—away from the tumult, no thought of overthrow, hoping for the best, whatever they might feel that to be—found themselves staring at twisted black or Vietnamese faces behind the walls of their eyes in the minutes before sleep?

People were dying, on both sides of the world; and nothing was changing except for the worse. Hence a new urgency on the left. It was nothing if not a time that screamed for choices and commitments, a time when not to act meant not to exist. As Gitlin put it, instead of Stop the War the agenda had to be: Start the Revolution. "It no longer felt sufficient—sufficiently estranged, sufficiently furious—to say no to aggressive war; we felt driven to say yes to revolt."[16]

As the Beatles cast about for their contribution, their *something else,* drawing lethargic sounds from the wilted noise-makers of last summer's party, the intellectual leaders of the counterculture sought to construct a program for social change from the debris of their disunited movements. Beyond the imperative of action, only a few things were certain. Black Power was an essential element; and there was no place for hippies.[17] Nor for the insular theoretics of left-wing intellectuals: even the militant Students for a Democratic Society, espousers of the "Port Huron Statement" of 1962—a prophetic antiwar position paper coauthored by student radical Tom Hayden—were now realizing that rational analysis on the order of Marx was wrong for this turning in history.[18] "Having tried available channels and discovered them meaningless," Hayden would say in October 1968, looking back, "having recognized that the establishment does not listen to public opinion—it does not care to listen to the New Left—the New Left was moving toward confrontation. The turning point, in my opinion, was October 1967, when resistance became the official watchword of the antiwar movement."[19] Desperation engendered a coming together between divergent camps, if only in spirit and the belief that there must be revolt, that democracy (as Lenin was paraphrased at the time) was lying in the street waiting for someone to pick it up—or snatch it away. The American counterculturalists were set to go radical en masse and define the moment. Thus were the new choices made: Guevara over Emerson; engagement over escape; aggression over passivity; energy directed outward instead of in.

Predicaments were aligned: How could the radicals stop the war? How could the Beatles stay engaged? Acting from a roil of anger, idealism, sadness, and ideology, the radicals came up with their answer; anger, idealism, sadness, and *instinct* formed the Beatles' answer. And into that unbridgeable chasm between ideology and instinct fell, finally, a good part of the Beatles' abiding romance with their greatest natural constituency: the white Western kids who, for most of their years, had sucked on rock and roll as if it were Mother's breast, Beatle music hardest of all. Given the divine synchronicity between the Beatles and their audience, it should never have happened. At this moment in time—when the stance was all, the choice everything—there was nothing else that *could* have happened.

The Beatles saw this coming too. More prophecy. We can never be what we were to each other, they implied in "A Day in the Life." We would love to turn you on—but we cannot. The turn-on has become too shallow, the need for it too deep. As the hippie wish gives way to the radical urge, fantasy and reality are too inextricable for one to be favored over the other—either one without its counterweight is a surrender to the facile, to the mere wish: a lie against the complex, contingent, and violence-ridden life which we all, in collusion with the other people and events of our time, have built around ourselves, and which we must be respond to, deal with—if possible, weigh ourselves against. The climactic piano chord is new reality shattering for good the old Beatle-audience synchronicity.

But: there's *something else.* Or its prelude. The Beatles tail their great song of doom with a ridiculous noise. Exactly two seconds of noise scratched into the *Pepper* end groove: party whistles and party laughter, one female voice singing what sounds like *There never could be any other love*— Turn it backward, any Beatlehead knows, and it says *We'll fuck you like a superman.* Translate the noise—not the words but the noise—in another direction and it may read imperfectly as: *Something else . . . something I must . . . don't know what.* A mere amoeba of a noise, a piece of aural scum oozing from a world in ruins, putting evolution on notice.

So we begin again.

As the Beatles will begin again. Because they are who they are and can effectuate any whim with a command, hold a mass audience without reaching for it, they have a choice. They can continue on the *Pepper* path and synthesize newer chemicals in sound—or they can return to the often grim work of pushing, resisting. To push and be pushed was always the essential; and the hallucinatory sway that is *Pepper*'s version of unity has been a dim substitute for the essential Beatle-audience push and pull. They will need to produce work that is not mere post-*Pepper* residue, not cold fantasy but fresh engagement. It will have to deal with what has happened and not happened over the halcyon summer and lethargic winter, size up the old push against the new sway, see through the lack of violence and volatility in Pepperland. It will have to engage with the world again and risk mucking once more in a mud of ambiguities, uncertainties, and holes.

But their music will again and again emerge through the distorting prism of the cover-up. They will seek simplicity while agonizing over complexities. *Pepper* was the first move in this final, defining push and pull. It spoke twice on the subject of holes. "Fixing a Hole" stated the record's spirit, the spirit of the movement for which the record was divine consummation; but the trivial recognition of four thousand holes stated a lone, obscure refusal to believe that anything could ever be so simple again. Now holes, of course, are anathema to any cover-up, and conspiracy exists to fill them. Because the audience willed it and the Beatles engineered it, the hole was fixed, the leak was plugged, and the cover-up prevailed. It was the last time the Beatles and their audience would ever find themselves in such accord.

But holes had a value: Who knew what you would see if you looked in? This became, sometimes very explicitly, the impulse in later Beatle music—to defy, parody, subvert, even outrage the cover-up—and it was foretold in words that, though heard many times by many millions, went unremarked: *I just had to look.*

□

I too once danced in a ring. It was in the spring of 1948. The Communists had just taken power in my country, the Socialist and Christian Democrat ministers had fled abroad, and I took other Communist students by the hand, I put my arms around their shoulders, and we took two steps in place, one step forward, lifted first one leg and then the other, and we did it just about every month, there being always something to celebrate. . . . Then one day I said something I would better have left unsaid. I was expelled from the Party and had to leave the circle.

That is when I became aware of the magic qualities of the circle. Leave a row and you can always go back to it. The row is an open formation. But once a circle closes, there is no return.

—Milan Kundera, *The Book of Laughter and Forgetting* (1981)

At the turning of the year—December 29, 1967—Bob Dylan released his new album and snapped an eighteen-month silence. It was a weird kind of country album, with stark graphics, a light sound, and a bushelful of Judeo-Christian symbolism. Debates commenced over whether it was irrelevant to its time or so relevant that its subtleties were undetectable. Doubts were instantly resolved in Dylan's favor, and he was welcomed back as the man of the moment. The album was such a refusal of the psychedelic standard—such a pop novelty—that, like other pop novelties, it left many people wondering what they'd been so excited about a few months before.

John Wesley Harding, in the words of Michael Gross, "sent listeners into long staring bouts with the LP's scratchy Polaroid cover, searching for the faces of Beatles in the tree branches, the *why* that had to be in Dylan's eyes."[20] That those listeners were looking for some encrypted link between the Beatles and *why* through the conduit of Dylan album art was as solid an indicator as any that *Pepper* was past—that it was the listeners themselves who wanted to know *why:* why the album and the counterculture it blessed had shriveled so quickly; why that pluperfect plum of fantasy had dried so fast into last summer's moldy fig.

There were many explanations for this, and only one reason. Jon

Landau said, "Dylan manifests a profound awareness of the war and how it is affecting all of us. This doesn't mean that I think any of the particular songs are about the war or that any of the songs are protests over it. All I mean to say is that Dylan has felt the war, that there is an awareness of it contained within the mood of the album as a whole." While the Beatles, in Landau's opinion, were *not* feeling the war. "Dylan's songs acknowledge the war in the same way that songs like 'Magical Mystery Tour' and 'Fool on the Hill' ignore it. . . . Bob Dylan, 1968, could not write a song analogous to 'Magical Mystery Tour,' just because he knows too much."[21]

Listening today, I don't hear what Landau heard. Not because I can't, but because I don't. What I hear in *Harding* is retreat. A well-earned retreat, no doubt considered and necessary, but retreat anyway. And not a frightened, harrowed escape from demons and doubts but a soft-souled settling-back that gives the record a thin, chastened sound.

Highway 61 had been a combination of tall tale, stand-up comedy, and gutter rhyme that nailed the Great Society in a series of exploding cartoon panels. *Harding* was a succession of pieties. What I hear in it is not an encounter with the unstable day-to-day realities of America at that point in its history, but the received wisdom of folklore. Its calm is a willed calm, in which homilies and stark symbols subdue reality, and moral insularity renders even the grimmer implications simple. The same Dylan who had warned you to *look out!* was promising you didn't have to worry anymore. With this, the drifter made his escape; and it would be years before the stale comforts of exile would force him back into fresh air to roar fresh heresies at his idolaters.

Escape is an eminently human response to chaos. The desire for accommodation and peace at the price of compromise—who hasn't taken that escape, struck the bargain with comfort? Who doesn't do it on some larger or smaller scale every day? But one thing the cultural and political movements of the '60s did was to render safety itself suspect as a goal, and peace questionable when divorced from context. After all, denial of chaos had been a prevailing dogma of the '50s, when it was presumed that any American family with sufficient means could live a reasonably comfortable post-atomic life in the cinder-block splendor of a fallout shelter. It took the '60s to make the shelter a symbol of retreat, complacency, false values; to make people realize that '50s security had been a spiritual tyranny. Though it created, or bought into, many myths of its own, the '60s counterculture was, at its *political* best, antimythic, for the efficacy of myth demands that no one look too closely at the seams where truth is joined to archetype. The radicals wanted, more than anything, to look closely—to get inside the Pentagon, peer into the holes.

Harding doesn't look too closely. Or, in musical terms, it doesn't *feel* too closely. When Dylan offers obsequious rapprochement to his dear landlord, the result is art that bypasses conflict and heads straight for resolution. Same for a title song about an outlaw from whose panegyric real blood, or even its corn-syrup Hollywood substitute, is conspicuously missing. (Maybe Harding wasn't known for foolish moves, but then neither was John Wayne—at least until 1968, when he thrust his craggy persona into the stew of American chaos with a heart-tugging thing called *The Green Berets*.) Though "All Along the Watchtower" arrays its ghouls and tricksters in medieval drag, it speaks to its own time and beyond by drawing a scene lowering with doom, busy with empty processions, rooms full of paranoia. But it is an aberration. For all their inscrutability the lyrics are thin on meaningful ambiguity, and Dylan's small-band sound—tamped down to a collective whisper—is another kind of regression, specifically to the very early '50s and Hank Williams, but without the starving-wolf moan of Williams' frightened voice.

Only at its most self-deluding points did the '60s counterculture attempt merely to replace one empty myth—say, Richard Nixon—with another—say, Mao Tse-tung. (Or the Maharishi.) If myths can be sustaining and unifying, they can also be limiting and deadening when the times outstrip them. *Sgt. Pepper,* for instance. *Harding* was Dylan's *Pepper.* Though it plundered a different set of archetypes, its methodology was identical: Dylan sought his answers in myths—the frontier, the outlaw, the saint—at a moment when nothing was that simple. Inasmuch as it predicted an impulse many would ultimately share, it's defensible that *John Wesley Harding* should be an evasion of fear. The problem is that within its boundaries fear is not imagined or sustained as a dangerous thing with immediate hungers: the evasion is all that's left. Like *Pepper,* it takes refuge in formalities and fictions from the mess outside its door; like *Pepper,* it is too certain of itself in relation to the world. Like *Pepper,* it fails as an artist's response to reality.

But more than that: it has failed to deliver that reality into history. Heard today, divorced from the heats of its moment, *Harding* is empty of what Landau's "profound awareness of the war" attributes to it. Those heats are lost to time, and perhaps not fully recoverable even by those who experienced them. But art lives so long as it communicates: the more it communicates, the longer it lives—and the more lives it will have. In popular art the prize goes to that work which, while enabling us to form our own meanings relevant to our own time and place, compels us to imagine what it made of the lives of people whose names we've never known, who lived in places we've never seen.

□

This is the United States, 1968, remember. If you are afraid of violence you shouldn't have crossed the border.

—Abbie Hoffman, in Norman Mailer, *Miami and the Siege of Chicago*
(1969)

Phil Spector once said of a record he'd produced that it sounded like God had hit the world and the world had hit back. 1968 was the sound of history striking—and the young striking back. It was the time for Western youth to show it was willing to make action out of rhetoric, and place its bodies where its ideals were. Surely there is no way to strike back at God or at history, so that it hurts, other than to risk everything in the attempt.

Anyone who was watching will confirm there was a moment—perhaps only a moment—in 1968 when it seemed the students of the world had the power to shut down not just the machinery of war but the very mechanisms of Western society. Spontaneously and independently, their moves linked by ties no more conscious or visible than frustrated desire and shared outrage, students sent a massed boot through the glass domes of the great cities of the West. From meager beginnings in Marxist cells or anarchist enclaves, radiating concentrically from colleges and universities in Tokyo, Munich, Prague, Paris, London, New York, San Francisco, and hundreds of smaller points in between, revolution coalesced as a daily possibility.

To survey the events of 1968 is to think mystical thoughts about the cosmic connections between disconnected events. Can any objective, deterministic view of history adequately explain such an awful chronology? First, in January, there was the Tet Offensive: a cluster of surprise attacks by the North Vietnamese on key installations, leaving many civilians dead and off-guard American forces badly damaged. State Department propaganda could not cover the loss, or make anything uplifting of the battles soon to occur in Hue and Khe Sahn: the Vietnam hole grew wider with every television transmission, and Americans slowly ceased to believe in the war. That the war nonetheless continued, that many millions continued to believe they believed when they increasingly did not, and that a smaller number of millions took this state of affairs as a call to ultimate action were the immovable facts of the year.

Many sources detail the events of 1968 in great depth. Suffice to say here that from Tet on down, things, unbelievably, got worse. Leaders were assassinated, revolts of the spirit burst forth and were blown to dust, and death hovered over the campus, the convention floor, the ghetto street, the public thoroughfare. The world, it seemed, had chosen its time to go insane.

The precise quality of everyday feeling in a person who cared about changing things in 1968 is impossible for another, of a different time and circumstance, to imagine. But in broader terms, we can posit a sense of the ultimate choice made by those who felt the fear the times imposed. If you cared, you either were paralyzed by the fear that came with inaction, or you took upon yourself the fear that came with action. You chose to change the world by choosing your fear.

Pragmatically, it was a fight over ideals. Symbolically, it was a battle over reality—that is, common consciousness of what reality was. The Western establishment, by pursuing or supporting war in Vietnam; by perpetuating racism and economic disparity; by selling out democratic oaths to ever-more degraded forms of capitalism and materialism; by plotting and sanctioning political assassination, suppression of dissent, corporate corruption—the establishment had written a reality it could control, under which its citizens, powerless and apathetic, were bound to live. But it had done this secretly, under cover of official lies, propaganda, cover-ups. The U.S. government would no more admit its activities in Vietnam than would the Soviet Union acknowledge that its occupation of Czechoslovakia was bound to cripple, not save, the country. Each would cover truth with silence or evasion, insane skews of the truth, and so recast the average citizen's reality as political fantasy. So the widespread outbreak of mass revolt in early 1968 was important: the students were attempting to rewrite in public the social and political realities that had always been written in private.

Student revolt had another powerful symbolic effect—as powerful as that achieved by the civil rights workers who had forced Southern bigots into showing their colors to the world. At the time, it was called "bringing the war back home." The establishment's reality, though sanitized, was composed of blood and intestines; obscenities were being committed in its name, grand and intricate cover-ups mounted to maintain its privacy. Student revolt, by pursuing an extreme, disruptive, often violent course, would bring that private reality to the surface, break the cover-up, and force the establishment to acknowledge on its own ground the chaos it was engineering in another, less real place, thousands of miles away.

For many, it was frightening as well as stirring, this revolutionary impulse coalescing worldwide, because the establishment seemed to hold all the levers, wield all the power—and effectively it did. Arthur Marwick is eloquent on the factor of fear:

> Most of those peace-loving people who found themselves trapped in a situation of violence had set out knowing that extreme and life-threatening violence was always a strong possibility in any kind of march or demonstration; while some felt a certain sense of exultation and even heroism, most suffered from a constant and debilitating sense of fear—yet such was their sense that they must bear testimony against evil that they fought against that fear.[22]

Many veterans of those days have spoken about how, as their country convulsed and their sense of themselves in relation to it shook apart, they felt increasingly like exiles. Wounded by the police and despised by the majority, their groups infested with long-haired moles from the FBI and CIA, even the most fervent among them must have privately questioned the wisdom of staking everything on such an uneven battle. Fear must have given more heat to the curses of a cop-baiting student than righteous indignation; self-doubt on the border of paralysis must have shadowed the bravado of radical leaders as they laid their battle plans. There were wounds that would never be salved by moral certainty or a rereading of the "Port Huron Statement." Paranoia was a constant low-burning blaze, kept in check by nothing but the absolute assurance of one's own rightness.

It's probable that never in this generation's days, then, had a community of like minds been so necessary. Blood lost to concrete and riot stick would be replaced only by regular transfusions of group unity. What these counterculture soldiers needed from their music, as they needed it from each other, was the assurance that they were right in their resistance—that their means and methods made sense, that heinous violence met with noble violence was finally the only defensible course.

Did those young people have any conception, going into the battles of '68, of what awaited them in Prague and Paris and Chicago, any notion of how brutally the establishment was prepared to protect itself? One suspects they did, and appreciates all the more their fierce need, in the face of such official violence, to believe in themselves. And to be told, by those they trusted and to whom they had always looked for some version of the truth, that, whatever might happen out in the street, they were the ones who were right.

□

It's with this in mind that we listen to "Revolution" today and try to understand how and why, when first heard, it made so many people so angry.

This may be the first song in the Beatle catalog that is consciously and with every calculation offered as a response to specific events in the public sphere; and, for reasons good and less than good, it suffered for that. John Lennon conceived it in Rishikesh, India, in March 1968, as the Beatles were attempting to live out their own, inevitably compromised version of what would soon become a popular post-hippie retreat: the rural commune. In May they recorded it in rough demo form, where despite its all-acoustic instrumentation it came out a rocker, tight and concise, with a classic radio-song structure. By

May 30, when initial studio tracks were laid, its tempo had slowed drastically; and the body of the song was followed by six minutes of hypnotic shuffle rhythm and instrumental squeal, over which Lennon ran the gamut of vocal display, an epic of whispers and whines, sexualized grunts and groans, and finally distended screams: *Right . . . RIGHT . . . RIIIII-AHHHHT*.[23]

The most crucial change was also the smallest. In this first studio version, one word was inserted to alter significantly the import of one line. On the demo John had said he could be counted out of any revolution that advocated destruction. Now, just after the word "out," he said "in."

This first formal incarnation of "Revolution" would remain unheard until nearly the end of the year, when it appeared on the Beatles' next album—at severely edited length—as "Revolution 1." The version the public first heard, taped July 10, was faster and funkier, and it rated the B-side of "Hey Jude," the Beatles' new summertime single. It also pulled a backstep and expunged that little word "in."[24] The revamped, commercialized, and out-leaning "Revolution" hit the radio late in August—the week of the Democratic National Convention in Chicago.[25]

No one has ever suggested that the Beatles could have calculated such coincidence. So fate is again the culprit. That "Revolution," a scolding response to the student uprisings of the spring, should first appear just as the radical left of the U.S. were being beaten on Michigan Avenue ensured that the Beatles' critique would be heard in a very particular way. As the sinister semblance of a political convention ground on inside the same International Amphitheater where two years earlier the Beatles had initiated their last tour, an eerie perverted circus tore through the streets outside: tear gas and battle gear in Grant Park, Vietnamese flags lofted in the Loop, long nights of rampaging police and screaming kids. Broken arms, broken faces, broken glass. For some cowboy country in the Third World this was routine. For America it was trauma: social insanity, the final feared collapse into chaos.

And here were the Beatles, last spotted following some swami up a hill, come to tell the protesters their tactics were all wrong. That waving Mao in people's faces made no sense; that all one had to do was free the mind and the institutions would follow. It sounded suspiciously like hippie talk—*Change consciousness, change life!*—and the time for that was past: free-your-mind as an activist strategy had gotten its tryout at the Pentagon and elsewhere, and had failed to cushion the blows or budge the machine. The Beatles were preaching appeasement in the manner of wealthy, dithering dilettantes, to some even sounding outrageously in league with the cops: Mayor Daley's stormtroopers wanted to change your head too—by smashing it in.

In the thick of those brutal few days in August, "Revolution" arrived like another swipe of the nightstick to batter every fresh wound. Reaction among the radicals and in the underground was immediate and hot. The pages of protest rags from Greenwich Village to Berkeley were flooded with animal metaphors. The Beatles were running dogs. Revisionist rats, capitalist pigs. Vultures in sympathy with the hawks. They weren't "in"; their song itself declared them "out."

Ramparts: "Betrayal."

New Left Review: "A petty bourgeois cry of fear."

Jon Landau: "Hubert Humphrey couldn't have said it better."

Berkeley Barb: "Sounds like the hawk plank adopted in the Chicago convention of the Democratic Death Party."[26]

Richard Goldstein was not comforted by the Beatles' promise that it would be all right. "For them it probably will," he wrote in the *Village Voice.* "But for the rest of us, those words delivered with such genial certainty must seem as consoling as a tract on the glories of national pride written in 1939."[27] Robert Christgau found "Revolution" "as artistically indefensible as, oh, 'Love Can Make You Happy,' and for many of the same reasons."[28] (Both Goldstein and Christgau immediately went on to extol the virtues of the radical MC5, bellicose metalheads who in this instance were found preferable to the Beatles despite what Christgau called their "rather dumb" political position, "based on an arrantly sexist analysis."[29] Well, you can't have everything.) At the same time, Establishment-organ-by-default *Time* magazine did the Beatles' underground credibility no great service by praising "Revolution," which it found to be a commonsense knuckle-rap to all those impetuous rabble-rousers.[30]

As if the events of Chicago weren't enough to splinter whatever soapbox the Beatles thought they were on, the Rolling Stones released "Street Fighting Man" that same week in August. The record was powerful, uncommonly thunderous for a Stones product, and its lyric, though shouted over a churning body of guitar and drum, came through sufficiently for radical radioheads to get the gist: Mick Jagger was saying, *Take it to the street.* The song reached its audience as an epic rock and roll battle march, conceived and executed to inspire the collective soul of a battered resistance.

But "Street Fighting Man" also had, it seemed, a share of ambivalence; it played with doubt. And that made it defensible as art—more so than "Revolution," which came across as an empty promise delivered from a political void. Jagger's simple musical question—What can I do, except do what I do?—expressed his suspicions as to the value of action, the possibility of one person effecting change, and his doubts reverberated with those of others: Can I do anything? Do I *want* to do anything? Is it worth the risk of trying? How far am I willing to go? These were all good questions, timely questions, and "Street Fighting Man" was embraced by the left largely because it seemed conscious of them. Whereas "Revolution" was heard as one thing and one thing only: denunciation, without doubt or question, of revolutionary action. The contrast was that plain—and that appalling. "The Beatles," Greil Marcus wrote, just weeks after the events of August 1968, "were ordering us to pack up and go home, but the

Stones seemed to be saying that we were lucky if we had a fight to make and a place to take a stand."[31]

Marcus likened "Revolution" to the protest songs which seemed now to belong to a much earlier time, though he and others his age had been singing them just a few years before. The words of those old songs were dead, he felt, because their easy answers and moral assumptions refused to acknowledge ambiguity. "There is nothing to understand in message lyrics of this sort, lyrics that are afraid to admit to the element of uncertainty and unpredictability that gives art—music, painting, poetry—the tension that opens up the senses." "Revolution," like the classic protest song, was lyrically dormant because its words offered "no space for doubt or illusion. . . . The words delivered a straightforward message, a command."[32]

But Marcus acknowledged that, to the extent popular music could effectively capture the complexity of real feelings in hard times, true communication was achieved not through words but through performance. "It's the experience of letting the rhythms of the music capture you, together, that affirms the group, strengthening the will to fight and keeping the struggle going. It is the act of singing, not the message mouthed as the words are sung." And as a performance, Marcus said, "Revolution" communicated a desire for movement, an anarchy of the spirit, which it didn't dare as a verbal statement: the music was "so immediate and ecstatic that I find myself singing along as my fingers pound out the beat. The music makes me feel happy even though its lyrics depress me."[33]

Then there was "Street Fighting Man," whose cachet surely lay partly in the fact that it had been banned in Chicago during convention week. Marcus valued it over "Revolution" because it did not take the easy protest-song escape: though in pure rock and roll terms it was as good as the Beatles' record, it refused to issue "commands"; it seemed to vacillate and admit to something less than certainty. "The Stones create a situation that seems absolutely clear-cut, but they accept just a hint of doubt, and that situation dissolves and becomes a challenging emotional jigsaw puzzle, not congratulations for being on the right side. The Stones won't do our thinking for us, as the Beatles tried to do with 'Revolution.'"[34]

Even so, Jagger and company could hardly fail to notch points with "Street Fighting Man." It was a subtle song as well as a loud one—ambivalent, but just enough and not too much. Doubt implies choice, and it's hard to hear a real choice being weighed: rejecting violent action—even just drawing back and reassessing its terms—are not tendered as true options. The political jigsaw puzzle it offered was easy to assemble, its conflict inevitably resolved on "the right side." Marcus called the song a gift—because it enabled him to find his own meaning within it.[35] But he and his radical like were clearly keyed, at that moment, to make a particular meaning; and it was that meaning which the song drew from and fed into. That the radical audience accepted the song's ambivalence not as a burden but as a gift—the way the hippie audience had accepted *Pepper*—suggests that like *Pepper* it gave that audience the affirmation it wanted, not the difficulty it didn't need. The Stones were subtly issuing an order of their own— *March!*—and that was the order its audience was ready, eager, needing to hear. "Sometimes you have to applaud yourself just to keep going," Marcus wrote of the activist's often miserable condition.[36] Somewhere in the clatter of "Street Fighting Man" is the sound of Stones and audience applauding each other, just to keep going.

In that way it was a good, useful piece of popular interchange: the Stones delivered what the moment needed and the audience expected, and expectations change according to needs. 1968 was not 1964—and if dreams were to live in the brute atmosphere of America and Vietnam and Europe, they would have to be hard, programmatic dreams, founded in a sense of real violence and backed with a willingness to suffer it. The new dreams would come with a price: heads would be cracked, noses flattened, the skies would go smeary with

23. July 17, 1968: while recording the White Album, the Beatles attend the premiere of *Yellow Submarine* at the London Pavilion. Keith Richards and Anita Pallenberg are in the next row.

tear gas, not marmalade. Impatient, scared, exhilarated, outraged daily, New Left critics were now at least as much political creatures as they were aesthetic commentators; and they needed the same reassurances as their kindred who did not have the luxury of expatiating on their angst in the pages of *Rolling Stone* and *Ramparts*.

But now these songs have long since drifted free of their specific topical associations; and if they survive at all, they survive as universalisms, expressing something (truth, passion, emotional reality) beyond their time. What such a song speaks must be deep enough, elusive enough, substantial enough to evolve, of itself, into something else.

"Street Fighting Man" is a smash to listen to, a terrific hurtling juggernaut of a record. But I find it unlikely that anyone innocent of '68 history can today experience its music as much more than that; or that anyone with a knowledge of that history can today experience its words as much more than an affirmation of the year's rebellions. May 1968 is its energy source—which means, among other things, that today I am less impressed by its doubts than by its righteous force. True that at the time, it assuaged the pain of many who needed acknowledgment. But it inflicts no pain on me.

"Revolution" does. To me, it is a musical scab—another kind of cover-up. An imperfect cover, a healing that won't take, drawing attention to what it tries to conceal: the wound shows, the pain is immediate, the blood is at the surface. Granted, the lyrics remain one-dimensional; their thrust is toward disengagement, or at least gradualism; and their prime geopolitical assertion is contained in the assurance that everything will somehow be all right. Lennon, you could say, was not as canny as either Dylan or Jagger, because unlike them he'd neglected to overlay his response to revolution with any self-exempting layer of obscurity or irony. You could also say that his were the most oblivious, politically inept words any rock and roll hero could have dredged from his personal pocket of positivist clichés.

Then why, *why* does the record remain such a bitch? Simple: the scabbiness of its performance. For a record of such fluidity, with such an automatic groove, it is incredibly abrasive to hear. "Revolution" has subversive meaning precisely because the words, all ideology, speak aphorisms, while the music, all instinct, howls violence.

Most immediately, there is its sound, as plain and raw as violence itself. Bass and drums produce a fat, rubbery bottom end; Ringo fills the anxious pauses with deadened, gutted beats; Nicky Hopkins plays a demented jazz; and everything forms itself around the scoop and scrape of the Lennon-Harrison guitars. Those guitars are distorted for the same reason the record starts with one piercing scream and ends with another. "Revolution" is formed of distortion and sonic abrasion because that is the sound that results when the sort of lie its lyric offers is forced through the Beatles' communal, instinctive sense of what is true. John Lennon, out of his fearful, hopeful heart, his drug-and-Maharishi-clogged brain-pan, produces a fantasy. And just like the dark-hearted *Magical Mystery Tour* fantasies, this one will not survive reality—the reality that is both *out there,* in the street, and *right here,* in the lawless, self-determining, instinctive coils of Beatle expression. Truth occurs beneath the surface, in some basement toilet of meaning and emotion, compression and expression, and it emerges not as what it started out to be, but as—yes, that mutant monster!—*something else.*

The record's ending tells its truth, even as it obsessively pushes its unifying lie. It's gonna be all right? John was quite probably that devoid of real perspective, that wistful and blank an ideologue. Just as his instinct was sufficiently profound to conjure the enveloping nightmare of "A Day in the Life," whose sole message was that it's *not* gonna be all right, his political consciousness was sufficiently amorphous to convince him, on another day, in another mood, that it truly would. What makes the difference, what makes "Revolution" live, is that he didn't say those words—he screamed them. Over and over: *ALL RIGHT!!!*

Few performers have brought more dimensions to the rock and roll scream than John Lennon. His "Revolution" scream was complex enough to produce irreconcilable responses even among ideological allies: while Greil Marcus heard it as a censorious command—*Pack up and go home*—Richard Goldstein heard it as embodying "genial certainty." But despite their differing responses to it, both heard the scream as the end of an argument, the closing of a dialectic. And I don't believe it. That is, I don't believe John believes what he is saying. He believes only in the scream.

That scream rips an opening in what appears to be a closed circle of meaning. A rent in John Lennon's cover-up, his attempt at de-frauding his audience and himself—that's where the action is. That hole is where we find the "space" in the song, the expression of doubt and division—not only between ideological camps but within the art-ist himself—which Marcus acknowledged but didn't particularly value in 1968; it's the space which exists between words that are dead and sound so alive it bleeds. What's interesting is that the radical crit-ics of 1968 were unable or unwilling to hear the pain in this record, its sound of a lie forced into voice and dying a quick, screeching death. But I may be staring into the biggest hole of all: the canyon separat-ing then from now. Then, it was probably impossible to hear any-thing but the lie, or anything contradictory in the distortion that ate into it like acid. Now the lie is a pile of bones, but the acid remains alive.

In 1968, movement fans had a right not to look so far ahead. They didn't want art later; they wanted results now. Long-term aesthetic questions were surely among the most pathetic of counterrevolu-tionary quibbles: they needed the Beatles to prove, as the Stones had, that they weren't bourgeois finks out to protect their millions. But the simple fact is that the Beatles—as distinct from John Lennon—were constitutionally incapable of such statements as the audience now needed. Certainly they were incapable of statements that came out untainted by equivocation; "Revolution" proved that.

What *could* they do? They could act as if there were still a world worth living in, creating from, giving to: they could do, as artists, what the radical audience were doing as activists. The difference be-ing that, as artists, they had the responsibility of creating work that would far outlast the immediate conflicts the radicals could not see past; the irony being that, in outlasting the moment, the art would be heard as irrelevant to it—even though the art was so forged of that moment that it would as much as any art deliver it into history, and into the imaginations of those to whom that history might one day matter.

The choice. As cultural leaders, the Beatles were expected by a good part of the audience to behave in one way; as artists they were bound to behave in another. "Revolution" was a failed attempt to have it both ways: its truth was in the performance, which had to work against and overcome a false verbal content. But now, acting wholly from instinct, they would avoid making statements and instead make art; and the art, whatever its form or content, would *be* the statement. In the terms of the time, it would have to seem the Beatles had chosen fantasy over reality, escape over engagement, when in fact they were choosing their art over their audience, the future over the moment—and thus an engagement different from any they had attempted before. It would be just as strong a rejection of audience demand as "Revolution" had been—just as much an offense against a faithful and beleaguered radical audience with its own psycho-ideological needs.

And this is the hole—between ideology and instinct, the political demand of now and the artistic demand of history—that those battered peace warriors and disheartened Beatlemaniacs of 1968 could not begin to encompass or envision, or the Beatles succeed in covering up.

□

Black birds, black clouds, broken wings, lizards, destruction.
—Tony Palmer, review of album *The Beatles,* London *Observer* (1968)

The White Album creeps and leaps from that hole. Its birth lay in those two seconds after "A Day in the Life," a noise issuing abruptly from silence and then retreating: chaos rendered microscopically, an aural microbe. The White Album was the same chaos of noises, gaiety, and mystery, not prediction but realization, late '60s chaos in its full measure of mutation.

It is about the events of 1968 the way Picasso's *Guernica* is about the Spanish Civil War. It both responds to and transcends its context. Like *Guernica*, the White Album is an excessive whole constructed of impacted vignettes, which finds its unity in radical segmentation and the discreteness of its parts. Like *Guernica*, it is black and white but mainly gray. Like *Guernica*, it is full of pain and melodrama. And as with *Guernica*, one need not be familiar with the details of its social circumstances to be overwhelmed by its power.

It's in the White Album that I hear what Landau attributed to *Harding*: a profound awareness. An awareness so profound, in fact, that it is profoundly confused. Awareness not just of the Vietnam war, and certainly not in the sense of a coherent social critique of issues plaguing the progressive mind in 1968; but awareness expressed in the decision to take on chaos as subject, animus, fuel, and fire—the arching of chaos over the span of a massive work, the transformation by chaos of every sound and emotion. The White Album is the concept album that *Sgt. Pepper* thought it was and wasn't. It seeps chaos, breathes it and voices it; fights it, exemplifies it, is overwhelmed by it, finally seeks a battered refuge from it. It tries to escape—tries *hard*—but can't. Like 1968, it screams, laughs wickedly, attacks, kills, cries, sighs, and dies.

The Beatles is their most fractured album, and their ugliest; their most unsettling and their most moving. It's their best album, and nothing else in rock and roll has ever come close to it.

□

The essential White Album track is a harsh, intractable piece of madness, a mashing together of absurd parts in which chaos builds by stages. It begins in suspension, briefly hovering over an indefinite terrain: a folk-delicate electric guitar whose soft, slanting chords are not picked but insinuated. Voice subdued and thoughtful: *She's not a girl who misses much . . . doo doo doo doo doo doo . . . oh, yeah.*

Wrrrack—a new chord strafes through, distorted and unnatural as the rip of metal. It lands the music but doesn't secure it. The first guitar dances in folkie circles, now a demented music box, as drums and bass thud dully in a congealed funk. The words, literal nonsense, are dreadfully sensual. Hands, a lizard, mirrors, boots, velvet—as a collection of fetish objects, the song is subtler, more insidious than "Venus in Furs." If the song is about fucking, as it seems to be, it is with a succubus. More so when the singing stops and there enters more distorted guitar: one string stretches itself in a continuous line over a broken-necked rhythm, and produces the sound of a horrible oozing.

The singer is going down. Despite the drag on the vocal, the disintegration it dramatizes, the music gains in impact and intensity. As musical performance it grows more fiendishly precise, the rhythmic contrasts between guitars and drums so complex and integrated they are hardly perceptible; while as emotion the track is all premature ejaculation, jumping the gun from one sweaty anxiety to another.

Suddenly we're in '50s land, and the form is doo-wop parody. But it is doo-wop parody as even the Mothers of Invention have never offered it—no abashed nostalgia or hip tease of adolescent devotion. If this isn't for real, it is nothing. Lennon goes into his doo-wop testimony: *When ah hold you in mah ahms . . . mah finguh on yaw trigguh.* Well, isn't this the secret wish behind every rock and roll love lyric ever sung, from Elvis to Sam Cooke to Gary Lewis and the Playboys, here in its purest animal noise? By main power, Lennon's tongue forces the words into life as the background voices sass him with their *bang-bang shoot-shoot,* so dirty and fun. The music suspends again, caught between comedy and fierce drama: the break into falsetto on the all-important word "gun"—rendered as *gah-oh-wah*—marks the highest and final point of frustrated spurt. With a flaccid thump of the drum, the song is over before it seems to have begun.

What was that?

It's a good question. Lennon growls and chokes his senseless antipoetry in an obscure language, while the music plunders the past only to outrage it, to sodomize the corpses of ethereal folk and sweet-hearted doo-wop. The song is about copulation, masturbation, body parts, body fluids, dark pleasure and awful pain. It's about handling meat and shooting holes. It's the music the Beatles should have been making in 1968, the music that brutalized year deserves.

It is only somewhat important that "Happiness Is a Warm Gun" is one of the few White Album songs traceable to a specific incident from the year 1968: Lennon told many times of spotting the title phrase on the cover of an American gun-enthusiast's magazine a few days after Robert Kennedy's assassination.[37] But the song's causal connection to an epoch-defining death isn't why I hear it as the true animal noise of 1968, as well as a great rock and roll recording. Rather, it is because "Happiness" is the ultimate expression of the Beatles' helpless fascination with and inclination to mutation.

We're back to the true underworld of even the sweetest Beatle dreams, that place they carried inside them, which they had never left even at their most romantic. Down to the caverns under Strawberry Fields—and indeed "Happiness" is the post-psychedelic son of that song. That place where the ideal meets the real and neither lives to tell: where the ideal is pulled inside out, its skull visible, its innards showing, its fingers crawling over forbidden regions. Acid fantasy's lizard slithers from behind the houseplant and clings to the glass, in full light, while doo-wop's starry vision of courtly love is stripped to what it always wanted to be in those sterile, benighted '50s—a cry for sex and touching, *as well as* a sincere expression of romantic feeling. Rock and roll had never nakedly acknowledged itself as the monster this song makes of it: not an organic body but a collection of badly matched limbs stitched into something approximating a recognizable form. Just like rock and roll; just like the bogs from which the Beatles emerged; just, in consequence, like the Beatles themselves. Each was a mutation, an unnatural, unprecedented combination.

The activist counterculture was another mutation, a freak being created of violence and unbidden desires. Civil rights came out of slavery, lynching, Jim Crow; idealisms were inflamed or sustained by official abuse, assassination, poverty. White New Leftists were often the progeny of Communist parents who sought to forge their own politics, envision their own, non-Stalinist social utopia. Alliances were attempted between vanguards of the Old Left, the New Left, the hippies and the Yippies, Panthers Black and White, moderates and extremists, cool academics and working-class firebrands. The radical vanguard of 1968 had, with only some success, melded itself from these far-flung parts into whatever unity it could be said to possess; and like the Beatles, that vanguard would not have become what it did had it not entailed so many unheard-of ideological and psychological collisions, and had its members not continued to push forward into newer and more encompassing combinations.

"Happiness" shows the Beatles driving to the heart of what they and their audience still share. The song is in one moment as gentle as the folkie soul of the New Frontier, in the next as brick-hard as the latest rad-punk noise, as white as John Lennon and as black as Willie Dixon. Yet it is no vision of peaceful integration, musical or racial or sexual. Each element shoves against another at some impossible angle, and the pervading unpleasantness does nothing to imply the success of revolutionary combinations in the real world. The song doesn't know what pushes its parts apart. It knows only that such harmony, such bliss as once existed in folk ballads like "I Gave My Love a Cherry" and doo-wop reveries like "In the Still of the Nite" are of the past, and now exist only as fantasies to be perverted by the rough facts of the present. It reaches for that ideal past, that matrix of memory, but can't help mangling the memory, transforming the past.

So I call it the defining song of the Beatles' greatest album. Inarticulate and instinctual, permeated with a sense of shared cultural history, it juxtaposes that past with this present and finds horror in the contrast. And it is about holes—hypodermic, vaginal, bullet. A year earlier the Beatles could speak, with every anticipation of success, of fixing a hole; now holes are everywhere, and the best they can hope for is a moment's fix to keep from going down forever.

The holes in this song stand in for the holes popping at the seams of all the dreams, from the first dream of the first Beatle, to the shrieking ecstasies of the fifteen-year-old girl, to the newest world-winning machinations of the radical left. All were dreams of transfiguration—a conjoining of communities in body and consciousness, the triumph of dreaming as a radical act, mutation as creation. And for a moment those dreams held: they were sustaining and empowering of their owners, and seemed capable of transforming the world in only the best ways. Then the nondreaming world began to fight back, and 1968 was the crash. Holes multiplied in a chaos of dead leaders, riot-cop rifles, hippie junkies, Vietnam horrors.

"Happiness Is a Warm Gun," in its disjunctive, near-psychotic way, really *was* about fucking: the sound of fantasy getting fucked by reality. For the Beatles' radical fans, that was the precise nature of the chaos encountered in 1968, and exactly what many of them didn't want to hear when the needle hit the vinyl.

□

What is happening is an evolutionary convulsion rather than a reformation. Young people are not correcting society. They are regurgitating it.

—Jeff Nuttall, *Bomb Culture* (1968)

A mutation requires at least two elements, preferably variables rather than constants. The Beatles' variables had always been Lennon and McCartney. Neither mirror images nor precise opposites, they were complementary coevals: two halves of a bipolar split, each with the potential to run manic or fall depressed, but each clinging to its fundamental identity when times got tough. Troubled, John always went back to rock and roll, the simplest wordings and most basic chords, the most immediate communication. At such times he favored reality—or his artist's idea of reality—over fantasy. Paul did the opposite, gravitating to the fantastic over the tangible, to impeccable pastiche over personal essay. John's songs on the White Album push the sense of an individual at odds with the world; in his struggle he speaks for the part of the audience that is striving to change the world, though consciously he usually speaks for no one but himself. If Paul speaks for anyone, it is for those resistant to or frightened of change.

Divided between them, the White Album is dominated by neither Lennon's biases nor McCartney's; each is qualified substantially by the other. Consequently there is a confusion of emphasis and shifting of focus, a relentless swing between confrontation and escape, resulting in a whole that is strikingly conflicted and angst-ridden even when its individual parts bespeak peace and certainty. Questioning and uncertainty are built into the music of the White Album; its character is defined by both sides of the Beatle brain.

But now, in response to a very new kind of external pressure, those sides are farther apart than ever. Thus emerge all the feelings that, for the Beatles' radical audience, so defined 1968: fear, anger, disorientation, death looming large. They emerge as feelings often do—naturally, implicitly, suddenly: acted out before they are articulated.

It is impossible not to hear the war and varying responses to it all over the White Album—never in explicit reference, always in feel. "Happiness Is a Warm Gun" conflates sex, drugs, weaponry, and a degraded notion of conquest. Contained in the jumbled *Come on come on come on come on*'s of "Everybody's Got Something to Hide Except Me and My Monkey," there is not only a nervous, drug-propelled echo of the cool and sexy "Please Please Me" urge (another measure of the space between old passions and new fears) but a platoon of soldiers rushing with heads down through a jungle clearing. Throughout "Revolution 9" are the noises of gunfire, stabbing, screams, explosions. "Revolution 1" revisits the scene of the Beatles' August offense against the radicals, though this time they are "in" as much as they are "out" of the desire for destruction in service of the antiwar cause.

Paul too has his piece of this action. Despite what he says, "Helter Skelter"—the scariest, the most monstrous of hard rock songs—is not about a playground slide, any more than "Revolution" was about its being all right. Even words as straightforward as these assume a vastly different meaning when performed over an echoing mass of chainsaw guitars and delivered in such a voice of reverberant cries and noble hysterics as McCartney summons. Here as ever in Beatle music, performance determines meaning; and as the adrenalized guitars run riot, the meaning is simple, dreadful, inarticulate, and instantly understood: *She's coming down fast.*

Sometimes the music or the words, usually both, conjure specific images. Listening to "Why Don't We Do It in the Road"—where Paul is certain no one will be watching—I think of those pictures of machine-gunned villagers lined up on the road through My Lai. And sometimes the war will loom in a quiet song, a long shadow at the edge of the scene. Hear how Paul queers the resolution of "Mother Nature's Son" with a dissonant seventh chord rather than the expected affirmative major. Something is wrong. The track overall has the tonal shadings of heavy skies, sinister lurkings in tall grass, with crepuscular horns and the underbeat of an unresonant drum; it is delivered in the disaffected voice and depressive mien of a shellshock victim. In its undermining of peaceful imagery with intimations of disturbance, it recalls Hemingway's war veteran clinging stoically to ritual and nature as he fishes the Big Two-Hearted River.

The White Album is also a black album: haunted by race. The prowling fingers of its songs never touch the issue directly, any more than they do the war, but black rage and black music are in the air these songs breathe. More elusively so than on *Beggars Banquet*, the Rolling Stones' contemporary release, because the Beatles are not as upfront as the Stones about their cross-racial references, and do more to transform them—for better ("Back in the U.S.S.R.," which breeds Chuck Berry's wit with the Beatles' musical muscle) and not-so-much-better ("Ob-La-Di, Ob-La-Da," whimsical bubblegum ska). "Piggies" is a shockingly caustic paraphrase of extremist black (and white) revolutionary rhetoric, though, characteristically for a White Album track, it contradicts even what would seem least mistakable about it. Harrison does this by casting such class-based vitriol in the quaintest European musical terms—chamber strings and harpsi-chord—which either renders the musical backdrop an effective surro-gate for the bourgeoisie the words attack, or compels music and lyr-ics to cancel each other into blankness. (Either way—subversive act or self-defeating paradox—the song is pure 1968, if not effective agit-prop.)

People were right to perceive "Blackbird" as a response to Black Power—whether Paul meant it that way or not. In fact the song is more apposite for being not a raised fist but an uncondescend-ing gesture, a perception that something new is in the air. That McCartney instinctively reconfigures the images and fond farewell of "Bye Bye Blackbird" by making the protagonist "you" rather than "I"—shifting the focus outward, acknowledging the movements of a neighboring presence in the world—is sufficient to suggest that the racial politics of the moment played into the song in ways he wasn't fully aware of.

Elsewhere, John chases the blues. With his White Album songs,

Lennon—as much as Jimmie Rodgers in the '30s, Hank Williams in the '40s, and Elvis in the '50s—defines a new kind of white blues. The style varies from track to track, but the emotional territory is the same. Lyrically, Lennon's blues are as mundanely detailed ("I'm So Tired") and nonchalantly surreal ("Happiness") as Robert Johnson's, and as apocalyptic ("Yer Blues"). Like older blues, they are highly sexual, though frustrated; and they are obsessed with honing the facts of feeling to the sharpest point.

But Lennon creates a *rock and roll* blues—which means a song's emotional weight is carried not by the guttural asides and vanishing vocal lines of classic blues singers, but by a hot and frenzied voice at the edge of its nerves. Even "I'm So Tired," all exhaustion and depression, is fired by that breakout impulse ingrained in the Beatles' rock and roll, when for an instant John's frustration overtakes him and he fires off a spurt of angst at the ceiling: *but I KNOW what you would do.* His blues are of the body—whereas the Beatles' 1967 music was almost entirely unphysical—and they are powered by the relentless need to dispel unbearable energies. These songs bring 1968 to its social paradigm: the destruction of bodies versus the liberation of bodies, with live, frightened flesh caught in between. John's body, as it achieves form in his voice, is not free at all; but it battles ferociously against whatever is attempting to destroy it.

The blues are implicitly accepting of misery, seldom convinced things could be any better; whereas John's blues are not accepting of anything—in fact are outraged that things could have gotten so bad. "Yer Blues" is brutally atmospheric: a storm-darkened, wind-driven hell on earth. It takes the nature references of classic blues (animals, skies, earth, elemental signs of doom) and damns them with an obnoxious, unforgiving sound. On the verses, Lennon's outcry is intercut with sharp guitar lines striking like lightning on either side of him—but he goes on bitching, hollering into the torrent. The refrain heaves against a crippled rhythm, guitar-bass figure following each vocal declamation like a dead leg; the beat breaks into freedom for just a few bars, becoming suddenly almost a boogie, a groove—only to stop cold again with a clumsy edit back to Ringo's drums. But the players bash away, Lennon shouts though he is barely heard over the din, and the song drags itself onward. Even as it fades, it wants to blow the trees over and stop the apocalypse in its tracks, fight thunder with louder thunder.

In the transformative process of White Album music, the Beatles take in the polluted atmosphere around them and exude it as naturally and sometimes as chokingly as their own breathing. The pollution becomes so much theirs that a charge of political irrelevance seems somewhat justified, though no less shortsighted. The White Album is livid with social terror, rank with social regurgitation, but on one level it is as irrelevant to 1968 as *Guernica* is to its specific inspiration. In transformations such as these, political acts, responses, and incoherent feelings endemic to a time of social cataclysm are employed as vehicles for an expressive, subtle, and enduring art. Expressive, subtle, and enduring art can never come about if viewed simply as a vehicle for politics. Ask the members of the MC5—or John Lennon, circa 1972.

□

> People like to say: Revolution is beautiful, it is only the terror arising from it which is evil. But this is not true. The evil is already present in the beautiful, hell is already contained in the dream of paradise, and if we wish to understand the essence of hell we must examine the essence of the paradise from which it originated.
>
> —Milan Kundera, "Afterword," *The Book of Laughter and Forgetting* (1981)

The White Album is a memory album: in aural terms, precisely analogous to the collage of Beatle imagery with which it is packaged—a formless clutter of past and present whose images are not always easily discerned, or understood. Much of its power comes from the way it sustains, often in ambiguous memory form, a simultaneous sense of past, present, and future. Through context and treatment and radical juxtaposition, it paints the past as something familiar but unstable; reaches for nostalgia without ever being merely nostalgic. Memory is present, in fact ubiquitous, but it is nothing very comforting.

This is the other half of the album's polarized brain. The first is defined by Lennon's hard blues and raw denunciations, Paul following John's lead with his own blunt rockers which promote the same sensation of an abrasive and overbearing reality. In this other, past-obsessed half, Paul calls the play, and the play is an end run around reality into the waiting arms of fantasy. Whereupon those arms disappear, a mirage. If reality is conspicuous in its absence from the album's more stylish stop-offs, it may mean only that reality, left unattended and uncontrolled over the rest of the record, is just as near and threatening in this fantasyland as it is in John's tight, airless room of misery. In other words, the White Album's fantasy songs attempt to deny *now* by invoking memories of *then*—but context kills the effort.

John, acknowledging this contradiction by carrying it close to the surface, comes up with fantasy songs that are sinister, sarcastic, defeated-sounding as they dredge the debris of earlier, easier dreams. "Cry Baby Cry" appoints its polite children and fairy-tale royalty as figures of malevolent potential, conducting séances and raising disembodied voices. That potential is again in the performance, since as a lyric the song is straight nursery rhyme. Nothing too weird, for instance, about the reference to the duke's message, lodged at the local pub, with which he is having some problem; except that neither message nor problem is explained—they're only glancingly referenced by Lennon in a spectral voice floating above an insistently mysterious instrumentation. The chord progression on the verses describes a nervous, doom-sensing downward movement, as of a frightened candle-bearer descending a staircase into darkness.

Lennon's (and the album's) most bilious performance, "Glass Onion," seeks to squash previous Beatle fantasy—though to do so, it must first place the thing squarely in view. Spitting a litany of references to recent Beatle characters and places as if they were living things with ongoing stories, Lennon indicts the late '60s passion of both ordinary fans and titled academics for crackpot fantasizing on Beatle images—as if that hadn't been an essential part of their allure from the start. But the song also registers as a self-indictment, since it can't help perpetuating the game, if only in jest: John tells us who the walrus was. In quashing fantasy the song allows a dollop of its essence to squirt free and squirm away, to renew itself elsewhere.

But that's another time, soon to come. Here and now, there is only the stench inside the glass onion, the stale air of old used-up fantasies. Great tiredness and desperation in John's voice as he references "Fixing a Hole," *Pepper*'s unofficial thesis tune. Oh, yes: remember last year, when we still thought the impossible was possible? Well—

Cut. The question splices into a coda of seasick strings sailing toward silence. Fade to black.

Even Lennon's trifles, like "Glass Onion," seem to have these peelable layers. McCartney's usually don't. But again, it's Paul who defines this other, fantastical aspect of the White Album, and brings it home. Paul's ballads are no harder to defend as *music*—as pure sound and surface—than Haydn's *Surprise Symphony* or Gershwin's *Rhapsody in Blue*. Even at their silliest, they are never less than thoroughly aware of their silliness, and have a gleam and free flow of humor which are close to sublime—at least for those whose tastes encompass the flossier end of pop.

Their value to the White Album as political statements-by-fiat is harder to justify—or explain—because, unlike John, Paul constructs fantasies that do not seem troubled by any countervailing reality. They are what they seem: there is no dark side, no negative to these whimsical interludes. But this is just why they are important. On the

White Album they benefit from their context as similar songs on *Sgt. Pepper* do not, because although they relate to chaos not as confrontation but as evasion, the White Album has all the confrontation *Pepper* lacks. And the record's painting of chaos is unthinkable without the fragility of Paul's ditties: fragility, too, is an aspect of chaos. Some songs evoke a historical past—"Rocky Raccoon" lampoons the gunslinger mythology Dylan played straight, while "Honey Pie" catches the fading echoes of empire—but generally their backward reach, their escapism, lies in attitude rather than reference. The attitude is wistful, hopeful, and as oblivious to ambiguity as it is embracing of love.

Songs like "Martha My Dear" and "I Will" sport the buffed surfaces and instant facility of an earlier Beatle music, and inevitably have the sound of a world, it now seemed, many years gone. As political artifacts they evoke, without trying, old naiveties and less tattered ideals; for as Paul has pointed out more than once, all love songs are antiwar songs. But they must fight harder, be heard differently, when they are elbowed on every side by songs that are themselves aural war, aesthetic brutality. Can these love songs survive war? Can the flower defeat the gun? That is the tension, the irreplaceable contrast, provided by Paul's escapist reveries and pillowy pastiches. If John's hard rock is the album's reality principle, Paul's balladry is its pleasure principle—only, pleasure is now heard not as something worth pursuing for its own sake but as a defense against reality, synonymous with escape, doomed to failure.

And Paul's agile, fragile songs of love do fail to escape. They never had a chance. That is why they are so lovely. They are lightweight because their function in the drama is as foil and failure. Every McCartney twirl has its negation in a Lennon thrust; every yearning for the past is countered by the oppressive noise of now. The contrast is made plainest in the juxtaposition of John's monumental noise-painting "Revolution 9" with a brief prelude in which Paul's high, graceful, spooked voice asks an emotional question of an existential void: he wants to know, pleads to know, if we can return him to the place he came from. Of course the question only narrows into silence: the White Album spends half its time concealing, the other half revealing—emerging from nothing, receding into nothing.

Few records are as layered as this, and the layers shift with independent life. A thing one notices instantly about the White Album is that it isn't pieced together as other records are—or were then. Seldom are there appreciable "rills" or silences between songs; and when there are, it is only to lay a noise trap (the space separating "Sexy Sadie" from "Helter Skelter"). Virtually every groove is filled by some fleeting, unaccountable noise, fillip, twitter, or hiccup; backward talk, mumbles, mild curses, musical doodles, exclamations hacked in the middle. From the traditional silences following banded tracks on normal records pops an underground zoo of id-like freak-squeals, rude noises from the bog. It is purposeful, clearly, this cramming of space and insistence on surprise, and remarkable as an artistic strategy: for most of us, the interjections define the record's identity as much as the songs themselves.

It's well to ask what, if anything, noises like these can *mean*. Aren't they the silliest of squeaks and squawks, random insertions of no weight, free of intended, let alone accidental, meaning?

Of course—but they are meaningful just because they are without calculation. They are unbidden, subconscious efforts at undermining the cover-up; attempts to voice, if not articulate, what can't be admitted in the conscious discourses of partisan times. The Beatles and the hippies had attempted a cover-up, and succeeded grandly, with the *Pepper* conspiracy. Could the individual Beatle now admit to what he had at that time covered up—that his dream of inclusion, of engagement, of winning the world with the rhythms of romance and sway of song was nearing its end? And what about the revolutionist of 1968: Could such a person admit the truth beneath his or her ideo-

logical cover-up—that history had shown violence in the service of social revolt, good cause or evil, to be ineffective and even insanity-
breeding as a long-term course?[38] For clear and all too compelling
reasons, both Beatle and radical had to perpetuate the cover-up, had
to *act* as if dream were reality: otherwise there would be no point in
going on at all.

But the little White Album noises make it clear that there are such
things, such doubts and accumulating fears, to *be* covered; that the
attempt has been and is being made; and that it is failing as it has not
failed before. What was always silent, successfully suppressed, is now,
in the grooves of the White Album, rife with mystery, contingency,
and absurdity. Shellacked and inviolable silences are now open holes
in music, life, ideology, desire, and deed—the essence of the irreconcilable, that open end of the circle which allows the hostile world its
point of entry, destruction and death their ingress.

□

"Revolution 9" has the force and violence of battle. Not only in its
specific sounds and sudden silences, but in its final sense of one reality having been taken over by another. If "Happiness Is a Warm Gun"
embodies the White Album's mutative principle, "Revolution 9" is its
ultimate realization of cover-up and breakdown—eight minutes of
the same freak-squeals, audio gremlins, and hole-popping night terrors that everywhere else appear for mere moments. It takes what is
implied in each two-second squawk between dysfunctional tracks
and makes it a universal vision.

Universal because "Revolution 9" is not only one thing or another.
Profoundly idiosyncratic, it is also all-inclusive: as a consummate
Beatle thing, it will be satisfied only when it encompasses the world
and every extreme within it. Ordinary existence, as well as cataclysmic
assault; classical music, as well as industrial whine; the birth in a
baby's gurgle, as well as the death in weapons of war.

John Lennon created "Revolution 9" out of the simultaneous feeding, in three different studios, of multiple tape loops into a master recording. Each loop contained its own set of sounds—music, effects, voices—and was elevated or lowered in the mix by arbitrary adjustments of the mixing console.[39] For his spontaneous and willfully random collage, Lennon had only one avowed goal: "I thought I was painting in sound a picture of revolution."[40] But as chaos theorists and people of common sense will agree, the perfectly random can produce sense as spontaneously as it generates chaos; and though the excitement of the accidental is part of its greatness, "Revolution 9" is not lacking in underground logic. It has ebb and flow, build-up and climax, comedy and drama, affirmation and despair. Threads of mystery run beneath its surfaces in tight skeins of coincidence and encounter.

This is my randomly logical response to it, on last listening:

I. APPROACH

Can you take me back leads into an exchange of voices—voices so low they disappear, conversation so secretive it scarcely registers as human interaction: two men, a plea for forgiveness, a whisper of "bitch," bad feelings beneath the surface. Behind a wandering piano played in minor key, the uninflected *Number nine* voice enters, swinging pendulum-like from one ear to another.

2. ENTRY

Announced by the sudden blurt of sinister quasi-classical music—distorted to dissonance, run backward, repetitive. Crash of cymbals and choir in repeated churchly ejaculation. Voices Lennonesque and Harrisonian appear, overlapping, hopelessly mired in the morass but for a snatch, here or there, of disconnected phrase:

—every one of them knew that as time went by they'd get a little bit older and a little bit slower—

Laughter of a female adult, and an infant's wet coo of happiness. *Who's to know?* George asks. *Number nine,* the voice says.

3. ANTICIPATION

Backward Mellotron and a doomy classical chord. *Informed him on the third night.* Blaring of a car horn, high screech of an air-raid siren. White noise to the rear, a nasal voice edging its way up from the bottom, struggling through the mud of the mix to assert a thin cry: *right . . . right . . . Right . . . RIGHT . . .* All other sounds fall away for an instant, the voice slithers snakily through the hole and escapes into the night: *—iiiighht—RIIIII-AHHHHT . . .*

4. CONFRONTATION

More car horns; bells; white noise of traffic, the desperate city. Are people fleeing? *With the situation—they are standing still. Upon the telegram from the late colonel—* A human throat is caught, seemingly, in the act of convulsing: *Huhnhh, huhnhh, huhnhh.* Mad forward rush of traffic noise. *Number nine.* Crescendo of the crowd, either in appreciation of some entertainment or the first stirrings of riot. *—couldn't tell what he was saying his voice was low and his eyes his eyes his eyes were closed—* The crowd of people turn away; and those voices in the basement, continuing, *All right, all right—*
—his hair was on fire his glasses were insane—
—which enabled him to move about—

5. PARALYSIS

More vocal convulsions—seizure in the larynx, attack of the heart. Everything grows louder as if someone has turned up the volume on the earth. The rough twisted beast of backward music lurching back and forth, lurching toward Bethlehem.

Time stops: the crowd applauds, stunned and excited. *the wife said he'd better go to see the surgeon* Some emotionless bass-toned machine thrums persistently at the floor of the mix—wires beneath the very floor of our civilization, control panel of the Combine, running efficiently or overheating? *so anyroad he went to see the dentist who gave him a pair of teeth* The upward-twisting sound, definitely, of a man as his scream is rewound live upon a spool of tape, or his body snatched whole and insignificant from the earth by the hand of God. *which wasn't any good at all so instead of that he joined the bloody navy and went to sea* The bass-tone breaks and throbs in bulbous measures.

A football chant, a malefic invocation: *Hold that line! Hold that line!*

6. EPIPHANY

in my broken chair, my wings are broken

And here, in the heart, the smoking crater, burning middle pit of every revolution, where the heretics are named and executions carried out. In this maze of madness is the unmistakable crackling of fire. The dull, chesty beat, once or twice, of stabbing, laughter. Overhead and on every side, missiles, machine-gun fire, an explosion at the periphery of time and trees.

only to find the night watchman   onion soup   of his presence in the building

Behind and above, a rounded curling and echoing chorus of silky sepulchral voices in a high hymn of mourning.

Number nine? Number nine? Number nine?

7. RETREAT

Move on past the crater if you have made it this far, and a doomsayer with schizophrenic features and preternatural calm stands wearing a doom-saying sandwich-board. He intones: *Industrial output. Financial imbalance.*

thrusting it between his shoulderblades
The Watusi. The Twist.

Glimpse the victory band practicing its paces on a far field. The doomsayer offers a sacrament—but what is it he hands you, what rests in your open palm?

Take this, brother, may it serve you well.

The dream ends here.

8. REALIZATION

A man awakens—*What? What? Ohhh*—and grumbles as a woman speaks. Elsewhere in the room there is a pop crooner on a staticky radio, lifting chest and voice-hole to the moon to sing some slop of syrup sweetness. Man and woman replicate the nightmare layers of the dream—she murmuring above, he grumbling rhythmically below.

Again all extraneous, all upper and lower reaches of sound fall back in randomly synchronized respite—and the woman's voice, uncertain, soft, but grasping at the edge of some thought that must be completed or at least begun, feels through the hole in the sound, and utters—

if . . . you become naked

9. RESTORATION

The emergence, or return, or renaissance, or simply the stoic endurance of the Great Silent Majority: *Block that kick. Block that kick! BLOCK THAT KICK!!* The sound of the crowd, the chant, hymn of the heaving beast, swings again from side to side, pendulum-like; fades.

□

"Revolution 9" is just as random and just as specific as that. To the extent that it is narrative, the narrative is all in pieces; yet it's full of stories, more than we can ever absorb, or even uncover. That I have determined there to be nine stages in the progress of the track is purest chance, a minor mysticism.

Randall Jarrell's famous comment on Whitman: "There is in him almost everything in the world, so that one responds to him, will-

ingly or unwillingly, almost as one does to the world."[41] I respond to
"Revolution 9," and to the White Album as a whole, as I sometimes
respond to the world: with fear, joy, awe, and exhilaration. That this
unfathomable montage, one of the Beatles' greatest achievements, is
perennially polled as their "worst song" says less about the average
pop fan's distance from the aesthetic tenets of the avant-garde than it
does about John Lennon's success in creating a picture of psycho-
social breakdown which is every bit as merciless, grotesque, and anti-
ideological as the rigors of art require that it be; in which the dullest
familiars of ordinary life beat a constant pulse beneath the most appalling noises of a world collapsing upon itself.

□

You know, you don't look like him at all.
—The Wardrobe Lady

Leftist critics had little use for the White Album. They couldn't hear
it—or could hear only those parts they were prepared to reject. Those
parts told them it was more denial, more anesthesia and trivia from
the oblivious Beatles. A few years later, Robert Christgau would call
the album "their most consistent [!] and probably their worst."[42] Jon
Landau compared it unfavorably to *Beggars Banquet,* fixing on the
Beatles' tendency to pastiche: "The Beatles have used parody on this
album precisely because they are afraid of confronting reality. It becomes a mask behind which they can hide from the urgencies of the
moment."[43] Richard Goldstein wrote, "Even if the Beatles had never
expressed doubts about youthful insurrection, it would have been
obvious from the tone of this new album that they are incapable of
producing relevant art in a revolutionary context." A flat statement
which presumes objective observation but in fact fairly crackles with
one man's anger. In Goldstein's view the Beatles had committed, if

not mortal sin, then the signal apostasy of revolutionary rock: the music on the White Album was "oblivious to its time."[44]

Such comments imply several things about what the radical audience expected and wanted of its rock heroes. That audience *expected* relevant art, a constructive contribution to the revolutionary project. What it *wanted* was balm. Surely the radical critics knew that no pop star could truly provide more than that; but this was another thing to go unacknowledged, to be covered up with the certitudes of ideology. These critics had no use for a work smacking of escapism—despite escapism being shown to fail, employed as a receding dream image and not the real thing. Yes, the White Album was by turns as banal, as oblivious as the commercials that filled space between televised abominations. But it was also hard with human perversity, violent and unanswerable, and each half of the contradiction was as important as the other. For reasons dictated by the moment, radical critics fixed on one half and, in a great collective failure of imagination and critical vision, ignored the other.

"People are always shouting they want a better future," Kundera writes. "It's not true. The future is an apathetic void of no interest to anyone. The past is full of life, eager to irritate us, provoke or insult us, tempt us to destroy or repaint it. The only reason people want to be masters of the future is to change the past."[45] As a generalization upon the motives of real people, this observation may be of arguable validity. But I think it explains much of why the White Album is a monumental work of art, and why so many of those who should have heard the most in it were so eager to disown it.

I believe that collective critical failure had to do with the White Album's unique and implicit sense of history. Dylan's mytho-Western synthesis sought metaphors in a past distant and conceptual enough to suit modern needs; and a Stones song like "Sympathy for the Devil" was as historically vague as it was musically dynamic, despite naming historical names. The Beatles reached into a past that was nearer than that, too near—the musical and emotional past they shared with the audience. Such a reach was bound to shake that audience's revolutionary confidence by reminding it of a time when it was less relevant than it now felt itself to be.

After all, every evil of 1968—Vietnam, racism, corruption, suppression—had existed a year earlier, two, three, four, ten years earlier. But many, perhaps most, rock and roll fans hadn't cared so much about them then; nor had they expected their rock idols to care. Come 1968 and many of those fans were now radicals, Marxists, Maoists; and embedded in their criticism was the assumption that the Beatles should have become radicalized, too—because their audience (at least a segment of it) had. Implicit were the questions: How dare the Beatles give the *impression* of not caring about what we care about, and in the same way? How dare they remind me of a time when I was freer than I am now?

A time like the previous summer. The White Album is the anti-*Pepper*. Its plain white cover opposes the earlier record's lavish spread, and where we open *Pepper* to find the full-color Beatles, bold and beautiful in their young manhood, posed in a tight grouping, inside the White Album hide four small, separate mug shots: black-and-white, faces scored and bewildered, unrecognizable as *Pepper*'s men. The title rejects the earlier record's false persona to reclaim the true persona, *Beatles*—whatever that might now amount to. Most powerfully, though, the White Album opposes *Sgt. Pepper* by swallowing it: it references both lyrically and musically the songs of the previous year, and some of Paul's contributions are pure *Pepper* pastiche. But the new meaning is that that fantasy has become antithesis, not thesis. As an allergic patient will be injected with a measure of precisely the offending virus, the White Album is infused with what it knows it must expel.

This is to say again that the album is wholly cognizant of history—

24. From a photo shoot in Studio Two, February 1968: hopeful smiles, caught in the
uncertain interim between hippiedom and harder times, Maharishi and Mao.

of the past from which it grows, and which it must acknowledge but also grossly transfigure. It absorbs the violence of 1968 while retaining a memory of what had gone before. That memory, again, was the radical audience's as much as the Beatles'; the difference was that one of those entities wished now to erase it. The White Album dwelled on the past, tongued the sore tooth of it, where its respondents were attempting just now to escape the past—in the case of *Pepper,* the recent history they had helped make, embraced as it was made, and which now seemed pathetically tangential to the course of historical action. Thus was "relevance" defined by those who found the Beatles to be lacking it.

Revisionism has always been revolution's fellow traveler. James

Miller describes the desire of latter-decade radicals to eradicate the very past which had made their movement possible:

> Ironically, the growing militance of blacks and young students made the achievements of the earlier activists seem, even to themselves, like an irrelevant, insufficiently radical pre-history. Increasingly ashamed of their middle-class origins, many were eager to deny the academic context of their original political interests. The spectacular demonstrations, riots and student strikes of the late Sixties, lavishly covered in the mass media, made memories of the early days seem pale by comparison.[46]

Relevance is a value assigned to what we think today; it may have no relation whatever to what is important. But a peculiarity of revolutionary rhetoric is that if a thing is classed "irrelevant," it is by definition unimportant. If, for instance, Richard Goldstein truly thought the Beatles "incapable of producing relevant art in a revolutionary context," it was necessary for him to believe equally that the whole of the decade to this point—those drear days of lunch-counter sit-ins and Free Speech rallies, Birmingham firehoses and blooming Beatlemania—did not qualify as a revolutionary context. That it was, in the end, unimportant.

Miller describes how, among late '60s radicals, "the intellectual foundations of the New Left were ignored, repudiated, forgotten."[47] Dropped, in other words, into the black hole of a generation's historical memory. The Beatles—who formed their phenomenon just as the civil rights workers and student democrats were forming theirs— were, in the minds of many in 1968, deserving of the same oblivion. But their curse at the time is now their credit: that they could, finally, endorse no program as simple as either *Change life, change consciousness!* or *Up against the wall, motherfucker!* The White Album's fantasy world encompassed both of these as possibilities, but also spotted the holes they sprang when asked to hold water. The Beatles, in other words, were confronting the impossible contradiction of their own existence. What had they ever said but that the largest dreams were, in fact, possible?

By the end of 1968 much had been lost, many dreams lay broken, and it would require one's whole being to reassemble them, re-believe in them. Who wished to be reminded of those dreams when they were whole and brilliant, hear again the sound of that world which would never return? Who cared to hear "Revolution 9" and experience the autopsy of one's own movement, envision the collapse of the very revolution upon which all hope had been staked? Who desired to know that, as Kundera said, hell could be contained in the dream of paradise?

"Good Night," the White Album's dreamy closer, is pure angelic fantasy: a Tinseltown production number, string-laden and harp-lush. But given what precedes it and the context in which it lives, it is also a morbid lullaby, a song of death. In 1968, some heard it as the final cop-out, the true saccharine soul of the Beatles. But a few may have asked, as I ask now, whether "Good Night" in fact represented the final triumph of fantasy, or its last breaths. A few may have wondered—even if they didn't ask—to whom, and to what, the Beatles were saying good night.

They just had to look. What they saw was their dream drawing to a close.

□

In Beatle history, 1968 was a moment of testing as well as truth—test of how an artist might deal with and thus contribute to a larger comprehension of immediate, history-making events; and of how an audience with very definite needs of its own might react to a split between its needs and those of the artist. The test was doubled by the intensely personal relationship between this audience and these artists; and it was necessary and correct that there come a time when those very people who had answered the Beatles' vow long ago would begin to ask questions of them, bring weightier expectations to bear, make demands more demanding than a lock of Ringo's hair, a flutter of Paul's eyelash.

Questions like: Why? What did we agree upon in that long-ago, and what end was it meant to serve? What, in fact, was the whole point?

Maybe the whole point was the revolt that was happening now. Radical critics were wrong in failing to acknowledge that the Beatles had done their bit for the revolution. Had begun doing it when they climbed their first coal wagon as the Quarry Men; had gone on doing it battling the crowd in Hamburg, banging a new sound against the Cavern walls, giving themselves to audience after audience, drawing in one here, alienating another there; and had paid for it in the rain of jelly babies and Manila fists and Jesus hysterics and mad love, in the sacrifice of their safety and the burning of their youth.

These were the Beatles' barricades, and upon them they carved out as a life model the tenets which the radical movement would one day declare as the essence of revolution. Jon Wiener expresses that essence: "Liberation, self-emancipation, participatory democracy. The plan was that people should take part in making the decisions that affected their lives. The plan was to break out of the system that required official plans, and instead to liberate the imagination."[48] As much as anyone in public life, the Beatles had written that plan; and instead of proselytizing had lived it, through all the rewards and terrors. The Beatles had done their bit for the revolution by acting it out before the eyes of the world.

But in the righteous, absolutist terms of '68 radicalism, if you weren't part of the solution, you were part of the problem. To many, the Beatles, unlike Dylan and the Stones, were now part of the problem—despite being the sole inhabitants of the rock pantheon who had ever said they wanted to change the world. That it was not right-wing zealots but rock and roll revolutionaries now casting the Beatles as the enemy marks the newest turn in their story. Who would have thought that the Beatles could be so hated by so many of their own most fervent following, the generation whose individual and collective lives they had transformed in virtually every way?

Because hatred emanates from the critics' expressions of sadness, anger, and disillusion that the Beatles could be so oblivious to the radical mission, so blind to the clear necessities of the historical pivot. It's the hatred of the betrayed. The Beatles would still be loved by their generation, still valued; but for the first time they would be disdained too, and in some quarters never again fully trusted.[49] Suddenly, and for many of this generation permanently, the Beatles were not just on the other side of the line but on the outside of the circle.

The circle, with its magical, terrible powers: *Leave a row, and you can always go back to it. But once a circle closes, there is no return.*

The Beatles had changed the world by voicing a vow and opening holes in mass consciousness that could never be closed. And there was no way they could have foreseen, as Liverpool kids, as mere Quarry Men—so hungry for absolute connection that only an audience as large as the earth could feed them—that in opening those holes they would end by digging their own graves.

"Here is a painting I happened to drip red paint on. At first I was terribly upset, but then I started enjoying it. The trickle looked like a crack; it turned the building site into a battered old backdrop, a backdrop with a building site painted on it. I began playing with the crack, filling it out, wondering what might be visible behind it. And that's how I began my first cycle of paintings. I called it 'Behind the Scenes.' Of course, I couldn't show them to anybody. I'd have been kicked out of the Academy. On the surface, there was always an impeccably realistic world, but underneath, behind the backdrop's cracked canvas, lurked something different, something mysterious or abstract."

After pausing for a moment, she added, "On the surface, an intelligible lie; underneath, the unintelligible truth."

—Milan Kundera, *The Unbearable Lightness of Being* (1984)

and we lived
_____

In the summer of 1969, an engineer from Atlanta, Georgia, named Dan Taylor arrived in the Inverness region of the Scottish Highlands. He traveled to a secluded valley nestled between the Corrigoe and Monad Liadh mountain ranges, bringing with him a one-man submarine. Taylor's goal was to use the tiny craft to determine whether a certain often-glimpsed but never-verified creature truly inhabited the waters of a local lake—as centuries of valley legend and many contemporary witnesses claimed it did. In fact the lake had long been known, in the Gaelic tongue of the natives, as Loch na Beiste—"the Lake of the Monster."

The mini-sub was originally christened the *Viper-Fish.* But popular favor had redubbed it the *Yellow Submarine* well before Taylor squeezed in and submerged his vessel to troll the murky, peat-thickened depths of Loch Ness for signs of something neither nature nor science could explain.

The summer passed. Dan Taylor never spotted the monster.[1]

5

O.P.D. / *DEUS EST VIVUS*

The Beatles and the Death Cults

> To reason about holes seems to involve reasoning about the shape
> of an object, but also about its dispositions to interact with other
> objects; about the way in which a hole is or can be generated,
> modified, used, destroyed; and, finally, about the ways in which it
> is or can be perceived, identified, re-identified. We will track all of
> these clues.
>
> —Roberto Casati and Achille C. Varzi, *Holes and*
> *Other Superficialities* (1994)

In the beginning was the Word; and the Word was *you*.

□

Fair notice: at this point, the Beatles—not "the Beatles" but the four
men themselves—pretty much disappear from the story.

And a prefatory word to those readers who may not know or might
not believe: aside from speculations on the part of myself or other individuals—always clearly marked—everything described in this chapter actually happened.

□

We are never content with mere deductive explanations for traumatic shifts in the lives of entire generations. Plagues, assassinations—reality and causality are not enough to deal with them: they frustrate our instinct for proportion. So we invent the crime to fit the punishment, the myth to justify the monument. It is the only way of assigning meaning—however creative, crackpot, or plain crazy—to something that defies reason: a search for truth in which the search becomes the truth, and endings have purpose.

Artists, like the Beatles, search by means of their art. The rest of us use myths and legends—instruments in one way more limited than art, in another far more powerful. Myth has been described as a waking dream, and dreaming on a mass scale may be most effective when an era is freest in its potentials, when none of its possibilities or limits is quite nailed down. Myth takes over when those potentials are realized, and tremors become quakes. The time comes when we must *speak* our fears by making stories of them: what was unrecognized in its dream form takes the shape of narrative. The volatile, far-flung community becomes a campfire; frightening times become the darkness surrounding it; and unity, if we're lucky, is a result.

1969 was the moment for such myths. Few would say it, but nearly everyone felt it: the end was near. The end of that world which a generation had worked to build for itself, in the process compelling the generations on either side to respond to what that world contained and implied. And many people, eager to cluster into tight, fanatical groups of like minds—cults, in the soon-to-be-common designation—made myths to prepare for and even welcome the end, but mostly to master it by writing their own scenario upon it.

Most of the myths had an element of religion to them—for religions have always rejoiced in detailing how the end will come and who will suffer hardest by it. That the ragged end of the 1960s produced such an apocalyptic impulse is easy to fathom. The most traumatic year in recent U.S. memory had just past; heroes were dead, and to all appearances the same forces of darkness were in power and only growing stronger. Death was already eating at the heart of this generation's common body, in its music, its political confrontations, its dwindling store of viable leaders. Unable just yet to deal with defeat and death as looming realities, many of this generation recast them in the terms of myth.

The myths were, in one way or another, all about death—also a subject that religion was invented to deal with. What the Beatles had lately been attempting to cover up, successfully with *Sgt. Pepper,* less so with the White Album—that history was turning, and death was coming—was an anxiety which had always found release in religious myth: in religion death is meaningful, never random, its causes noble and divine. But there's no God without some sense of the devil: So it came to pass that midway into the year 1969, the holy and the profane were made to fuse. The angel and the demon of this generation, the good and evil of the time it had defined, came together for the End. And in the End, it fell again to the Beatles to midwife a mutation born of needs and desperations. It fell to them because in their unity the Beatles contained, and in their music expressed, the best of their generation's spirit—its most transformative values, its largest visions. It fell to them also because they had been, for some time, prophesying the compromise of those values, and the dimming of those visions.

Late 1969: the chronology of these few months is so irretrievably bizarre, so cosmically screwy with synchronicities and scattered insanities, that one is now tempted to reconceive of it as a mammoth conspiracy fiction handed down as historical fact. The substance of these few months was itself constructed of parallel fictions—the fictions around which two groups of people, far removed in space, circumstance, and ideology (or lack thereof), chose, for a time, to structure their lives in whole or in part. These community fictions made sacred truths of the most gruesome fantasies; they were equal parts Holy Bible and *National Inquirer*. For both groups, the wildest flights of Beatle-sparked imagination became both the stuff of life and the rationale for death. And though both fictions had everything to do with the Beatles, neither required the participation, consent, or acknowledgement of the Beatles themselves to rise and thrive.

Why do we make myths? We might as well ask why we make wars, or why we build gods. It is simply something we have always done: apparently we've had no choice. The other thing we've had no choice in is dying; and surely we make myths for the same reason we make wars and gods, or write books, or preserve our songs and paintings, or in some other manner mark our spot of earth in ways that will reach into the lives of those we'll never know: to defer as long as possible the certainty that one day, fairly soon, we'll be only another set of bones in the boneyard.

We have got to leave a trace behind.

□

> Attempting to classify holes is an important part of our work. It is convenient to have a general idea of what holes look like and of the various forms they can come in.
>
> —Casati and Varzi, *Holes and Other Superficialities*

Suddenly everyone was looking for a hole. Once there had been any number of circles to join; now, in 1969, a hole was the spatial metaphor of choice. In some ways a hole was the same as a circle: a space in the imagination. In other ways holes and circles were opposites. Circles were large, round, and flat against the earth; holes were deep, dark, and narrow. A circle was for inclusion; a hole was for keeping other people out.

That is how this theory of holes in the late '60s begins. But it doesn't end so simply. A taxonomy of 1969 holes is called for—an inquiry into types, methods, functions.

The Beatles, seeking a hole in their fame, began the year by going underground. They spent all of January rehearsing and recording songs for their next album, an album advertised with the tag-line "The Beatles as Nature Intended." *Get Back* was its symbolic title: the songs would be rock and roll primitive, free of overdubs and post-psychedelic fairy dust. By so stripping their music, they obviously hoped to renew their unity—but also to cleanse themselves of the mythic barnacles history and fantasy had placed upon them. It was both a search for the bog and another late-'60s escape attempt: the Beatles needed a hole for shelter, but, as always, their own needs had to be justified in terms of music and audience. In earlier passages their penchant for exotica had resulted in rich and strange diversities of sound; now their psychic need for the clean and simple would be channeled through music whose populist ethic was its basicness.

And *basic* meant *basic*. Even the White Album songs hadn't gotten back far enough. Those had been hard rock, often incredibly simple, but laden with a mature sense of doom and bewilderment. *Get Back* was meant as unadorned, head-in-the-sand rock and roll. Among the songs they focused on, performing it dozens of times in search of its essence, was "One after 909," a number John and Paul had written as teenagers, and first recorded in Paul's living room.

Meanwhile, thousands of miles away in southern California, Charles Manson was dreaming of a hole in the desert. The Hopi Indians of that region had for centuries retold a myth about the hole, which they believed lay hidden somewhere in the vast floor of Death Valley. Manson was obsessed with finding the hole, and at a certain point this jailhouse prophet and flower-power fascist began to tell people he had found it. He described the hole as an underground paradise where water cascaded and the very dirt was made of gold; and his plan was that he and his followers would descend into the hole, there to live until the apocalypse had come and gone and the band of underworld-dwelling gypsies would emerge to assume control of what was left.

"I found a hole in the desert," Manson is reported to have said. "I covered it up and I hid it. I called it . . . The Devil's Hole."[1]

Meanwhile, two thousand miles away in the American Midwest, another group of young people was searching for another kind of hole. Like a lot of holes, this one came in the shape of an O. This group kept searching for the O on the covers of Beatle albums, where, if you could find it, it was damaged, and if you couldn't, it was notable in its absence.

O was a letter you needed to form the word "love." And Paul McCartney, people now realized, was the only Beatle without an O in his name.

□

How do you describe what you see? A spot in the wall, darker than the rest, filled with shadow, that goes deep inside (though you cannot really tell how deep). It looks unitary and complete, compact, though less dense than the wall. A thing, perhaps, but a bit mysterious.

—Casati and Varzi, *Holes and Other Superficialities*

Most Americans first heard of a bizarre rumor involving Paul McCartney in the latter days of October 1969, when brief items began to appear at the margins of major newspapers.

It was a rumor like other rumors: no one knew quite where it had begun. But it began for the same reason that rumors always begin: someone, somewhere, dreamed up a notion. The myth of Paul McCartney's death materialized out of nothing because that someone, in whatever manner or measure, wanted it to be the truth. It then gathered force, turned nothing into something, because a large number of people found they *liked* the idea of its being the truth. At the time, some truly believed that Paul was dead, and that the Beatles were subtly and systematically revealing this fact in words and pictures. Many others suspected that Paul was as alive as you or me, but felt the clues were nonetheless there, planted by mischievous Beatles for no goal grander than their private amusement. Still others bypassed the factual question of death altogether, caring only to hunt up new clues. The rumor allowed all to take part, whatever their belief; it enabled fun from any position.

But that's too flippant, because in another way this was *not* a rumor like other rumors. Quickly, and mostly quietly—away from conventional media, passed by mouth, in the smoke and hush of dormitory rooms after midnight—it accrued a wealth of arcana, explanation, elaboration, mystification, and solemnization which put it well past the league of any other rumor one can name. Obviously it was not only fun the rumormongers were after. It was also a sense of involvement, being in on the creation of something excitingly bigger than any of them, which was nonetheless theirs. *All* theirs, since one didn't actually need the Beatles to play the game. You had no more need of the Beatles than the authors of the Gospels had needed Jesus: you needed only their artifacts, and the creative faculty to make narrative of them.

The death rumor, I like to believe, was the unconscious pursuit of a mystery—a historical mystery that was unfolding as it was being investigated. Unlike other rumors, it was a trivial exercise with a profound impulse. The conscious, articulated mysteries—Is Paul dead? If so, how did he die? How have the Beatles been telling us this?—were manageable, ostensibly answerable (and yes, fun) surrogates for other, deeper mysteries. Is our time, our moment in history, dead? If so, how did it die? How have the Beatles been telling us this? The rumormongers were generational detectives working on a case that had not been named. The crime scene, where traces would be sifted and fingerprints lifted, was the Beatles' post-1966 art. The corpse was the world their generation had dreamed, and so very nearly fought into being.

But who was the murderer?

☐

> The identity of a hole over time will have to be traced to some delicate interplay between the identity of the host and the identity of the filler.

—Casati and Varzi, *Holes and Other Superficialities*

Like most Americans, Charles Manson discovered the Beatles in the spring of 1964. Unlike most Americans, he was in prison—specifically the U.S. Penitentiary at McNeil Island, Washington State, where he'd been incarcerated since June 1961. He may have seen the Beatles' pictures in *Life* magazine, or heard their voices coming from a transistor radio. Instantly, he was excited by them. Some said obsessed. One of his friends, the legendary Alvin "Creepy" Karpis—in the '30s a member of Ma Barker's gang, now the fellow inmate who taught Manson guitar—said later, "He was constantly telling people he could come on like the Beatles, if he got the chance."[2]

The intensity of Manson's reaction was not unusual in that feverish spring; the precise quality of that reaction was. Manson's urgent response to what the Beatles were setting off was more akin to jealousy than joy—the sense not that something had been given him, but that something had been stolen. Those screams, he was implying to whoever would listen, were rightfully *his*. The Beatles seem to have awakened a latent sense of entitlement in this 29-year-old petty crook. Suddenly, with Alvin Karpis' guitar in his hands and the Beatles' music in his head, he had a purpose.

But where did it come from, this fierce certainty, unprecedented given Manson's record as an inveterate small-timer, that he had something to say that was worthy of being attended to by those awed millions? From what interior palette did this determinedly insignificant man—who had spent more than half his life in juvenile institutions and prisons, who had never aimed at any success higher than the next stolen car or forged check, and whose musical tastes ran to Perry Como and away from Elvis Presley—draw such a grand rock and roll vision of himself? What self-discipline enabled him to do honest time for the next three years, earn release in early 1967, and methodically recruit a cluster of fanatical followers over the next two years, all the while constructing an elaborate personal cosmology *and* staying clear of prison longer than he had since reaching his majority, long enough to orchestrate crimes that would place him near Hitler as a madman of the age?

Perhaps he drew the discipline from the dimensions of his prison cell. Unlike those experiencing the Beatles on the outside, those who could *do* something with their excitement, Manson found himself imprisoned with a burgeoning sense of possibility: torture, of a kind, to know that there is something out there to be done, and have no arms or legs with which to do it. But probably the sense of mission was most attributable to the fact that nothing like the Beatles had occurred in his lifetime. If they were truly something new, it was obvious that, as a result, other *somethings* would take shape; and that in among all the *somethings* wholesome and harmless there would be coiled others which were cruel, diseased, fixed on destruction.

So it's quite possible that Manson, wavering always between lucidity and psychosis, gifted equally in cool calculation and mystical fancy, was turned on by the Beatles because he knew instantly that something had changed: a hole had opened. It's quite possible that he saw as deeply into the potential of the Beatle phenomenon as anyone, far deeper than any objective newsman or social commentator, and knew that a universe of potentials, dormant the day before, had now come to trembling life. And it's quite possible that he took that opening as the personal cue which he, like the fifteen-year-old girl, had been waiting for his whole life. His chance to make a mark on his time, to influence mass consciousness. His time to go insane.

□

A discontinuity breaks in, and you can imagine how to restore the natural continuity of the surface so as to make the hole disappear. Thus, it is by perceiving discontinuity in the surface of the wall that you seem to perceive the hole.

—Casati and Varzi, *Holes and Other Superficialities*

The University of Michigan at Ann Arbor had been a pulse point of the New Left long before such a thing was perceived to exist—though it trundled through the '50s as a classic American "multiversity" of the time, explicitly devoted to producing useful technocrats for direct insertion into Cold War society.[3] An odd confluence of events and individuals—the civil rights movement, Old Left professors in fringe departments, a student subculture enamored of '50s rebels from Dean to Camus—bent the school into new forms as the '60s loomed. At a human rights conference in 1959, a tattered group called the Student League for Industrial Democracy was rechristened Students for a Democratic Society. Six years later, the campus sponsored the first anti-Vietnam teach-in. Ann Arbor produced the scene that produced the hyper-radical MC5 and John Sinclair's White Panther Party. Key movement people like Tom Hayden (once editor of the campus newspaper, the *Michigan Daily*) gravitated to Michigan as a community for both intellection and action. Todd Gitlin wrote that he moved from Harvard to Michigan "not so much to study political science (my ostensible purpose) as to breathe the air of the SDS circle."[4]

Ann Arbor, a spiritual birthplace of the student movement of the '60s, at the other end of the decade became the spiritual birthplace of the Paul McCartney death rumor—if not its true point of origin, then certainly the magic circle from which the myth and its details were dispersed. How did things travel, on one fairly representative American campus, from life to death—from programs to myths, pragmatic detail to mystical apocrypha?

It was perhaps the essential trajectory of this generation, in this decade: from ideals to action to retreat. Things had been heady once, Ann Arbor as rich with idealistic intrigue and world-moving plots as any point on the American map. But by late 1969, it was pretty much over—the action, if not the talk. Michigan's radical spirit was inextricably bound with the fate of SDS; and SDS, like a lot of other things, died its true death at Chicago's Democratic National Convention in 1968, where prime philosopher and strategist Hayden was arrested and prosecuted, along with the other Chicago Eight, for the crime of "conspiring to cross state lines with intent to incite riot."[5] Then came the coup de grâce: in June 1969, SDS staged its own convention in Chicago, and was effectively chewed asunder by its increasingly violent and doctrinaire factions. The group was taken over by the Weatherman contingent, a force of paramilitary extremists whose program amounted to radical reform through the most violent revolutionary means possible—direct, destructive attack.

That attack was made, again in Chicago, between October 8 and October 11—the so-called Days of Rage. "Against all reason and good sense," wrote Weatherman Bo Burlingham, "some four hundred of us donned hard hats, padding, and work gloves, picked up chains and rocks, and went wild in the streets—before the astonished eyes of America's roughest, toughest police force." It started with a march and a chant. It progressed to the destruction of shopfronts, cars, lobbies, and streetlights, and the firing of shots. It ended with a siege of Haymarket Square that lasted, Burlingham thought, "all of twenty-five minutes."[6]

A replay of Chicago the year before—but with a difference. The 1968 riot had begun as a cluster of mostly peaceful assemblies and vigorous protests pushed into anarchy by official paranoia; violence for its own sake had not been the goal of most protesters. Whereas the Days of Rage were conceived as a suicide mission. "We felt," remembered Burlingham, "like miners trapped in a terrible poisonous shaft with no light to guide us out. We resolved to destroy the tunnel even if we risked destroying ourselves in the process." In the heat of the riot, Burlingham foresaw his own death, and the death of his movement. "I have yet to encounter a single participant in that day's action who did not believe he or she was going to die on October 11, 1969."[7]

Each stage of the radical movement's decline into factionalism, bloodlust, and hysteria tracked back in some way to Ann Arbor, to the wild notions sprung by a few willful idealists in some early '60s student enclave. And from out of Ann Arbor, late in 1969, on the other side of time—three days after the climactic Day of Rage—sprang another wild notion, one having to do with death, not birth. On October 14, a student named Fred LaBour published an article in the same *Michigan Daily* that had run Tom Hayden's earliest editorials on participatory democracy. LaBour's piece was no less sensitive to the signs of its time.

"McCartney Dead," its banner proclaimed. "New Evidence Brought to Light."[8]

□

> Now, our suggestion is that this shift is pretty close to what we need in order to overcome the apparent complexity of the hole problem. . . . We do, however, need a better way to characterize it. We need a general criterion that tells us, given a certain hole, what its skin is.
>
> —Casati and Varzi, *Holes and Other Superficialities*

On March 21, 1967, Charles Manson walked out of prison and went to Los Angeles. After a few days he made his way to Berkeley, and there, playing his guitar in a university plaza, he met a young librarian named Mary Brunner. The plain-faced bookworm from Eau Claire sat and listened as he sang, charmed, flattered, spun tales, and expounded wonders. Just like that, Manson had bagged his first zombie.[9]

Almost constantly on the move, sucking strays into his cult with absurd ease, he and those he collected would blaze a strange trail through the year of *Sgt. Pepper.*

That summer, Manson zeroed in on Haight-Ashbury. The hippie hub was on its way to the point where drugs and sex ceased to be experimental subversions of the status quo and became habitual indulgences; runaways from the split-levels of Middle America lined the curbs, waiting. The Haight became Manson's Hamburg: the teeming toilet where he decided his potential, sized up the game, honed his act, and found his audience. Like Hamburg, "Hashbury" was vice-ridden and pulsing, filled with fried brains and sick souls. An ex-con with long hair, guitar, imp's grin, and line of religioso blather could not have landed himself in a richer field of opportunity than the accumulating wastelands of the drug culture. But Manson did not stay: he saw, correctly, that the Hashbury high was turning ugly. So he decided to take his band of gypsies out of this overstimulated environment and hit the road for some Merry Prankster–type adventures. Just as well: soon enough the same lost boys and girls would be spilling out of the urban centers and into the country, trickling through the suburbs and out to the deserts. There would be no shortage of candidates for indoctrination, no dearth of guru-hunger.

By the way: the little Manson mob left Haight-Ashbury not long before George Harrison arrived for his own epiphany at summer's end.

The next months were spent driving up and down the California coast in a converted school bus, picking up eager young bodies. Patricia Krenwinkle, Susan Atkins, Bruce Davis: along with a few others, they came to form the hard core of Manson acolytes. All were from straight backgrounds—families, college, Bible study. But Atkins' family was broken, Davis was a dropout, and Manson soon had Krenwinkle plumbing the Bible for its seediest sediments, its meatiest rhapsodies on submission, violence, apocalypse. Everything straight about these post-adolescent drifters was in some way crooked, and Manson found he had a gift for locating the twisted nerve of a straight influence and twisting it harder, so that a hatred of family became love of the Family, and a passion for the Bible became a course of study in righteous massacre.

Manson's best-connected pickup during this period was Bobby Beausoleil, aspiring rock musician and occasional pornography stud.[10] He had been used by the avant-garde filmmaker Kenneth Anger in a Satan-slanted short film which was eventually screened in 1969 as *Invocation of My Demon Brother*. Beausoleil educated Manson on what Anger had taught him about the diabolical philosophies of the pioneer satanist, sensualist, and "magick" theorist Aleister Crowley. "'Do what thou wilt,'" ran Crowley's most familiar axiom, "shall be the whole of the law."[11]

By the way: Aleister Crowley's gloomy countenance, sagged by dope and the Devil, can be seen among the other famed faces on the cover of *Sgt. Pepper*.

"The Beatles to the rescue," Ed Sanders writes of the Manson gang's response to *Magical Mystery Tour*. By December 1967, they had been traveling and living in their bus a good while, and here were the Beatles, as if by magic—or "magick"—pulling up in their own bus to validate the vision and join the trip. Sanders places *Tour* as "the first Beatles album from which Manson drew philosophical guidance. The whole black bus trip came to be called 'The Magical Mystery Tour.'" And where were the Beatles guiding this burgeoning family? Toward what horizon? In Sanders' characterization, "[The Family] were into such a trip of mystic transformation that [they] evidently believed that there was an archetypal core personality in each human that could be discovered through acid-zap, mind-moil, role-playing, bunch-punching, magic, blasting-the-past, and commune-ism. This was the Magical Mystery Tour."[12]

Paul Watkins, an early Family recruit and, for a time, its de facto second-in-command, defined Manson's use of *Tour* thus: "From the beginning, Charlie believed the Beatles' music carried an important message—to us. He said their album *The Magical Mystery Tour* expressed the essence of his own philosophy. Basically, Charlie's trip was to program us all to submit: to give up our egos."[13]

Where did Manson find all this? Were such things truly implied in "Your Mother Should Know," "Blue Jay Way," "The Fool on the Hill"—acid-zap, mind-moil, et cetera? Bunch-punching, whatever that is? Program? Submit? Did these wicked pastimes and nefarious goals have anything to do with what the Beatles were meant to be about?

Well, obviously they did—for one person. "Sleazo inputs" is the term Sanders employs for the Hashbury drugs, twisted religion, hip California Satan worship, all the stimuli which Manson poured eagerly into his personal churn of psychosis, social resentment, and self-glorifying domination fantasy.[14] Sleazo inputs—like rock and roll, come to think of it, or Liverpool cellars, or all-night Hamburg hell-raisings—are often what make mutations happen. And precisely because they are unstable, they will shift shape in interaction with other components, particularly when combined in the crucible of a sick mind bent on revenge. Though Sanders doesn't categorize them as such, it's clear that the Beatles were another sleazo input.

But not *just* another—one of the most critical. Of Manson's defining '60s influences, the Beatles were among the most intensively studied and longest-lived. Their presence in his hateful odyssey stretches from first American mania to the end of the decade: He seems to have derived a highly personalized interpretation and drawn a very particular sustenance from almost everything they did, post–McNeil Island. Again and again, their paths and stars somehow cross; at each stage Manson is a hellhound on the trail of the Beatles' apparently happy trip through the '60s, the psychotropic fiend let loose in their psychedelic dream.

Or maybe it's the other way around.

On the evening of March 21, 1967, three Beatles were in Abbey Road's studio two, recording vocals for the *Sgt. Pepper* track "Getting Better." John, Paul, and George stood at their mikes, chanting the song's queasy mix of gaiety and fatalism. Suddenly John said he felt sick. Courtly George Martin, in all innocence and kindness, escorted Lennon to the studio roof for some fresh air, whereupon he returned to the control booth. An interval passed. Paul and George wondered where John was. "Looking at the stars," Martin replied.

Mark Lewisohn describes the next anxious moments: "What Martin said suddenly struck the two Beatles with force. They knew *why* John was ill—he was in the middle of an LSD trip—and yet he had been left alone on the roof of studio two which has no rails or barriers, just a sheer drop of about thirty feet to the ground below. He was quickly fetched down to the studio before he killed himself."[15]

Whew. Just a little acid indigestion, a minor freak-out nearly resulting in the untimely obliteration of John Lennon's skull, here in the midst of *Pepper* magic and the year of the flower and everything getting better all the time, the very day Charles Manson leaves McNeil Island to stake his claim on eternity in southern California.

□

MYTHING IN ACTION: FIRST DIGRESSION
We have seen that holes do not necessarily depend on their hosts.
But they do necessarily depend on having actual hosts.

—Casati and Varzi, *Holes and Other Superficialities*

On October 18, 1969, an article appeared in *Rolling Stone* under the byline of T. M. Christian. Its first sentence: "They began months ago, the rumours of an event that at first seemed hardly believable but which in the end was accepted as all but inevitable."[16]

Christian's piece was not about the death of Paul McCartney. It was a review of a new album, the eponymous debut of a supergroup called the Masked Marauders—whose line-up, Christian assured the incredulous, consisted of John Lennon, Mick Jagger, Paul McCartney, Bob Dylan, George Harrison, "and a drummer as yet unnamed." The unimaginable assemblage had held a three-day jam session "in a small town near the site of the original Hudson Bay Colony in Canada"; fashionable progressive-rock mastermind Al Kooper had served as producer. Among the songs recorded were Donovan's "Season of the Witch" (sung by Dylan); Dylan's "Masters of War" (a Jagger-McCartney duet); and James Brown's "Prisoner of Love" ("an indescribable twelve-minute John Lennon extravaganza"). There were nods to '50s nostalgia, including "Duke of Earl" and "I Am the Japanese Sandman (Rang Tang Ding Dong)." There were even new songs, penned especially for the Marauder sessions: Dylan's "Cow Pie," and Jagger's "I Can't Get No Nookie."[17]

Now these historic recordings were seeing the light of commercial issue, on a two-record set from the obscure Deity label. In Christian's estimation, the results were astounding, ineffable, beyond the beyond: "It can truly be said that this album is more than a way of life; it *is* life."[18]

Only, "this album" didn't exist. Not yet, anyway.

Ralph J. Gleason blew the whistle in his San Francisco *Chronicle* column: "It was intended as a joke. That's right, son, a joke." But a lot of people bought the T. M. Christian account, despite its unlikely details and the writer's overwrought gosh-wowisms. "Allen Klein, the business manager of the Rolling Stones and the Beatles, called and wanted to know where he could get [the album]. Albert Grossman, Dylan's manager, had his secretary ring through and ask, and one of the local KSAN disc jockeys wanted to know when they were going to get their copy. Al Kooper ... refused to comment to a reporter in New

York, thus adding to the mystery." Gleason, wrapping up his kibosh, saluted the Marauders as "a delightful bit of instant mythology."[19]

But it didn't end there. Stunned by the outbreak of Marauder-mania, the engineers of the hoax convened some local musicians and made a tape which more or less fit the original review's specifications. The hoaxers then, says Robert Draper, "took the tape to KMPX-FM, San Francisco's hippest station, and the session was aired. More hysteria. Motown Records offered to pay $100,000 for the tape. Instead, the Marauders cut a $15,000 deal with Warner Brothers. Phony press releases were drummed up and faithfully printed in *Billboard, Record World,* and *New York.*"[20] And so the album appeared, the album that hadn't existed when it was reviewed. Same jacket design as seen in *Rolling Stone;* liner notes by the same T. M. Christian; same Deity imprimatur, with its obscure Latin motto: *Deus est vivus.* "God lives."

Hopeful consumers listened to *The Masked Marauders* and discovered it sounded precisely like what it was: something tossed together by a chain-pulling *Rolling Stone* writer and a few musician friends, all blowing a weekend by doing their best rock-star impersonations in between cans of beer. I.e., it was musical dog food. At that point—the limit of gullibility being directly related in the case of many people to the actual outlay of money—the jig was up. This wasn't any supersession.

Eventually it was ascertained that "T. M. Christian" was the alias of critic and merry prankster Greil Marcus. The record itself ended with the Marauders' auto-epitaph, growled by a brusque voice in a transport of indignation, to the accompaniment of a lone piano and uproarious boozy laughter: "I paid five dollars—and eighty-six cents—for a record that has Bob Dylan . . . Paul McCartney . . . George Harrison . . . John Lennon . . . and an unbilled drummer—ooh—plus Mick Jagger. And what do I get? *This piece of shit!*"[21]

"Be nice if they play it on the air," a calm, wistful voice says as the record ends. Be nice, too, if this singular instance of spontaneous creation-participation—fabricated by fans for their own delight, hijacking their rock deities as unwitting conspirators—were not completely forgotten; if this piece of insanity were to survive in the dimmer regions of pop's collective memory.

Maybe it does, even now; maybe it only waits to rise again. Robert Draper finishes off the saga of the Masked Marauders—or rather, passes on its last recorded installment.

> Years later, Greil Marcus's brother met some fellows who insisted on playing for him a truly rare bootleg recording. Steve Marcus laughed, and told them the tale of the Masked Marauders. The fellows shrugged, saying they didn't know anything about that but what Marcus was about to hear was a genuine Lennon/Jagger/Dylan supersession.
>
> As the first notes sounded, Steve Marcus exclaimed, "This is it! I'm telling you, this is my brother's band!"
>
> But his new friends refused to believe him. The Masked Marauders, darling of the critics, would live on.[22]

As last words and aesthetic judgments go, *This piece of shit!* may not be unjust. But here is another, nobler epitaph for the band that never really was—more fitting for a delightful bit of instant mythology:

THE MASKED MARAUDERS

1969–?

"More than a way of life; it *is* life."

Deus est vivus

□

Holes are spacious; they are made of space; they consist of "bare," unqualified matter. They are—we shall say—immaterial bodies, "growing" parasitically, like negative mushrooms, at the surfaces of material bodies.

—Casati and Varzi, *Holes and Other Superficialities*

Not all of Fred LaBour's evidence was, strictly speaking, new. The rumor of Paul McCartney's demise had been circulating among rock-fixated Midwestern college students for at least a month before his article appeared in the October 14 *Michigan Daily*.

Thanks to the prodigious efforts of Andru J. Reeve, author of *Turn Me On, Dead Man: The Complete Story of the Paul McCartney Death Hoax*, the story's trail may be traced back—to a point. Reeve discovered that the death rumor and many of its core clues had been propagated prior to LaBour's article, in a UPI wire release sourced back to John Summer, an Ohio Wesleyan University student. Summer had heard the rumor at a party, from a stranger who claimed Paul's death was the excited talk of Drake University in Des Moines, Iowa, hundreds of miles away.[23] Indeed, what Reeve identifies as the first college newspaper article to detail the rumor—in fact probably the first media mention of any kind, anywhere—had appeared in the Drake *Times-Delphic* on September 17.[24] Its author, Tim Harper, had gotten the story from one Dartanyan Brown, Drake student and aspiring rock musician.

And how had it reached Brown? There the trail pretty much ends, on a blank face and a nonentity. Brown, whose home often served as headquarters to whatever band was passing through Des Moines, came home from class one Friday night to find a group of strangers— "long-haired musicians and their girlfriends"—crashing in his living room. "Brown didn't recognize any of the people who visited the house that night," Reeve writes, "and he never saw them again." Among those never to be seen again was a girl who "spent the entire evening talking about some supposed secret messages on Beatles albums and how they suggested Paul McCartney's death."[25]

This girl—not known to Brown, her name unremembered—is the nonentity; hers is the blank face. She made the first recorded utterance of what became a signal myth of her time, and as far as anyone knows she is the hole from which it sprang—as well as the hole into which it disappears if one attempts to know it fully, understand and dismiss the myth by means of names, dates, places, precise origins. Where had the girl come from? Where was she going? Had she invented the story herself, or was she merely passing on what she'd heard somewhere along the bar-band interstate?

Harper's article was picked up and, with minimal adjustments, rewritten for Northern Illinois University's *Northern Star* of September 23.[26] The rumor had sown a solid row through the field of Midwestern academia. Now it moved north. On the night of October 12, there was an unusual broadcast on WKNR-FM, Detroit's underground rock station.[27] Disc jockey Russ Gibb took a call from a young man who identified himself as Tom, a student at Eastern Michigan University.

> *Gibb:* Yeah, hello, Tom, what's going down.
> *Tom:* Oh, well, I go to school at—
> *Gibb:* Have you got your radio on?
> *Tom:* Uh, yeah, some—
> *Gibb:* Yeah—yeah, turn it off, man, 'cause you're giving us feedback.
> *Tom:* Um . . . I was gonna rap with you about, uh, McCartney being dead and what is this all about.[28]

Gibb knew nothing of the rumor; before the evening was over, he knew quite a lot. The caller gave him very specific instructions on which Beatle songs to play, at which speed and in which direction, so as to reveal some of the more striking "clues."

> Well, the youngster said would you play one cut for me on the air, forward. And he said take the album *Revolution,* and—what we call the White Album. Play a cut called "Revolution #9." And play it forward. And as you do so, a guy comes on and says, "Number nine, number nine, number nine." He repeats it . . .

> And at that point the kid said, "Now, play that back-
> wards." And I played it backwards, and man, I freaked. I
> went—I went crazy because of the fact—it says, "Turn me
> on, dead man." And I just flipped out.

So, evidently, did a lot of people who were listening that night,
among them Fred LaBour. "At that point," Gibb said, "the switch-
board at the station started to light up like crazy and kids started to
call in—"[29]

That is how rumors catch fire and spread; that is how something
like Paul-is-dead becomes, in Nicholas Schaffner's phrase, "a genuine
folktale of the mass communications era."[30] But it could not end
there, a mere folktale, as other rumors had. The Beatles had always
taken whatever they did a step beyond—beyond the obvious into
something else. Their rumormongering fans, spotting their chance to
write Beatle history, create a whole new Beatle myth, followed suit
and took a step beyond—into the mythifying impulse of the past. Get
back, indeed.

For centuries the practice of creating epochal narratives which
would give coherence to whole stretches of common history, imaginatively explaining a people to itself, was efflorescent in societies all
over the world; in fact it was seen as a conscious and meaningful *function* of society. The impulse had always dictated not just beholding an
image of worship or documenting earthly disaster but recreating
them, with back-story, detail, elaborate systems of interpretation.
But while classical myth might attempt to explain a great flood or the
rise of a deistic regime, thereby making the random or calculated appear natural and inevitable, it knew it could not understand everything: only the gods held all the keys. Myth in its grandest sense,
then, was the recounting of a mystery which might be explained but
never resolved. Then came whole sweeping ages of renaissance and
reformation, enlightenment and reason: myth took other forms,

25. London, 1966: Worshippers in tribal dress and occult markings make an early, unsuccessful attempt at securing Paul McCartney's eternal soul as the ultimate Beatle souvenir.

scientific hypothesis or philosophical tract, more limited forms which believed mystery could be subdued by objective analysis. The mythic tradition of *Gilgamesh* and the *Odyssey* and the Bible was lost to antiquity. Few seemed to miss it.

Yet now, toward the end of the twentieth century—spacemen on the moon!—the Paul McCartney death ghouls were, like comic-book archeologists, working their way back to that first mythic drive, partly because the process was fun and partly because their bones told them that the move was right for this moment. Technology could disseminate the rumor, deductive inquiry enlarge it, but nothing short of a surrender to the fantastic would explain the hole this generation was sinking into—the ultimate failure it felt impending.

With the WKNR broadcast, Paul-is-dead had nearly reached the point where it would cease to be the property of a clued-in campus underground extending from Des Moines, Iowa, to DeKalb, Illinois, to Delaware, Ohio, to Ypsilanti, Michigan. What it now needed was its own Homer, someone to gather the dangling strings of theory and all the scattered intimations into a streamlined piece of modern myth. This meant that, in the telling, everything would be made to seem the logical outcome of divine, or at least Beatle-directed, processes. It meant that religion was invoked—for how else to deal with what seems past temporal understanding? It also meant inventing the *how,* the *when,* and the *where* to go with the *what.* The earlier articles had merely listed the clues; LaBour fabricated the dates, places, and chain of events that would connect them. Finally, his was no small achievement: imagine having written, as an unassuming college undergraduate, what for all time will be the "official" story of Paul McCartney's death.

It began: "Paul McCartney was killed in an automobile accident in early November, 1966, after leaving EMI recording studios tired, sad and dejected." There'd been a fight at Abbey Road. "Paul climbed into his Aston-Martin, sped away into the rainy, chill night, and was found four hours later pinned under his car in a culvert with the top of his head sheared off." Myths have always gloried in violence; not enough that Paul is dead—his upper cranium is missing. "Thus began the greatest hoax of our time and the subsequent founding of a new religion based upon Paul as Messiah."[31] (Let that sentence lie, for the moment.)

The surviving Beatles were not prepared to go gently into Paul's good night. The death was kept secret, the period of mourning brief: George dug the grave, Ringo lowered the coffin, and John—who else?—conceived a monumental scheme after three days in seclusion. The survivors would locate a McCartney imposter, integrate him into public life as McCartney per se, "then slowly release the information of the real Paul's death to the world via clues secreted in record albums."[32]

This presented LaBour with a logistical problem: How to explain the Paul McCartney who had been seen in public and on television fairly recently, who had been heard in the months since November 1966 singing "Penny Lane" and "Lady Madonna" and "Hey Jude"? LaBour's solution was inspired. "A Paul Look-a-Like contest was held and a living substitute found in Scotland. He was an orphan from Edinburgh named William Campbell." Our student journalist is flying now, making myth on the wing. "Minor plastic surgery was required . . . mustache distracted everyone who knew . . . nearly erased entirely his own speech patterns."[33] With a slap and a tickle, Paul McCartney's shadowy doppelgänger is born.

An annotated list of death clues follows. The clues themselves, collated in sequence, given the appearance of logical development, go well beyond the audio freakeries that so blew Russ Gibb's mind. Many clues required LaBour to fabricate abstruse rituals and cultic symbols from foreign lands, which teased the undergrad mentality with a whiff of erudition and no troublesome specifics. A sampling:[34]

Inside the *Pepper* gatefold, Paul's shoulder patch apparently reads

O.P.D., a British acronym for Officially Pronounced Dead. (Yes, but why a *patch?*)

There is a hand over McCartney's head on the front cover: "The hand behind the head is a symbol to mystics of death." (Which mystics?)

"Empty shoes, as appear next to Ringo's drums on page thirteen [of the *Magical Mystery Tour* booklet], were a Grecian symbol of death." (When?)

"'Walrus' is Greek for corpse." (Hellenistic Greek? Biblical? Modern?)

"'Octopus's Garden' is British Navy slang for the cemetery in England where naval heroes are buried." (What's the address?)

Obviously it was not sufficient that these signs of death be present merely for their own macabre sake; there must be a rationale, and none presented itself more readily than the deistic. In LaBour's reading, the just-released *Abbey Road* is a New Testament proclaiming the new Beatle religion, conceptualized by John and predicated on Paul's dead body and risen spirit. "On the cover is John Lennon, dressed in white and resembling utterly an anthropomorphic God . . . followed by Paul the resurrected."[35] The suite of songs on side two "announces the principles upon which the religion will be based: beauty, humor, love, realism, objectivity."[36] A utopian synthesis of the best hippie and radical urges, the core values of two youth movements presently in the process of decay.

But decay, Fred LaBour assures his readers, will lead to renaissance under the benediction and guidance of the reconstituted Beatles, John-God at the karmic wheel, Paul-Jesus walking as a holy wraith among the living. "And at the end, Paul ascends to the right hand of John and proclaims, 'The love you take is equal to the love you make.'" Ah!—but what, then, of "Her Majesty," the one-verse McCartney morsel slipped in just after *Abbey Road*'s divine peroration, as if to puncture its pretenses, ground its grandiosity? "But in the VERY end, they are joking about the Queen. The Beatles are building a mighty church, and when you emerge from it, you will be laughing, for Paul is the Sun of God."[37]

That explains that. *Deus est vivus.*

"McCartney Dead" was a joke, and a good one. Though the *Michigan Daily* coupled it with an artist's rendering of Paul's disembodied head—cribbed from a photo in the White Album collage—LaBour's article contained so many absurdities that it's hard to see how anyone bought it. But often jokes are good because they tap into truths, and there were two assertions buried (apt word) in the article which, because they were not paused over, suggest the writer was on to more than he knew. Those who took the rumor from LaBour and got to work excavating their own clues may have been responding to the joke, to the creative opportunity it offered, but they were acting on those buried assertions—the hidden truths that gave immediacy to the joke and resonance to the excited hunt for any vague trace of death.

The first was the author's blasé promotion of myth over man. It is important only that the Beatles offer the symbology of resurrection at Abbey Road, not the fact of it. Beatle flesh, animate or not, is irrelevant to the mythic project: "The real Paul is still dead, of course, but his symbolic resurrection works fine without him."[38] A for insight, Mr. LaBour.

The second was his interpretation of the *Sgt. Pepper* cover shot. If anyone looking at the picture back in the Summer of Love, when *Pepper* ruled the earth, ever saw the Beatles' bed of soil and plot of multicolored flora as anything but a garden of plenty, promising limitless growth and endless bloom, they didn't mention it. Only now, in 1969, were people claiming—in just such a flat, earnest voice as LaBour's, as if the matter had never been in question—that the cover of *Sgt. Pepper* depicted not a garden, but a grave.

□

An analogous problem is the famous Peircean puzzle of the color
of the line dividing a black spot from its white background on a
continuous surface. We do not have any reason to say that the line
is either black or white, and we could choose among some alternatives. It could be meaningless to attribute any color to the line. It
could be that the line is both black and white, so that there would
be true contradictions in nature. It could also be that the line is
neither black nor white, thus allowing for indeterminacies in
nature.

—Casati and Varzi, *Holes and Other Superficialities*

"When I met him, there was no violence in the Family, no talk of Helter-Skelter; in fact, it was the complete opposite. Charlie's love then
was real."[39]

Such was Paul Watkins' impression when he first met Manson, in
March 1968. The Family were by then living in an abandoned house
in the hills of Topanga Canyon, near Santa Monica. Under Manson's
direction they were stuck in a post-hippie, *fin-de-siècle* rut of aimless
sensualism: there was nothing to do, nothing to be desired, beyond
getting high and making love. Group sex was a nightly ritual, drugs
grossly abundant. Music was forever in the air: jam sessions ended
with Manson and his hordes howling at the moon.

Watkins was impressed by Manson—"a jovial little dude," as he
first appeared.[40] Founder and leader of what looked like a peaceful
commune and hedonist's paradise, he must have appeared masterful
to the teenage searcher already thrown by both establishment and
hippie perversions of the psychedelic idyll. Manson was drug dealer,
bandmate, lover, father, doctor, advisor—and he used each role as a
wedge into the immature, drug-loosened, all-accepting, deeply hungry, and poorly protected heads of the driftwood kids who came his
way. His manipulative brilliance lay in his ability to tailor his tech-
niques to the needs of each initiate. Watkins describes Manson's skill

in talking one frightened girl through her first LSD horror: he begins with the blunt command, "Look at Death!" and ends with the tender instruction, "Don't let anyone into your head but me."[41]

Then there was Manson's articulated philosophy. "Charlie's rap about life," Watkins admitted, "was in direct harmony with my own feelings: 'I am you and you are me,' he said. 'What we do for ourselves, man, we do for everyone. There's no good in life other than coming to the realization of the love that governs it. . . . Coming to 'Now,' dig?"[42] All of this was Manson's hippie face, sparking with cosmic wisdom and boundless love, great humor and unashamed sex—a thin layer concealing another, deeper face.

Things took their first turn for the weird, it would seem, in early May 1968, when Manson moved the Family to a place called the Spahn Ranch, near the town of Chatsworth, California. By every account, this was a miserable site for anyone's existence. Though in its very filth the ranch qualified as "authentic" under hippie ethics (nothing plastic about its squalor), it was also antithetical to those ethics because it so reeked of death: the stagnant landscape—rocky hills, scrub brush, choked weeds, mud-thickened streams—bespoke the agricultural equivalent of a rotting, bony corpse. As if Nature itself had given up on this world.

It's certain Manson chose the Spahn Ranch for its isolation: he needed a protected perch from which to hatch his plans. It could also be that he chose it for the same reason the Beatles had chosen their own pockets of filth years before: *because* it was foul, *because* it was underground, *because* reaching the heights of adulation meant serving a dues-paying period of abjection in the lowest of conditions. If Manson's ambition was the world's submission, then he must be first to submit to ambition's demand. Watkins wrote of days at Spahn when "Charlie used to sit on the boardwalk in the sun and laugh, letting the flies crawl all over him: 'Man, you gotta submit to the flies. . . . Let's face it, they own this place.'"[43]

Whoever submits to Manson's music will find this a theme near to his heart. He recorded a number of original songs at a studio in Van Nuys, California, on August 9, 1968—one year to the day before the murders that would imprint him on history.[44] The Family is a presence throughout the songs—occasional backing vocal, odd percussive gesture—but for the most part it is only Manson, his voice and guitar, singing for you. It is a bit disconcerting. This is Charlie the hippie philosopher, the easy smiler and embracer of life who had so little difficulty making all the children fall in love with him. Yet you know this is a voice capable of horrible violence, belonging to someone who committed such violence, who ordered it committed in his name. Even if it sounds like Manson is singing about love, what he is really singing about is murder.

"My own admittedly unprofessional appraisal," wrote Vincent Bugliosi, "was that Manson was no worse than many performers in current vogue."[45] He was right: Manson's voice, guitar, and song-sense even now sound "no worse," and on occasion even a little better, than many folk-inflected, schmaltz-infected singer-songwriters of the period. Had Helter Skelter never happened—had Charles Manson grown up differently and been encouraged toward music and away from evil—he might well be recalled now, with some fondness, as a purveyor of refreshing if fuzzy-brained acoustic preachments from the nuttier realms of the late '60s drug religion. One of his songs might have been a hit, and might now be a staple of classic-rock radio and reissues from Rhino Records.

Except for that submission thing. "Cease to Exist" is the best of Manson's songs, the least precedented and the most haunting—the one that, on feel alone, might have been a hit. Manson's voice here is strong, sensual, and wooing. He picks his notes tenderly, as a distant electric guitar creates wisps of blue smoke behind him. The tempo goes from a languid sway to an insistent thrust; the girls support him with a near-silent wail and echo. Manson sings a few well-chosen words of love, death, and domination—*Give up your world* is the theme—the far-off guitar quivers between two notes and dematerializes, and that's it. The song is very brief, really only the beginning of something—the first phrases of an invocation never completed. It is either the soundtrack to the sleaziest Satan-porn movie in existence or the creepiest thing ever laid on a piece of recording tape. It could be both.

It is Manson in all of his evil charm and liquescent appeal. All his warmest promises are here, all his come-ons, all his domination mania. Also here, perhaps, are two layers of the doubtless infinitely complex motivation behind Helter Skelter. The words of the title imply that submission equals death; and therefore that death is the only means of fully experiencing life. Such was his mystical rationale for a creed of peace based, ultimately, on the most savage destruction of life. But the core of that creed was submission—not, as in other alternative philosophies of the time, to the beat of one's own heart, or even the shifts and cycles of some unfathomable universal karma, but to *me*. While another line of lyric, recalling what McNeil Island witnesses reported as Manson's intense Beatle-jealousy, states it more bluntly: *We all get our turn*. Left unsaid: *And my turn is now*.[46]

As it came about, "Cease to Exist" almost *was* a hit. Through the intercession of drummer Dennis Wilson, a Manson enthusiast whose mansion the Family were currently inhabiting, the Beach Boys recorded it as "Never Learn Not to Love."[47] They sweetened Manson's hemlock with their trademark swirls of California harmony and conventionalized the Svengali lyrics, but otherwise the song came through remarkably intact—i.e., still a bummer. Sinister has never been the sound of the Top 40. Hidden on the B-side of an unsuccessful single and the middle range of an unsuccessful album, "Never Learn Not to Love" sank into the oblivion reserved, in 1968, for the morbid and ungroovy leftovers of last year's hippie-think.

With it went Manson's best chance of usurping by musical means the Beatles' audience and seizing the power radiating from those young female bodies. By October, Dennis Wilson had evicted the Family from his mansion, and none of his industry friends seemed interested in the creepy Family album. It is really anyone's guess what prompted Manson, in the next several months, to turn his final corner; but the failure of his musical ambitions certainly played a role in accelerating his descent, into both irretrievable psychosis and the dry, loveless wastes of Death Valley, where he moved the Family on October 15.

At the time of Manson's trial in 1970, his lieutenant Gypsy described what she perceived to be the geological history and physical features of Death Valley: "There have been these gigantic explosions there. A whole mountain will fly off and leave this giant hole. The Fault runs right through Death Valley, and in the last time, there will be an earthquake that will open up the earth for all those who love."[48]

By the way: there is a "fault," a crack, running through the word *BEATLES* on the rear cover of *Abbey Road*.

"There is this pool in Death Valley which goes down to the center of the earth, where the aware live forever. . . . There will be a door of water that will open up for us to enter. You know the Beatles song 'Glass Onion'? Well, the glass onion is the door of water, and the 'hole in the ocean' is the pool in Death Valley."[49]

Unlikely as it seems, there is some basis for Gypsy's colorful survey: Death Valley did hide secrets beneath its surface. Robert Murphy, former superintendent of Death Valley National Monument, writes, "Not one of the streams that flow down the slopes into the valley ever reaches the sea. It is a land of upside down rivers, with stream beds on top and water beneath the sand and gravel."[50] Upside-down rivers, subterranean waters: not quite the Atlantean wonderland evoked by Gypsy via Manson and the Hopis, but myth needs only the seed to sprout vines from dust. It was here in the lowland of natural death and hidden waterlines that such a living extension sprang up, and

Manson became obsessed with locating the hole of the Hopis. "The family would go out on Hole patrol," Sanders says, "to try to find hidden openings to The Hole. Manson seems to have claimed that he had personal access to The Hole and was able to go down there, or so he got his followers to believe."[51]

It was a lie, but a meaningful one. He had emerged, on March 21, 1967, from a hole, and now he was looking to get back into one: a hole enabling him to escape from the world which had spurned and imprisoned him, but a hole leading as well to the material realization of the mystical world in his head. If the hole signified escape, it also meant a return to confinement. It was a confirmation of the world's opinion of Manson, but it also represented a vindication of his greatness. The hole was his Shangri-La; it was also the final dungeon of death.

The Death Valley expedition was a failure. Manson never found the hole he was looking for—not there. But a month later, back in a Los Angeles suburb, he found it in the White Album. The Beatles to the rescue: what Death Valley had withheld, they would provide. Literally within days of first exposure, Manson had seized upon the White Album, along with the Bible, as his main source of world-revolutionary inspiration.[52] From the Book of Revelation, Manson derived a programmatic picture of how the apocalypse would come; what numbers it would involve; who would die, who survive. From the Beatles, he drew moral support; the assurance that his vision of revolution-as-apocalypse was valid; and that he was the one to bring it about. For him, the White Album was a psychotic's fun-house of holes and tunnels, portals bearing different signs but routes all interconnected, leading ultimately to the same cache of revelations: Charlie is Christ, and the apocalypse is his. *Deus est vivus.*

Most have written of Manson's turn as a radical shift. But again we find that hell is contained in the dream of paradise, and that hate emerges as love's demon brother. The two compulsions driving Manson to psychopathy and his Family to murder had been voiced in earlier, more loving days, when Charlie guided his frightened novitiate through her acid ordeal.

The first of these he shared with the Beatles of 1968, and probably it was what he heard singing to him through the holes and tunnels of the White Album: *Look at Death!*

The second, though, never came from the Beatles. It belonged to Manson alone: *Don't let anyone into your head but me.*

□

MYTHING IN ACTION: SECOND DIGRESSION
Our suggestion is that putting something into a hole is, in some way or another, filling the hole, just as one cannot fill a hole without putting something into it. And just as something can be said to be partly in a hole if some parts of it are in the hole, something can be said to partially fill the hole if some parts of it fill the hole (though not completely).

—Casati and Varzi, *Holes and Other Superficialities*

In mid- to late 1969, strange pieces of musical reproduction began appearing in head shops and underground record stores, mainly on the East and West Coasts. While they had the look of long-playing records, they bore no artists' names, sometimes not even titles. Persons unknown had slipped thick, badly pressed plates of cheap vinyl between blank white covers and neglected to provide documentation as to the contents—save, on occasion, a mimeographed sheet with typewritten list of usually incorrect song titles. The records had fanciful rubber-stamped names like *Great White Wonder, LIVEr Than You'll Ever Be,* and *Kum Back.* People bought them on word of mouth or a moment's curiosity, took them home and listened, and discovered the unmistakable noises of their favorite rock gods struggling through a sludge of indifferent sound and bad wax. But they were noises unheard anywhere else—noises made in private, never intended for pub-lic distribution. These illicit taps on the wires of the gods became known, instantly, as bootlegs.

You almost—*almost*—wonder how that anonymous Bedouin shep-herd felt when he found a collection of ancient jars in a cave in Qumran, Israel: the jars containing the Dead Sea Scrolls.

For like the scrolls, bootleg material is addenda to a story long es-tablished (or so people believed), and constitutes the leavings of ex-traordinary beings whose stories cannot be known to any fullness without the interpretation of such material. And like the scrolls, some bootlegs required scholarship and intense study to be deci-phered, because often those who produced them had little or no idea what they were distributing. In the case of the Beatles, songs were not only misnamed but misattributed: often a song was passed off as their work despite its provenance being wholly doubtful. Occa-sionally one slipped through a crack in the common knowledge and became, briefly, something it was not. A case in point is the song called "Have You Heard the Word?"

Bootlegged since 1970 as, among other things, the sole fruit of the Beatles' final recording session, "Have You Heard the Word?" is a great track, and surpassing strange.[53] It cuts in after it has begun. Me-tallic guitar strikes and a slippery-limbed bass; two nasal British voices mixed no higher than any other instrument, wailing ungraspable words in perfect non-unison:

and the love inside you happy singing now heard the word and the love inside you and the love inside you ahh ahh ahh

Now, a fast beat and honky-tonk piano. The voices speed up, grow almost furious. Climax—the tempo mellows again. The voices resume their wail, each repetition of the title question more comical than the last, the voices attempting new shapes and personalities. Very sud-denly guitar, piano, and percussion fall away—simply spontaneously stop—the bass throbs on a bit further, and the voices mutter privately as the beat dies on someone's off-key whine.

First voice: *Have you heard the word then?*

Second voice: *I've heard the word, yeah.*

Metrically askew, textually incoherent, close to tuneless, it is objectively a shoddy product, a palsied sketch of no identifiable subject. Yet it has vitality and humor and oddity; it moves and bounces and is catchy as hell. And it sounds just like them. If this isn't their last session, it ought to have been: it's appropriate in every way that they should end their life together by extolling unity in radically disunited voices, couching their last mysteries in a recording made up of such compelling incongruities.

As far as anyone knew in 1970, that breakup year, this was the Beatles. It had to be. So what if they no longer existed—surely the music would keep coming? Not until later did a few facts, or eminently reasonable suppositions, emerge to confirm the widespread suspicion that "Have You Heard the Word?"—however tantalizing and exact in sound, spirit, and lyrical quote—was *not* the last epistle of the gods themselves but a ventriloquial vocalization of Beatle motifs by an obscure band of fans and celebrants.

Have *you* heard the word? Is this the Beatles or not? Is it two of them, or one of them, or none of them? Is this singular recording driven by their physical presence, or is it only their musical spirit which animates it? Is this the word of the gods or the enraptured tongue-speaking of their proselytes? Is this music an aural apparition in bootleg form, a tattered and unreadable text left behind, trailing the Beatles as they drift out of sight and on to their celestial reward? Could it be that what masquerades as a cheap vinyl Frisbee in dirty cardboard covers contains, in fact, *the Beatles' very own Dead Sea Scroll?*

Hallelujah!!

□

> Of course this new theory needs to be further scrutinized. Our pu-
> tative "immaterial bodies" threaten to turn out to be a sort of
> philosophical phlogiston, another—to come closer to their real na-
> ture—ether. Are they so ethereal as to vanish altogether?
>
> —Casati and Varzi, *Holes and Other Superficialities*

Paul's death broke free of the college underground on October 18—
the birthdate of the Masked Marauders—with another phone call to
another radio personality from another student. The personality was
Alex Bennett of WMCA in New York City, host of an overnight call-in
talk show, and the student was Lewis Yager of Hofstra University, on
Long Island.[54] Yager was not content this night merely to rehash the
past, rack up old clues, and run down old theories for the benefit of
those who had arrived late. He was out to give his own twist to the already well-knotted narrative.

One twist was Yager's announcement that he had formed something called the Is Paul McCartney Dead Society. Its purpose, he explained, was not to ask the question, but to answer it in the
affirmative—to *prove* that Paul was dead, and, further, to establish
that the Beatles were doing a dance of the seven veils through their
lyrics and album art. The fact that the death rumor was now inspiring such fantasy (an investigative cabal? a cryptic agency of card-
carrying death sleuths?) spoke loudly that this was no ordinary
rumor. Paul-is-dead would not end once the luster had gone off
someone else's daydream. Instead—because it so invited refinement
and embellishment, offered so many openings for the insertion of
oneself—it gave signs of going on, in some form, so long as there were
others with sufficient imagination and leisure time to take up its
challenge.

Since Alex Bennett seemed unaware of the death rumor, it was easy
for Yager's other myth-twist to go unquestioned. It was a bold claim,
even heretical given the history of the rumor as we have tracked it.

Yager, it seemed, had not learned of Paul's death from any of the usual sources: rather he had, as Nicholas Schaffner reported, "been awakened in the night by the screams of a Beatlemaniacal girlfriend to whom McCartney's dire fate had been revealed in a dream."[55]

Lewis Yager was up to some serious revisionism. His even newer testament added unique features and a sprig of the supernatural to the rapidly growing mythology of Paul McCartney's death. For one thing, the rumor now had a precise point of origin—Yager's girlfriend (whose own version of things, so far as I know, has not been heard to this day). Most mysteriously: in his telling, McCartney's death had entered his consciousness, and therefore the public's, not as a frivolous fantasy but as a true revelation—a gift, or curse, from the unconscious—the collective unconscious, perhaps, of Beatle fandom itself. And by the lights of Lewis Yager, that revelation, once tendered, was a solemn responsibility: it called at once for the creation of an Is Paul McCartney Dead Society. No self-satisfied laughter here; only the midnight scream of a dreaming girl.

But we can bet money that, speaking on the phone that night with Alex Bennett, the collective radio ear of the Big Apple quivering at his every word, Lewis Yager had the time of his young life.

What had happened earlier in Detroit now happened in New York. WMCA's listeners were fascinated, and Bennett's show became a nightly death-rumor symposium. Other East Coast outlets pounced on the public's infatuation with this odd news from the heartland. Within days, the rumor was national, and thousands of initiates raced to dive into the myth pool—either as observers, reporters, or participants.

For a week—or two, or three—they all felt the buzz of a shared hallucination. The novelist Richard Price, in college at the time, recalled getting caught up in the sudden phenomenon of Beatle mortality as public entertainment, as a local station staged its death-clue phone-a-thon.

> All the phone-ins sound earnest—everybody's trying to come off like he's not having a ball. The deejay dutifully mangles the cuts according to instructions. I've never heard my voice on radio before, and I want to play.
>
> "Yeah, hi, uh, I just thought of this. I don't know what it means . . . but you know what eighty-four percent of all the coffins in England are made of?"
>
> "Lay it on me . . ."
>
> "It might even be eighty-seven percent. . . . Norwegian wood."[56]

There was fun in the thousands of phone calls lodged at hundreds of radio stations. There was fun in dormitories, fun in the pages of *Rolling Stone*. Fun in what Nicholas Schaffner called the "slew of sick novelty records . . . hurriedly recorded to cash in on the macabre fad"[57]—records with titles like "The Ballad of Paul" (the Mystery Tour), "Brother Paul" (Billy Shears and the All-Americans), "We're All Paulbearers" (Zacherias and the Tree People), and "So Long, Paul" (Werbley Finster—a pseudonym for, of all people, José Feliciano).[58] There was fun in the Thanksgiving-weekend TV special "Paul McCartney: The Complete Story, Told for the First and Last Time"—a mock trial examining the death evidence, with superstar defense attorney F. Lee Bailey soberly pressing album jackets and backward voices on everyone from Russ Gibb to the president of Capitol Records. Whole segments of American humanity were caught in the swerves of a morbid mini-obsession, eager to see how far the mystery could take them, how far they could take the mystery.

The old clues were disseminated anew and became writ, as new ones were added to the swelling concordance. Some showed real ingenuity in the forging of iron-clad syllogisms from pieces of apparently unrelated "evidence." For an example, follow the walrus trail. John sings "I Am the Walrus," therefore must *be* the walrus. Not so fast: *No you're not said Little Nicola,* someone has handwritten in the *Mystery Tour* book. But if not John, then who? Without fully knowing what it is doing, "Glass Onion" lifts the walrus mask to reveal Paul's innocent visage. Like a paranoid's worldview, Paul-is-dead was not illogical once you had accepted the lunatic premise: "walrus," remember, was Greek for "corpse." Paul = walrus = corpse. Q.E.D.

Most clues were merely tossed into the forum by those eager to contribute *something,* even if it was only the sound of their own voice. But all were really the same: darts thrown at a board. Either in jest or in earnest, but always with the desire to hit some kind of bull's-eye: locate something weird, absurd, disturbing, and on some level undeniably *true.* Most darts went wild or, at best, hit the outer rim. A very few landed dead center. These few, although promulgated in the prevailing Paul-is-dead spirit of straight-faced bushwa, crank calls, and red herrings, pierced the generational anxiety at the heart of all the fun.

There is that plot of ground on the cover of *Sgt. Pepper,* gone in two years from garden to grave without displacing a single clod of earth.

There is "Glass Onion," which ridicules the forging of spurious meaning, but which in its deconstructive process has only bolstered the most spurious meaning of all by offering the key to unlock any number of adjoining doors: the name of the walrus-corpse. There may be no song in rock and roll that has rebounded so neatly on its creators.

There are those other tracks which became the sacred gospels of the death myth, relating whole chunks of the story in sound and image. "A Day in the Life" (apocalyptic car crash); "I Am the Walrus" (Shakespearean death scene); "Revolution 9" (rifles, knives, fire, collapse). With or without the rumor to highlight their morbid peculiarities, these are undeniably the most deathly things the Beatles have recorded; and except for the first song's brief middle passage— an escape route from death which finally only circles back to it—Paul is conspicuously missing from all of them. Which means that love in the old sense is also missing. In its place is something else: a different energy, an anxious pulse, perhaps the sudden intense awareness of the mundane that is said to visit those staring at death.

There is the mystery around the word "love." On the back of *Pepper,* it was said, George's fingers form an L, John's a V, Ringo's an E. Paul is turned away: both his face and the O are missing. Now turn *Abbey Road* over—see how the O is chipped? Paul, unlike his fellows, has no O in his name. Again the heart, if it is not damaged, is missing altogether, and only a hole is left.

There is the black carnation. Look in the *Magical Mystery Tour* book and see the Beatles in white tuxedos: John, George, and Ringo wear red boutonnieres, but Paul's is black. This is late 1967, the time of bleary, weary after-*Pepper* noises and incipient hippie rot; consider this mini-mutation of a significant historical shift with a trivial real-life contingency ("They ran out of red ones," said Paul)[59] and the edge of death myth–mania comes into view. You feel the attraction, the frisson, the hint of millennial doom. And you almost—*almost*—wonder the unwonderable: Are forces other than coincidence truly at work here? For how could any young person regard Paul's dark flower in these dark hours and *not* see a little bit of black death burning a hole where his heart is? A black O of death usurping the red O of love, the O which other Beatle iconography implied had been missing since sometime late in 1966?

Now turn back a few pages. Paul, in military getup, sits at a desk, and on the desk sits a sign. On the sign are three words and a face. The face is that of a Victorian Englishman with walrus mustache and pointing finger; and the words, according to clue-hunters of the time, proclaim "I WAS"—the "I" in this case being the man behind the desk, Paul McCartney, O.P.D. But in fact (as the LaBour article pointed out but didn't interpret), the sign reads "I YOU WAS." And the finger of the man between the words points not back at Paul but straight at YOU.

What is the scrupulous investigator-mythographer, following his clues wherever they may lead, to make of that? Who is dead—who WAS? I or YOU? HE or ME? Or is it WE? Grab your King Death de-coder ring, and dig the first line of one particularly suggestion-heavy song for the answer:

I am he as you are he as you are me and we are all together. Even in death, apparently.

Uh—yeah, man, right on, uh-huh. . . . Listen, that foreign bit in "Sun King"? Esperanto for *He who hath croaked.* Pass it on.

□

Still a different way of bringing holes into existence, or transform-ing a holed object into a differently holed object, is through pierc-ing, punching, or puncturing.

—Casati and Varzi, *Holes and Other Superficialities*

By early 1969, the Family were in Canoga Park, inhabiting a house of rancid margarine color which had come to be called the Yellow Sub-marine. (Manson knew a good hole metaphor when he found it.) There the White Album was spun continually, providing background noise and foreground discourse, as the rhetoric grew more heated. Manson's early love philosophy had never given his ego all it needed, and the music industry had failed to recognize the vast dimensions of his talent. The world was all but breaking apart and here he was, still on the fringe of the fringe, his scraggly band scrounging dump-ster food and stealing credit cards as he paced and pontificated in a suburban squat.[60]

Like a lot of people in the '60s, he wanted his piece of the action—but the Beatles had shown him that the world itself was the only piece that meant anything, the human race the only audience worth fighting for. Ego and psychosis took over from there. The demons in Manson were stronger, far stronger than any angels: they determined the mark he would leave on the world, and now they turned him toward destruction. Suddenly the line he fed his followers was not love, or even the sensuality of submission, but mayhem. And not puny riot or insignificant upheaval but the honest-to-Jehovah, blood-and-guts end of the world, civilization blazing to ash in the fires and slaughter of an all-out race war.

The first official mention of a possible link between the Beatles and the murders that took place in Los Angeles on August 8 and 9, 1969, was this brief note in a preliminary report submitted by one of the investigative teams: "Investigation revealed that the singing group the Beatles' most recent album, No. SWBO 101, has songs titled 'Helter Skelter' and 'Piggies' and 'Blackbird.' The words in the song 'Blackbird' frequently say 'Arise, arise,' which might be the meaning of 'Rise' near the front door." The connection, Vincent Bugliosi recalled, was so outlandish as to be beneath consideration. "The idea was just sort of tossed in, by whom no one would later remember, and just as promptly forgotten."[61]

Listening to the White Album is a disturbing sojourn—even for those of us of sound mind and placid nature who have heard it more times than we can count. It is not within our well-adjusted capacities to know how Charles Manson felt upon hearing it for the first time. We consider a damaged mind and criminal instinct, a cerebrum and sensibility wired tight by drugs and paranoia, driven by all variety of artistic frustration, unguided ambition, delusions of omnipotence, antisocial energy, and a taste of real power—and are left wondering how such a mind responds to what we in our *sanity* cannot fully fathom. All we know to any certainty is that when Manson met the White Album, there was mutation.

This is no guess. Bugliosi quotes Manson telling several followers that the record had arrived to "set up things for the revolution."[62]

Paul Watkins was among those present to witness Manson's first night with the White Album. "After that," he remembered, "things were never the same." By the first of the new year, the record "had turned his head around."[63] But turned it, perhaps, 360 degrees—leaving his head where it had been for a long time, but now wound tighter and set to spin out of control. Manson had been incipiently psychotic since adolescence; but the late '60s intensified his mania by giving it its ideal history-making window. Like many white convicts, he was a racist; but at some point in 1968 fear of black revolution began to pervade his delusions, and his own ultimate domination of the black race became a primary element of the apocalypse he would orchestrate. The Bible had long been central to his thoughts; but now, Manson became fixated on the Book of Revelation, the New Testament's horrific, imagistic vision of Judgment Day.

Nor was his Beatle obsession new. What was new was that, with the White Album, the group became a vehicle for Manson's demons, not his angels. The Beatles had begun as the Family's fellow magical mystery tourists, spiritual comrades in school-bus adventure. Now they were, to hear Manson tell it, right at the wretched heart of all the darkness to come: "Are you hep to what the Beatles are saying? . . . Dig it, they're telling it like it is. They know what's happening in the city; blackie is getting ready. They put the revolution to music. . . . It's 'Helter-Skelter.' Helter-Skelter is coming down."[64]

The meats in Manson's primordial stew—fear, ambition, resentment, insatiable ego, the twin drives toward creation and destruction—were those found in any genius, any madman. Given this, and given that here was a madman who believed himself a genius, what did he hear in the White Album that no one else heard?

Let Manson explain himself first:

> At the end of each song there is a little tag piece on it, a
> couple of notes. Or like in "Piggies" there's "oink, oink,

oink." Just these couple of sounds. And all these sounds
are repeated in "Revolution 9." Like in "Revolution 9," all
these pieces are fitted together and they predict the violent
overthrow of the white man. Like you'll hear "oink, oink,"
and then right after that, machine gun fire. [*He sprays the
room with imaginary slugs.*] AK-AK-AK-AK-AK-AK-AK!

Do you really think the Beatles intended to mean that?

I think it's a subconscious thing. I don't know whether
they did or not. But it's there. It's an association in the
subconscious. This music is bringing on the revolution,
the unorganized overthrow of the Establishment. The
Beatles know in the sense that the subconscious knows.[65]

From the incidental symbols and random utterances of the White
Album, Manson discerned a voice and drew a prophecy. The voice
was that of the Beatles speaking to him, and its prophecy was annihi-
lation. Manson took the same prophecy from the Book of Revelation, particularly Chapter 9, where the narrative was laid out in much
plainer language, no code or symbol to get in the way: the straight
dope on the end of days.[66] Charlie—the prophecy ran, courtesy of the
Beatles and the Bible—take your Family into the Hole: the end is
coming. The black man has had enough, and soon he will fight the
white man in the streets. He will win. But the black man, having lived
so long in chains, will not know how to officiate in whatever world is
left to him. Then you will emerge from the Hole, return the black
man to his chains, and rule forever in paradise.

By the way: in 1965, Paul McCartney expounded on the historical
inevitability of racial table-turning. "I believe Negroes will be in control one of these days. . . . Then they'll make the white people suffer as
they've suffered. It may sound cruel, but it's only natural, isn't it?"[67]

*And the fifth angel blew his trumpet, and I saw a star fallen from heaven to
earth, and he was given the key of the shaft of the bottomless pit.*[68] The Beatles
as the first four angels; Manson as the fifth. *He opened the shaft of the*

bottomless pit, and from the shaft rose smoke like the smoke of a great furnace, and the sun and the air were darkened with the smoke from the shaft. Manson as gatekeeper to the final hole, the hole at the end of the '60s, at the end of the world; the hole of the Hopis, the mouth of Hell at the floor of Death Valley. *Then from the smoke came locusts on the earth, and they were given power like the power of scorpions of the earth.* The Beatles.

In appearance the locusts were like horses arrayed for battle; on their heads were what looked like crowns of gold; their faces were like human faces, their hair like women's hair, and their teeth like lions' teeth; they had scales like iron breastplates. The Beatles with their long hair and guitars, the teeth of their violent White Album music. *They have as king over them the angel of the bottomless pit; his name in Hebrew is Abad'don, and in Greek he is called Apol'lyon.* Fifth angel and gatekeeper, Abad'don, Apol'lyon, Exterminans, Manson: in any language, "destroyer."

So the four angels were released, who had been held ready for the hour, the day, the month, and the year, to kill a third of mankind. The Beatles instigate black riot with their white album full of orgasm and explosion, revolution and death. The black man hears the call and responds by killing a third of mankind: the white race.

The rest of mankind, who were not killed by these plagues, did not repent of the works of their hands nor give up worshiping demons and idols of gold and silver and bronze and stone and wood, which cannot either see or hear or walk; nor did they repent of their murders or their sorceries or their immorality or their thefts. "The rest of mankind": the Family. They survive to ascend as rulers of the earth, Manson as ultimate conqueror, repenting of nothing.

The myth Manson wove out of Revelation, the White Album, and his own paranoid fever drove the Beatle-audience symbiosis to its last extreme: past the merely rational and into that other land where no one walks but the dreamer himself. In the White Album, Manson heard terror, destruction, anguish, bloody glee, redemption sought in vain; he found not just God but Satan in its details. He had renamed Susan Atkins "Sadie Mae Glutz" sometime in the fall of 1967;

here, a full year later, was a song about "Sexy Sadie." "Honey Pie" begged for the magic (or "magick") of someone's Hollywood song: Who else could that someone be? In "Don't Pass Me By," Ringo—even Ringo!—was listening for someone's footsteps in the driveway; and "I Will" found its singer yearning for the transforming arrival of a loved one's music. Manson heard the word *arise* in "Blackbird" and fixed on it. He believed "Glass Onion"'s *hole in the ocean* was the bottomless pit of Death Valley, and that "Helter Skelter" described the Family's eventual emergence from the depth. He homed in on any mention of weaponry, utensilry, cutlery—"Happiness Is a Warm Gun," "Piggies," "Rocky Raccoon"—and when in "Revolution 1" the Beatles said they were *in* on destruction, Manson didn't miss it. He exhumed the near-buried *RIIIII-AHHHHT* of "Revolution 9" and was sure it said *RISE.* Manson played the track over and over, attending to its every stab and shriek, nestling each noise as the Beatles' blessing on his madness.

This may be only a partial enumeration of the voices Manson heard in the White Album. He was not the first fan to read very precise and personal meanings into the Beatles' work; probably not even the first to believe they were speaking directly to him. Past that, he was on his own.

Mutation was defined earlier as the painful, unnatural transformation experienced by living organisms forced to join. In mutation something is born, or wrenched into life. What had never been so obvious before Charles Manson came along was the reciprocal fact that, in this kind of birth, something else is destroyed.

Gary Hinman was a thirty-four-year-old music teacher, doctoral candidate in sociology, musician, and occasional friend of the Family.[69] On Friday, July 25, 1969, Bobby Beausoleil, Mary Brunner, and Susan Atkins showed up at Hinman's small hillside house in Malibu, demanding money: he had, they said, a stash of thousands in drug money. Hinman resisted, and Beausoleil began to beat him with a pistol. This went on for a few hours, as Brunner and Atkins searched the house. Late into the night a call was placed to the Spahn Ranch; soon after, Manson appeared. When Hinman again claimed ignorance of any stash, Manson pulled out a saber and cut a five-inch swath through his ear and jawbone.

He departed. The others bound Hinman with rope and continued searching the house. Beausoleil from time to time would administer another pistol-whipping. All the time Hinman was bleeding and screaming; eventually they gagged him. This went on until Sunday night, when Beausoleil made another call to the ranch. *Informed him on the third night.*

Gary Hinman was stabbed to death. Susan Atkins later testified to seeing him stagger into the kitchen, bleeding from the chest. His body would not be found for another four days. By then it was filled with maggots. The "gentle musician," as Ed Sanders called him,[70] mutilated and killed by a failed ex-con troubadour and a failed satanist acid-rocker, was the first casualty of Helter Skelter. He died chanting a Buddhist prayer. He died with the words *POLITICAL PIGGY* written on the wall in his own blood.

A snapshot from the Family album:

A year or so after Hinman's death, a group of filmmakers have come to the Spahn Ranch to make a movie about the Family. Three hard-core Manson girls—Sandy, Squeaky, and Brenda—stand behind a table, holding enormous hunting knives. Their hair is cut close to the skull in the current style of their leader, and their faces are a mesmerizing mix of stone and flesh, the infantile and the insane. Nothing comforting in their high, feminine voices.

"Aren't you worried about the police?" the off-camera interviewer asks, sounding a little scared. Instantly all three of the girls smile.

Sandy even starts to sing, edging into the refrain of a recent hit song: "If you want it—"

Quickly, as if they've done this before, Squeaky picks it up: "Here it is—"

All three join for the punchline: "Come and get it."

Squeaky ends it by adding a lyric of her own. "But you better hurry. *'Cause it won't be here long, you motherfuckers.*"[71]

By the way: on July 24, 1969, the day before Gary Hinman began to be murdered, Paul McCartney—soon to be dead himself—recorded a song he'd just written, called "Come and Get It."[72]

□

MYTHING IN ACTION: THIRD DIGRESSION
Here we cross the border into a new territory where geometrical or morphological concepts alone prove insufficient for orientation.
—Casati and Varzi, *Holes and Other Superficialities*

The fantasist, writes Stephen King, responds to a mystery by playing with it "as a child would. . . . It's a child's toy, something bright and shiny and strange." The fantasist is drawn by instinct and interest to whatever goes unexplained—any object, event, or phenomenon whose mysteriousness leaves it an empty vessel waiting to be filled by someone's imaginative discharge. The fantasist regards a mystery and says: "Let us pull a lever and see what it does. . . . Let us turn it over and see if it will magically right itself again."[73]

> *I'm looking at the candle burns a flame to meet the sky*
> *I leave the candle laughing, I turn my face to cry*

"The Candle Burns" is the title most often assigned to a piece of music that began to appear on Beatle bootlegs in the early '70s.[74] By this point, "Have You Heard the Word?" seemed to have run its course as an object of Beatle-related inquiry. Facts of its creation were unearthed by a few intrepid seekers after truth, and speculations were replaced by explanations. Just then, magically (or "magickally"), "The Candle Burns" appeared to fill the gap and give new focus to the same question: Is it them or isn't it?

The song had come from nowhere; to this day, it remains there.

A safety pin returns my smile, I nod a brief hello
While you are building molecules with your garden hoe

It is a sustained swirl of psychedelic acid-folk. Like "Have You Heard the Word?" it has no real starting point, fading in on a buzz of acetate scratch and unsynchronized vocal moanings twisted in reverse. An acoustic guitar dances a circular pattern on two chords. Two voices coalesce to intone lyrics which combine a mundane surrealism with vague hippie invocations. With each verse the tempo is quickened and the key changed by someone's hand on a knob, altering the tape speed on playback. Voices, guitar, tempo—all share a druggy lassitude which distorts the song's circle, bulging its ellipses.

Once the lyrics are exhausted, the voices drift apart. *Hush,* one of them whispers; the other releases a series of high cries, like long thin fingers reaching out of the circle as it fades from view. The song retreats into the scratch of acetate, which lingers for a few seconds before itself vanishing.

Why can't this last forever, these things repressed inside
One feels it almost instantly unless one of us died

"The Candle Burns" must rival the Knickerbockers' "Lies" as the most convincing Beatles pastiche ever recorded. The tape effects and thick-throated vocals make it a stoned, sluggish brother to "Strawberry Fields." The voices are credibly close to George's and John's, and the sound overall—while far less pop-oriented and more avant-garde than anything on *Pepper*—seems more than plausible as a product of Beatle psychedelia, circa summer 1967.

So much more than plausible that, early on, the authenticity of "The Candle Burns" was taken for granted. The necessary "facts" were supplied by those required to explain where such an oddity—unnoted in any Beatle conversation or documentation—had come from. In 1975, discographers Harry Castleman and Walter Podrazik identified it as "Peace of Mind," a studio outtake from mid-1967 containing "intriguing lyrics woven around very complicated beat changes. In spite of the very bad recording available, it still deserves close attention."[75] Six years later, Charles Reinhart identified the recording's genesis in one terse and unattributed sentence: "Recorded June, 1967, and found in the Apple trash can in 1970."[76]

> *It's over, it's done, we are meeting again*
> *Just please, please, please, oh, don't keep me from the end*

But that was a long time ago, when collectors and fans knew a lot less. More contemporary researchers like Mark Lewisohn and Allen J. Wiener do not mention "The Candle Burns" at all, even to dispose of it as a hoax. Some have suggested it came from a private reel produced in a Beatle rumpus room; others that it is a demo by the Syd Barrett-era Pink Floyd. The point is: we still do not know. After all these years no artist, no entity has come forth to lay hands on it and say, "This is mine."

By far the strangest speculation I have seen on the matter comes from Steve Belmer, a.k.a. Belmo, editor of *Belmo's Beatleg News*. "I am absolutely convinced this is not John Lennon or the Beatles," he writes. "After years of mindless research I have come to the conclusion that it is either an outtake from Trash (Apple recording artists) or a soundtrack song from a film about witches. Really!"[77] This crosses in an odd way with an earlier, conflicting source: according to Belmo, the song may have been recorded by Trash at Apple, while Reinhart claimed the song was recovered *from* the trash at Apple.

> *I need to hear the colors red and blue and whispered words*
> *To fly all day and sing in tune and not hear what I heard*

Fantasy often is inspired by great acts and heroic personages. Often it is something found in the trash. A bit of debris fluttering in the vacuum of the fixed and immutable may compel the creation of facts, the imagining of stories. This is fantasy in its commonest, least monumental form: it will neither move mountains nor affect the course of history. But it is open to anyone with the willingness to take on the fantasist's role. Such minor controversies and limited mysteries as were kicked up around the Masked Marauders, "The Candle Burns," and "Have You Heard the Word?" constitute another manner in which the Beatles enriched the imaginative life of their time.

There is no way of quantifying the changes the Beatles catalyzed in private lives. The affairs begun or ended to one of their songs; the career paths and passionate avocations inspired by their creative example; the spiritual inquiries spurred by one Beatle's famous blasphemy; the filial bonds deepened by a common love of their music. Because they don't move mountains, such things fall into the vast wastebasket of unrecorded history. Are we to consider them unimportant for that reason? I think we may consider them as important as any history ever recorded. They are the changes that determine how people live within history, day to day—as opposed to how populations live *because* of history, era by era.

If unrecorded history is important, then so are the Masked Marauders, "The Candle Burns," and "Have You Heard the Word?" These singular instances of vinyl mythology were indicators of change at the same mundane, private level. They were graspings after mystery, openings for the imagination; affirmations of the power and fun and richness of living life in an awareness of the unknown, of feeling blindly for holes in reality. Ordinary fantasies at play, for a time, in a world where fantasy, potential, and a constructive sense of the unreal had become the transformative nutrients of ordinary life.

If the Beatles changed the course of world history by inspiring mass fantasy, and by driving mass aspirations toward an ethic of radical possibility, they also changed the history of ordinary, evanescent fantasy in ways that were themselves evanescent and ordinary. They turned rational people into fantasists, fans into creators. For a few years in that most rational of centuries, the human imagination in all its colors ruled, and anyone who dared take a step could turn his own world into a funhouse, or a madhouse.

> *To see you all around me and to take you by the hand*
> *And lead you to a brand new world that lately has been banned*

The only other words I've seen on "The Candle Burns" belong to a former bootlegger calling himself Mr. Nurk Twin. "It beats me," he said, asked if he thought the song was the creation of the Beatles. "That's one that really kind of bothered me."[78]

Why? It's only another mystery, no more or less meaningful than the other mysteries we find in the wastebaskets of everyday life, where they have landed after slipping through reality's holes, anomalies on which we meditate briefly before forgetting them forever. "The Candle Burns" is forgotten today, and there is no melancholy in that. Except for the one irreducible fact that it has never been claimed, and never explained.

> *We'll build things never built before, we'll do things never done*
> *And just before it's over, it's really just begun*

□

But are we saying that immaterial bodies are individuals proper in other worlds only?

—Casati and Varzi, *Holes and Other Superficialities*

Mikhail Bakhtin devised the notion of the "carnivalesque" to characterize those texts in which a range of voices other than the author's shape the reader's experience of the narrative. As J. A. Cuddon formulates the theory, "The element of carnival in literature is subversive; it disrupts authority and introduces alternatives." Quoting Bakhtin, he explains that in the process of carnivalization "many different characters express varying, independent views which are not 'controlled' by the author to represent the author's viewpoint. They are 'not only objects of the author's word, but subjects of their own directly significant word as well.'"[79]

Paul-is-dead hit its unreal apogee when, for a moment, it achieved the variety and clangor of carnival. We've heard the voices of many who spoke up just to hear themselves, try their luck at the dartboard, maybe win a prize. Then came the voices of those who sought to sell tickets to the carnival: the barkers, touts, and snake-oil salesmen. The rumor may have reached back several centuries for its mythological formula, but it was utterly contemporary in its availability for commodification. It was being widely reported, after all, that the Beatles themselves were profiting nicely from the rumor they seemed so reticent to put down: *Sgt. Pepper* and *Magical Mystery Tour* had both undergone a commercial resurgence sufficient to put them back on the album charts, and *Abbey Road* was on its way to becoming one of their top sellers. Death has always sold, and the Werbley Finsters of the world have always been around to shovel dirt either in or out of the grave—whichever is selling this year. But it was further evidence of resilience that commercial exploitation, far from suffocating the myth, only added fresh facets to it.

"Paul McCartney: The Complete Story, Told for the First and Last Time," the F. Lee Bailey television special, cashed in while managing to throw some new shadows on the already murky plot. A few of them came courtesy of Fred LaBour, up to his old tricks. In a diffident monotone, he embellished further on his original set of death clues. The cover of *Magical Mystery Tour*, he said, showed Paul, as the black-clad walrus, "in crucifixion pose—with his arms out like this." Religion was not new to the rumor; crucifixion was. LaBour continued to lead Bailey (playing the credulous initiate) by the nose:

"Now there's a lotta speculation that the walrus is a symbol of death in Roman mythology, in Dutch mythology, in Eskimoan mythology. So that would be significant."[80] Did he say *Eskimoan?*

An odd side story was detailed by Paul Cannon, program director of WKNR, the Detroit undergrounder whose Russ Gibb show had sent the rumor on its way to national attention. Cannon described receiving a phone call from someone identifying himself as Paul McCartney. What had Cannon asked him?

> *Cannon:* Of course, we were interested in the symbolism, if there was any, and why they had done certain things, and he said that there was no symbolism, nothing intended, it was very spontaneous.
>
> *Bailey:* Denied it all.
>
> *Cannon:* Yes, he did. . . . [He said,] "It's whatever anyone reads into it, is what it is."[81]

A subsequent witness, Beatles business manager Allen Klein, attempted to clear up this mystery within the mystery, and only left more obscurity in his wake. It was not McCartney talking to Paul Cannon, he said. Bailey asked who it was.

> *Klein:* I think it was Tony Bramwell, a promotion man.
>
> *Bailey:* Why do you think he would make such a call?
>
> *Klein:* I think that you have a lot of people with no authority who make a lot of statements about the Beatles because they're interested in their own self-adornment.[82]

Which very succinctly explains why *many* people got involved, in some way, with the rumor.

Singer-producer Peter Asher took the stand to concur with Klein that the WKNR caller was not, in fact, his friend McCartney. He went on to insist that not only was the pre-death Paul identical to the subsequent model, but that the rumormongers were gullible fools. Still, when asked if he thought the half-heard phrase toward the end of "Strawberry Fields" was *I buried Paul,* as the fools maintained, Asher was stuck for a retort. "Uh, it sounds like it is to me," he said nervously. "Yes, it sounds like John is saying 'I buried Paul.'"[83]

Into the thick of the fad, so hastily assembled its pulp was still wet, came an uplifting item called *Paul McCartney DEAD: The Great Hoax,* a one-shot fan magazine produced by Country Wide Publications of New York. As cash-ins went, it was typically shoddy in its fact checking, graphic layout, and photo captioning; it was also atypically philosophical in its ruminations, referencing the Hindu Upanishads and other mystic precursors on the subjects of death and reincarnation. Despite its pretense of objectivity, the magazine announced its own position with a cover which assigned prominence to two features: Paul's frowning, downcast face, and the word *DEAD.* The writings inside also were informed by a consistently pro-death bias.

"There are those Beatle fans with hope," one article began, "and there are those who no longer have hope."[84] The writer was speaking in the limited sense of the death rumor, but went on to quote a "young lady from Chicago named Rita Randol" on a more general anxiety:

> From the time of the reported death, the music, which had previously been written mostly by Paul, changed completely, as if a different person entirely had been writing it. If it had been a slow, evolving process, I could understand it. But the style changed so radically. . . . You must remember that it was at this time that the Beatles lost many of their fans as a result of the change. From *Rubber Soul* to *Revolver,* everything about the Beatles' music became different. I'd like to believe that Paul is alive, but I just can't— because of this.[85]

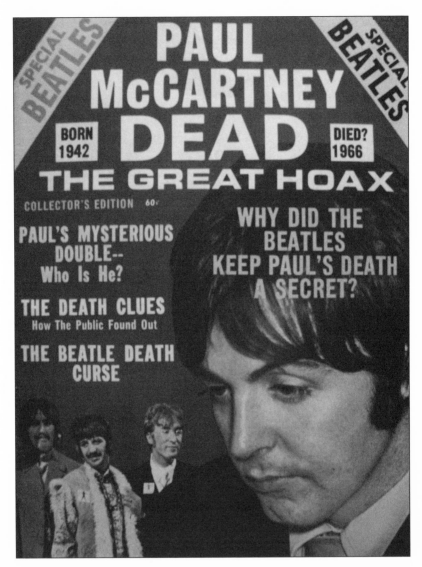

26. Pulp mythology, 1969: fan magazines have come a long way from *Teen Beat*.

If, after reading such stilted speech, you accept the existence of Rita Randol, you may also be a close personal friend of T. M. Christian's. Those lachrymose lines doubtless were written by some anonymous, paid-by-the-inch Country Wide Publications wordslinger, not spoken by any fan—a ghost fabricated to regard a ghost. Nevertheless the words *were* written; someone thought they held truth. And they did— truth reaching back to the recoil that Ron Schaumberg experienced at seeing the aged faces of *Rubber Soul,* his repulsion at the death they suggested; reaching back to the sense of death that followed the Beatles through 1966, and that had since accounted for most of the depths in their music. "As if a different person entirely had been writing it."

Another of the stories introduced a new element to the myth by crossing it with a classic American legend: the phantom hitchhiker. Fred LaBour had had Paul dying when his speeding car shot off a slippery road. This version was bound to strike some as too arbitrary, a mere rough draft of a death: the destruction of Paul McCartney deserved something more symbolic, more *appropriate* than that. Again narrative necessity was the mother of morbid invention: as LaBour had invented William Campbell, orphan and contest winner, to fill his needs, someone else came up with the hitchhiking girl. "According to one of the rumors surrounding the accident that allegedly took Paul's life, he stopped that night to pick up a hitchhiker."

> Maybe he should have been warned by the way she got into his car, without the usual hesitation natural for a girl alone on the road. . . . Maybe if he'd been more suspicious, more careful . . .
>
> Then, according to the stories surrounding Paul's fatal accident, the girl recognized Paul and became hysterical, throwing her arms around his neck and kissing him. Paul tried to calm her, but the car swerved off the rain-slicked

road, and crashed, head-on, into a stone fence, killing both
Paul and his unknown companion.[86]

Take a moment to appreciate this amended version of the myth—
its poetic correctness, the circularity it achieves with the introduction
of the hysterical girl-fan. No mere failure of wet-road traction
brought down the magical McCartney, god of love and music, whose
almond eyes moistened a million panties. The fatal component was
the sudden passion and unstable sexuality of an unnamed girl—a
girl, the excerpt suggests, with some sinister, Loreleian allure. A faceless girl, who could be any girl; a runaway, perhaps, running toward
death, her appointment in Samarra with Beatle Paul.[87] An anonymous nymph and innocent bringer of doom, who now joins her love
object in the spirit world, where they will ascend to the skies in
mythic marriage, bonded through eternity.

The unknown artisan who added this touch, daubed in this inspired refinement, may be smiling even as we speak.

Such was the distance the rumor had taken its subscribers into the
realm of utter weirdness. Fans were at the point of deciphering a telephone number from within the starry lettering of the *Magical Mystery
Tour* jacket, coming up with any number of alternate permutations
depending on who was looking, on the particular angle, and on
whether a mirror was used—for some said the numbers were printed
in reverse. Unfortunate Londoners reported being harassed with
midnight calls (collect, of course) from addled Americans demanding due reward for having completed the puzzle.

Eventually there came the point when Paul had to step from the
shadows, stand before a camera, and redeclare his existence to the
world. In a pleasing reversal of the *Great Hoax* cover, the rumor of his
death was "definitively" denounced in the mass-market magazine
whose large letters proclaimed it to be about *LIFE*. Thus was the ru-

mor returned, as found news, to the Middle America whence it came. The November 7 issue bore the promise "Paul is still with us," and showed a rustic Beatle posed with wife and children against a gloomy, windswept backdrop of deep Scottish farmland. Inside, along with the inevitable recap on major death clues and theories, were McCartney's denials of both his own morbidity and the Beatles' mischief.

It should have been enough to kill death. Of course it wasn't. Too many people were still having too good a time; too many felt they were onto something big. LaBour had written that Paul's symbolic resurrection worked fine without him: so, it turned out, did his ongoing death. The rumor had gained such momentum that it was no longer necessary—if it ever had been—to believe in that death; all that mattered was a belief in its signs, a belief that truth would be found if the signs were interpreted correctly, and a belief that the Beatles had hidden that truth in plain sight.

"I think Paul McCartney is alive," Russ Gibb told his listeners on the night of October 26. His theory was that the Beatles had orchestrated the hoax in response to the Christ controversy: an elaborate and purposeful sham on messiah hunger. "I'm overwhelmed by the intensity of thought that has gone into this, and I'm also overwhelmed by the idea that the general public has taken this long to catch on to the Beatle game . . . or the Beatle Plot, if you will."[88]

So the carnival would go on. Voices would fade in and out, but there would never be a lack of fans eager to build molecules with garden hoes. Nothing wrong with that. That's the imaginative faculty at work, the sound of people making myths and constructing meanings; and meanings are never, if you will, meaningless. They are the prints we leave on history so that someone else, thirty or a thousand years later, may dust them off, read them, and wonder what we were thinking. Paul-is-dead may not live as long in human memory as that, and if it does its print will be smudged, barely readable, all but invisible—a latent, as the detectives call it. But who's to say it *won't* live? Already it straddles two centuries.

Thus the positivist view of overinterpretation, which says there is generally no harm and perhaps some good in a fan's claiming that, for example, "glass onion" is British slang for a coffin handle. But there are other, less sanguine ways of looking at it. There may be something very wrong indeed with the fan who claims that, for example, the Beatles' "hole in the ocean" refers to a great pool of water in a paradise beneath Death Valley.

The unnamed scroll-writers of *The Great Hoax* cheerfully remind us of this duality: "Every coin has two sides. . . . As the young lady from California pointed out, the songs could be interpreted in other, more frightening ways!"[89]

□

> Holes are part of the world, and language has to cope with them if it is to describe the world.
>
> —Casati and Varzi, *Holes and Other Superficialities*

Friday, August 8, 1969.

Manson is depressed. Two of his people are in jail. He's just been informed that Bobby Beausoleil was arrested a few days ago, driving Gary Hinman's Fiat.[90] And it's one year since his recording session— the one that was intended to make him the latest and last oracle of world revolution, spearhead of plague and apocalypse, and a bigger star than the Beatles. But it hasn't worked out that way. Hinman was not the big statement but only its vague prologue, an accidental rehearsal turned to their advantage: he had had them leave *POLITICAL PIGGY* on the wall, along with a little cat's paw, so the police would think the Black Panthers had done it.[91] But now, with Beausoleil's arrest, even murder is tainted by failure and incompetence.

Back at the ranch, things are tense. As darkness falls he surveys his

B-movie domain: crabgrass and rotten planks and tired horses. Part of him is white with fury and another high with elation as he realizes, *This is it.* He gives them the Word:

"Now is the time for Helter Skelter."[92]

Secreted on one of Hollywood's most exclusive hilltops, 10050 Cielo Drive had been the home of Terry Melcher, ace L.A. record producer.[93] Melcher was number one on Charles Manson's death list: an emissary had brought Melcher to the Spahn Ranch to hear the Family's ballads of psychic submission and dumpster-diving, and Manson hadn't heard from him again. On March 23, 1969, Manson appeared at the Cielo Drive guest house and attempted to interest Melcher's business manager in his music. Sharon Tate was in the main house that day; it would later be established that she had seen Manson as he loitered on the porch.[94]

He's chosen four of them to visit Cielo Drive: Susan Atkins, alias Sadie Mae Glutz; Patricia Krenwinkle; recent addition Linda Kasabian; and Tex Watson, killer zombie. They take with them a few knives, some rope, and a .22 caliber revolver.[95] They reach the house, locate and sever the telephone wires. The house is protected by an electric gate which the crawlers avoid by climbing an embankment to the side. They are about to descend to the driveway inside when a car appears, approaching the gate. Watson leaps down and shoots the driver, eighteen-year-old Steven Parent, four times.

Leaving Kasabian outside as a lookout, Watson, Atkins, and Krenwinkle steal into the house. Its inhabitants—Voytek Frykowski, Abigail Folger, Jay Sebring, and Sharon Tate—are herded into the living room. Watson ties them up. He then instructs Atkins to kill Frykowski. The latter has loosened his bound wrists, and he attacks. Atkins and Watson stab and shoot Frykowski multiple times, driving him out to the lawn, where he collapses. Abigail breaks free and Krenwinkle chases her through the house. Watson stabs Sebring to death. Abigail is brought back; Watson stabs her. Frykowski is screaming for help on the lawn. Watson runs out, kills him. Inside, Abigail rises and staggers outside. Krenwinkle kills her on the lawn. Sharon Tate is the last. She's stabbed to death by all three killers. Before exiting the house, Atkins dips a towel in blood and writes *PIG* on the front door.

Like the Weatherman attack on Haymarket Square, the murders have taken about twenty-five minutes. Twenty-five minutes for three zombies to do what so many of their generation have, in their worst fantasies and deepest rages, only dreamed of doing.

The next night Manson drives.[96] His anointed killers are Krenwinkle, Watson, and Leslie Van Houton; the night's tools are four bayonets, two strips of leather thong, and the saber used to slice Gary Hinman's ear. Manson drives them to the Los Feliz section of Los Angeles, where he once visited an acquaintance's home. In the house next door live Leno and Rosemary LaBianca. They happen to be home. Manson steals in quietly, and ties husband and wife together. He goes outside, orders Van Houton, Krenwinkle, and Watson into the house, then drives away with the others.

Using the saber and bayonets, in addition to a two-pronged carving fork and butcher knife from the LaBiancas' kitchen, the killers end two more lives. Before leaving, they lay on the last touches. Leno LaBianca's corpse is mutilated, and three messages are left. All are again written in blood, in large letters and in plain view.

On the refrigerator: *HEALTER SKELTER.*

On the living room wall: *DEATH TO PIGS.*

On the opposite wall: *RISE.*

□

That was it: Helter Skelter. That was the fantasy Manson enlisted the Beatles to musicalize, fetishize, energize, and formalize. As long as he is remembered, the Beatles will be a part of his story; as long as they are remembered, he will be a part of theirs. The Beatles had no choice in it.

Eventually the murderers were caught, and a trial was held. Among the exhibits brought into evidence was Apple Records No. SWBO 101, *The Beatles,* a.k.a. "the White Album." Among the motivational factors whose meaning and relevance were contested were the Apple recording artists the Beatles, a.k.a. the four angels of the Book of Revelation. Prosecutor Bugliosi invoked the Beatles' music and Manson's interpretation of it as key determinants in the cosmic psycho-scam that was to be Helter Skelter; in response, Patricia Krenwinkle's attorney announced that he would call John Lennon as a witness in his client's defense.[97] Once deliberations had begun, the jury would make two requests of the judge: that they might visit the scenes of the murders; and that they be given a phonograph upon which to study the White Album.[98]

By the way: the accordion player on the *Magical Mystery Tour* bus was named Shirley Evans. Among the Tate-LaBianca jurors was a woman named Shirley Evans.[99]

The Family—laying curses and promising vengeance as they waited out the trial—sent desperate transmissions across the ocean in hopes that the musical communicants of Helter Skelter would rally to Manson's aid. David Felton and David Dalton described Manson sitting in his cell at the Los Angeles County Jail, "occasionally entertaining a disturbing thought: Why haven't they gotten in touch? A simple phone call would do it. Surely they've received the telegrams, the letters. Surely they realize that he knows, he *understands* their glorious revolution; that he understands the whole fucking double album."[100]

Gypsy was asked by the same writers what she would care to say to the Beatles. The words she began with expressed frustration, an inability to understand how the tuned-in authors of the White Album could fail their transatlantic soul brother by refusing to make themselves visible: "They have the power—and this is directed to them—if they would realize how much they're the ones, then just the point of their finger could send 144,000 people back to the desert. They could point to Charlie and say, 'This is the man who's saying what we're saying. Let's all get together on it.'"[101]

Suddenly her tone changed. Now Gypsy sounded hurt, betrayed. The undertone was: How could the Beatles have enabled me to believe, only to leave me here unfulfilled, wasting among the weeds, my leader on trial for his life? Is this the world I was promised? "They had the power to make everyone love each other. When *Sgt. Pepper* came out, there was so much love—everyone in the street and in the parks loving and hugging each other. There was no end to it. . . . 'All you need is love.' We were the only ones gullible enough to take the Beatles seriously. We were the only people stupid enough to believe every word of it."[102]

Now Gypsy was angry. But also resolute, pragmatic. Things had come too far: Helter Skelter would happen with or without the Beatles. Yes, they had urged it along, helped it take shape in Charlie's mind; but now its life was its own. The dream was *not* over. And if the Beatles would not dream it too, Gypsy's implication ran, they would be choosing to place themselves outside the last, the most magical and terrible circle of them all. And their necks, when the time came, would crack along with everyone else's.

"What can I say to the damn Beatles?" asked Gypsy, slightly exasperated. "Just get in touch, man. This is their trial. And all the things they've been hearing—there's something happening here; they should see it by now. It's hard to see through the negative, but just tell them to call. Give them our number. It's not that there's anything to say except hello to your brother, and how are we going to get this thing together? Because it's coming down fast. Don't let it break you."[103]

John Lennon did not testify in defense of Patricia Krenwinkle. She, Manson, Atkins, and Van Houton were found guilty on all counts and sentenced to death. Watson, who had fled to Texas, was extradited after a long delay and tried separately. He too was given the death penalty. Then, on February 18, 1972, the State Supreme Court of California repealed capital punishment on constitutional grounds, thus enabling the Helter Skelter killers to live out their years as Bachelors of Science (Krenwinkle), born-again Christians (Atkins, Watson), quiltmakers for the homeless (Van Houton), and faces on T-shirts (Manson).[104]

□

Police removed a door from the Spahn Ranch on November 25, 1969. Painted on it in red letters were "the lines from a nursery rhyme, '1, 2, 3, 4, 5, 6, 7—All Good Children Go to Heaven'; and, in large letters, the words 'HELTER SKELTER IS COMING DOWN FAST.'"[105] *Abbey Road* was released in the United States on October 1. There's no way to know whether the Family had heard that album's "You Never Give Me Your Money"—which fades on a recitation of the same rhyme—before they painted those words on the door.

It's tempting and frightening to wonder what atrocities might have been committed in the Beatles' name if Helter Skelter had not ended when it did: to wonder if *Abbey Road* would have been as fertile a field for Family fantasy as the White Album had been. Assuredly the Family would have found all manner of mind-blowing significance in one fact, had they but known it. The same day Cielo Drive became a charnel house, the Beatles gathered in the London sun and strode across Abbey Road as photographs were taken for their new LP.[106] In Beverly Hills, three killers and an observer crossed the driveway; in London, three Beatles and a corpse crossed the street. The acts were separated in time by a few hours, in space by half a planet, and virtually any signification of death, rebirth, and fan mania at its outer limit may be read into them.

You listen to *Abbey Road,* with the White Album and all those screams echoing somewhere behind it—and, after long immersion in the history of Helter Skelter, you're not certain anymore what you're hearing. Manson seems to be all over the record: in Old Flattop of "Come Together," long hair and disease, his incomprehensible acts preceded by a whispered *Shoot me.* "Sun King" with its soothing vocal and zombie serenity is a fulsome tribute to the golden god of the post-Revelation world. "Maxwell's Silver Hammer" is no more or less than a cartoon celebration of Manson's silver saber. "I Want You (She's So Heavy)" mushrooms into the abandoned howl of an obsession out of control, a desire that will devour everything to fulfill itself. While elsewhere, the mastermind of Helter Skelter haunts the Beatles' shaded summer street in the derelict rags of mean Mr. Mustard, who sleeps in a hole in the road.

Does the Devil lurk in these immaculate productions and comic asides? Or would their influence, had Manson been free to absorb it, have acted only for the good?

I have my opinion. Another person went on record with the opposite opinion. Among those who were, for a time, under Manson's thrall was a Hollywood producer who was given, or requested, the pseudonym of "Lance Fairweather." Take Lance Fairweather's comments, not as any kind of truth or last judgment, but simply as an anonymous individual's grasp at the possible, his answer to the unanswerable.

> I asked myself many times, "What made Charlie change? What was the main cause?" And one thought kept recurring: If *Abbey Road* had come out sooner, maybe there wouldn't have been a murder.
>
> That's far out, I know. But *Sgt. Pepper* was such a happy album, such a happy acid trip, and it made Charlie very happy. And then the white double album was such a down album. I know it affected Charlie deeply. And then *Abbey Road* was another happy one.

And I just can't help thinking: If *Abbey Road,* another happy album, had come out sooner, maybe Sharon Tate would be alive today.[107]

□

Not all abstract objects are perceivable; and if we perceive abstractions at all, we do not perceive them directly but only via the perception of some material object or entity (which instantiate them or with which they might be co-localized).

—Casati and Varzi, *Holes and Other Superficialities*

We must ask: How did the roving eye of myth fix on Paul's inoffensive face? Why was he chosen as the victim of the first (and thus far the last) pop-myth death—as opposed to, say, John Lennon, who many more might have wished dead? Why not, for that matter, George or Ringo? One answer is evident enough. In many post-1966 Beatle photographs, Paul is singled out by some detail, insignificant in itself, that distinguishes him from his companions: raised hand, turned back, black carnation, bare feet. Cross enough of these details with a vigorous imagination and—presto—they are points in a plot.

But what dull evidence *that* is.

In Richard Avedon's book *The Sixties,* there is a two-page spread captioned "Cape Canaveral, Florida, September 8, 1963."[108] It shows a deserted stretch of archetypal American highway at twilight: darkening sky and telephone poles, cars idling at an Esso station. In the foreground, a tall neon sign topped by a white star and three rings of extraterrestrial light advertises the Polaris Motel. A sad, strange image: the noble moon-quest of the New Frontier is equated with an empty motor lodge, cheap American neon aspiring to an empty sky.

The next picture is the last thing you expected to see: Paul McCartney, summer of 1967—and he is *wearing a NASA spacesuit.* Paul's head is tilted slightly, and his eyes have never looked less like they contain the real burdens of real life; never looked more like loving orbs of sweet supernatural acceptance. Instantly, he resembles the fetal star-child of *2001: A Space Odyssey,* with its wide eyes, just as innocent and monumental, hovering in space as it regards its own earth-womb.

The sequence of images is jarring, suggestive. The Cape Canaveral shot, taken weeks before the assassination which seems fated in its lowering sky, catches the last days of the American 1950s: an ethos of Eisenhower and Edsel, crewcuts and crude oil, outer space as un-tapped marketplace—everything the Beatles arrived to render old and dry and dead. The next shot casts Paul McCartney as astronaut in the new decade, stellar voyager into the next realm, first face of a new and unsullied order of human: Paul as star, child, and star-child. With ex-ploration of space (outer and inner) as the shared thread, these two photographs dramatize, in one leap, the supplanting of one con-sciousness by another.

In 1967, Timothy Leary proclaimed the Beatles to be "prototypes of a new race of laughing freemen. Evolutionary agents sent by God, en-dowed with a mysterious power to create a new human species."[109] A year earlier, a girl had explained her painting of Paul as the depiction of "A start, a new dawn. . . . And here is the thing—if you notice, he's like growin'." Both Leary and the girl may have been crazy—each in his or own way—but the point is belief. A lot of people, from acid evangelist to middle-class girl, believed that the Beatles were avatars of evolution's next turn, heralding a whole new mode of style, thought, and action. We're aware of the many '60s beliefs, and know something of their power. Among these was the belief, held for at least one spinning interval, that the Beatles' example would trans-form the shape and dimensions of the human mind.

And if the Beatles were seen as a new breed, it had to be Paul who was the cream of that breed. Physically he was the most beautiful of them, owner of a face crafted by nature to waft in the amniotic haze of a girl's dream world. Though his psychology was certainly as com-plex in its way as Lennon's, he had the public-relations professional's ability to coat psychology with charm. As a musician he was never,

27. Paul, 1967: alive and well in the Summer of Love, with the world on a string.

even at his greatest, an eccentric: his songs translated to any language, any taste. In short, he was brilliant but not offensive, erotic without being very sexual, he gave substance but always in a lean and easy-to-swallow form. He was born for mass appeal: "All Paul McCartney has to do," Jann Wenner wrote, "is wink or wave, and he'll set the world smiling."[110]

A power he shared with the infant—and Paul with his baby eyes and baby face, star-child and sprout, was as much new infant as new man, if not more. And so even better as a mythic surrogate: the world the '60s generation fought to create was, for the years it breathed life, likewise an infant. Like the star-child, a new imagination tenuously circled the earth, enormous but uncoordinated, powerful but vulnerable: it is life, but will it live?

A myth is a circle which inscribes beginnings in endings and vice versa, which searches for the ideal, the elusive fusion of birth and death. Joseph Campbell quoted Thomas Aquinas: "The name of being wise is reserved to him alone whose consideration is about the end of the universe, which end is also the beginning of the universe." Campbell continued:

> The basic principle of all mythology is this of the beginning in the end. Creation myths are pervaded with a sense of the doom that is continually recalling all created shapes to the imperishable out of which they first emerged. The forms go forth powerfully, but inevitably reach their apogee, break, and return. Mythology, in this sense, is tragic in its view. But in the sense that it places our true being not in the forms that shatter but in the imperishable out of which they again immediately bubble forth, mythology is eminently untragical.[111]

Paul-is-dead, then, followed a great mythic pattern: extracting from death a resolve of life. Out of death, real and symbolic, came the new life of communal narrative, the fixing of sense and significance. Tragic in its premise but "eminently untragical" in its methods, Paul-is-dead was a macabre playground, a place of fun, carnival, absurdity, invention. As the '60s died, clue-seekers dug for life among what they suddenly perceived as artifacts of death, thereby reversing, as all myth wishes to do, a biblical axiom: *In the midst of death we are in life.* Thus does the death-ridden community assure itself that life continues— by exercising imaginative power over reality, by dreaming, as one, the waking dream of myth. "True being," Campbell says, defining the self-creative, the self-constructive lure of mythmaking, "is not in the shapes but in the dreamer."[112]

By the time a myth of '60s death became necessary, the Beatles had served as changeable shapes for so many dreamers that they really had no competition as death messengers. And there was no Beatle whose combination of traits both real and perceived, personal and popular, positioned him better as designated corpse than Paul McCartney. John was too loud. George was too quiet. Ringo was too human. Paul was perfect—perfectly beautiful, so beautiful he was not quite real. Beautiful enough for the death to have a tragic dimension, unreal enough for it to function as pure myth and magic. Like his generation and its great social experiment, he was an infant in a grown body, both flesh and spirit, an ethereal presence circling the earth in a radiant membrane of evanescent purity. What had once made Paul a god among humans now placed him squarely on his back upon the altar of myth.

Life *does* go on, and something *is* sacrificed. For his beauty, he had to be the one.

□

> Suppose that, while walking along a street, you come across the following strange phenomenon: Beside you, on the ground, human footprints are being impressed one after another, accompanying your path.
>
> —Casati and Varzi, *Holes and Other Superficialities*

In fact, it was John Lennon who was the new *man* of the 1960s. He was the new in all its abrasive and irresolvable reality: the portrait to Paul's Dorian Gray, face bearing all of the decade's elations and exhaustions. He embodied its bruised idealism, its constructive pugnacity and righteous fervor, but also its violence and darkness; its radical hunger for power as well as its passive hippie-headedness; its hatred as well as its love. Name any extreme of the 1960s, and it lay in him by nature.

Except for the glasses, of course, Charles Manson and John Lennon did not look too dissimilar, that year of 1969.

Both Manson and Lennon were born in medium-large, industrialized river cities—Cincinnati and Liverpool. Both had youths marked by petty crime, social maladjustment, belligerence against authority, and the absence of parents. Both were deserted by their fathers, and both had fraught relations with mothers to whom they were close despite frequent separations. Lennon's mother is remembered as a free spirit; Manson's was known as loose. Both boys were left, in the mother's absence, with strict maternal aunts, whose discipline they were driven to rebel against all the harder. Turning points came for both at the age of sixteen. Manson, on the run from an Indiana reformatory, headed to California for the first time; Lennon heard Elvis Presley for the first time. Manson was caught; Lennon was freed.[113]

Compare the lyrics of Manson's "Cease to Exist" and Lennon's "Tomorrow Never Knows" for two blatant instances of crypto-spiritual, psycho-cultic indoctrination in a pop context. Each is posed as a psychic tutorial: how to relinquish autonomy to the whims of a greater power. Manson favors the word "submission," Lennon "surrender"; but each promises that not death but a higher form of conscious life is the reward for such existential capitulation. Ceasing to exist is not so far from turning off your mind; maybe it is the same thing.

Manson and Lennon shared similar thoughts on death. "Death to Charlie," Bugliosi was told in 1969, "was no more important than eating an ice cream cone."[114] "I'm not afraid of death, because I don't believe in it," John said the same year. "I think it's just getting out of one car and getting into another."[115]

They also had in common a pronounced Christ complex. Lennon in 1966: "We're more popular than Jesus now." And then, "There's something else I'm going to do, something I must do—only I don't know what it is." Manson four years later: "I may have implied on several occasions to several different people that I may have been Jesus Christ, but I haven't decided yet what I am or who I am."[116]

Bugliosi had an unidentified "folk-song expert" listen to Manson's music. The expert reported: "Somewhere along the line Manson has picked up a pretty good guitar beat. Nothing original about the music. But the lyrics are something else. They contain an amazing amount of hostility ('You'll get yours yet,' etc.). This is rare in folk songs, except in the old murder ballads, but even there it is always past tense. In Manson's lyrics these are things that are *going to happen.* Very spooky."[117] The expert is, of course, quoting a line that is also prominent in "Sexy Sadie," John Lennon's poisonous epistle to the giggling Maharishi—a song which also contains "an amazing amount of hostility."

Linda Kasabian was questioned by Bugliosi on the methods by which Manson had consolidated his extraordinary influence over the Family. Sexual manipulation and psychological domination through constant drug use, she said, were the most powerful of Manson's means. "Linda then added one statement," says Bugliosi, "which went a long way toward explaining not only why she but also many of the others had so readily accepted Manson. When she first saw him, she said, 'I thought ... "This is what I have been looking for," and this is what I saw in him.' Manson—a mirror which reflected the desires of others."[118]

In "Group Psychology and the Analysis of the Ego," Freud wrote, "Even today the members of a group stand in need of the illusion that they are equally and justly loved by their leader; but the leader himself need love no one else, he may be of a masterful nature, absolutely narcissistic, self-confident, and independent." Mark Edmundson expands on this: "Freud saw the self-abasing 'longing for the father,' on which our attraction to dictators, among other authoritarians, is based, as connected to the religious drive. And so long as we sustained religious beliefs, he believed, we would continue on in a state of protracted childhood. Our collective psychological task was to grow up by exchanging comfort for freedom, superstitious assurance for noble, if harsh, autonomy."[119]

Manson pushed the first half of that contrast—the religious belief over the collective psychological task. His mythos was all about comfort (the paradise beneath Death Valley), superstitious assurance (he had *found,* he said, the hole which led to said paradise), and above all the nourishment and protection of his own lordly ego (to say nothing of his all-too-human skin). Like his secret hero, Hitler, Manson was a pathological narcissist in the guise of father, lover, leader, savior; while through the "implication" that he was God or Jesus, he exploited the religious drive which Freud believed attracted fascist masses to their dictators.

Lennon, too, was some of this: a sybarite always in search of physical comfort, a narcissist with a weakness for faddish superstitions. But he agitated for the harder, nobler task of mass communication and involvement—for emotional freedom and autonomy (sometimes *very* harsh), and psychological growth past the false assurances of religion (hence his attempted demystification of the Christian savior). His narcissism was anything but pathological. He did not have Manson's mastery and cold self-containment; he was too aware of and fascinated by his own contradictions to keep any mask in place for long; and his communications to his audience were meant to direct that audience's energies outward into the world or inward into themselves, not back upon himself. Unlike Manson, he never asked you to give up your world to be with him; and while he may have advised you to surrender to the void, it was the color of your own dreams you were meant to hear.

And unlike the "absolutely narcissistic, self-confident, and independent" (and inevitably fascist) leader who "need love no one else," John Lennon desperately needed a return of the love he gave out. His resentment of his audience was genuine, but so was his love of it, and so was his need to be repaid by that audience in the rare coin of deep and constant communication, in whatever form—adulation, hatred, reverence. As his fans needed him to be their distorting mirror, he needed his audience to show him, again and again, what he looked like to them, what he was to them.

Manson and Lennon gave complementary shapes to the messiah-mania their era was made to embrace; both also carried an explosive mix of the angelic and the demonic. Manson was more demon than angel, John more angel than demon. But just as the whispers of the angel drew people to Manson, it was the shade of the diabolical that attracted so many to John Lennon, and his combustive potential that made him a defining figure of his time. These are the demon brothers of the '60s because in their constant swing between love and violence, music and mindfuck, the messianic and the mad, both absorbed and lived out the secret struggle of their decade. Creation against destruction, life against death, *Deus est vivus* versus *O.P.D.*

Of course John, unlike Manson, was not psychopathic; just unstable, just unpredictable. Nonetheless it was common in the late '60s for onlookers to raise serious questions about his soundness of mind. Following the appearance in 1968 of *Two Virgins,* whose famous cover showed John and Yoko in all their unclothed splendor, actress Sissy Spacek recorded a novelty item (under the *très* hippie sobriquet of "Rainbo") called "John You Went Too Far This Time."[120] During the peace campaigns and extended media copulations of '69, words like "mad" and "deluded" had a habit of reappearing in press reports. But the first suspicions of imbalance may have appeared as early as the *Revolver* songs. Nicholas Schaffner wrote of the reaction to John's mangled, magnificent 1966 acid-pop: "At the time some people thought Lennon was spouting incomprehensible gibberish, and concluded that the poor lad had slid off the deep end."[121]

In the '60s, pop was centralized by direct dialectic communication between artist and audience, and for that reason John Lennon was a dangerous presence in public life—a transforming and vitalizing presence. He knew there was madness in himself and his generation, madness in the epoch they were making, and he played with the radical possibilities of controlled madness from within the privileged role of the Beatle. Love is real, one of his lyrics said; he let you know how real it was to him. His hate was likewise real, as were his foolishness, his heedlessness, his hubris, and his madness. Perhaps no other figure of the time walked so exposed a line between offering the blessings of an artist and the provocations of a lunatic. Walking that line, he pushed, tested, outraged friends and enemies alike.

And in the end, as his blood hit the sidewalk, he may have known he had gone too far.

□

> Another question left open by our preceding discussion of holes is this: We examined the case of a holed object located in the hole of another holed object, but exactly what is meant by the expression "in a hole"?
>
> —Casati and Varzi, *Holes and Other Superficialities*

The 1960s—not as a sheaf of calendar pages but as a continuing project of the counterculture that made them—ended because they had to. With each universe of possibilities came a galaxy of contradictions, and the counterculture could not support the central contradiction it found itself living out: love and hate. Or luv 'n Haight, as Sly Stone titled a song, cleverly twinning pre-*Pepper* innocence and post-*Pepper* decadence, rendering the generic syndrome specific to his generation. Built into the social rebellions and cultural transformations of the decade were coeval drives toward creation and destruction; and in the end—under drugs and hedonism, abuse and backlash, ideology and dogma, paranoia and despair—the two melded into a single beast with thrashing body. From its overburdened gut came the vomits of 1969 and 1970: Weathermen, Manson, Altamont, Kent State, Nixon, and war ascendant.

Creation meant love meant life. Call it social justice or human compassion, but everything the movements of the '60s called for was based on the assumption that an ethic of love was the best way to run a society. Destruction, in a neat dichotomy, meant hate meant death. Call it righteous provocation or sticking it to the man, but everything the movements of the '60s called for demanded that old structures be smashed—and along with them, countless people both guilty and innocent. Creation meant embracing ambiguity, imagining options; while destruction meant stomping ambiguity, eliminating options until only one remained, and finally denying the humanness—however flawed or wretched one might feel it to be—of those who were hated precisely for denying the humanness of others.

"It's a wonderful feeling to *hit* a pig," said student radical Mark Rudd at the Christmas 1969 Weatherman conference. "It must be a really wonderful feeling to *kill* a pig or blow up a building."[122] A month earlier, Weatherwoman Bernardine Dohrn described a courtroom encounter with one of the cops who had arrested her. "And he turned around to look at me and I turned around to look at him, and we got locked into this staring thing. I hated him so much. And we just got locked into this thing and him looking at me was totally sexual and my looking at him was . . . was wanting to kill him. A lot."[123]

These are extreme examples of counterculture hatred, but they are examples of it. The Weathermen came out of that culture, as did the zombies who carried out Manson's murders. All right: so the love generation turned out to have as much hate in it as any other. Shocking insight. Isn't each of us an alternating current of love and hate? I don't know, but even to ask the question is a reflex we have taught ourselves in a post-'60s world—a pop-postmodern presumption of human duality that did not really inform the counterculture ethics of the '60s.

In other words, I'm not certain things were as obvious then as they may seem now. I believe most of the counterculture saw itself as good and its enemies as evil, and that the times themselves made it natural to distinguish sides with such Manichean clarity. I believe most of those who fought on the side of love believed their energies were not powered, in any part, by hate. I believe the hippies believed in flowers and quailed at aggression as one would at anything that was felt to be horribly alien to oneself. I believe many radicals believed the ruthless destruction of "the system" to be an act of enormous love, and that they would have found this attitude in no way comparable to that of the American forces who were bombing Vietnamese villages in order to "save" them. I believe John Lennon believed "that love would save us all."

Such beliefs—and the very *fact* of believing, a belief in the power of belief itself—were what enabled the '60s counterculture to alter the world's conception of itself. But it was partly the evasions these beliefs necessitated that forced the crescendo of madness at the decade's end. Pressing to itself these beliefs and more, the counterculture remained for a long time innocent of its own capacity for hate, of its drive toward destruction as an uncontrollable release of mass hostility and blind anger and not merely a deplorable necessity—which is how counterculture violence always was justified, once it became inevitable. By which time it was too late for the counterculture to do anything constructive with its hatred. Too late to do anything but stand back—as did SDS in capitulating to the Weathermen, as did much of the "alternative" press when it celebrated Manson as a culture hero and generational martyr. Stand back, and hope you don't get mistaken for a pig.

Helter Skelter and Paul-is-dead came directly out of these contradictions; out of this awful ending to a brilliant time; out of luv 'n Haight. Meaning that the Beatles, even in decline, dissolution, and disembodiment, were still at the essence of everything underlying the official history of the '60s; were again the ready focus of anxiety, illusion, myth, and monstrosity, fantasies both rational and anything but. As the counterculture turned bestial and the decade issued its last death-rattles, architects of creation and destruction found their raw materials in the bodies and voices of the Beatles.

Both Manson and Paul-is-dead returned the Beatles' story to its beginnings, while taking it to the furthest endings imaginable—or unimaginable. The Beatles began under the ground: the death cults were themselves underground, non-mainstream obsessions. Both were drawn by some magnetic pull emanating from beneath something else: hidden holes, hidden clues, *the real truth*. In both cases *the real truth* would, if discovered and deciphered, reveal *the ultimate truth*. And in both cases, *the ultimate truth,* such as its seekers found/made it, pointed at death. Both involved doppelgängers, demon brothers—Charles Manson and William Campbell. One group of seekers was a despised band of social dropouts who committed physical murder to serve one man's myth of himself. Another comprised unconnected clusters of middle-class college students who committed an intellectual murder in order to create a myth for their time.

Both groups heard the Beatles sending them the same message—the same *word,* really. Each was sending that word back, amplified, willing a concept into being through acts of imaginative fancy and physical violence, luv 'n Haight, creation and destruction. The word portended, for one group, violent insurrection; for the other, transformative resurrection. The word was preceded by *O.P.D.* and followed by *Deus est vivus.* For both groups, it was the dream held dearest as other dreams died their deaths—the one dream that, for those who had lived it once, would never come again.

In the ending was the Word: and the Word was *RISE.*

□

Holes die hard, we said. But how do they die, if ever? There are various cases. For instance, the matter that surrounds the hole may contract and simply close up on itself.

—Casati and Varzi, *Holes and Other Superficialities*

So they were standing on the rooftop, playing to an audience of television antennae and clouds. The human audience on the street—consisting, as ever, of fans and detractors, the curious and the concerned, those who felt blessed by their presence and others irritated by their audacity—looked skyward to discern the source of the wind-muffled sound, the stymied shouts of rock and roll. And saw nothing but sky.

The Beatles' final album, *Let It Be,* was a dank and dispirited patch job drawn from the masturbatory dribblings of the *Get Back* sessions. Its moments of simplicity and beauty—"Across the Universe," John's sunset valedictory on the deathless power of dreaming; "Two of Us," in which Paul looked to a future with Linda but sang across the past to his first partner—were left to languish in a thin mud of compromise. The final film, *Let It Be*—a dank and dispirited patch job, etc.—was worse. Unlike the other Beatle films, it had no periphery-story or under-meaning; no unconscious, and no symbols but one. In *A Hard Day's Night* the Beatles had been anti-icons who ascended finally to the skies. Here on the rooftop, lifetimes later, they are prisoners of that aerie, disembodied specters pushing their music against the wind. Whereas they had started by embodying a nascent revolution of the spirit, they were now the invisible spirits of a revolution officially pronounced dead: its wind-blown figureheads, voices without bodies, hollering last rites from a stage their audience could neither touch nor even see.

In one sense, then, breaking up was the only practical thing: they had no more to give. In another, better sense, it was their final gift to the audience. For there was much more they could have taken, had they chosen to: they could have continued as a commercial commodity long past the point where they had perished as a creative force, reaping the rewards of their very uselessness. Instead they abdicated the shelter of their collective identity, and began lives as private citizens who also happened to be world-famous rock stars. The ex-Beatles—particularly John and Paul, who made acknowledgment of their wives requisite to any acknowledgment of themselves—announced immediately that they would be functioning on a different scale: that they would pursue whims, try on clothes, succeed and fail on terms more modest than their audience was accustomed to.

In abrogating their exalted status—helping to push the audience past its need for them—they would, throughout the '70s, expose themselves to every imaginable charge of deceit, betrayal, banality, irrelevance. But their message to the audience was the familiar, the great Beatle message: into the breach, and on to *something else.*

□

"There comes a time—I believe we are in such a time—when civilization has to be renewed by the discovery of new mysteries."[124] The utopian sociologist Norman O. Brown said those words to the graduating class of Columbia University in 1960; four years later, the Beatles appeared to answer his vision. They fought, through the media of rock and roll and their own personae—constructed by them, continually reconstructed by their audience—to pose mysteries, embody them, conceal and reveal them. The audience, lovers and haters alike, fought too—harder than it had ever fought with or against any pop influence in its midst—because the mysteries were so many, the possibilities so unnerving, the adventure so fantastic.

The Beatles brought mystery, all right. More than their era could handle; certainly more than it could resolve in the few years allotted to it by history. But that was the burden of the '60s—too much mystery, too much ambiguity, too much *new* to figure out in too little time—as it is to a great extent the burden of those of us who missed the '60s but whose adolescent years were bathed in the run-off of its culture and politics. But would we have wanted it any other way? Imagine what the legacy of the '60s would be if the Beatles had not descended into their first cellar hole, back in those mythical days before there *were* Beatles. Imagine what that legacy would be if they had not then pushed themselves to rise. Imagine where the '60s would have gone if the Beatles had disbanded in late 1966, after they stopped touring. And imagine, for the sake of completeness, what the Beatles would have turned into had they not broken up until 1976. To the extent we may envision such hypotheticals at all, every idea, emotion, intuition, or suspicion we have ever had of what the Beatles or the 1960s *were* dissolves into dust.

What we now know—what seems obvious—is that the two were never separable. When the decade ended, other bands went on; but the Beatles, like the '60s, ended because they had to. History itself had become the only thing that could kill them; and when the time came, it did.

On New Year's Day, 1981, the body of a thirty-five-year-old woman was found in an apartment in Seattle, Washington. The corpse, clothed in striped pajamas, lay face-down on a couch in the bedroom. The coroner estimated the death had occurred at least two weeks prior to the discovery.

Police gathered routine information. The woman had earned a law degree from Stanford University, where she was active in campus causes. She had defended members of the local Menominee Indian tribe against charges stemming from a 1975 occupation of tribal ground in Colville National Forest, near Laurier, Washington. She had then worked for the Legal Aid Society of Seattle, handling the cases of impoverished tenants in class-action suits. A client described her as "a warm person. She would always help with legal advice, or bread if that's what you needed. She didn't mind listening to people's problems." She left the Legal Aid Society in August 1980; it was not clear whether she had sought employment since that time.

Friends were at a loss to explain the suicide, though none appeared to have had extensive contact with the woman in her final months. "I called one night after having not seen her for a year," said a college friend. "She sounded tired and depressed. Her words were kind of slurred. I thought she was drunk, so I said goodbye." Another acquaintance, thought by police to be the last person to see the woman alive, said she had responded with "shock and dismay" to the recent murder of John Lennon in New York City, but knew of no other reasons for the apparent depression.

A note was found on a dressing table near the body. It read: "Forgive me, my friends, for saying it—but I just don't care about this world anymore. We let each other down. Peace."

Decomposition prevented a definitive finding on the cause of death, but the coroner's pharmacological report noted that the dead woman's blood bore excessive amounts of two substances: vodka, and Phenobarbital capsules—also known as Nembutals, once also known as "yellow submarines."[1]

6

FANTASY INTO FLESH

A Life and an Afterlife

We'd better figure out what there is for us now that we can't be
Beatle fans any longer.
　　—Robert Christgau, *Village Voice* (1971)

I spent years living, much of the time, in someone else's past. That
past was the 1960s, and it came to me gradually, assembling itself
from the atmosphere; materializing from photographs and television specials, movies and music, paintings and books, the collected
memories of relatives and strangers. Before my teens even began, the
'60s had become nearly all I thought about. I hated and loved them.
They drove me to frustration, at times even modest despair, and I
didn't care to think how barren my life might have been had they not
happened.

　　I was born in 1966, about a month after the Beatles gave their final
concert. This situated me between the postwar generation whose history fascinated me and the generation labeled X by the media—that
generation which some people thought had briefly found its common tongue lodged between the sore throat and soft palate of the

late Kurt Cobain. I found this "between" a strange place to be (or not to be). From an early age I had the feeling of one who arrives at a party after most of the revelers have gone and there is nothing left but cigarette smoke, empty bottles, and a few moaning casualties. I was too young to have witnessed the events of the '60s, to have seen with my own eyes all the magic made, the curses laid; too old to feel that the events of my own time were anything more than tabloid fodder and dreary disaster. Too young to claim the '60s as mine by right of birth; too old—or melody-oriented—to feel that the exponents of grunge, rap, metal, hip-hop, trip-hop, trance, house, world-beat, techno, or any other style of '80s and '90s popular music spoke either to or for me.

Too young to remember the '60s; too old for them not to loom over me as a mythic measure against which my own era was in every way meager and inconsequential. So here I was ensconced, as few my age seemed to be, in a past not my own but close enough to be discerned in the pale second-hand droppings of the culture that was supposed to be mine.

It was easy for me to *imagine* the '60s because, despite being over, they were all around me. Everywhere I looked in the early '70s, there was some leaving of the decade just ended—from my father's modish sideburns to the growing number of feminist books on my mother's shelves, from the picture of Martin Luther King on the wall of my grade school to the Watergate hearings that were on TV when I came home. Among the few recordings my parents owned were '60s LPs by the Kingston Trio and Frank Sinatra, Glen Campbell and Ray Conniff—the middlebrow taste of Middle America for which I would forever be burdened with an undue affection.

In my parents' magazine rack was the issue of *Life* that sought to encapsulate the previous ten years: *The '60s—Decade of Tumult and Change.*[1] So many times—at first idly, then compulsively—I had taken it to my room, savoring the immediacy of the images with an illicit relish more appropriate to some dampened issue of *Playboy*. On one page, a group of young people in dirty street clothes were gathered in a cluster of shouts, the shirtless boy at the center raising his middle finger to punctuate the oath leaving his mouth. On another page, a blond man's spooked eyes and gaping mouth were imposed on a giant soup can.

This, I thought, excited, mystified, was *too strange*.

A boy with mustache and dark glasses smoked a cigar behind an impressive desk as other boys peered out a window behind him. A boxer raised his arms and bellowed bellicosities at the world. Vividly colored frames from a blurry filmstrip showed a woman in a pink outfit climbing out of a black car. People on a balcony, an assassinated man lying before them with face covered, their fingers straining toward the shots as desperately as if the devil himself were getting away. Pictures from what looked like some jungle in Hell, one-eyed bandaged faces and exposed bloody limbs, the gory mural suffused in colors of military olive, mud brown, pale red. On a street that looked like any street, an Asian man stood with hands bound, taking a bullet in the head. His face—tragic and twisted as it perceived the fang of the bullet—was one it would have taken a painter of demented genius to capture.

Years later I would, along protracted paths of undirected research, garner the information that explained each of these images. But they needed no facts to convey their essence to seven-year-old eyes. To me, the '60s became a place—not even so much a time—of horror and majesty and magic. All kinds of magic: good and bad. Magical not only in their seemingly unlimited creativity but in their surfeit of violence and transgression, the braving of the obscene and realizing of the impossible. My *Life*-styled view of the '60s was romantic, but only as *Wuthering Heights* or *Oliver Twist* was romantic: into it was built an apprehension, if far from an understanding, of madness and murder. It was the extremes of the time that drew me to study it; and the romance depended on my sense of how much horror had been touched in that time—that short time which by some awful fluke of generational scheduling lay only a few years behind me, yet in a way might as well have been a century distant.

Therein lay all the lure of this past. One: its extremes, from one end of creation to the other end of destruction. How a single unit of time could have seen so many eruptions, birthed so many traumas; how such intensities of individual genius, mass insanity, and the reverse of each could have crossed in a webwork of synchronicities and culminations so mind-boggling even Jung would have scoffed at its theoretical proposal. Two: that like a dream chimera, the '60s were within temporal distance and yet would never be touched by me, let alone grasped, however intense my attempt. One and two together: the '60s were a lifetime's supply of mystery meat. A limitless bounty of questions and quandaries, existential enigmas and antic occultisms, the ultimate mythic-romantic fusion of birth and death, dream and nightmare. And it was *all true*. It was *history*, freshly minted, and there for the taking.

The '60s might be untouchable, but it became clear to me that I would need, in some way, to make the attempt. This would mean acknowledging the decade's incoherence while seeking its unities; creeping along the entangled live-wires of anger and idealism that ran through the decade, in the hope and foolish confidence that all would reach a common terminus, a control center from which the decade's good and bad energies could be seen to radiate. It would mean asking, and answering—to my own satisfaction, if no one else's—the question, *Who invented the '60s?*

What I didn't know was that my effort to touch the '60s would finally mean creating my own myth from the facts and fancies of the time: my own Book of Revelation, starring the Beatles as the four angels of the apocalypse. Even less did I know that making myth of another's past would have the ultimate personal result of making me

more at home in my own time, that foolish and desolate era in which
I had once believed myself so unfairly misplaced.

□

Of all the washed-up, moribund, self-pitying, self-parodying erstwhile pop giants to survive the Sixties, the four splintered Beatles
may well have weathered the pall and decay of the Seventies the
worst.

—Lester Bangs, *Creem* (1972)

The unassuming wellspring of my rock and roll obsession was a second-hand store in Davenport, Iowa. On a Sunday in the summer of
1973 my father and I drove there from our hometown of Waterloo, a
few hours to the west. We visited a National Guard armory museum,
mausoleum to hulking Howitzers and ancient pea-shooters. We also
stopped at a Goodwill store, where my father bought me my first radio: a toaster-sized artifact of the '60s, with stylized Zenith name-
plate, large translucent dial, and hard shell of beige plastic. The radio
was in battered shape, static its major export, but it was something
new and exciting in my life. I listened to talk stations and classical
stations and country stations, sounds not of great interest to me,
merely to hear them issuing from my own private box of random
voices. Soon enough I landed at KWWL, 1330 on the AM dial, a me-
dium-wattage station in the heart of Waterloo that played the Top
40. I'd never paid particular attention to pop music before; now I did.
For years, the dial would seldom see another frequency.

From my radio came the hits of 1973–1976. Hearing these records in
later days, as '70s vogues came and went and came, I would be revisited by a feeling that was equal parts nostalgic warmth and judgmen-
tal discomfort. Some of the records I loved from those years were
simply not good. Some were indeed shamefully bad, and a handful I
knew I would detest had I encountered them at any time other than
my own childhood, whose memory sheen transformed everything in

its range into emblems of a happiness as much figment as fact. As my critical consciousness formed, I grew queasy with the pleasures of my musical youth and resisted the pleasure they still gave me. For how could I justify my preference for the Carpenters trifle "Top of the World" to "Sweet Home Alabama," the race-baiting hit of those critical favorites Lynyrd Skynyrd? How could I feel comfortable with the surge of emotion I got from Maureen McGovern's "The Morning After"—a record that much older and wiser critics seemed always to have recoiled from as if it were a pox-bearing monstrosity?

But that was what nostalgia was—or what it *could* be, when it wasn't behaving: an upending of critical distinctions, an agnostic zone of wish, garbled recollection, selective reconstruction, and emotional profit and loss in which rational calibrations of taste played no very powerful part. If something reached you *then,* the chances were good it would reach you always, no matter how far you believed you had traveled in the interval. "SOS" would always have the baleful power to hack two feet off my height, "Kung Fu Fighting" the ability to scoop decades of education and maturation neatly from my surrendering brain. That, I guessed, was only one of the funny tricks memory would play on you if it got the chance—and somehow it always got the chance.

Elton John was my first concentrated musical interest, and *Goodbye Yellow Brick Road* the first rock and roll album I ever owned. In the early '70s, Elton was in his golden age, and unrecognizable from today's eunuchoid purveyor of kitschy bombast for corporate boardrooms: outrageously imaginative eyewear, pudgy body ridiculous with feathers, sequins, and platform heels, head free of any apparent hair plugs or Disney aspirations. Elton's talents were of a kind common in pop music, but uncommon in such fecundity—talents for melody, nasal-glottal voice trickery, hard-pop production value, and plain vinyl showmanship: he knew how to write songs, how to sing them, and finally, crucially, how to sell them. I found flight in his melodies, flash in his piano, sweep in his melodramatic orchestrations, wondrous irritation in his vocal mannerisms and coddled peculiarities. Even his record jackets were elaborately detailed epics of pop clutter and Hollywood nightdreams, with booklets, gatefolds, bright art, and pieces of interlocking cardboard. On show were a sense of humor, a pop appreciation of focused grandiosity, and most of all a delight in play and fancy. As Elton stepped from the concrete sidewalk to the golden path on the cover of *Goodbye Yellow Brick Road,* all I wished was to go with him. This was a true rock and roll hero.

Another cluster of hits stuck in my ears during this time—all tuneful and pleasant, some silly, some with a layer of what could only be called melancholy. All seemed inexplicably similar despite obvious differences, like waters drawn at different banks along the same river. "Band on the Run," "Whatever Gets You through the Night," "Give Me Love (Give Me Peace on Earth)," "You're Sixteen," "Jet," "#9 Dream," "Listen to What the Man Said," "Sally G," "Photograph." Eventually, names joined with sounds: Lennon, McCartney, Harrison, Starr. I determined further that the latter three had once been members of the Beatles—a group I was vaguely aware had once existed, since their music was a staple even on the chart-based KWWL. The name of the fourth member, though, remained a mystery.

In 1975, two things happened that changed my world. The first was that my parents broke up. The second was that I became entranced by a book—*The Beatles: An Illustrated Record*—whose cover showed four men in shiny suits.[2] Every trip to the mall was an excuse to fondle this glossy, oversized production, turn its pages and stare at the album covers, all the photographs of these strange, handsome, astonishingly changeable faces. After several visits the book's spine was cracked, and pages were coming loose. Leaving the store, I always hid it behind other, larger books, so that no one would buy it.

On my next birthday my father presented me with the book, cracked spine and all. Then I started to read, and was able to reach

**28. Ringo, kit, and flowers: head bobbing in the shadows, peace and love
without nonsense, the uncommon common man.**

one grand resolution—and here in my tenth year, as my outer world
came apart, my inner world came together. It was John Lennon who
was that fourth, elusive member.

Too much. I'd sensed that McCartney was a major talent, since his
records were on the radio like jam on a sandwich. But Lennon *too?*

Wow, was roughly my thought, *that must have been some group.*

□

I say in speeches that a plausible mission of artists is to make people appreciate being alive at least a little bit. I am then asked if I
know of any artists who pulled that off. I reply, "The Beatles did."

—Kurt Vonnegut, *Timequake* (1997)

Guess what? I have a theory:

Each child feels he is the center of his own universe, and so anything he experiences seems natural, be it pain or pleasure, simply because it is happening to *him*. He does not know what his or the world's darker themes are; he has no way of distinguishing between dark and light. Therefore there *is* no dark or light—only a monochrome that is the undeveloped self. No dualities—only a spectrum containing all extremes.

Such godly innocence doesn't last. As consciousness accrues, the world inserts a wedge into that childish self-possession and slowly adjusts it to the fact that, as divisions exist in others, so they exist in the child himself. Thus it is axiomatic that fear, like hatred and prejudice, must be taught. If parents do not teach the child fear, something will; and when the lessons commence, it will be an unsentimental education. The child's only response as an outside force begins to toy with the gears of his psychic mechanism is to be as viscerally afraid as an adult would be of finding himself isolated in a foreign country. The child's first intercourse with some disruptive agent of the world outside his own fastened frame of reference will place him squarely on the terrain of his own divides, at a time when he is unable to identify, let alone integrate them; when he can do nothing but stare, stupefied, into the cracks.

For me, John Lennon was that agent. At a certain point my fascination with the Beatles began to grow daily; yet I was frightened of Lennon. In every particular, from the teeth of the smile to the flat of the unimpressed voice, he was an unaccountable presence in my universe, seedy and exotic, with the suggestion of something truly perverse in the inner workings. Studying his face, I feared Lennon would materialize in some wraith form to devour me.

At nine, I stumbled into the boudoir of my primal Beatle scene. *Help!* was shown on television. Nervously, I turned it on; and instantly realized that my fear of Lennon was bilious, overwhelming. I winced as I watched, for the camera seemed always too close to Lennon, his face ever growing, shifting, advancing. I switched between the movie and "Saturday Night Live," and each return to John's taunting, meat-eating grin brought new dread, a new thrill: this Lennon had weird designs on me. Finally the intensity was too much. I quit the Beatles and calmed myself with "Samurai Dentist."

Only much later did it dawn on me that these thoughts were, well, *irrational.* What was the precise shape and character of this fear? Was it not fear at all but some other raw emotion, one interpreted as fear by an immature mind? My guess is that it was something which, had I been an adult, would have pointed to paranoid schizophrenia: the unreasonable fear of infiltration and domination by an outside force. Lennon in his perversity and humor, attractiveness and brutality, impressed me as pure rapacious ego, an amoral organism with a basic need to dominate. I resisted as best I could the wholesale invasion of my consciousness he and his three co-conspirators seemed to intend—even while I relentlessly encouraged it. This was why I fled the TV image, then hurried back, only to flee again. It was also why I became obsessed with the Beatles: I was being invaded and could do nothing to stop it. I grew used to positioning my gaze somewhere between looking at them and looking away, and in the obliquity of the angle I formed a personalized Beatle image of shifting psychic layers, multiple exposures of fear and exhilaration.

So it was not only entertainment the Beatles were bringing into my world—it was the conflicted, yet-to-be-articulated sense that one thing could, in fact, be many things. They were bringing me knowledge of two worlds, one outside, one inside: the mysteries out there, the darknesses in here. And one day the two were conjoined. My first deep experience of a Beatle song occurred when both the song and I were ten years old. Home alone on an autumn afternoon, I lay on the floor with my head less than an inch from the better of two badly wired, simulated-woodgrain-finish stereo speakers. I played the first song on the first side of my first Beatle album: "Strawberry Fields Forever."

This would never quite become my favorite Beatle song—it remains fifth, behind "Yes It Is," "A Day in the Life," "Please Mr. Postman," and "She Loves You"—but it was the instrument of my first consciously experienced cosmic epiphany. As I lay listening and the song built itself into reality from a funny kind of marshmallowy movement, muffled voice and marginal noises, the floor beneath me began to liquefy. The walls curved inward over my head. My eyes swam, my legs vibrated, and my hands, without moving, lost contact with the floor. The descending guitar chimes between verses touched my temples like silver raindrops. I felt cleansed by them.

Cleansed of what? Innocence, or ignorance, or simply an old way of thinking and feeling? How could I know? But when I stood and looked out at the gray Midwestern sky, unchanged from minutes before, its thunderheads were pendulous with a wondrous weight of doom; those dark clouds promised the same silver rain that even yet was forming wells in my ears. The mysteries out there and the darknesses in here had come together, and I had realized that in some final sense the two were, had to be, the same: I'd been to that place where world and self were connected. After hearing "Strawberry Fields Forever" as I had heard it, anyone with two synapses to snap together had to realize that worlds unseen lay many leagues distant, that worlds unknown teemed just outside the window. That Experience held promise far beyond the beery languor of a college-football Sunday in an off-ramp Rust Belt town; and that there was something of Eternity in the precise, verdant lines of an Iowa cornhusk.

Within a few months, a large part of my identity had been formed—a basic need implanted, a prize glimpsed that I would spend my life pursuing in the hope of recapture. It was formed first by fear, then by exhilaration; by the primal and the epiphanic; by the dangerously erotic and the excitingly exotic. Some things were clearer upon receipt of these gifts, others more mystifying. Life itself was infinitely worthier of being lived and pursued. It was the child's first great revelation.

Revelation has different uses, I would someday learn, and all manner of practical result. One was that, within two years, the child who had known cosmic fusion on the living-room floor would be embezzling cash from his paper-route collection-bag to buy Beatle records, and wind up owing the crippling sum of $56 to the Circulation Department of the Des Moines *Register*.

□

Instead of using his musical brilliance for good, Lennon chose evil. Those deifying him need to seriously consider what it is they feel worth canonizing. His atheism? His gross immorality? His drugs? His social rebellion? His world view? If we could answer this question, we could also discover why Western civilization is crumbling.

—David A. Noebel, *The Legacy of John Lennon* (1982)

In the late '70s, my father shot pool with a man who was a Vietnam veteran. He wore a field jacket, Fu Manchu mustache, and sunglasses even in the dark of the local pool hall. His voice was a murmur. He drank beer and uttered the subtlest of sardonicisms while moving in quiet circles around the table, lining up shots with utter detachment before sinking them decisively. For one so recessive, the vet was not easy to forget. He threw off an aura of not being quite a complete human being, making me think that if I were to look behind his shades there would be nothing but two more black lenses.

At one point my father missed a shot, and cursed how close he'd come. The veteran—reclining against a pillar with his cuestick at parade rest—breathed a smirk and murmured, "Close only counts in horseshoes and hand grenades."

The meaning of that deathless phrase was chilling to me as a young discoverer of the past, a '60s past close enough to haunt me in its closeness, and that meaning was: Close doesn't count at all. Proximity to such danger as the '60s held mattered only if you were near enough to be damaged by it, burned and twisted by it.

Neither horseshoe nor hand grenade, I could never comprehend the '60s, because I had never been close enough to have suffered by them. I hadn't been there to take my position and run my share of the risk, be beaten down for standing up. To me, the '60s could never be reality; they could be only Beatle music and flashy movies, the historical snuff-porn of war, assassination, and a thousand other thrilling brutalities. I told myself I wasn't just a day-tripper in the tourist land of the '60s, that I truly respected the time and its makers. Which I did. What I could not so easily acknowledge, or justify, was that I was getting turned on by another generation's traumas. Something told me that that man in the pool hall who would not bare his eyes to the world was the *only* one who knew what the '60s were about, and it was not for a kid barely in his teens to trespass on this man's emotions by attempting to "understand" or—worst sin—"enjoy" what leftovers of the '60s he could scrounge from library shelf or record rack or TV tube. This is what I sometimes thought: that I had no right to this history.

Then something happened to make all that feel like wasted energy. Late one night my sister appeared at my bedroom door and said, "Someone just shot and killed John Lennon." Exactly those words. My reaction was probably not unusual: a sharp, violent exhalation of scared laughter. This was followed by the sensation that my insides had fallen out somewhere. Then numbness set in, and over the next couple of hours the insides crawled back, one by one, to resume their niches. I expelled a few hot, unfulfilled tears before drifting into light sleep. In the middle of the night I woke with dry heaves, and when they passed I slept as soundly as if I'd been beaten.

Two solid weeks followed, or perhaps three, in which the story was seldom out of the news. Reports filtered through as the killer underwent psychological observation and his murderous life-journey was rapidly reconstructed. Inescapable were the views of Dakota vigils, mass sing-alongs and red faces boiled in winter tears; peace fingers lofted, candles aflame, cardboard lettered with inevitable words: *GIVE PEACE A CHANCE. REMEMBER. IMAGINE. WHY?*

The popular press was by now geared to, and largely produced by, the baby boomers, and most of its obituaries pushed the same culminating point. People were reacting as they were, the commentary went, because *this,* at last and finally, was the death of all those dearly held '60s dreams. Nothing so simple as that a man had died, or even a man who through his work had enlightened and enlivened the public life of two decades in ways that could be expected to resonate far beyond his passing. No, it was the *dream* that had died, the very idea of the '60s itself. In death, Lennon became once again what he had for years stoutly resisted being: a symbol.

Even though I sensed its falseness, I found the whole idea in some morbid way appealing: if I hadn't been around to see the '60s live, at least I could watch them die. I even tried, very briefly, to construct Lennon's death as my generation's "answer" to the Kennedy assassination. Same loss of innocence, right? Same trauma, same shock? I remembered where I was when the news came. And hadn't that become the piece of shared history by which '60s people identified themselves to each other? But it was all crap: the parallels simply were not there. My generation was never as innocent as the '60s people claimed to have been at the dawn of Kennedy time, and the awful fact was that John Lennon's death was neither as traumatic nor as shocking to someone my age as it should have been.

I was too young to have imagined growing old with Lennon—to have imagined, that is, growing old—but it was more than that. My generation was already familiar with assassination as a social reality, death as a gratuitous media spectacle. We'd seen the bodies of Jonestown cultists and American soldiers in Iran. We knew about the lone gunman; and the loss of John Lennon to a moronic nobody simply fit too well into the history we had inherited to be shocking for anything more than its disheartening inevitability. It hurts to sound blasé—for blasé is not how I feel—but the plain truth is that my generation had been prepared too well to accept that John Lennon should die by a fanatic's bullets.

I felt differently about the '60s. They'd given me something, and now the looming '80s had taken it away. One person might have said there was no great loss, because all that was taken was something I'd never really known anyway; another might have said that the loss was as hard and meaningful for me as it was for any '60s person, inasmuch as that person hadn't *known* John Lennon either. One person might have said that I, like other Beatle fans my age whose obsession would always include an aspect of mourning for the absent figurehead, could now fairly count myself a victim of '60s (or at least '60s-derived) suffering. Another might have said that I was the victim of nothing but tough shit.

I suppose that I and my generation of Beatle-lovers fell somewhere in between suffering and tough shit: our pain was neither epochal nor trivial. But whatever else it was, the loss felt by a second-generation fan in December 1980 and forever after was personal—it was not parasitic on anyone else's history. John Lennon's murder, for all that it robbed me of, enabled me to feel for the first time that I could approach the '60s on something like my own terms.

□

I don't know which is more pathetic, the people of my generation who refuse to let their 1960s adolescence die a natural death, or the younger ones who will snatch and gobble any shred, any scrap of a dream that someone declared over ten years ago.

—Lester Bangs, Los Angeles *Times* (1980)

If pushed into a corner and threatened with a knife, I would have to admit that though I hated the '80s, I liked a lot of their pop music. It was the golden age of U2 and Prince, and the blue period of Bruce Springsteen. Elvis Costello produced much of his best work, and REM could be counted on for one or two superior songs per album. The decade began with the brief flowering of MTV as a strange new thing, an almost funky outlet for ephemeral innovations that had all the basement charm of cable access. The decade ended with *Do the Right Thing*, Spike Lee's camera zooming in on a dancing Rosie Perez as Public Enemy drilled into "Fight the Power." There were stellar 45's from the likes of Madonna, the Pretenders, Tracy Chapman, Culture Club, Eurythmics, the Go-Go's, INXS, the Cars, Terence Trent D'Arby, Crowded House, and John Cougar Mellencamp. Febrile indie rock was all over the place—Dead Kennedys and Dinosaur Jr., Pixies and Pogues, Hothouse Flowers and Hüsker Dü—as well as a solid stream of the one-hit wonders which form, if not the backbone, then the ribs and femurs and radii of any body of rock and roll time.

Throughout the decade, loathing Ronald Reagan and the culture of jingoism, piety, and consumerism that seemed to have sprung up at his silent beck, I tried to care deeply about the best new music I was hearing—because I knew that, good or bad, it was *my* music, and would form my pop adolescence. This realization was of some urgency: if I hoped to go through life with any pop memories of my own, I'd better work hard to make '80s music work for me. It did and it didn't. I cherished the good singles that came on the radio in those years, before the medium was demographized into shopping-mall units; and I prayed to the marketplace gods for any sign of a unifying genius, a culture hero around whom we all could rally. Michael Jackson was to me as much a creative cipher as he was a commercial fact. Springsteen wrote good songs and had a good heart, but there was finally something too retrograde about him for me to embrace him as a character indubitably of the day, let alone the future. U2 hit their *Achtung Baby* peak long past the point where I had given up hoping for my own Beatles.

Beyond the '80s lay the '90s, and the '90s were, to my Beatle-trained ears, almost unrelieved tedium. There were good records—passionate, quirky, chaotic, or merely catchy records; but as pop became ever more of a "universal language," it also drove toward a stylistic self-segmentation and avoidance of mutative potentials which indicated it was taking its cues from an increasingly segregated marketplace. Rap moved in to declare itself the dominant sound of the millennium, and as its gangsta subgenre became more of a cultural monolith I found less and less place for myself in its cramped and cartoonish worldview, its mindless, apolitical thumping of thuggish hatreds. I liked a handful of Nirvana songs and appreciated Cobain's sorrow and violence; but neither he nor his indie ilk had anything generationally personal or emotionally specific to tell me. While the other unavoidables of these years—manufactured divas, boy bands, and belly-baring girls, all vocal hysterics and spastic dance moves—were too musically mediocre to inspire my hatred, they were too commercially popular to evade my contempt. As self-important as a liberal movie producer, as monotonous as cancer, '90s pop reached the point where it was sucking more out of the world than it was pumping into it.

So I gave up trying so hard to "relate" to the music of my moment. I listened to my '60s music even harder—embraced it first as an antidote to Reagan poison, then as a tonic against the self-referentialism and bullet-headed aggressiveness of '90s pop culture. For me, the old stuff sounded stronger as time passed. It had never enervated, only empowered me; never been a roadsign to regression, always been a spur to the next thing in life. I couldn't see that changing now. It didn't.

□

Phony Beatlemania has bitten the dust.
—The Clash, "London Calling"

As the well-hyped millennium lumbered near and the '60s receded ever further, I came to accept that I would never know the self-conscious sense of age-based unity that had made the '60s what they were. Certain realms of knowledge and experience were simply not open to those majorities consigned to the great blank spaces in between periods of world-shaking, world-making transformation. The best I could do was to reach peace with myself as an actor within my own stretch of time, whose choices were my own and whose era, whatever its shortfalls and banalities, was and would continue to be unlike any other in history.

The peace was both calculated and organic, in part formulated and in part just accepted. Formulated, because it depended on growing older and the recurrent recognition that one *had* grown older; and accepted, since in truth it was there to be found all along, through all the old envies and the false hopes of a '60s sequel—if only I'd been prepared to receive it. Any number of personal transformations conspired in working this out for me, but two in particular bore relevance to the Beatle vein of my own story.

First: In the early '90s I moved to New York—partly to attend graduate school, partly because I wanted to be a writer and that's where writers went, and partly because New York was, if such a place could be named, the Beatles' American hometown. It was where they'd made their U.S. debut, where they'd played Shea Stadium, and where John Lennon had lived and died. I sought out those physical signifiers of the Beatles' previous existence that were now available to me: the Dakota, of course, the Gothic spook-trap familiar from vigil footage and *Rosemary's Baby;* Strawberry Fields, the Lennon-dedicated walkway in Central Park across 72nd Street, with its memorial plaque on a piece of sloping green; the Plaza Hotel, where the Beatles roomed and jived with Murray the K; Carnegie Hall, where they played their first American concert; the Delmonico on Park Avenue, where they had lit up with Dylan; the Ed Sullivan Theater on 52nd

Street. For me, New York was imbued with Beatleness. When, quite by chance, I spotted Yoko Ono on a street corner, it seemed the least surprising thing in the world.

The sites and sightings drew one kind of arc between the Beatles' history and mine. New York City had been forward guard to their land of dreams, immovable gargoyle at the gate of their destiny—and now, on more modest scale of course, it was mine. My scouting of Beatle places had the sensation of a return to roots—doubled in strangeness, since the roots were ones I had given myself, and, more than the past, they seemed to point to a future.

Second: In 1995, the news came through that the three "surviving" Beatles would collaborate on their official autobiography. It would take varied and successive forms: three-part TV show with ten-hour home-video box to follow; three double-CD soundtrack installments composed of unreleased studio outtakes and live performances; and finally a coffee-table book. Though duly excited, I placed only the lightest of expectations upon the Beatles' ability to tell their own story in an interesting way. And they did not disappoint, failing to deliver a radical self-examination—though the ultimate product was a good deal more absorbing than might have been expected coming from three people who evidenced little more than a dutiful, flame-keeper's interest in the whole enterprise. Each of the *Anthology*'s incarnations was a larder stocked with flavorful goodies for the Beatle fan. But their interest lay in a wealth of unseen and unheard material, and many wicked flashes of post-Fab sarcasm—not in a particular willingness to delve, let alone dive, into the total raw texture of the mania and what it had done to its three breathing beneficiaries.

For me, the emotional as opposed to archival riches of the whole *Anthology* slew lay in the first "new" Beatle music in a quarter-century: two Lennon demos, recorded solo shortly before his death, and embellished by McCartney, Harrison, and Starr fifteen years later. Though no one agreed with me, I was certain that "Free as a Bird"

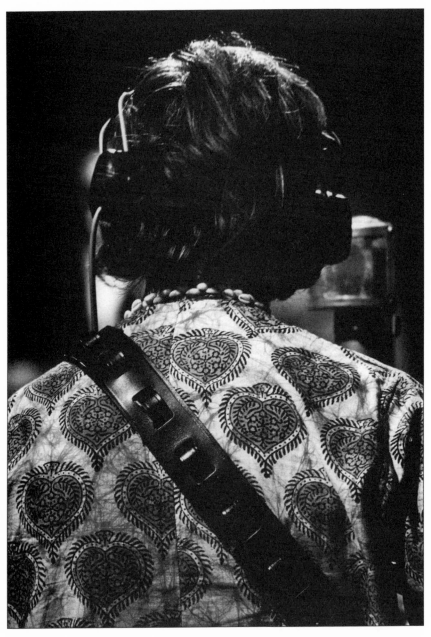

29. George Harrison, 1943–2001. R.I.P.

and "Real Love"—particularly the latter—were among the best things in the Beatle catalog. They were emotionally transporting, first of all, as pop records. Unutterably sad, they offered the sound of wraiths commingling: one dead, tape-preserved ghost, and three live ghosts living in a post-Beatles world. In part because their components were so hazily meshed, both recordings had a legitimate quality of lostness that rendered the artless and even simple-minded lyric sentiments dry, elusive, and haunting. Both recordings were contrived of studio tricks, equalizations and enhancements, decorative overdubs and deceitful mix-arounds; yet because the quality of both past and present performance was so intuitively delicate and supportive of every other part, both felt organic in sounding so spectral. These Beatle voices, separated by time, acrimony, history, and death, were shadows touching in air. Somehow the touch was felt, and the love felt real.

More than this: "Free as a Bird" and "Real Love" extended me another Beatle revelation. On the one hand, they were from their opening notes (sharp Ringo snare-crack for the first, befogged circular piano phrase for the second) unmistakably the work of the Beatles—whatever virtual, incomplete, even false form they were now forced, by love or money, to assume. Yet they did not sound remotely like any pathetic appeal to the past. They sounded instead like the expression of four wise and humbled humans of just that state which the writer-listener had, for all these years, been feeling toward—an accepting and harmonious resolution on the predicament of seeming historically adrift, miscast in time.

"Real Love" overturned my whole sense of what was past and what was present, what was historically mine and what was not. Unlike all the old Beatle songs that to me sounded new, this was a new song that sounded old—old as a tombstone is old, whatever its vintage. It was a transitory merging of yesterday and today, a fusing of histories that was appearing, for the first time anywhere, before my eyes, then instantly vanishing. Was the '60s veteran, the original Beatle fan, hearing the song in just this way? I'd have bet my life not. So the revelation was: though as a historical object "Real Love" belonged to me, as a live emotional organism it belonged to anyone who saw into it, who felt that it saw into them. Upon the smooth deceptive history-haunting surface of this record, all were equals, all would be equally adrift. But my drift in this strange water, its speed and bounce and salt content, would be my own.

Wait—it had *always* been my own—? Obviously! I could not have felt all these feelings, or heard the Beatles' songs as I had always heard them—could not have felt *anything I had ever felt about the Beatles or their time*—if I had been anything other than what I was: an ordinary American Beatle-besotted second-generation fan-fanatic destined by fate to miss out on the '60s.

Now *here* was, as they said, the meat of the matter. I had always coveted the direct experiences, earned wisdoms, and epochal blessings bestowed on the '60s veterans. At any point in my growing up, I felt I would have given all I had to trade places with the merest and most marginal of them. What I had never realized or appreciated until now—alone in a cramped Manhattan room, suddenly pushing thirty—was that trading places in the historical line would have meant giving up the precise set of psychological biases, intellectual limitations, aesthetic prejudices, and personal experiences that had shaped me into the possessor of a relationship with the Beatles and the '60s unique from that of anyone who had ever given thought to either.

What had been my sweetest and bitterest fantasy was now almost horrifying. Without this identity, after all, I would never have been able to twist the Beatles into the many private shapes I had asked them to assume. Never have been able to construct, through an interpretation of dream and study of history, my own version of the story they had once imagined and enacted. Change an instant of my experience, and the Beatles—*my* Beatles, my customized version of their meanings and metaphysics—would be stolen from me.

That decided it. What I could say, at last, was that I would *not* trade my place in history, whatever this place was or wasn't, for any other.

This helped me get clear on what I had and hadn't done with myself. As much as my embrace of the '60s had been, I still thought, a healthy response to certain imaginative and social deficits in my own time, it was also an escape from the choices and responsibilities I knew would be required of me as an adult. It was one thing to explore another's past in order to enlarge one's sense of the present and future; something else to take up permanent intellectual residence in that other past in order to feel superior to whatever future one might take a role in shaping. My willful envy of the '60s veterans was a way of deferring the need to add anything new and vital to the life of my time, to set my own small weight against the inevitable and ongoing deficiencies of my culture by deploying whatever talents I had in whatever might be the right places.

I had finally taken my highest cue from the Beatles and decided to live my life as if it were not predetermined but yet to be made, neither craving nor cursing another's past. I was whatever I was. I would never experience the '60s, and my time would likely never see such extremes. The '60s would never be a part of my past, but some of their soul could remain a part of my present, and my future—unavoidably, unforeseeably, thrillingly—would be *something else*.

□

Much have I seen and known; cities of men
And manners, climates, councils, governments,
Myself not least, but honoured of them all;
And drunk delight of battle with my peers,
Far on the ringing plains of windy Troy.
I am a part of all that I have met.

—Alfred, Lord Tennyson, "Ulysses" (1842)

On December 8, 2000, I attended my first John Lennon death vigil. It was held, as always, in Central Park. I'd been to a birthday vigil there a few years before, alone, and found it pleasant and utterly unexciting, a commune of hoarse-throated boomers trying to keep their candles lit in a roaring wind. But this time I'd be meeting friends—and besides, this was the *deathday* vigil. It might be different somehow. For good and bad, it was.

I met my companions at the sing-along outside the Dakota, and we walked across Central Park West to the pathways near Strawberry Fields. There in the middle of the concrete walk was a clutch of people in overcoats and scarves, some standing on folding chairs or benches, some with small children or babies. They formed a vague circle around a flowery shrine of lit candles and a minimal band—two men with acoustic guitars, a woman with a tambourine, someone else holding up sheet music. A TV news helicopter wove circuits in the sky. My friends and I moved toward the center, trying to discern from the jumble of embarrassed or inept voices just which song was in progress. "With a Little Help from My Friends"—a Paul song, but appropriate. Then came "Yesterday." The crowd made a fumbling pass at "You've Got to Hide Your Love Away," then swung into "Hey Jude," its chorus ideal for any mass of people joined together in the pursuit of song.

The three of us, feeling crowded and cold but wishing to pay tribute, wondered why the preponderance of McCartney ballads. The answer seemed apparent: Paul's songs were far better suited than John's to what this middle-aged, Beatle-nostalgic concord wished to make of the occasion. To them, the occasion called for gentle reverie and reminiscent uplift—which was fair enough. But it wasn't John. Wasn't snarky or funny or disruptive. We called out, in voices edging up to boorishness, for more John songs—weird choices like "She's So Heavy" and "I Am the Walrus," the opposite of sing-along material—but no one else took up the cry. In fact no one else was calling out for anything. My friends and I exchanged looks: *Let's beat it.*

Then we heard unruly noises from the other side of the circle. Music, without a doubt, but obscure. We made our way to an outer region situated on a dark, confined patch of walkway. There we found a smaller circle, cosmetically identical to the larger—guitarists and tambourine-banger at the center, candle-holders in common sway—but the whole tone was different. Here all the funkier sorts had collected, the oddballs and misfits: college girls with eyes closed, swaying in candlelight, grinning with indescribable sweetness from atop marijuana clouds; tanked-up tourists looking to get silly on vacation; grizzled Leary lookalikes who seemed to have donated entire cranial lobes to the lysergic sciences. Searching out a discordant din, we'd located the fringe festival of the John Lennon deathday vigil.

And this circle was singing raw Lennon rock—"Mother," "Remember," "I Found Out." And finally, "God." The three of us joined in on its climactic litany of denunciation, all voices gaining power as the small circle pulled itself, nervous and turned on by its own transgression, toward the inevitable: *I don't believe in Beatles.* No song could have been more irreverent to sing at the John Lennon deathday vigil than the dead man's own hymn of emancipation from the collected corpses of his past—except possibly for comedian Allen Sherman's long-forgotten and little-lamented exercise in direct address, "I Hate the Beatles."

I felt myself and all the other singers wondering together, as the words drew nearer, how it would feel to sing those lines loudly and proudly in such a place, on such an occasion. Well—if I was in any way typical, and if the height of vocal volume achieved by the gathering was any indication, it felt fantastic. To shout disbelief in the very thing that had brought us to this place was to crack into a contradiction that was funny, unsettling, and liberating. By voicing so joyfully John Lennon's disdain of his Beatle history, we denizens of the outer circle were reaffirming our own devotion to that history—or at least its artifacts, its myths, its traces. Or were we? Did we rather sing so heartily because we all knew the hidden wisdom of the words—that a "disbelief" in Beatles did not have to mean the denunciation John intended, but could mean, and mean well, the determination to live life in consciousness of the past while refusing to be tyrannized by it?

However one chose to feel about it, the bet was safe they wouldn't sing "God" over at the big circle if they stayed there all night.

The tribute went on, and the songs stayed hard, unsentimental: "You Can't Do That," "Don't Let Me Down," White Album work. Suddenly a terrific time was being had here in the park. Nothing polite or reverential on this side of the vigil; it was all an occasion for profane fun and good-natured rudeness. The little circle swelled as curious passersby stopped and stayed, and new defectors from the central circle drifted across. David Peel—minor Beatle-related celebrity, longtime Lower East Side fixture, and creator of such musical milestones as "Bring Back the Beatles," "The Pope Smokes Dope," and "Howard Stern for Governor"—showed up with a small retinue of groupies to expound on how Yoko's disaffiliation from Paul, George, and Ringo either was or wasn't identical in its tragic particulars to Dean Martin's break with Jerry Lewis. As my friends got to know other circle-singers, I was assailed by the subversive urgings of a small, consumptive-looking man who happened to be a dead ringer for Charles Manson. ("Everyone should sing a different Beatle song, all at once—just a big noise, right?—and we'll tape-record it and send it up to Yoko . . .")

The bigger our circle grew, the rougher its noise became. Eventually someone appeared—one of the guitar players from the inner circle, an old peacenik from the look of him—and asked the instrumentalists if they'd like to come back and join what was being implicitly defined as the "real" vigil. And just like that, the fringe festival was over. Guitars fell vertical and tambourine rattled tinnily as the musicians, sluggishly and without visible enthusiasm, capitulated. Some of the misfit crowd went with them. Some, those who had been just passing by, now continued on their way; the tourists laughed their way to a cab.

My friends were ready for a drink, but I was almost outraged—I couldn't leave just yet. I thought I had just seen some rotten kind of social metaphor in action. A miniature of capitalist hegemony, in which the determined minority expresses its own identity as an explicit alternative to the bland centrism of the mainstream. It grows in number and strength of voice, and once it begins to make too much of the wrong noise, up sidles the mainstream to suck the fringe into its all-containing membrane. It was the Beatles' whole magnificent story in reverse—or perverted: an offense against the man to whose memory the entire event was consecrated.

Screw you, was my silent farewell to the fringe-dwelling backs as they slouched off to join the inner circle.

But that's our world now, isn't it? The Beatles' jostling, welcoming, dangerous circle is now no more exciting or creative a thing than "the mainstream"; while the smaller, overlapping outer circles—musical, artistic, philosophical, political—are either startup guppies eager for a big fish's swallowing, or outposts of antisocial irony so contemptuous of mass communication that the sound of their voices will never carry past the armor of their pose.

If this was the '60s—if they were—if I were—

It was tempting, oh, very tempting, to fall back into the old thinking. *If. If. If.* The old time-machine thinking. But I caught myself. *These aren't and I'm not. It's John's deathday. Show some respect and cut the crap.*

I could remain unmoving, indignation rooting me to this cold, dark spot; or I could move. Not caring to freeze, I moved. My friends and I jumped a fence, laughing loudly. In abandoned imitation of a scene from *A Hard Day's Night,* we ran like insane children into the dark, stomping circles in fresh snow.

□

Ex-Beatle George Harrison and his wife, Olivia, were sleeping soundly in their upstairs bedroom when they were awakened at

3:30 A.M. by the sound of breaking glass. Dressed only in pajama bottoms, Harrison went downstairs to investigate while his wife phoned for help. On the first floor of his Henley-on-Thames mansion, Harrison encountered a knife-wielding intruder, and a horrific struggle ensued. The musician received a near-fatal stab wound to the chest before Olivia came to the rescue.

—*People* Magazine (January 17, 2000)

The one fact common to all heroes is that they have gone ahead and done it, in spite of all the danger. The danger which promises that, though their lives and works will fill the majority of people who respond to it with strength, with a sense of what they might be able to achieve given the example, these same heroic endeavors will fill others with hatred—a sense, instead, of their own weakness, self-loathing at what they are, rage at their failure to be what they are not.

Part of me has always envied that apparent majority of my generation who seem able to do without models of heroism—who call on no figurehead to spur their own aspirations. Sometimes I think those people see the world more clearly than I do, and are certainly less vulnerable once heroism is exposed as equivocal—as it always will be. But another, more fundamental part of me believes heroism is a genuine and miraculous thing, when genuinely found; that for all the disappointments encountered elsewhere, it's worth holding dear, when genuinely found. And I know there will never be another thing like the Beatles because there will never again be such popular heroes as they chose to be.

Perhaps in great part because of the dangers they set loose, forged through, and paid for, there will never be another pop figure to voice such a vow as theirs, or to venture such promises as they made and kept. There will be no one to time and again compel mutation on a world scale and stand tall against its uncontrollable fallout; none with the audacity to pierce such broad holes in time and consciousness, and then look inside to see what has been exposed; none willing to suffer the last punishments of mutilation and murder for the crime of having made such a vow at all, and the aggravated offense of having attempted to honor it.

The contemporary view, all but irrefutable in its broad acceptance, is that time can't be beaten. There has been too much time, and we have occupied too little of it to think that we may be transcendent of it. Our earth is absurdly young after all, our race itself barely old enough to be called infantile, our endeavors a sad inconsequence to the pitiless mechanisms of the random galaxy. This is the contemporary view.

It was never my view. My view is that time can in fact be transcended—that in its tyranny and terrorism it can be subverted, suspended, even destroyed, by an act of the imagination. Imagination engaged in the pursuit of old facts, new suppositions, the traces of discarded fantasies from anywhere, the wildest of inferences drawn from across the expanse of years, decades, centuries. Arcs of such passionate pursuit can encircle time and soften its implacability, expand it imaginatively where it is most restrictive physically. For in the completion of such arcs affiliations might be found with people, places, and events far removed from ourselves; bonds formed with strangers we've never met, sorrow felt for losses we never suffered, pride taken in victories we never abetted. In such pursuit we might begin to know that we stand not alone on the earth but rather in the midst of a great race, an immense chronology. In such pursuit we might begin to have the sense that there is, indeed, such a thing as human history; such a thing as time, which defeats us; and such a thing as the immortal, which defeats time.

That is my view of time, and how I decided it could be transcended. Who showed me this, who made me believe it against all evidence of rational sense and hard science, if not the Beatles?

Then again, maybe this is only a pretentious shell game I play with myself. Maybe it's only more generational penis envy, delusional fanaticism, a pipe dream.

But maybe it isn't. Maybe it's true. Maybe everything I've imagined about the Beatles, every crazy speculation, is on or near the mark.

Maybe the truth is beyond anyone's ability to capture it.

Maybe the Beatles were a hallucination that actually happened: the telepathic projection of a million desires, the willed gratification of a generation's boldest and basest fantasies. A creature synthesized from the popular unconscious of its age which was meant to take form for only a brief interval, after which it would return to the nether regions of imagination and the obscurity of dreams.

Maybe the Beatles were soldiers of love on the battlefield of history.

Maybe John Lennon had it right all along. "We were just a *band* who made it very, very big—that's all."

Maybe history is an ocean of maybes we can navigate only by thrusting precariously from one bobbing buoy of hopeful truth to another, in search of a way to the shore, a way to ourselves.

Maybe I have nothing more to say, except this:

I circle back to a passage from Milan Kundera, veteran of the Prague Spring of 1968 and the Soviet invasion which crushed it. I respect Kundera because he is not only a consummate artist but a wise and loving man who knows a thing or two about history, and about feeling exiled in time and space. In *The Book of Laughter and Forgetting* he wrote the finest words I've seen to characterize my own historical dilemma, as well as the cherished confidence hidden within, waiting for the day I would find it. The words also crystallize what I now realize I have always found most inexplicable, most magical in the music and lives of the Beatles, most transcendent in the history of their history.

"And the thought went through his mind that beauty is a spark which flares up when two ages meet across the distance of time, that beauty is a clean sweep of chronology, a rebellion against time."

in our yellow submarine

Kathy and I are watching *Yellow Submarine* in a Manhattan multiplex. This is the first time I've seen it as part of an audience—most of which is made up of boomers and their offspring.

It's the best time I've had in ages. I have always liked the cartoon, but good sense told me to resist its corn, its sad redolence of flower power gone to rot. But tonight, it's as if I've never seen *Yellow Submarine.* Was it always this funny, this Python-ridiculous, this erudite? Have I ever noticed the chief Meanie's Hitler mustache, or the Beatles hiding behind a thorny tree that has the precise and unmistakable form of a Communist hammer and sickle? More than once I am close to choking up at the beauty of the visuals, the magnificence of the songs. So full of color and ideas, so open and absurd.

And the kids are really getting into it. These kids, who will go home to instant entertainment of every kind; who will absorb from the news a blasé familiarity with rape, bombing, and atrocity; who will grow up on movies that insult their intelligence and suffer in schools that murder their creativity; who are offered terminal irony, canned sensation, and fashionable arrogance as their chief character-defining options in this new era of world history—this corny, dated movie has grabbed them. They are clapping, laughing, singing. A pair of preteen girls nearby knows every word to every song. Giggles drift from the balcony, and excitement is all around: the theater itself is poised in space upon the arch of each five-year-old spine drawing closer to the screen.

Among the snatches of child-voice:

"Oh, no! Here come the apples!"

"Is that one George?"

"Their legs are so big!"

"Glasses and a fur coat?"

"Look out!"

"Did you like that?" "Yeeeess." (The affirmative uttered by a wide-eyed child whose T-shirt bears the word TECHNOGIRL.)

"All together now, all together now!"

"We all live in a yellow submarine . . ."

When the movie ends, everyone claps. No one feels embarrassed at applauding these celluloid strips as if they were live people who have been present before us. The audience leaves the theater in a shared glow, and the kids—the kids are so excited. The Beatles have found them; they have found the Beatles.

What wonders await them.

What wonders await them?

The sub sails on in a sea of time.

NOTES

So we sailed

1 Barry Miles, *Paul McCartney: Many Years from Now* (New York: Henry Holt / Owl, 1997), pp. 286–287.

2 Bruce Spizer, *The Beatles' Story on Capitol Records, Part 1: Beatlemania and the Singles* (New Orleans: 498 Productions, 2000), p. 100.

1. Rude Noises from the Bog

1 *The Playboy Interviews with John Lennon and Yoko Ono,* ed. G. Barry Golson (New York: Playboy Press, 1981), p. 44.

2 William Butler Yeats, "The Second Coming," in *The Collected Works of William Butler Yeats,* ed. Richard J. Finneran (New York: Scribner, 1997), p. 189.

3 Nik Cohn, *Rock from the Beginning* (New York: Stein and Day, 1969), p. 150.

4 *Lennon Remembers: New Edition,* ed. Jann Wenner (New York: Verso, 2000), p. 146.

5 For surveys of postwar British politics and culture through the prisms of (respectively) pop, radicalism, and social conservatism, see George Melly, *Revolt into Style: The Pop Arts in Britain* (London: Penguin, 1970); Jeff Nuttall, *Bomb Culture* (New York: Delacorte, 1968); and Christopher Booker, *The Neophiliacs* (Boston: Gambit, 1970).

6 See Ray Coleman, *Lennon* (New York: McGraw-Hill, 1984), pp. 61–64; and Chris Salewicz, *McCartney: The Definitive Biography* (New York: St. Martin's, 1986), pp. 42–44.

7 Mark Lewisohn, *The Beatles Live!* (New York: Henry Holt, 1986), p. 12.

8 Ibid., p. 14.

9 Jim O'Donnell, *The Day John Met Paul: An Hour-by-Hour Account of How the Beatles Began* (New York: Penguin, 1996), p. 136.

10 Cohn, *Rock from the Beginning,* p. 177.

11 Lewisohn, *Live!,* p. 21.

12 Ibid., pp. 19–23.

13 Mark Lewisohn, liner notes, *The Beatles Anthology 1* (Apple/Parlophone CD, 1995), pp. 6–7.

14 Lewisohn, *Live!,* p. 22.

15 Ibid., pp. 31–32, 44–45.

16 *The Beatles Anthology* (Apple/Capitol Video), vol. 1.

17 Ibid., p. 36.

18 Ibid., p. 37.

19 Allan Williams and William Marshall, *The Man Who Gave the Beatles Away* (London: Elm Tree, 1975), p. 201.

20 *Mondo Cane* (Cineriz [Italy], 1963; MPI Home Video).

21 Pete Best had been hired to replace Tommy Moore as drummer. See *Beatle! The Pete Best Story* (London: Plexus, 1985). On Hamburg, see Hunter Davies, *The Beatles,* 2nd rev. ed. (New York: Norton, 1996), pp. 75–88; Philip Norman, *Shout! The Beatles in Their Generation* (New York: Simon and Schuster, 1981), pp. 81–102; The Beatles, *The Beatles Anthology* (San Francisco: Chronicle Books, 2000), pp. 45–62; and David Pritchard and Alan Lysaght, *The Beatles: An Oral History* (New York: Hyperion, 1998), pp. 35–55.

22 Williams, *The Man Who Gave,* p. 166.

23 "Scouse" (or "scouser") is slang for "Liverpudlian"—particularly one of less than high birth—and comes from the name of a beloved British beef stew.

24 Ibid., pp. 173–197. The misspelling is Williams'.

25 Lewisohn, *Live!,* p. 119.

26 Williams, *The Man Who Gave,* pp. 229–230.

27 *The Beatles vs. The Third Reich* (V-E LP, 1987).

28 Ibid.

29 On the Beatles' success in 1963, see Michael Braun, *Love Me Do! The Beatles' Progress* (New York: Penguin, 1995 [1964]); and Allan Kozinn, *The*

Beatles (London: Phaidon, 1995), pp. 57–76. Braun's book is easily the best, most candid firsthand account of Beatlemania; Kozinn's is a factually accurate, critically astute, and photographically sumptuous career survey.

30 *Lennon Remembers,* pp. 108–109.

on to the sun

1 Todd Gitlin, *The Sixties: Years of Hope, Days of Rage* (New York: Bantam, 1993 [1987]), pp. 209–210.

2. Ascension/Sacrifice

1 Buddy Dresner, "Eight Days a Week," *Rolling Stone* (February 16, 1984), p. 47.

2 Quotes in Nicholas Schaffner, *The Beatles Forever* (Harrisburg, Pa.: Cameron House, 1977), p. 10.

3 Geoffrey Stokes, *The Beatles* (New York: Times Books / Rolling Stone Press, 1980), p. 71.

4 Preferable video versions of *A Hard Day's Night* and *Help!* are from MPI Home Video. (Avoid Miramax's lifeless digital "enhancement" of the former.) *You Can't Do That! The Making of "A Hard Day's Night"* (MPI) is a fine supplement. *The First U.S. Visit* (MPI), directed by Albert and David Maysles—a reconstituted version of the 1964 TV special *The Beatles in America*—combines fantastically immediate documentary footage with enhanced video of the initial "Ed Sullivan" appearances and the first full-scale American concert, at the Washington Coliseum. For the first film's screenplay (both shooting and final versions), with accompanying stills, see *A Hard Day's Night: A Complete Pictorial Record of the Movie,* ed. J. Philip Di Franco (New York: Penguin, 1977). For historical perspective, see Alexander Walker, *Hollywood, England: The British Film Industry in the Sixties* (London: Harrap, 1986 [1974]). Also useful is Bill Harry, *The History of the Beatles on Film: An Illustrated Filmography* (New York: Avon, 1984).

5 Mark Lewisohn, *The Beatles Live!* (New York: Henry Holt, 1986), pp. 172–177.

6 Ibid., p. 172.

7 Ibid., p. 177. The same article notes that Dallas Chief of Police Jesse

Curry—whose sad, sunken visage was familiar to television viewers from the previous winter's JFK assassination coverage—attended the concert that night with his daughter and two grandchildren. What was going through the mind of a man on close terms with celebrity homicide and mass trauma, as he heard the screams and saw the heaves directed at these four favorites of post-Kennedy youth?

8 Lewisohn, *Live!,* pp. 172–177.

9 *Lennon Remembers: New Edition,* ed. Jann Wenner (New York: Verso, 2000), p. 105.

till we found

1 *Sympathy for the Devil* [a.k.a. *One Plus One*] (Cupid Productions [U.K.], 1968; Abkco Video).

3. Meat

1 Quote from a news clip in the video compilation *Fun with the Fab Four* (GoodTimes Video, 1986).

2 Tony Barrow, liner notes, *Don't Touch That Dial 2: The History of Music Radio* (Jumbo CD, 1995). This CD also contains the interview quoted here.

3 Nicholas Schaffner, *The Beatles Forever* (Harrisburg, Pa.: Cameron House, 1977), p. 55; Barrow, *Don't Touch That Dial 2;* Ron Schaumberg, *Growing Up with the Beatles* (New York: Pyramid, 1976), p. 57.

4 Schaffner, *The Beatles Forever,* pp. 55–57. See also Bruce Spizer, *The Beatles' Story on Capitol Records, Part 2: The Albums* (New Orleans: 498 Productions, 2000), pp. 111–135.

5 Robert Whitaker and Martin Harrison, *The Unseen Beatles* (San Francisco: HarperCollins, 1991), pp. 6–12. The fourteen-year-old girl turned out, upon achieving success in the 1970s, to be Olivia Newton-John.

6 Robert Whitaker, interview with Roger Taylor, November 1998, National Gallery of Australia website (www.artgallery.com.au).

7 Whitaker said the cages were meant to show that McCartney and Harrison "had beautiful singing voices—they literally sang like canaries." In fact the birdcaged head was a Surrealist trope, appearing in avant-garde films like Sidney Peterson's *The Cage* (1945) and Kenneth Anger's

Inauguration of the Pleasure Dome (1954). More generally, Whitaker's displacement or violation of heads is in a Surrealist tradition running from René Magritte to David Lynch. See Whitaker and Harrison, *Unseen,* p. 143.

8 This shot accompanies Whitaker's National Gallery interview; see also Whitaker and Harrison, *Unseen,* pp. 144–145.

9 Whitaker, National Gallery interview.

10 See Sue Taylor, *Hans Bellmer: The Anatomy of Anxiety* (Cambridge, Mass.: MIT Press, 2000); and Therese Lichtenstein, *Behind Closed Doors: The Art of Hans Bellmer* (Berkeley: University of California Press, 2001). For Whitaker's acknowledgment of Bellmer, see Spizer, *The Beatles' Story on Capitol Records, Part 2,* p. 112.

11 "That's all them wife-beaters need is an anthem," said TV star Roseanne of "Run for Your Life" on one of her shows—though the line she quoted was lifted from Elvis' "Baby Let's Play House."

12 Ellen Willis, "Dylan," in *Beginning to See the Light: Pieces of a Decade* (New York: Knopf, 1981), p. 5.

13 Schaumberg, *Growing Up,* pp. 52–53.

14 Mark Lewisohn, *The Beatles Live!* (New York: Henry Holt, 1986), p. 199.

15 Peter Brown and Steven Gaines, *The Love You Make: An Insider's Story of the Beatles* (New York: McGraw-Hill, 1983), pp. 192–193.

16 Ibid., p. 192.

17 Nik Cohn, *Rock from the Beginning* (New York: Stein and Day, 1969), p. 110.

18 The Hamburg press conference is on *Germany 66* (4 x 4 Soundz CD, 1998).

19 Ibid.

20 Brown, *The Love You Make,* p. 193.

21 Ibid., p. 194.

22 Edward Seidensticker, *Tokyo Rising: The City since the Great Earthquake* (Cambridge, Mass.: Harvard University Press, 1991), p. 253.

23 Ibid., p. 330.

24 Philip Norman, *Shout! The Beatles in Their Generation* (New York: Simon and Schuster, 1981), p. 263.

25 Raymond Bonner, *Waltzing with a Dictator: The Marcoses and the Making of*

American Policy (New York: Times Books, 1987), p. 26. For another version of history, see Ferdinand Marcos, *The Democratic Revolution in the Philippines* (Englewood Cliffs, N.J.: Prentice-Hall International, 1979).

26 Bonner, *Waltzing with a Dictator,* pp. 23–27.

27 The war was being fought just across the South China Sea from the upper tip of the Philippine archipelago—only 600 miles from where the Fab Four would stand singing "Baby's in Black" and "Day Tripper."

28 Eric Gamalinda, "Sod Manila!" in *In My Life: Encounters with the Beatles,* ed. Robert Cording, Shelli Jankowski-Smith, and E. J. Miller Laino (New York: Fromm, 1998), pp. 47–64.

29 Brown, *The Love You Make,* pp. 119–120.

30 Ibid., pp. 196–200.

31 Mark Lewisohn, *The Beatles Recording Sessions: The Official Abbey Road Studio Session Notes, 1962–1970* (New York: Harmony, 1988), p. 77. The Internet Movie Database (www.imdb.com) gives September 16, 1966, as the U.K. release date for Truffaut's *Fahrenheit 451;* Martin's string arrangement was recorded April 28.

32 The song's first arrangement, a cool, self-mocking avant-gardism dominated by organ and contrapuntal vocal trickery (an uncanny augury of *Smiley Smile–Wild Honey*-era Beach Boys), was entertaining but tonally incorrect for *Revolver:* it radiated peace in a hippie vein, while the second burst with tension in a post-hippie vein. See *The Beatles Anthology 2* (Apple/Parlophone CD, 1996).

33 *The Beatles Digest,* compiled by the editors of *Goldmine* magazine (Iola, Wis.: Krause Publications, 2000), p. 38.

34 The July 29, 1966, *Datebook* cover is at the website entitled "The Internet Beatles Album" (www.beatlesagain.com).

35 Maureen Cleave, "How Does a Beatle Live? John Lennon Lives Like This," in *The Lennon Companion,* ed. Elizabeth Thomson and David Gutman (New York: Schirmer, 1987), p. 72.

36 Ibid., p. 75.

37 Ibid., p. 73.

38 Mark Lewisohn, *The Complete Beatles Chronicle* (New York: Harmony, 1992), p. 213.

39 "The *Playboy* Advisor," *Playboy* (March 1965), p. 38.

40 *Dear Beatles,* ed. Bill Adler (New York: Grosset and Dunlap, 1966), un-numbered page.

41 *Lennon Remembers: New Edition,* ed. Jann Wenner (New York: Verso, 2000), pp. 103–104.

42 Anthony Scaduto, *The Beatles* (New York: Signet, 1968), pp. 98–99.

43 *John Lennon in His Own Words,* ed. Barry Miles (New York: Quick Fox, 1981), p. 59.

44 Hugh J. Schonfield, *The Passover Plot* (New York: Bantam, 1978 [1965]), pp. 57–58, 56, 53, 76.

45 Ibid., pp. 239, 196.

46 *John Lennon in His Own Words,* p. 59.

47 *The Beatles Anthology* (Apple/Capitol Video), vol. 6.

48 Cleave, "How Does a Beatle Live?" p. 72.

49 *Imagine: John Lennon* (Warner Brothers, 1988; Warner Home Video).

50 *Lennon Remembers,* p. 111.

51 Linda Rosen Obst, ed., *The Sixties* (New York: Random House / Rolling Stone Press, 1977), p. 166.

52 See Lewisohn, *Live!,* p. 196; and Brown, *The Love You Make,* p. 204.

53 See Barry Tashian, *Ticket to Ride: The Extraordinary Diary of the Beatles' Last Tour* (Nashville: Dowling Press, 1997). p. 45.

54 See *The Beatles Anthology* (video), vol. 6. Ten years later the TV reporter, Leonard Harris, would appear in Martin Scorsese's *Taxi Driver* as Senator Palantine, the initial target of Travis Bickle's murderous breakdown—acting out the collision of public life and private fantasy that in 1966 the Beatles were living.

55 Tashian, *Ticket to Ride,* p. 68.

56 Though they did support that struggle privately. They refused to honor a Jacksonville, Florida, engagement until assured that audience seating would be integrated (Lewisohn, *Live!,* p. 176), and they routinely declined lucrative South African offers—twenty years before "I Ain't Gonna Play Sun City." "As far as we're concerned," Ringo said on the 1965 tour, "people are people, no different from each other. We'll never play in South Africa if it means a segregated audience." See Julius Fast, *The Beatles: The Real Story* (New York: Putnam's, 1968), p. 184.

57 News clip, *Fun with the Fab Four.*

58 Ralph J. Gleason, "Like a Rolling Stone," in Edward E. Davis, ed., *The Beatles Book* (New York: Cowles, 1968), p. 200.

59 Elizabeth Hess, "The Women," *Village Voice* (November 8, 1994), p. 91.

60 For contemporary newspaper reviews of the concert by Philip Elwood and Ralph J. Gleason, see Eric Lefcowitz, *Tomorrow Never Knows: The Beatles' Last Concert* (San Francisco: Terra Firma, 1987), pp. 84, 88.

61 *Shea! / Candlestick Park* (Spank CD, 1994).

62 Ibid.

63 Ibid.

64 Schaumberg, *Growing Up*, pp. 51–52.

65 Lefcowitz, *Tomorrow Never Knows*, p. 76.

66 *Shea! / Candlestick Park* (CD).

67 As readers may know, "she" started out as "he"—specifically Peter Fonda, with whom Lennon shared an acid experience. But John, in re-writing, transgendered his imaginary foil, and an instinctive (though canny) universalist impulse prevailed over personal detail. See *The Playboy Interviews with John Lennon and Yoko Ono*, ed. G. Barry Golson (New York: Playboy Press, 1981), p. 152.

   Jacqueline Warwick's "*I'm* Eleanor Rigby: Female Identity and *Revolver*" gives a quite different (and rewarding) interpretation of the song's internal dialogue. See *"Every Sound There Is": The Beatles' "Revolver" and the Transformation of Rock and Roll*, ed. Russell Reising (Hampshire, England: Ashgate, 2002), an excellent essay collection combining academic and general approaches.

68 Barry Miles, *Paul McCartney: Many Years from Now* (New York: Henry Holt / Owl, 1997), p. 269; William J. Dowlding, *Beatlesongs* (New York: Fireside / Simon and Schuster, 1989), p. 132.

69 Lewisohn, *Recording Sessions*, pp. 87–91.

70 *How I Won the War* (United Artists, 1967; MGM Video).

the sea of green

1 Paul Watkins with Guillermo Soledad, *My Life with Charles Manson* (New York: Bantam, 1979), p. 137.

2 Ibid., p. 144.

4. The Unintelligible Truth

1 Barry Miles, *Paul McCartney: Many Years from Now* (New York: Henry Holt / Owl, 1997), pp. 303–304.

2 Todd Gitlin, *The Sixties: Years of Hope, Days of Rage* (New York: Bantam, 1993 [1987]), p. 213.

3 Robert Christgau, *Any Old Way You Choose It: Rock and Other Pop Music, 1967–1973,* expanded edition (New York: Cooper Square Press, 2000 [1973]), p. 45.

4 Ibid.

5 Greil Marcus, "One Night with You," in *Rock and Roll Will Stand,* ed. Greil Marcus (Boston: Beacon, 1969), p. 66.

6 Richard Goldstein, *Goldstein's Greatest Hits: A Book Mostly about Rock 'n' Roll* (Englewood Cliffs, N.J.: Prentice-Hall, 1970), p. 152.

7 Ibid., p. 153.

8 Marcus, "One Night with You," pp. 66–67.

9 Greil Marcus, "Epilogue: Treasure Island," in *Stranded: Rock and Roll for a Desert Island* (New York: Da Capo, 1996 [1979]), p. 258.

10 Greil Marcus, "The Beatles," in *The Rolling Stone Illustrated History of Rock and Roll,* ed. Jim Miller (New York: Random House / Rolling Stone Press, 1976), p. 180.

11 Nik Cohn, *Rock from the Beginning* (New York: Stein and Day, 1969), p. 239.

12 *The Beatles Anthology* (Apple/Capitol Video), vol. 7.

13 David Caute, *The Year of the Barricades: A Journey through 1968* (New York: Harper and Row, 1988), pp. 3–7.

14 Norman Mailer, *The Armies of the Night* (New York: Signet, 1969 [1968]), p. 108.

15 Gitlin, *The Sixties,* p. 244.

16 Ibid., p. 263.

17 In *The Strawberry Statement: Notes of a College Revolutionary* (New York: Avon, 1970 [1969]), James Simon Kunen tells why his SDS cadre refused to cooperate with *Life* magazine's plan for a major article on campus radicalism: it would "relegate us to the route of the hippies. Next thing they'd have Mark Rudd sweatshirts" (p. 131).

Printed on the paperback edition: "Soon, a new kind of movie from MGM!"

18 The "Port Huron Statement" is reprinted in James Miller, *Democracy Is in the Streets: From Port Huron to the Siege of Chicago* (Cambridge, Mass.: Harvard University Press, 1994), pp. 329–374.

19 Gitlin, *The Sixties,* p. 285.

20 Michael Gross, *Bob Dylan: An Illustrated History* (New York: Tempo, 1980), p. 114.

21 Jon Landau, *It's Too Late to Stop Now: A Rock and Roll Journal* (New York: Random House / Straight Arrow Press, 1972), p. 52.

22 Arthur Marwick, *The Sixties: Cultural Revolution in Britain, France, Italy and the United States, c. 1958–c. 1974* (London: Oxford University Press, 1998), p. 536.

23 Mark Lewisohn, *The Beatles Recording Sessions: The Official Abbey Road Studio Session Notes, 1962–1970* (New York: Harmony, 1988), pp. 135–136.

24 Ibid., p. 142.

25 Another layer of the "in"-"out" onion: On September 4, days after the convention ended, the Beatles filmed a promotional clip for "Revolution," performing live vocals over the prerecorded backing track. Though he was promoting the song's "out" version, John—singing directly into the camera, baring his teeth at the pivotal moment—followed "out" with a very clearly enunciated "in." Therefore an "in"-"out" combination was seen by British viewers on the September 19 "Top of the Pops" and by American audiences on the "Smothers Brothers Comedy Hour" of October 13. Meanwhile the "out" version reigned on radio, with the "in" version ("Revolution 1") awaiting its release on the White Album. Talk about mixed messages.

The promo film is seen in volume 8 of the *Beatles Anthology* video set. Airdates are given in Mark Lewisohn, *The Complete Beatles Chronicle* (New York: Harmony, 1992), p. 297.

26 Quotes in Jon Wiener, *Come Together: John Lennon in His Time* (New York: Random House, 1984), p. 60.

27 Goldstein, *Greatest Hits,* p. 183.

28 Christgau, *Any Old Way,* p. 101.

29 Ibid.

30 Wiener, *Come Together,* p. 61.

31 Greil Marcus, "A Singer and a Rock and Roll Band," *Rock and Roll Will Stand,* p. 94.

32 Ibid., pp. 91, 95–96.

33 Ibid., pp. 91, 97.

34 Ibid., p. 101.

35 Ibid., p. 104.

36 Ibid., p. 91.

37 *Lennon Remembers: New Edition,* ed. Jann Wenner (New York: Verso, 2000), p. 115.

38 In an exchange of open letters with Lennon upon the release of "Revolution," British radical John Hoyland asserted that "In order to change the world, we've got to understand what's wrong with the world. And then—destroy it. Ruthlessly." See *The Age of Paranoia: How the Sixties Ended,* compiled by the editors of *Rolling Stone* (New York: Pocket Books, 1972), pp. 143–147.

39 Lewisohn, *Recording Sessions,* p. 138. Among the tidbits Lewisohn isolated in listening to the four-track master—most of them buried so deep in the mix they are imperceptible to you and me—was George and John whispering six times, "There ain't no rule for the company freaks!" Those words *must* have some symbolic bearing on the Beatles' predicament vis-à-vis the radicals of 1968, though I have no idea what it is.

40 Elizabeth Thomson and David Gutman, eds., *The Lennon Companion,* (New York: Schirmer, 1987), p. 167.

41 Quoted in Brooke Allen, "Criticism and the Age," *New York Times Book Review* (August 1, 1999), p. 4.

42 Christgau, *Any Old Way,* p. 237.

43 Wiener, *Come Together,* p. 65.

44 Goldstein, *Greatest Hits,* p. 182.

45 Milan Kundera, *The Book of Laughter and Forgetting* (New York: Penguin, 1981), p. 22.

46 James Miller, *Democracy Is in the Streets: From Port Huron to the Siege of Chicago* (Cambridge, Mass.: Harvard University Press, 1994), pp. 15–16.

47 Ibid., p. 16.

48 Wiener, *Come Together,* p. 61.

49 A full year after the release of the White Album, *Rolling Stone* balanced John Mendelsohn's rave review of *Abbey Road* with an attack by Ed Ward which, though its complaints were aesthetic rather than political, was pure '68 invective. Calling the album "garbage," Ward dismissed the Beatles as studio-bound pop mandarins, implicitly phony, contrived, vapid, and passionless. "They've been shucking us a lot recently," Ward concluded, not saying precisely what he meant because he didn't have to: What reader with similar biases wouldn't remember all too clearly the betrayals of '68?

    See *The Rolling Stone Record Review,* compiled by the editors of *Rolling Stone* (New York: Pocket Books, 1971), pp. 24–26.

and we lived

1 Elwood D. Baumann, *The Loch Ness Monster* (New York: Franklin Watts, 1972), p. 138.

5. O.P.D. / Deus est Vivus

1 Ed Sanders, *The Family: The Manson Group and Its Aftermath* (New York: Signet, 1989 [1971]), p. 101.

2 Ibid., p. 19. See also Vincent Bugliosi with Curt Gentry, *Helter Skelter: The True Story of the Manson Murders* (New York: Bantam, 1994 [1974]), pp. 195–198.

3 James Miller, *Democracy Is in the Streets: From Port Huron to the Siege of Chicago* (Cambridge, Mass.: Harvard University Press, 1994), pp. 24–26.

4 Todd Gitlin, *The Sixties: Years of Hope, Days of Rage* (New York: Bantam, 1993 [1987]), p. 103.

5 David Caute, *The Year of the Barricades: A Journey through 1968* (New York: Harper and Row, 1988), p. 443.

6 Bo Burlingham, "Bringing the War Back Home," in Linda Rosen Obst, ed., *The Sixties* (New York: Random House / Rolling Stone Press, 1977), p. 298.

7 Ibid.

8 Fred LaBour, *The Michigan Daily* (October 14, 1969), reprinted in Andru J. Reeve, *Turn Me On, Dead Man: The Complete Story of the Paul McCartney Death Hoax* (Ann Arbor: Popular Culture Ink, 1994), pp. 17–23. The au-

thor wishes to thank Mr. LaBour for granting permission to quote from his article.

9 Sanders, *The Family*, pp. 20–38; Bugliosi, *Helter Skelter*, pp. 221–223.

10 Sanders, *The Family*, pp. 34–35; Bugliosi, *Helter Skelter*, p. 639. See also Bill Landis, *Anger: The Unauthorized Biography of Kenneth Anger* (New York: HarperCollins, 1995), pp. 142–148.

11 Landis, *Anger*, p. 26.

12 Sanders, *The Family*, pp. 37–38.

13 Paul Watkins with Guillermo Soledad, *My Life with Charles Manson* (New York: Bantam, 1979), p. 47.

14 Sanders, *The Family*, p. 57.

15 Mark Lewisohn, *The Beatles Recording Sessions: The Official Abbey Road Studio Session Notes, 1962–1970* (New York: Harmony, 1988), p. 104. The incident is also recounted in Hunter Davies, *The Beatles*, 2nd rev. ed. (New York: Norton, 1996), pp. 270–271.

16 T. M. Christian [Greil Marcus], "The Masked Marauders," in *The Rolling Stone Record Review*, compiled by the editors of *Rolling Stone* (New York: Pocket Books, 1971), p. 392.

17 Ibid., p. 393.

18 Ibid., p. 394.

19 Ralph J. Gleason, "On the Town" column, San Francisco *Chronicle* (October 8, 1969), reprinted as insert to *The Masked Marauders* (Deity/Reprise LP, 1969).

20 Robert Draper, *Rolling Stone Magazine: The Uncensored History* (New York: Doubleday, 1990), p. 92.

21 The Masked Marauders, "Saturday Night at the Cow Palace," on *The Masked Marauders* (LP).

22 Draper, *Rolling Stone Magazine*, p. 92. As for this being the "last recorded installment" of the Marauder saga, I may have spoken too soon: subsequent research reveals a new twig on the myth's hardy branch. Vernon Joynson's e-book *Dreams, Fantasies and Nightmares*, described at its website as a "guide to Canadian / Australian / New Zealand and Latin American psych and garage music 1963–1976," currently lists the Masked Marauders in its Canadian subsection as an actual band—though without providing names or sources of information. Joynson says the band's single self-titled late '60s album "benefitted

from some hype: it was rumoured that the group [included] Bob Dylan and other big names. Their sound was supposedly somewhat 'Dylanesque.'"

Joynson gives no indication he is joking. So which category would this bit of invention fit—dream, fantasy, or nightmare? See www.borderlinebooks.com/canada/m5.html#Masked_Marauder.

23 Reeve, *Turn Me On,* pp. 25-29.

24 Ibid., p. 28.

25 Ibid., pp. 27-28.

26 Ibid., p. 28n.

27 Ibid., pp. 1-5.

28 *And Here's Another Clue for You All* (Dinosaur CD, 1995).

29 Ibid.

30 Nicholas Schaffner, *The Beatles Forever* (Harrisburg, Pa.: Cameron House, 1977), p. 128.

31 Reeve, *Turn Me On,* p. 17.

32 Ibid., p. 18.

33 Ibid.

34 All of the following details are from Reeve, *Turn Me On,* pp. 19-22.

35 Ibid.

36 Ibid.

37 Ibid., pp. 22-23.

38 Ibid., p. 22.

39 Watkins, *My Life with Charles Manson,* p. 16.

40 Ibid., p. 17.

41 Ibid., pp. 50-51.

42 Ibid., pp. 35-36.

43 Ibid., pp. 42-43.

44 Bugliosi, *Helter Skelter,* p. 287.

45 Ibid.

46 Charles Manson, "Cease to Exist," on *LIE* (Awareness LP, 1970).

47 Sanders, *The Family,* pp. 45-49, 72-75; Bugliosi, *Helter Skelter,* pp. 338-341. See also Steven Gaines, *Heroes and Villains: The True Story of the Beach Boys* (New York: Da Capo, 1995 [1986]), pp. 201-220.

48 David Felton and David Dalton, "Keeping Up with the Mansons," in *The Age of Paranoia: How the Sixties Ended,* compiled by the editors of

Rolling Stone (New York: Pocket Books, 1972), p. 395. See also Sanders, *The Family,* pp. 96–103; and Bugliosi, *Helter Skelter,* pp. 167–173.

49 Felton and Dalton, p. 395.

50 Bob Murphy, *Desert Shadows: A True Story of the Charles Manson Family in Death Valley* (Morongo Valley, Calif.: Sagebrush Press, 1993), p. 18.

51 Sanders, *The Family,* p. 101.

52 Watkins, *My Life with Charles Manson,* pp. 134–138.

53 Tin Tin, "Have You Heard the Word?" on *Spicy Beatles Songs* (Trademark of Quality LP, 1973).

54 Reeve, *Turn Me On,* pp. 36–37.

55 Schaffner, *The Beatles Forever,* p. 127. Now this is funny (strange more than ha-ha) because, although ostensibly unconnected to it, the "girlfriend"'s version of the death had, as Yager related it to Bennett on October 18, the same details as Fred LaBour's, documented in the *Michigan Daily* a mere four days earlier: car crash, November 1966. There is a chronological puzzler nestled here. Assume Yager got his "facts" from LaBour, and fabricated his girlfriend story on the very day he called Bennett. Could the LaBour version have traveled from Michigan to Long Island in only four days? Possible, though not altogether probable. But the only other explanation is that Yager's girlfriend (or Yager himself) truly *did* have a dream about Paul's decapitation on the motorway—and that the nocturnal revelation was, by fan telepathy or Beatle magic (or "magick"), identical to LaBour's facetiously calculated, fully deliberate death scenario.

It could also be that a friend in the Midwest simply phoned Yager and told him about the LaBour story. Ockham was not necessarily wrong.

56 Richard Price, "It's Never Too Late," *Rolling Stone* (February 16, 1984), p. 76.

57 Schaffner, *The Beatles Forever,* p. 127.

58 Reeve, *Turn Me On,* pp. 82–88.

59 John Neary, "The Magical McCartney Mystery," *Life* (November 7, 1969), p. 105.

60 Sanders, *The Family,* pp. 110–120; Watkins, *My Life with Charles Manson,* pp. 137–144.

61 Bugliosi, *Helter Skelter,* pp. 89–90.

62 Ibid, p. 325.

63 Watkins, *My Life with Charles Manson,* pp. 134-135.

64 Ibid., p. 135.

65 Felton and Dalton, "Keeping Up with the Mansons," pp. 370-371.

66 Bugliosi, *Helter Skelter,* pp. 321-331.

67 Julius Fast, *The Beatles: The Real Story* (New York: Putnam's, 1968),
    pp. 183-184.

68 Holy Bible, Revised Standard Version (New York: Thomas Nelson and
    Sons, 1953), Revelation 9:1-11, 20-21.

69 Details of Hinman murder in Sanders, *The Family,* pp. 204-212; and
    Bugliosi, *Helter Skelter,* pp. 137-139.

70 Sanders, *The Family,* p. 209.

71 *Manson* (American International Pictures, 1972).

72 Lewisohn, *Recording Sessions,* p. 182.

73 Stephen King, *Danse Macabre* (New York: Berkley Books, 1983 [1981]),
    p. 408.

74 "The Candle Burns," on *20 x 4* (Ruthless Rhymes LP, 1981).

75 Harry Castleman and Walter Podrazik, *All Together Now: The Only Com-
    plete Beatles Discography, 1961–1975* (New York: Ballantine, 1975), p. 258.

76 Charles Reinhart, *You Can't Do That! Beatles Bootlegs and Novelty Records,
    1963–1980* (Ann Arbor: Pierian Press, 1981), p. 169.

77 Belmo, *Not for Sale: The Beatles' Musical Legacy as Archived on Unauthorized
    Recordings* (Owen Sound, Ontario: Hot Wacks Press, 1997), p. 213.

78 Jim Berkenstadt and Belmo, *Black Market Beatles: The Story behind the
    Lost Recordings* (Burlington, Ontario: Collector's Guide Publishing,
    1995), p. 134.

79 J. A. Cuddon, *The Penguin Dictionary of Literary Terms and Literary Theory:
    New Edition* (London: Penguin, 1991), pp. 119-120.

80 *And Here's Another Clue for You All* (CD). T. M. Christian, too, had a pro-
    nounced Eskimo fixation—his liner notes to the Masked Marauders LP
    mentioned Nanook of the North and Hudson Bay. Given that the al-
    bum was released in the interim between LaBour's initial article and
    the Bailey special, we might speculate where LaBour got his timely in-
    terest in "Eskimoan" mythology.

81 Ibid.

82 Ibid. Tony Bramwell was not just any promotion man, but a child-

hood friend of George Harrison's who was later employed by Brian Epstein before taking charge of promotion at Apple Corps. Klein, who began managing the Beatles' affairs in early 1969, was apparently less than tactful in his reorganization of their corporate structure, which may explain his dismissive tone. See Bill Harry, *The Ultimate Beatles Encyclopedia* (New York: MJF, 1992), pp. 119–120.

But Bramwell's status as a Beatle insider makes you wonder what role, if any, the Beatles may have played in his fraudulent phone call to WKNR—assuming it *was* Bramwell. But if not he, then who? And why?

83 *And Here's Another Clue for You All* (CD).

84 *Paul McCartney DEAD: The Great Hoax* (New York: Country Wide Publications, 1969), p. 58.

85 Ibid. For the record, "Rita" errs rather widely in her assertion regarding the Beatles' pre-1966 songwriting: up to and including *Revolver,* John produced nearly twice as many of their original songs as Paul.

86 Ibid., pp. 11–13.

87 See the epigraph from John O'Hara's novel *Appointment in Samarra* (1934), quoting W. Somerset Maugham: "*Death speaks:* 'There was a merchant in Baghdad who sent his servant to market to buy provisions and in a little while the servant came back, white and trembling, and said, Master, just now when I was in the market-place I was jostled by a woman in the crowd and when I turned I saw it was Death that jostled me. She looked at me and made a threatening gesture; now, lend me your horse, and I will ride away from this city and avoid my fate. I will go to Samarra and there Death will not find me. The merchant lent him his horse, and the servant mounted it, and he dug his spurs in its flanks and as fast as the horse could gallop he went. Then the merchant went down to the market-place and he saw me standing in the crowd and he came to me and said, Why did you make a threatening gesture to my servant when you saw him this morning? That was not a threatening gesture, I said, it was only a start of surprise. I was astonished to see him in Baghdad, for I had an appointment with him tonight in Samarra.'"

88 Reeve, *Turn Me On,* pp. 108–109.

89 *Paul McCartney DEAD,* p. 56.

90 Sanders, *The Family,* p. 220.

91 Bugliosi, *Helter Skelter*, p. 139.

92 Ibid., p. 433; Sanders, *The Family*, p. 230.

93 Bugliosi, *Helter Skelter*, pp. 306–310.

94 Ibid., p. 309.

95 Details of Cielo Drive killings in Sanders, *The Family*, pp. 238–253.

96 Details of LaBianca killings in Sanders, *The Family*, pp. 276–280; and Bugliosi, *Helter Skelter*, pp. 361–363.

97 Bugliosi, *Helter Skelter*, p. 510.

98 Ibid., p. 554.

99 Ibid., p. 417n.

100 Felton and Dalton, "Keeping Up with the Mansons," p. 334.

101 Ibid., p. 395.

102 Ibid., pp. 395–396.

103 Ibid., p. 396.

104 Bugliosi, *Helter Skelter*, pp. 678, 684–690.

105 Ibid., p. 399.

106 Mark Lewisohn, *The Complete Beatles Chronicle* (New York: Harmony, 1992), pp. 328–329.

107 Felton and Dalton, "Keeping Up with the Mansons," p. 389.

108 Richard Avedon and Doon Arbus, *The Sixties* (New York: Random House / Kodak Professional, 1999), pp. 172–175.

109 Schaffner, *The Beatles Forever*, p. 71.

110 Jann Wenner, in Ben Fong-Torres, ed., *The Rolling Stone Rock 'n' Roll Reader* (New York: Bantam, 1974), p. 72.

111 Joseph Campbell, *The Hero with a Thousand Faces* (Princeton, N.J.: Princeton University Press, 1973 [1949]), p. 269.

112 Ibid., pp. 269–270.

113 Details of Manson's childhood in Bugliosi, *Helter Skelter*, pp. 184–188.

114 Ibid., p. 301.

115 *The Beatles Tapes* (Polydor LP, 1976).

116 Bugliosi, *Helter Skelter*, p. 345.

117 Ibid., p. 287n.

118 Ibid., p. 438.

119 Mark Edmundson, "Lacks Interpersonal Skills," *New York Times Book Review* (December 17, 2000), p. 32.

120 Schaffner, *The Beatles Forever*, p. 107.

121 Ibid., p. 63.

122 Caute, *The Year of the Barricades,* p. 442.

123 Avedon, *The Sixties,* p. 149. Dohrn also weighed in on the revolutionary value of Helter Skelter: "Dig, first they killed those pigs, then they ate dinner in the same room with them, and they even shoved a fork into a victim's stomach. Wild!" (Caute, *The Year of the Barricades,* p. 441).

124 Norman O. Brown, quoted in James Miller, *Democracy Is in the Streets: From Port Huron to the Siege of Chicago* (Cambridge, Mass.: Harvard University Press, 1994), p. 7.

beneath the waves

1 In the interest of full disclosure: the woman written of here is a fictional character. She didn't live, let alone die. In the months after John Lennon's murder, there were several suicides reported to have been catalyzed by that event, but this wasn't one of them.

6. Fantasy into Flesh

1 *Life* (December 16, 1969).

2 Roy Carr and Tony Tyler, *The Beatles: An Illustrated Record* (New York: Harmony, 1975).

DISCOGRAPHY

This is a list of recordings that are relevant to the text, and I append to it a familiar disclaimer: "No attempt at comprehensiveness," et cetera. The canonical Beatle releases are established and accessible, but the bootlegs which augment them are in constant flux, and their availability varies. So I have cited only the titles I consulted in my research, even though in some cases they have been supplanted by more up-to-date releases. In the bootleg business, flux is an assumption and "up-to-date" a relative concept at best.

The list is chronological, and—like the main text—keyed to the Beatles' U.K. discography. Albums analyzed at length in the text are merely cited here. For singles, songs are usually listed only if unassessed elsewhere, and are followed by the album where they are most conveniently located.

1. Rude Noises from the Bog

The Songs We Were Singing—The Music That Inspired the Beatles (unlabeled Internet bootleg, 2001). Exhaustive, and necessary to any (attempted) understanding of where the Beatles' music came from. The four discs collect the most Beatle-influential versions of virtually every song known to have been covered by the group in its various permutations—beginning with Lonnie Donegan's "Puttin' on the Style," and ending with the Coasters' "Besame Mucho." In between are whole swaths from the works of the pioneers (Presley, Berry, Holly, Richard, Perkins, Williams, Alexander); obscurities of the British '50s (Ritchie Barrett's "Some Other Guy," the Vipers Skiffle Group's "Maggie Mae"); and outer-genre marginalia ("The Honeymoon Song" by

Marino Marini & His Quartet, Lenny Welch's "A Taste of Honey"). Small miracles happen (the Donays' "Devil in His Heart," both funky and forlorn), and large questions arise (why didn't the Beatles cover more Everly Brothers?). We're reminded of how John, just as much as Paul, loved singing songs originated by women (Ann-Margret, Little Eva). We see that the Beatles were as familiar with British folk music as Bob Dylan was with American; and that if they played almost nothing but rock and roll from the start, it was simply because they preferred it.

More than manna to the Beatle collector, this is a broad survey of post–World War II popular song styles in America and Europe, and valuable on that basis alone.

The excerpt of "Puttin' on the Style" from July 6, 1957, is heard on the bootleg *Puttin' on the Style* (Black Dog, 1998).

All of the known spring 1960 Liverpool rehearsals—some of which may, in fact, date from Hamburg later that year—are collected on the bootleg *Wildcat!* (Madman, 1996). Three of the songs were released, slightly abbreviated, on *The Beatles Anthology 1*.

The Early Years Featuring Tony Sheridan (Polygram, 1971). Billed as "The Beat Brothers"—with Pete Best still on drums—they backed Sheridan, Liverpool's own Elvis epigone, at Polydor's Hamburg studios on June 22–23, 1961. At the same time, they made their first professional recordings as the Beatles. John sings "Ain't She Sweet"; the group perform their instrumental "Cry for a Shadow" (Shadows-inspired but amazingly surf-sounding); and they lend rhythm and inimitable background shouts to "My Bonnie" and other souped-up songbook standards.

March 5, 1963 Plus the Decca Tape (Vigotone, 1994). The best source for the failed Decca audition of New Year's Day, 1962. The twelve cover versions and three originals are performed energetically; there is verve, there is polish; and I, for one, don't blame the unfortunate Dick Rowe for taking a pass. Magic flashes for a moment, then it's gone. Would *you* have known what you were hearing?

The Cavern Club Rehearsals (Early Years, 1990). Five self-taped performances from the cellar, fall 1962. They run through an unmemorable "I Saw Her Standing There," and take two passes each at "One after 909" and the instrumental "Catswalk." Each performance improves just slightly on the one before. A brief study of four happy obsessives.

"Love Me Do" / "P.S. I Love You" (*Please Please Me*); single released 1962. The Beatles' first single is an unassuming pop-blues with something pretty dark and—dammit—revolutionary in the sneering slide of the harmonica, the thump of the drum, the way Paul puts his throat into *doo-hoo*. On the other side is one of their best early ballads, a lovely set of chord changes and silver harmonies.

For the Star-Club show, I am working from two sources: the "official" release, *The Beatles Live! At the Star-Club in Hamburg, Germany; 1962* (Lingasong [Germany], 1977), and a bootleg called *The Beatles vs. the Third Reich* (V-E, 1987), which offers unedited versions of many of the same songs. Both are necessary—the first for the music, which is brought out but not prettied up, the second for the real-time ambiance of the performance, which is noisy and intimate, full of pregnant pauses and rowdy noise-making.

Note: It is now widely held that the Star-Club collection comprises two or more performances from the last week of 1962, and that they were recorded by King Size Taylor's guitarist, Adrian Barber. I confess ignorance of the proof for this; but I also feel the consistent energy level and sound quality (or lack of it) suggest a single performance, and that is how I have always heard it. See the bootleg *Farewell to Clubland* (Silent Sea, 1999) for what some believe are the dates of recording for each song.

"Please Please Me" / "Ask Me Why" (*Please Please Me*); single released 1963. A growling sex heathen crawls up behind the Everlys and slips amphetamines to their backup band, then seals his takeover with a sincere love song.

"From Me to You" / "Thank You Girl" (*Past Masters Volume One*, Apple/Parlophone); single released 1963. On the shrill, smarmy A-side they stumble, but do not fall; on the B-side they are so full of love they leap into the sky.

Please Please Me (Apple/Parlophone, 1963). It's gotten better with time. The ballads that once seemed soft now sound sinister, the rockers that were once monotonous now boom with excitement. And it all reeks of humanity: at least two Beatles have mid-winter colds, and throughout, sentiment is redeemed by snot. Give Ringo credit for knowing how much better "Boys" rocks when it's shouted, not sung—and give all of them points for being so innocent of the sexual ambiguities they were splitting open with such a song-choice.

"She Loves You" / "I'll Get You" (*Past Masters Volume One*); single released 1963. One of the few rock and roll singles that will still be around when you and I are not.

"I Want to Hold Your Hand" / "This Boy" (*Past Masters Volume One*); single released 1963. On one side, the heaviest musical hand, and the clumsiest come-on, ever to constitute a Beatle hit—and just the bludgeon to tap America's thick skull. On the other, their super-sophisticated refinement of the '50s prom-night lament, their dream of a golden oldie. The Beatles can play dumb, they can play smart—whatever works.

With the Beatles (Apple/Parlophone, 1963). Love letters to Motown in the form of hard rock; George sounding as nervous and earnest before Chuck Berry as he would, years later, before God; and further subliminal gender play with the requisite girl-group covers—all pronouns discreetly adjusted, but nevertheless sung without idiot affect or macho stance, as if the Beatles knew how girls felt. In retrospect, the album sounds mainly like a study in what the Beatles would have done with and to black American pop if they had made such a pursuit their life's work. Nothing would have been the same. Nothing *was* the same.

Live at the BBC (Apple/Capitol, 1994). All told, this is the best way to hear the Beatles' work for various BBC radio shows, recorded and broadcast between early 1962 and mid-1965. In a body of work daunting in size and impressive in breadth, the group take on rock classics and nonclassics, along with contemporary pop oddities and fresh versions of their own current material. Occasionally a song emerges to join the Beatles' best work from any period ("Keep Your Hands Off My Baby," rough and all-out—and destroyed, unfortunately, by digital cleanup; "I Got to Find My Baby," in which the Beatles out-swing Chuck Berry's rewrite of a Louis Jordan jump blues; "I'll Be on My Way," Paul's winsome Everlys pastiche; and "I Forgot to Remember to Forget," Elvis' country weeper, transformed by George into the quintessence of Beatle joy).

If your interest in this material is more than passing, a good recent multi-disc bootleg archive is *The Complete BBC Anthology 1962–1970* (Beeb, 2001).

The Beatles Anthology 1 (Apple/Capitol, 1995). Like the other *Anthology* installments, loaded with sounds unheard, in some cases believed to have been destroyed. Starting with "Free as a Bird," it reaches back to "That'll Be the Day" and "In Spite of All the Danger," and follows with selections from the Liverpool rehearsal tape and the Decca audition. From there, madness and magic. Highs include a drum-heavy, near-hysterical set from Stockholm, October 1963; a charging, dramatic, sadly incomplete version of "And I Love Her"; and an alternate arrangement of "Eight Days a Week" in which John and Paul banter boyishly, attempt a new vocal overture, fail, try again, and finally succeed in a soar of orgasmic harmony. Ringo's drums stumble in with their unmistakable drunken modesty, and the Beatles proceed to obliterate the version we have always known.

2. Ascension/Sacrifice

The Beatles Tapes Vol. II: Early Beatlemania 1963–64 (Jerden, 1993). Sound bites from both the cusp and the crest of world history. The Beatles are at their cheeky pinnacle, but the nicest surprise is eighteen seconds of Maryland teenager Marsha Albert introducing "I Want to Hold Your Hand" on "The Carroll James Show," WWDC-AM, December 17, 1963: the first airing, it is claimed, of the song on American radio.

"Can't Buy Me Love" / "You Can't Do That" (*A Hard Day's Night*); single released 1964. An irritating Beatle perennial (the better, harsher take is on *Anthology 1*) backed with a first-rate Lennon rocker. John's guitar solo on the latter is a minor classic, and a major convulsion.

"Long Tall Sally" / "I Call Your Name" / "Slow Down" / "Matchbox" (*Past Masters Volume One*); extended-player released 1964. A direct challenge to the rock pioneers—almost a concept EP. The Beatles don't come close to vanquishing Larry Williams or Carl Perkins, but on "Long Tall Sally" they break even with Little Richard. "I Call Your Name"'s lanky, skanky rock beat opens into a still-surprising ska midsection: crunchy and chewy, like a Tootsie Pop.

"A Hard Day's Night" / "Things We Said Today" (*A Hard Day's Night*); single released 1964. Judging by the trade-off between their voices, Lennon and McCartney are vocalizing upper and lower regions of one man's brain as he motors homeward, envisioning his love abed, in *Playboy* pose. John sings lean and cool, all innuendo; Paul cries emotional and physical basics from the top of his throat. Confident John readies for sex; desperate Paul craves warmth and safety. This is the Beatles' version of cock rock, in which the phallus coexists with the emotions.

The B-side is adult romance with thoughtful vocal and hard, sobering guitar flourish—exactly the kind of serious song much of Paul's solo career has encouraged us to consider aberrational.

A Hard Day's Night (Apple/Parlophone, 1964). The album swings between extremes of hammering rock and sophisticated balladry, and everything integrates because each style takes something essential from the other. On the rock songs the hammer falls with nuance and grace; on the ballads, acoustic guitars are strummed like electric guitars and single notes are pulled boldly, as if amplified. So "Tell Me Why" has its flawlessly timed drum rolls and kick-steps, "I'll Be Back" its folk ambiance calibrated somewhere between chime and churn; while "Any Time at All" shares its single-string guitar throb with the elegant "And I Love Her" solo. A rich album we probably haven't begun to rate properly, it turns pop to wine, and vice versa.

Hear the Beatles Tell All (Vee-Jay, 1964). Vee-Jay, a black-owned outlet for Chicago soul and gospel—and the Beatles' erstwhile U.S. label—released, at the height of the mania, the first album of "Beatle talk." Recorded in Los Angeles at the end of the first American tour, the album offers one side of Lennon chat, which is less revealing than simply relaxed, and another with all four Beatles, which is fan-magazine airport babble caught on the fly: useful for atmosphere, not insight. Background drumming by the legendary Hal Blaine.

"I Feel Fine" / "She's a Woman" (*Past Masters Volume One*); single released 1964. Following the leap of *A Hard Day's Night,* both sides of this brilliant single seem elemental enough to pass for roots rock, if not simple regression. But in fact both slip into the modernist skin the Beatles will be wearing for at least the next two years. The reliance on fundamentals (a few chords, a few lyric clichés) as a bed for innovation (feedback overture on the A, further rock-ska meld on the B) marks this as active experiment, not entropy. But anyone who has heard these songs knows *that.*

Beatles for Sale (Apple/Parlophone, 1964). The band press the limits of their club- and stadium-muscled voices ("Mr. Moonlight," "Kansas City"); the limits of their ability to push commitment through exhaustion ("Rock and Roll Music," "I'm a Loser"); and the limits of the pop, rock, and country formulae they have long since decided can encompass any innovation they care to bring to them ("No Reply," "Baby's in Black," "What You're Doing"). On other songs, the Beatles are not pressing, they're accepting, letting the music come from them, or to them ("I'll Follow the Sun," "Words of Love," "I Don't Want to Spoil the Party"). For the rest, they sound cranky and obligatory. So it's half a great album; but that half is so great it shoots energy through the rest and elevates the field.

"Ticket to Ride" (*Help!*) / "Yes It Is" (*Past Masters Volume One*); single released 1965. The hit is high-modernist power pop so strong and absolute it smashes most of what passes for rock today. It wrestles perfection from clashing shapes and crossed purposes: the harmonies are steep slants, the riff is a turning wheel with broken spokes, the drum rolls are hard immovable objects. Even today, it sounds as new as tomorrow.

The B-side, which comes to us from another world, surpasses its lachrymose genre to achieve a searing sadness whose only rightful precursor may be *The Sorrows of Young Werther.*

"Help!" (*Help!*) / "I'm Down" (*Past Masters Volume One*); single released 1965. Many fans count it a favorite, but "Help!" has not matured especially well: the ingenuities of voice and instrument, on other contemporary songs still cutting and immediate, register here as Beatle clichés, ripe for Rutle parody. Paul's hysterical rocker is far better, funny despite being a painful experience in sound: he nearly chokes to death trying to cough up Little Richard, who has somehow crawled in and taken over his body.

Help! (Apple/Parlophone, 1965). The soundtrack songs are best: pop exuberance that shimmers like the film's Alpine snow, shines like its Bahamian sun ("Another Girl," "The Night Before," "You're Gonna Lose That Girl"). John brings the meat with "Ticket to Ride" and "You've Got to Hide Your Love Away." "Yesterday" is what it is. But this is a Beatles album—two sides, fourteen songs—and that isn't good enough. The band are limp when not selling the movie, a few too many songs loiter in some vague space between forgettable success and noteworthy failure, and the worst tracks ("Act Naturally," "Dizzy Miss Lizzie," "I Need You") are as close as the Beatles came—until the deepest doldrums of *Get Back*, anyway—to true mediocrity.

3. Meat
"We Can Work It Out" / "Day Tripper" (*Past Masters Volume Two*, Apple/Parlophone); single released 1965. The conciliatory A-side glows with intelligence but feels contrived, compromised, fussed over—like most peace proposals. While the deceptively simple B-side takes the modernism of "Ticket to Ride" and subjects it to the concentrated flame of Beatle minimalism.

Rubber Soul (Apple/Parlophone, 1965).

Revolver (Apple/Parlophone, 1966).

The Circus-Krone-Bau show is on the bootleg *Germany 66* (4 x 4 Soundz, 1998).

The Beatles' 1964-1965 Hollywood Bowl performances appear in their undoctored entirety on the bootleg *The Complete Hollywood Bowl Concerts*

(Repro Man, 1997); *Live at the Hollywood Bowl* (Capitol, 1977) collapses each year's highlights into a continuous performance. *Live from the Sam Houston Colosseum* (Audifon / Ruthless Rhymes, 1979) and *Atlanta/Munich/Seattle* (Spank, 1995)—to pluck examples from the vinyl and CD ages, respectively—feature representative shows from 1965. For 1966 ambiance see *"Make as Much Noise as You Like!"* (FLO, 2001), a bootleg with live excerpts of varying quality—poor to abominable—from shows in Munich, Hamburg, Detroit, Memphis, and New York; and *Vinyl to the Core* (unlabeled Internet bootleg, 2000), with further '66 noises from Essen, Cleveland, and Boston.

An unedited recording of the Beatles' August 22, 1964 Vancouver press conference is on the bootleg *Vancouver 1964* (Trademark of Quality, 1972). The Hamburg press conference is on the aforementioned *Germany 66,* and several other 1966 press conferences are available on bootlegs and quasi-legitimate releases: Essen (June 25) is on the boxed set *Mythology—Vol. 2, 1964–66* (Strawberry, 1999); Tokyo (June 30) on *The Definitive Collection: Japan 1966* (unlabeled bootleg, no date); Chicago (August 12) on *The Lost Beatles Interviews* (Durkin Hayes, 1994); Seattle (August 25) on *Inside Interviews* (LaserLight, 1995); and Hollywood (August 28) on *The Lost Beatles Interviews.*

Both the June 30 and July 1 Budokan concerts are on *The Definitive Collection: Japan 1966.*

The San Francisco concert is best heard on the bootleg *Shea! / Candlestick Park* (Spank, 1994), which also contains Brian Epstein's "happiness and tragedy" quote.

A sequence of John's home demos for "She Said She Said" is on the bootleg *Revolving* (Silent Sea, 2001).

For the history of "Strawberry Fields Forever" from earliest fragments to finished version, see the bootleg *It's Not Too Bad—The Evolution of "Strawberry Fields Forever"* (Peg Boy, 1997).

The Beatles Anthology 2 (Apple/Capitol, 1996). New Beatle chemistry takes root and grows in the deep soil of *Help!* balladry; takes an honest break with a high-spirited, good-natured "Night Out" in Blackpool; lies fallow and frustrated as the young Tom Edisons shout Stone Age rock at the stadium hordes; comes into immature but definite presence with *Rubber Soul* experiments. And then—*and then*—the brilliance bursts, the release springs, genius spurts, shoots, and shatters in your ear as they create Take 1 of "Tomorrow Never Knows."

These outtakes from *Help!, Rubber Soul, Revolver, Sgt. Pepper,* and *Magical Mystery Tour* constitute, if not the whole essence of the Beatles ("She Loves You" is in there somewhere), then the essence of the essence. Some of which is best flushed: "If You've Got Trouble," the musical equivalent of a prolonged groin pull; and "12-Bar Original," a six-minute cop of Booker T. and the MG's, here cut by half and *still* endless. But virtually all of these tracks—many, remember, marked as failures—are bolder and tighter, more immediate and fully realized than what most groups offer as official product. Some are better than the familiar versions ("It's Only Love," "Your Mother Should Know," "The Fool on the Hill"), and there is one great song never released in any form: "That Means a Lot," a dramatic McCartney showcase with jet-age guitar overdubs and flaming rebound on the voice, precisely how the Beatles would have sounded if produced by Phil Spector at his mad-science peak. How brilliantly well, though, George Martin did by them: this is a hell of a cliché—but feel the skull-pop of the drums, the depth and detail of all those sound-waves and audio layers, and the cliché comes alive.

The best *Anthology* volume, from their best period. And it leads off with the priceless "Real Love."

4. The Unintelligible Truth

Sgt. Pepper's Lonely Hearts Club Band (Apple/Parlophone, 1967).

"Hello Goodbye" / "I Am the Walrus" (*Magical Mystery Tour*); single released 1967. Could it be that the essential cleavage which makes rock and roll interesting is summed up right here? On top, one of the great summertime singles: a hazy guitar-driven, organ-charged shaft of light. Underneath (in every sense), a drug-deranged pop-culture war-baby's dark night of the soul.

Magical Mystery Tour (Apple/Parlophone, 1967). The TV show soundtrack, plus all '67 singles: psychedelia so unimpressed with itself it has hardly dated at all.

"Lady Madonna" / "The Inner Light" (*Past Masters Volume Two*); single released 1968. Paul's piano-based workout on a Fats Domino theme is lively, though the turn-on is in Ronnie Scott's babbling, grinning sax solo, and the chicken-throated backing vocals of John and George—whose witty, imaginative counterpoint to McCartney leads was a terrific late strength. On the reverse, Harrison's *echt*-Bombay scoring of an uncredited Basho poem is precious and self-enchanted—until the end of each stanza, when it gets impatient with its own serenity and runs through the jungle. But not fast enough to save itself from that hungry beast called Tedium.

The "Revolution" demo is best heard on Disc 1 of the bootleg *From Kinfauns to Chaos* (Vigotone, 1999), along with twenty-two other demos, mostly of songs destined for the White Album. Disc 2 features approximately twenty-five minutes from the "Revolution 1" mixing session of June 4. In a live, off-line recording made surreptitiously during the song's playback, the slow White Album version is heard in numerous long and short excerpts—all, unfortunately, overlaid with an unceasing stream of Yoko Ono chatter. (Some of which is nonetheless interesting: she describes Paul's kindness, Ringo's smile, John's sexiness.)

"Hey Jude" (*Past Masters Volume Two*); single released 1968. Paul's epic of ordinary generosity is the most unassuming of rock anthems, and the greatest. I used to think it was overrated; now I can't listen to it without trembling.

The Beatles (Apple/Parlophone, 1968).

Yellow Submarine (Apple/Parlophone, 1969). All but one of the performances collected here stretch back to *Pepper* days or before—though coming as late as this, they are not Summer of Love Revisited but shadows beckoning shadows. (Except for "All Together Now," which resists any attempt to darken it via oppositional reading or contrarian double-negativizing: it may be a better children's song than "Submarine" itself.) Best is "Hey Bulldog," a Lennon stomp in proto–White Album style.

Interesting that the title track and "All You Need Is Love" sound far more limp, far less inventive and colorful, in this bookend context than they do anywhere else—the import of which, here in January 1969, seems to be: It's later than you think.

5. O.P.D. / *Deus est Vivus*

"Get Back" / "Don't Let Me Down" (*Past Masters Volume Two*); single released 1969. The Beatles strip down to unadorned muscle and form; to clean lyrical enigma (Paul) and new emotional maturity (John). Not getting back so much as getting straight.

"The Ballad of John and Yoko" / "Old Brown Shoe" (*Past Masters Volume Two*); single released 1969. Two more fantastic late-period grooves, astonishingly tight and fluent. John and Paul play as one and infuse every note with humor and empathy, making the diaristic gripes of the ballad lovable, even jubilant. For the B-side, Paul's bass and George's guitar are so free and loose they're like kites, while John and Ringo remain on the ground, holding the string, watching. This is a band that was breaking up?

Abbey Road (Apple/Parlophone, 1969). Side 2, even the less dazzled among us will admit, is really something: chaotic yet seamless, epochal yet terse. If Paul, along with George Martin, takes the credit for this bangup, stops-out finale to the Beatles' real-life Mondo Hollywood musical—as well as some of the best electric bass-playing ever—let him also take the blame for the moronic "Maxwell." George blesses us with "Here Comes the Sun"; John scares the hell out of us with "I Want You (She's So Heavy)."

"Let It Be" (*Past Masters Volume Two*); single released 1970. The horny Phil Spector mix found on the LP is bombastic enough for a telethon. (In fact the song became the rough Brit-pop equivalent to "I Shall Be Released," topping off charity rock concerts throughout the '80s.) But the 45 is beautiful schlock, with a nice built-in alienation effect: like Diana Ross's version of "Ain't No Mountain High Enough" or USA for Africa's "We Are the World," it's proof positive that in pop music we needn't buy into a record's self-importance to be moved by it.

Let It Be (Apple/Parlophone, 1970). Neither woodshed jam nor full-out production job, the album is distressingly half-assed. To hear what could have been—and was—locate one of the many bootlegs based on the original, scrapped album. The tracklist, assembled by co-producer Glyn Johns, includes lovely stringless versions of "Let It Be" and "The Long and Winding Road," and the finest available takes of "Don't Let Me Down," "I've Got a Feeling," and "Get Back." This is the great lost Beatles album: muted, sad, and intimate without trying, it sustains a fragile mood over a modest length; it leaves you wanting more, and knowing you can't have it. See *As Nature Intended* (Vigotone, 1994).

Get Back—The Glyn Johns Final Compilation (Vigotone, 1999) contains the producer's second, refined (and again rejected) draft of the album.

For the Beatles' last public appearance—on the Apple Corps rooftop, January 30, 1969—find *The Complete Rooftop Concert* (Yellow Dog, 2000). In addition to the Beatles' songs and interstitial conferences, it features interviews with various Londoners responding to the impromptu gig, and the Beatles themselves listening (with surprising enthusiasm) to a playback of the performance the following day.

Bits and pieces of the bottomless *Get Back* sessions have seen official release on *Anthology 3,* and illegal release on dozens of bootlegs. Of the latter, by far the most exhaustive, and exhausting, have been *The Get Back Journals* (Vigotone, 1993), *The Get Back Journals II* (Vigotone, 1996), and *The Twickenham Sessions* (Yellow Dog, 2000)—each an eight-disc set composed of mostly unedited tapes. Then there is *Thirty Days—The Ultimate Get Back Sessions Collection* (Vigotone, 2000), an encyclopedic seventeen-disc set that excises talk, false starts, and rehearsals in favor of complete performances.

Among the highlights of the sessions are a delightful bossa nova medley incorporating "Brazil," the Rascals' "Groovin'," Elvis' "I Got Stung," and much improvised silliness; a torrid whorehouse rocker called "Suzy's Parlour"; an absurd, spirited version of Paul's first song, "I Lost My Little Girl"; and a furious extended jam, recorded an hour or so after George had blandly quit the group, that germinates from an idle pick at the Who's "A Quick One" riff, gradually centers itself on John's guitar, and escalates into noisy terror by stacking Ringo's hysterical drumming and Paul's feedback atop Yoko's inspired screech. It's an exorcism—though of what, precisely, only the people involved can know.

There is music here to place beside the best, and certainly the most unusual, of the Beatles' output; also enough dull chitchat, sluggish rehearsal, and depressed run-throughs of mediocre songs to wear the patience of even the most devout fan.

Audio of the November 1969 television special "Paul McCartney: The Complete Story, Told for the First and Last Time" was issued on the CD *And Here's Another Clue for You All* (Dinosaur, 1996).

"Cease to Exist," on Charles Manson LP *LIE* (Awareness, 1970). I listened to this album precisely once, for purposes of research.

"Never Learn Not to Love," on Beach Boys LP *20/20* (Capitol, 1968). A terrific album—better than the overrated *Wild Honey* or *Sunflower*.

The Masked Marauders, *The Masked Marauders* (Deity/Reprise, 1969); Tin Tin, "Have You Heard the Word?" on *Spicy Beatles Songs* (Trademark of Quality, 1973); unknown, "The Candle Burns," on *20 x 4* (Ruthless Rhymes, 1981). Ancient vinyl may be your only source for these scratchy hoaxes: the songs come and go as music files on Internet sites, but if you care, you'll want the originals, with flaking spines and obscene underground-comix art. A marvelous piece of pop history that is vanishing fast.

The Beatles Tapes (Polydor, 1976). In these 1969–1973 interviews with BBC correspondent David Wigg, the Beatles—interviewed separately—are found in gentle voice, good humor, and forgiving mood. A soothing listen, the chat equivalent of *Rubber Soul*.

The Beatles Anthology 3 (Apple/Capitol, 1996). Pepperland drifts out of sight as we sail into "A Beginning," the George Martin theme that was intended to introduce Ringo's country banger "Don't Pass Me By" (a complete mismatch—perfect for the White Album). Out to the suburbs with some un-plugged demos, and back to town for studio outtakes that make it clear how little alteration most White Album songs went through in the studio. (Exceptions: "While My Guitar Gently Weeps," the noble Harrison heart-breaker, here performed solo; and "Helter Skelter" as a bass-heavy vamp, a phallic strut). From there into the shallow waters of *Get Back* and the anti-experiment of *Abbey Road.* Something is missing. Maybe it's that sense of rid-ing a tiger: the Beatles are now at ease with their talents, settling back to sources, and they seldom reach for anything they're uncertain of grasping.

That said, it's touching to be reminded of how simple and fine their end-ing was. George demos "All Things Must Pass," Paul one-man-bands "Come and Get It," John revisits "Ain't She Sweet" with cracked voice and sleepy smile. Stoned-choirboy loveliness of "Because"; "Let It Be" free of angel trill; a three-way guitar battle as exciting, concise, and generous as we could want from the Beatles; and a final audio gimmick that makes a magic circle of the doomiest chord in the history of popular music.

6. Fantasy into Flesh

John Lennon, *John Lennon / Plastic Ono Band* (Capitol, 1970); Paul (and Linda) McCartney, *Ram* (Capitol, 1971); George Harrison, *All Things Must Pass* (EMD/ Capitol, 1970); Ringo Starr, *Ringo* (Capitol, 1973). These are the solo albums I have always recommended friends buy first. Next stop would be each man's greatest hits.

Turn Me On Dead Man—The John Barrett Tapes (Vigotone, 1999). John Barrett, an engineer at EMI's Abbey Road studios, was diagnosed with inoperable cancer in 1983. Seeking distraction in his final months, he set about docu-menting every Beatle recording in the EMI vaults—every session, every take of every song. In the process, he made cassette copies of hundreds of outtakes, most intended to accompany an audiovisual tour of Abbey Road, others apparently for personal enjoyment. Upon his death these were leaked, and began to appear on bootleg compilations. They were a hit. By now, the illicit releases based on the Barrett tapes are beyond numbering.

It's probable that the steady underground flow of this material over ten years' time forced the completion of the long-deferred *Anthology* project, thus making failed takes, informal chatter, improvisations, and off-mike noises into approved pieces of an authorized biography. Barrett's alternative canon, a doppelgänger history of the Beatles, has changed the way we hear, think, and feel about them; refreshed and revitalized our perspective on something we may have thought we knew too well; and touched off new wonderings—such as this book.

John Barrett died having opened a new circle. It remains open, and we who love the Beatles walk around in it every day.

CREDITS

1 Michael Ward / Rex Features.
2 Michael Ward / Rex Features.
3 Terry O'Neill / Rex Features.
4 Monty Fresco / Rex Features.
5 Pierluigi Praturlon / Rex Features.
6 Rex Features.
7 Emilio Lari / Rex Features.
8 Pierluigi Praturlon / Rex Features.
9 Emilio Lari / Rex Features.
10 Emilio Lari / Rex Features.
11 Monty Fresco / Rex Features.
12 Kevin Cole / Rex Features.
13 Bob Orchard / Rex Features.
14 Bob Orchard / Rex Features.
15 Bob Orchard / Rex Features.
16 Kevin Cole / Rex Features.
17 Kevin Cole / Rex Features.
18 Kevin Cole / Rex Features.
19 Kevin Cole / Rex Features.
20 Rex Features.
21 R. Wilson / Rex Features.
22 David Magnus / Rex Features.
23 Harry Myers / Rex Features.
24 Rex Features.

25 Rex Features.
26 From the author's collection.
27 Reg Wilson / Rex Features.
28 David Magnus / Rex Features.
29 David Magnus / Rex Features.
30 (page 371). Mondial / Rex Features.

INDEX